CW01240229

THE AMSTRAD PC1512/1640 ADVANCED USER'S GUIDE

A PROGRAMMER'S GUIDE

THE AMSTRAD PC1512/1640 ADVANCED USER'S GUIDE

A PROGRAMMER'S GUIDE

Jim Reid

HEINEMANN
NEW·TECH

Heinemann Newtech
An imprint of Heinemann Professional Publishing Ltd.
Halley Court, Jordan Hill, Oxford OX2 8EJ

OXFORD LONDON MELBOURNE AUCKLAND SINGAPORE
IBADAN NAIROBI GABORONE KINGSTON

First Published 1989

© J. T. W. Reid 1989

British Library Cataloguing in Publication Data

A CIP catalogue record for this book is available from the British Library

ISBN 0 434 91998 5

Produced by SC&E Morris Computer Services, Bodenham, Hereford

Printed and bound in Great Britain

Table of Contents

List of illustrations	**13**

Foreword	**17**

1. Overview	**19**
SCOPE OF THE BOOK	**19**
MS-DOS	20
Assemblers	20
Sample programs	21
Tables	21
Hexadecimal notation	22
THE AMSTRAD PC RANGE	**22**
Compatibility	22
Components	23
SOFTWARE	**25**
Operating systems	25
Bundled software	25

2. The Amstrad PC System Unit	**27**
THE MAIN SYSTEM BOARD	**27**
The 8086-2 CPU	27
System bus	29
PORTS	**30**
THE AMSTRAD PC COMPONENTS	**33**
MEMORY	**42**
System RAM variables	45
THE SYSTEM CONFIGURATION	**48**
The PC1640 system unit DIP switches	48

3. Programming the 8086	**55**
DATA TERMINOLOGY	**55**
BINARY CALCULATIONS	**59**
ASCII	**66**
MEMORY ORGANISATION	**70**
ELEMENTS OF 8086 PROGRAMMING	**71**
The registers	72

Table of Contents

The stack	72
Segment registers	76
The general purpose registers	77
The pointer and index registers	77
The flags register	78
ADDRESSING MODES	**80**

4. The 8086 Instruction Set — 85

THE SYNTAX OF INSTRUCTIONS	**85**
ARITHMETIC OPERATIONS	**91**
LOGICAL OPERATIONS	**95**
FLAG OPERATIONS	**96**
BRANCHING AND LOOPS	**98**
MOVING DATA	**103**
THE STACK	**105**
ROTATE AND SHIFT	**106**
TYPE CONVERSIONS	**108**
STRING OPERATIONS	**108**
COMMUNICATING WITH PORTS	**112**
CHANGING THE PROGRAM FLOW	**112**
PAUSING AND STOPPING	**114**

5. Interrupts — 117

INTERRUPTS	**117**
Interrupt handlers	117
Interrupt vectors	118
The INT instruction	120
The 8259 interrupt controller	120
HARDWARE INTERRUPTS	**121**
Maskable hardware interrupts	121
Non-Maskable Interrupt (NMI)	121
Interrupts 00h - 04h	122
SOFTWARE INTERRUPTS	**123**
Replacing interrupts	124

6. Compiling and Running Programs — 145

ASSEMBLERS	**145**
COM and EXE files	146
The A86 assembler	146
DEBUG	149
THE PROGRAM SEGMENT PREFIX (PSP)	**149**

Ending a program	151
RUNNING A SUBPROGRAM	**155**
ALLOCATING MEMORY	**157**
Critical errors	158

7. Multi-tasking and Resident Programs 161

MULTI-TASKING	**161**
TERMINATE AND STAY RESIDENT (TSR) PROGRAMS	**164**

8. Boot Procedures 169

TYPES OF BOOT	**169**
COLD BOOT	**169**
POWER-UP PROCEDURES	**170**
Self-tests	170
Initialisation	172
WARM BOOT	**174**
LOADING THE OPERATING SYSTEM	**178**
ROM boot routines	178
MS-DOS boot routines	179
COMMAND.COM boot routines	181

9. Components of MS-DOS 183

THE DOS BOOT RECORD	**183**
THE MS-DOS FILES	**183**
THE ENVIRONMENT	**187**
Modifying the environment	196
The environment in memory	196
OTHER DOS VERSIONS	**196**
A note about PC-DOS	197
COMPATIBILITY CONSIDERATIONS	**199**

10. The Clock and NVR 201

THE CLOCK HARDWARE	**201**
TIME	**201**
DATE AND TIME	**206**
Date	206
Time	208
THE NON-VOLATILE RAM (NVR)	**211**

Table of Contents

The clock information	213
The alarm	217
The NVR system data	218
Loss of power in NVR	218

11. The Keyboard — 221

KEYBOARD HARDWARE	**221**
Keyboard test	222
Keyboard layout	222
Keyboard operation	222
Interrupt 09h	223
The modifying keys	225
The keyboard translation table	230
SPECIAL COMBINATIONS	**235**
Key indicator lights	238
The key-repeat action	239
Duplicate keys	240
Control codes	241
The Alt codes	241
THE KEYBOARD INTERRUPTS	**242**
Accessing the buffer	242

12. The Mouse, Light Pen and Joystick — 253

THE MOUSE	**253**
Mouse operation	253
MOUSE.COM and MOUSE.SYS	256
The mouse cursor	259
Mouse buttons and position	265
Light pen emulation	267
THE LIGHT PEN	**268**
THE JOYSTICK	**269**

13. The Screen — 271

DISPLAY HARDWARE	**271**
PIXELS AND RESOLUTION	**271**
MONITORS	**273**
ADAPTER MODES	**275**
VIDEO RAM	**278**
Creating the screen display	279
Changing the screen display	280

Colour	282
THE VIDEO STATE	**285**
Display modes	285
Text modes	285
Graphics modes	290
Display pages	294
PALETTES	**298**
DISPLAYING CHARACTERS	**302**
THE CURSOR	**310**
Cursor types	310
Changing the cursor	311
WINDOWS	**314**
Scrolling	315
GRAPHICS DISPLAYS IN MEMORY	**316**
WORKING WITH PIXELS	**317**
THE VIDEO PORTS	**319**
CONCLUSION	**320**

14. Sound   321

THE PRODUCTION OF SOUND	**321**
PROGRAMMING THE 8253 TIMER	**322**
DIRECT CONTROL OF THE SPEAKER	**327**

15. Disks and Disk Drives   329

FLOPPY DISK HARDWARE	**329**
DISKS	**332**
Floppy disks	332
Hard disks	333
Non-standard devices	333
DISK ARCHITECTURE	**334**
How the disk is used	335
FORMATTING	**336**
FLOPPY DISK TYPES	**337**
Preparing a hard disk	339
HDFORMAT	339
FDISK	339
FORMAT	340
FORMATTING A DISK TRACK	**341**
Accessing a disk	344
Working with sectors	345
Disk buffers	350
The disk status	351

Table of Contents

16. The Disk Directory — 355

DISK STRUCTURE INFORMATION — **355**
    How directories are created — 356
THE FILE DIRECTORY — **357**
    Directory structure — 358
    Displaying the directory — 365
VOLUME LABELS — **365**
SUB-DIRECTORIES — **365**
    Sub-directory structure — 366
    The current drive and directory — 367
THE FILE ALLOCATION TABLE (FAT) — **371**
    Structure of the FAT — 373
    FAT and disk information — 375
    Changing the directory and FAT — 377
    Deleted files — 377

17. Files — 381

FILE SPECIFICATIONS — **381**
    How DOS interprets file specifications — 383
FILE TYPES — **384**
    Sequential files — 384
    ASCII files — 385
    Random access files — 385
DATA TRANSFER AREAS (DTA) — **386**
STANDARD ERROR MESSAGES — **387**
AMBIGUOUS FILENAMES — **388**
FILE HANDLES — **391**
    Finding a file — 392
    Creating and opening files — 393
    Moving the file pointer — 399
    Writing to a file — 400
    Reading files — 400
    Closing files — 401
    Locking and unlocking files — 402
    Duplication of file handles — 403
FILE CONTROL BLOCKS (FCB'S) — **403**
    Creating and opening files — 404
    Finding files — 405
    Sequential files — 406
    Random files — 408
    Closing files — 410
    Determining the file size — 410
SWAPPING DISKS — **411**

RENAMING FILES	**411**
DELETING FILES	**412**
CHANGING THE TIME AND DATE STAMPS	**413**
REDIRECTION, PIPES AND FILTERS	**414**
Filters	414
Redirection and pipes	415

18. The Serial and Parallel Ports   423

THE PARALLEL PORT	**423**
Parallel printer internal ports	424
PROGRAMMING THE PARALLEL PRINTER	**427**
The print-screen service	429
Echoing output to the printer	430
THE SERIAL PORT	**431**
PROGRAMMING THE SERIAL PORT	**433**
The time-out error	437

19. Device Drivers   439

OPERATION OF DEVICE DRIVERS	**439**
Device types	441
Redirecting input and output	443
INSTALLATION AND EXECUTION	**443**
Structure of device drivers	443
The strategy routine	446
The interrupt routine	446
Using a device driver	448
The Bios Parameter Block (BPB)	448
Input/output control (IOCTL)	449
THE DEVICE COMMANDS	**450**
INSTALLABLE DEVICE DRIVERS	**460**
ANSI.SYS	460
MOUSE.SYS	461
RAMDRIVE.SYS	461

INDEX   467

List of Illustrations

2.1	Organisation of the Intel 8086-2 CPU
2.2	Internal ports
2.3	Internal device ports
2.4	Expansion bus ports
2.5	Operation of the DMA Controller
2.6	The PIT ports
2.7	The PPI ports
2.8	User RAM codes
2.9	Displaying the contents of the PPI ports
2.10	The power supply socket
2.11	The Amstrad PC memory maps
2.12	System RAM variables
2.13	Allocation of low memory areas
2.14	The PC1640 dip switches and related ports
2.15	The configuration list codes
2.16	Displaying the configuration list
2.17	Reporting the RAM size
3.1	Hexadecimal representation of bytes and words
3.2	Decimal-to-hex conversions
3.3	Hex-to-decimal conversions
3.4	Decimal/hex conversion routines
3.5	Binary representations
3.6	Standard ASCII characters
3.7	ASCII control codes
3.8	The 8086 segment addressing system
3.9	The 8086 registers
3.10	Using the stack
3.11	The flags register
4.1	The 8086 instruction set and the effect on flags
5.1	The interrupt vectors
5.2	Replacing an interrupt
5.3	Standard interrupts
6.1	DEBUG commands
6.2	The Program Segment Prefix (PSP)
6.3	Locating program parameters

List of Illustrations

6.4	Subprogram control block
6.5	Return codes after ending a subprogram
6.6	Critical error codes
6.7	Detailed critical error codes
7.1	The shell of a TSR
8.1	Language links
8.2	Confirming a reset
8.3	System reset routine
9.1	Boot record disk information
9.2	The environment variables
9.3	DOS 3 country codes and keyboard programs
9.4	Listing monetary values
9.5	DOS 2 country-dependent information
9.6	DOS 3 country-dependent information
9.7	Structure of the country information buffer
9.8	Checking the DOS version number
10.1	A time routine
10.2	Generating pseudo-random numbers
10.3	Interrupts for changing the NVR
10.4	The RTC data
10.5	Range of RTC data
10.6	RTC Registers A-D
10.7	The NVR data
11.1	The keyboard connector
11.2	The keyboard status bytes
11.3	Modifying the effect of Caps Lock
11.4	Inspecting the keyboard status
11.5	Effect of special key combinations
11.6	Scan code translation table
11.7	The keyboard interrupts
11.8	Getting a character
11.9	Clearing the buffer
11.10	Entering a filename and extension
12.1	The mouse connector

List of Illustrations

12.2	The mouse interrupts
12.3	The mouse defaults
12.4	The light pen connector
12.5	The joystick connector
13.1	The video connector
13.2	The adapter dip switches
13.3	The language font dip switches
13.4	The external adapter dip switches
13.5	Adapter switch settings byte (0488h)
13.6	The screen interrupts
13.7	The IRGB colours
13.8	Drawing boxes
13.9	Encoding character attributes
13.10	Writing a block of text to the screen
13.11	Clearing the screen
13.12	Video mode statistics
13.13	Switching between work areas
13.14	Video mode palettes
13.15	The default EGA palette (rgbRGB)
13.16	Display routines
13.17	Using the cursor
14.1	Sound frequencies
14.2	Generating sound
15.1	The disk interrupts
15.2	The floppy drive links
15.3	The effect of port 03F2h
15.4	The disk parameter table
15.5	The DRIVPARM directive
15.6	Disk formats
15.7	Sector address marks
15.8	The disk status
15.9	DOS disk error codes
16.1	Directory interrupts
16.2	Root directory entries
16.3	Directory structure
16.4	Valid filename characters

List of Illustrations

16.5	The file attribute byte
16.6	Valid file attributes
16.7	Displaying the disk label
16.8	FAT disk codes
17.1	File interrupts
17.2	Standard error messages for DOS functions 38h onwards
17.3	DOS 3 extended error codes
17.4	Reserved DOS file handles
17.5	The DTA after finding a file
17.6	Finding matching files
17.7	File use codes
17.8	Structure of File Control Blocks
17.9	Parsing control bits
17.10	File-handling routines
18.1	The parallel printer connector
18.2	The parallel printer status port
18.3	Parallel printer status codes
18.4	The serial connector
18.5	The data transfer code
18.6	Serial port status codes
19.1	Standard MS-DOS devices
19.2	Structure of MS-DOS device drivers
19.3	The request header
19.4	Meaning of device attributes word
19.5	Meaning of device status word
19.6	The BIOS Parameter Block
19.7	The IOCTL functions
19.8	IOCTL device information
19.9	IOCTL BPB
19.10	IOCTL device parameter block
19.11	Use of request header data area by device commands
19.12	The ANSI.SYS command set

Foreword

The aim of this book is to provide an introduction to the inner workings of the Amstrad PC. Its object is to show you not only what can be achieved but also *how* it may be achieved. The emphasis is on the practical, rather than the theoretical side of the computer. That is, there is no detailed explanation of the individual components of the machine except where an explanation of the system's construction will assist in understanding the operation of the computer or provide an explanation of why certain procedures are necessary.

This book is aimed at the advanced Amstrad user; that is, someone who is familiar with the basics of computers, their operation and how to program them. To that extent the emphasis must be on programming, for that is how we can mould the computer and use it to achieve our aims. It is only through intelligent programming that the Amstrad can become a versatile machine, capable of such diverse activities as the preparation of the annual accounts and the playing of tunes, not to mention its quite acceptable standard of chess!

One half of the book covers the operation of the hardware, showing how each individual component operates and how it is integrated into the system as a whole. The other half looks in detail at the operating system - the software upon which all computer operations are dependent. By careful programming of the hardware and by using the in-built facilities of the software it is possible to achieve some interesting results. An understanding of the mechanics of the system as a whole opens up whole new horizons and provides the user with a range of exciting new possibilities.

Unfortunately space has not permitted me to include the many programs that I would have liked to use to demonstrate the features of the machine. Those that are here are fairly rudimentary and certainly not guaranteed to be perfect. They are intended as a guide for the user and not as complete programs, to be copied blindly into the computer.

However, there is nothing more frustrating than keying in a long listing, only to discover that it is full of typing errors or does not work as well as you may have hoped. For this reason there is a disk offer associated with this book. The disk comes with all the routines included here, in both their original form and in a more sophisticated format. There are also many routines that had to

Foreword

be excluded from the book due to lack of space. This disk provides a good starting point for building up a programmer's toolkit. Details of how to obtain a copy are given at the back of the book.

A book of this type is inevitably an undertaking that is not undertaken lightly and requires a great deal of work and thought. I am extremely indebted to Stephen Morris and Robin Kinge for the tremendous amount of work they have put into this project and for their assistance throughout the preparation of the book.

Disclaimer. Every effort has been taken to ensure that the information given in this book is accurate and complete. However, in any work of this size there will inevitably be ommissions and errors, for which I apologise. Obviously I cannot take responsibility for any problems that may arise from use of the information contained in this book.

The book has taken a great deal of time to prepare but it has been a thoroughly enjoyable experience. I hope that all who read this book and delve into the intricacies of Amstrad-based programming find their time is equally well rewarded.

1. *Overview*

Much has been written about the capabilities of the Amstrad PC range of microcomputers. For those who want to find out more about how the Amstrad works there is certainly no shortage of information. The main problem is in finding the information that you want *when* you want it.

Several books exist that document the workings of these machines and their operating system, MS-DOS. Amstrad have also produced their own technical reference manuals which catalogue the components of the range and their most important features. There are a number of excellent reference book relating to the IBM PC and later compatibles, and to the generalities of MS-DOS.

The aim of this volume is to bring together the wealth of technical information that has been collected over the years, along with much new information and new ideas, into a single reference manual. This information is intended primarily for programmers who want to make the most of their machines.

A few notes on the contents and layout of the book are given below. It is recommended that all readers should scan these few paragraphs in order to gain a better understanding of the book's style and its contents.

SCOPE OF THE BOOK

My intention is that this book should be both a technical reference manual and a practical guide. As a technical reference it aims to include as much information as possible, presented in a compact, simple format. As a practical guide, it includes a number of sample programs that demonstrate features of the computers and their software. These should also provide the reader with some useful utility programs.

However, it must be stressed that this book does not claim to be a full tutorial. Some basic knowledge is assumed, such as the operation of the MS-DOS commands and how to write a basic assembly language program. That said, it should be possible for the intelligent user to glean much of this knowledge from the book.

Overview

It is always difficult to know where to draw the line in any work of this magnitude. Clearly it is impossible to cover every facet of the Amstrad PC range and its software. Therefore this book covers all information relating to the computer and its operating system but only in as far as it relates to the way in which the machines operate.

MS-DOS

MS-DOS is clearly an integral part of the Amstrad PC. Supplied with it, it provides access to many routines that can make the programmer's life easier. Why work out a whole new file structure when DOS can do it all for you? For this reason there is a small section on how to bypass the operating system but in the main there is extensive coverage of DOS and its features.

Further complications arise from the many different DOS versions. Although the Amstrad PC's are all supplied with the same version of DOS, the same is not true of all other computers. However, because of the very high degree of IBM-compatibility of the Amstrad range, programs written for the Amstrad PC should be portable to other machines, providing certain rules are followed. There is generally some trade-off to be made between portability and enhancement; for example, you may wish to directly access the locations that store the current time but you will find that such programs will probably not work on other machines. However, DOS provides a good set of instructions for dealing with this subject.

ASSEMBLERS

Most importantly, a working knowledge of assembly language is assumed. While this is not essential, much of the book must, of necessity, cover the way in which information is passed to the computer in its lowest form. There is detailed coverage of assembler features, such as the computer's registers and addressing modes, and there is a full list of assembler commands. In short, almost all of the information needed for assembly language programming is contained here, but the inexperienced reader would do well to consult a good assembly language programming book, lest he adopt bad habits that may, later, be difficult to shake.

Similarly, there is no list of MS-DOS commands nor instruction in the DOS user interface. However, there is a detailed appraisal of how MS-DOS works and many important commands are referenced. The aim is not to show you how to use MS-DOS in your day-to-day operation (there are already many very good guides that do this) but rather how MS-DOS works.

In this way, by getting under the skin of the computers and their operating system, the programmer should be able to use the features that are available to their fullest extent, creating fast, efficient and friendly programs.

SAMPLE PROGRAMS   The best way to demonstrate any feature is by example. Therefore, this book is liberally sprinkled with small assembly language routines that make use of particular features. Each of these routines is fairly basic in its operation. The routines achieve a purpose but not necessarily in an elegant fashion; each would therefore benefit from some additional improvement.

The error handling has also been kept to a minimum so the routines given here will not cater for all the things that a new user might do (nor those of an experienced programmer hell-bent on finding bugs). Some of the routines are re-used several times throughout the book. In these cases the programs issue a call to the relevant routine and the page number on which it will be found is indicated in the comments. Inevitably some routines (such as those to display text on the screen) must be used before the principles behind them have been fully explained.

Companion disks   Unfortunately, space does not allow us to include long listings. Anyway, this would be boring for the reader and frustrating for those who have to type them in, only to discover that the program takes hours to debug because of minor typing errors. To overcome these shortcomings a separate disk is available that contains not only the routines given in the book but also some fuller, more elegant versions. A description of some of these programs is given along with the basic routines. This disk is also bundled with a copy of the A86 assembler that has been used to compile the routines. Details of how to obtain these disks are given at the back of the book.

TABLES   Once the programmer becomes familiar with a particular set of features and their operation, usually all that is required is some form of table detailing the various options. As a general rule such tables are relegated to the back of the book. However, recognising that such information is ultimately to be the most widely used and therefore warrants more than just

Overview

an appendix, I have reversed this process. For any particular topic it is the summary and general description that come first. Individual items of interest are covered in detail later. For example, when interrupts are first encountered they are shown as a table in their entirety. Each interrupt is expanded upon in its own particular section as the text progresses.

HEXADECIMAL NOTATION

As you will see the aim of this book is to provide an exploding view of the Amstrad PC. In each section we look at a particular part of the system and then move in to look in closer detail, expanding the description at various stages as and when necessary.

It is assumed that any serious assembly language programmer will work mainly in hexadecimal. Great confusion can be caused by mixing hexadecimal and decimal notation. Therefore, all references to locations in memory, interrupts and so on are usually given in hexadecimal. All hexadecimal numbers are notated with the letter 'h'. Any other 'natural' numbers will appear in standard decimal format.

THE AMSTRAD PC RANGE

The Amstrad PC was first launched in the autumn of 1986. The first machines in the range were the Amstrad PC1512's. These were followed, at the beginning of the next year, by the enhanced Amstrad PC1640's. Since then we have also seen the launch of the Amstrad PPC portable and more recently the Amstrad 2000 series. It is only the Amstrad PC1512 and Amstrad PC1640 that are covered in this book. However, the programs produced here will work - in the vast majority of cases - on the Amstrad PC2086 or, for that matter, on most IBM-compatibles.

COMPATIBILITY

Amstrad PC's have been designed to be as IBM-compatible as possible. This means that any program written for an IBM PC or true compatible should run identically on the Amstrad PC without modification. Likewise, any program written for the Amstrad PC should work satisfactorily on any other compatible. However, this will only be the case if you ignore some of the special features of the Amstrad PC, such as its method of storing information in an area of battery-backed memory.

Overview

The features that are unique to the Amstrad or may cause compatibility problems are clearly marked in the text. If you steer clear of these few sections then there should be no fear that the programs will not run on any other IBM-compatible.

Amstrad PC programs can also be transferred to $3\frac{1}{2}$" disk for use on the Amstrad portable, and should work to a certain degree on the IBM PS/2 range (though obviously they will not make any use of the PS/2's many enhanced functions).

The Amstrad PC is totally incompatible with the Amstrad PCW word processors.

COMPONENTS A number of separate units build together to make an Amstrad PC. You can mix and match within the various Amstrad models with relative ease (with the exception of the monitors).

System unit At the centre of the Amstrad PC is the main system unit, which houses the following items:

- The 8086-2 central processing unit

- The user RAM and the resident operating system (which is stored in ROM)

- The system clock, which regulates all processing

- A variety of other integrated circuits for dealing with specific devices (such as the keyboard, screen, etc.)

- The video adaptor, which deals with all output to the screen

- The floppy disk drives

- A hard disk unit, if attached

- Up to four expansion slots for adding extra hardware cards

Each of these components is explained later in the text.

Overview

Memory
The Amstrad PC1512 is supplied with 512K of user RAM as standard. This can be expanded to the maximum 640K. The Amstrad PC1640 is supplied with the maximum 640K user RAM, which cannot be expanded.

Disk drives
Each Amstrad PC is supplied in a number of configurations: single floppy drive, double floppy drive or hard disk drive with one floppy drive.

The monitors
There are a number of different monitors available for each type of Amstrad PC. In the case of the PC1512, we may have either a medium resolution colour monitor or a similar monochrome monitor, capable of displaying up to 16 shades of grey. The PC1640 is also supplied with a medium resolution colour monitor, as well as a high resolution true-monochrome monitor or, at the top of the range, the enhanced colour display (ECD) which provides high resolution colour graphics.

Keyboard and mouse
The keyboard is an IBM look-alike, with the addition of one or two extra keys. In most respects it is fully IBM-compatible. In addition, all Amstrad PC's are supplied with a two-button mouse. It should be noted that this mouse is not standard and is not Microsoft-compatible.

Input/output ports
Two standard input/output ports are supplied, one for serial communications and one for parallel output.

In addition, there is a joystick connector at the rear of the keyboard.

Expansion slots
Four expansion slots are provided on the Amstrad PC1512, with three available on the PC1640. These will take a variety of additional standard devices, such as a modem, hard card, alternative graphics cards and so on.

External devices
Many devices can be connected to the Amstrad PC through its ports and expansion slots, including printers, plotters, digitisers, modems and various other control devices. There is also a connector on the main board for attaching a light pen.

Overview

SOFTWARE

Most software that will run on an IBM PC or compatible will run quite happily on an Amstrad PC, and vice versa. In particular the Amstrad PC is supplied with one industry-standard operating system and a variety of other software.

OPERATING SYSTEMS

The main operating system supplied with the complete range is MS-DOS version 3.2. This has recently been superseded by the slightly enhanced DOS 3.3, though this is not provided as standard on any Amstrad PC. DOS 3.3 is used, however, on the Amstrad PPC. DOS 3.2 provides complete compatibility with most other versions of MS-DOS.

In addition, the Amstrad PC1512 was supplied with an alternative operating system, DOS Plus. The aim of DOS Plus was to combine compatibility with both MS-DOS and the now infrequently-used CP/M. However, DOS Plus has not been an overwhelming success and most applications still tend to be written with MS-DOS in mind. Since most programs written under MS-DOS will run quite happily under DOS Plus there seems little point in delving into the intricacies of DOS Plus. A program that runs under DOS Plus may not necessarily run under all MS-DOS installations. Therefore, this book concentrates heavily upon MS-DOS, with little reference to the capabilities of DOS Plus.

Any other operating system that is suitable for PC's can of course be run on the Amstrad. Such operating systems include CP/M, Xenix and Unix.

BUNDLED SOFTWARE

A variety of software has been supplied with the Amstrads during their history.

The Amstrad PC1512 and PC1640 are both bundled with the GEM user interface, including the GEM Paint drawing program. Again, the main interest here is to the user and no coverage of these packages is given in this book.

Later versions of the Amstrad PC1512 were supplied with the Ability integrated package and the US Gold games package. The PC1640 has been bundled at various times with SuperCalc 3, WordStar 1512 and Accounts Master.

Overview

This concludes the overview of the Amstrad computers. The remainder of this book will concentrate on the Amstrad PC hardware, the MS-DOS operating system and how we may best make the most of their capabilities.

2. *The Amstrad PC System Unit*

The Amstrad PC is based on a main system board that contains a large number of individual chips, each with their own part to play in the running of the system. This chapter gives a short description of each of the main components. It also shows how memory is allocated within the Amstrad PC and takes a brief look at the central processing unit itself.

THE MAIN SYSTEM BOARD

The large number of individual components on the main board also connect to the various standard devices that form part of the Amstrad PC. Although the main operation of the computer is carried out by the 8086-2 Central Processing Unit which forms the core of the system, much of the work when dealing with the external devices (including the keyboard and screen, for example) is dealt with by additional processing chips that are dedicated to individual tasks. This means that the 8086 can get on with its main task (that is, processing) while all the minor details of handling communications with other devices are dealt with by other chips that have been designed specifically with those uses in mind.

THE 8086-2 CPU The main *Central Processing Unit (CPU)* is an Intel 8086-2 processor. This has a 1 megabyte memory-addressing capability. It operates at a clock frequency of 8 MHz.

An outline of the internal organisation of the 8086 CPU is shown in Figure 2.1. Broadly speaking the CPU falls into two main parts:

■ The bus interface unit

■ The execution unit

Each of these performs a number of major functions.

Bus interface unit The *bus interface unit* is the part of the CPU that is used for general control within the computer. It contains the following:

The Amstrad PC System Unit

```
                        BUS INTERFACE UNIT
┌─────────────────────────────────────────────────────────────┐
│   ┌──────────┐   ┌───────────┐   ┌─────────┐  ┌───────────┐ │
│   │ SEGMENT  │   │INSTRUCTION│   │ CONTROL │  │INSTRUCTION│ │
│   │REGISTERS │   │  POINTER  │   │ SYSTEM  │  │   QUEUE   │ │
│   └────┬─────┘   └─────┬─────┘   └────┬────┘  └─────┬─────┘ │
│     Data              Increment     Processing    Instructions│
│   transfer                                                   │
└─────────────────────────────────────────────────────────────┘
           ↕                 ↕              ↕            ↕
  ⇐═══════════════════════════════════════════════════════⇒
                   16-BIT SYSTEM DATA BUS
                  ↕                ↕
              Data             Results
            transfer
┌─────────────────────────────────────────────────────────────┐
│   ┌──────────┐        ┌───────────┐      ┌──────────┐       │
│   │ GENERAL  │        │ ARITHMETIC│ ←────│ OPERANDS │       │
│   │REGISTERS │        │ AND LOGIC │      └──────────┘       │
│   └──────────┘        │   UNIT    │                         │
│                       └─────┬─────┘                         │
│                          Update                             │
│                             ↓                               │
│                         ┌───────┐                           │
│                         │ FLAGS │                           │
│                         └───────┘                           │
└─────────────────────────────────────────────────────────────┘
                        EXECUTION UNIT
```

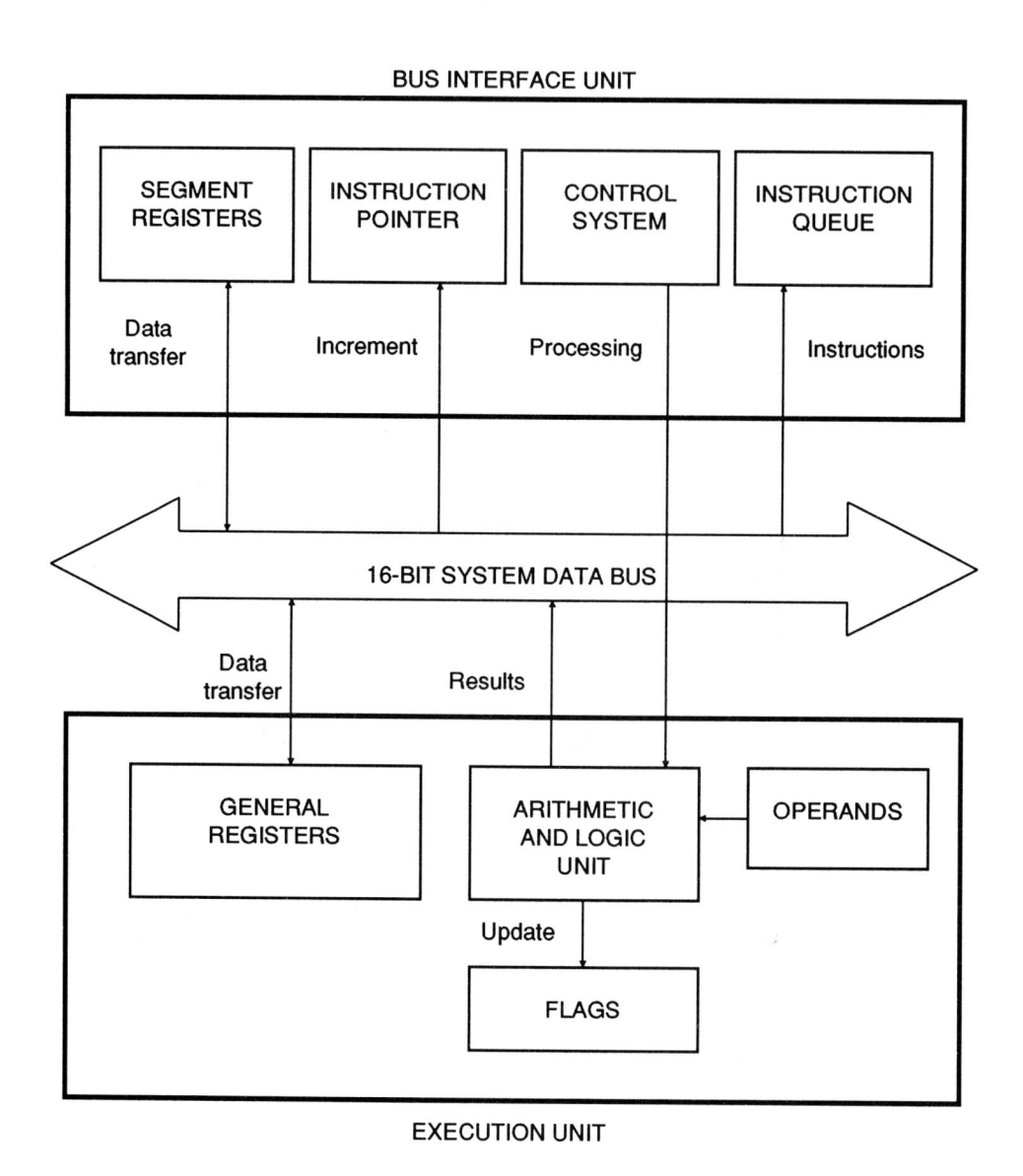

Figure 2.1 Organisation of the Intel 8086-2 CPU

- The *segment registers*. These store the addresses of programs and their associated data.

- The *instruction pointer*, which is used to keep track of the next instruction to be processed.

- The *instruction queue*. This is where instructions waiting to be processed are placed.

- The *control system*. This controls the computer as a whole.

This part of the CPU is also responsible for control of the system bus, which is described later.

Execution unit

The *execution unit* is the part that actually processes the instructions. It contains the following components:

- *General registers*. These are the main variables of the system, where information is temporarily stored.

- *Operands*. The actual instructions to be carried out are translated into a series of simpler operations here.

- *Arithmetic and Logic Unit (ALU)*. This is the part of the system that does all arithmetic and logical operations, such as adding two numbers together or comparing their values. From these simple instructions all other operations are built.

- *Flags register*. A variety of flags are stored, each of which tells us something about the current status of the system.

Any instructions received by the bus interface unit are stored in the instruction queue. When the processor is ready for another instruction the control system hands over the next instruction in the queue to the execution unit. The operands are transferred into the ALU, along with the contents of any registers that are to be used and data from memory; the calculation is performed and the results are then passed back to the appropriate device or memory along the system bus. The flags are updated according to the result and the instruction pointer is incremented.

SYSTEM BUS

All information is passed from the 8086 to the other parts of the system along its 16-bit *data bus*. This is simply a set of 16 parallel lines which will take 16 individual items of information at the same time. Since the 8086 itself works with 16-bit information the inclusion of this 16-bit bus makes the Amstrad PC a true 16-bit machine (unlike the IBM PC, for example, which uses a 16-bit processor but has only an 8-bit data bus).

Whenever any information is sent along the bus, the destination of the information is attached at the head of the data itself. All components of the system check the information that passes them and pull off whatever data is intended for their use. The fact that a 16-bit data bus is used means that complete memory addresses and 16-bit data can be sent unhindered.

Note that some parts of the system also have an 8-bit data bus.

Both of these buses are used for three separate purposes:

- To send control information from one part of the system to another

- To send addresses indicating where information is to be collected or sent

- To transmit data from one part of the system to another

All information comes into and out of the CPU via its 64 pins.

PORTS

All communication between the CPU and the other devices is done via the *ports*. These are locations connected to the data bus that can be used to input and output data values to and from the devices. For example, when a key is pressed the keyboard controller places the appropriate code in one of its ports. The CPU checks the port and reads the value. The same principle is applied whenever the CPU is sending or receiving any type of data or instructions. The only exception is when data is sent directly to memory locations, or read from them.

Amstrad PC System Ports		
Numbers	I/O	Use
00-0F	IO	8237 DMA Controller
10-1F	-	Reserved
20-21	IO	8259 Interrupt Controller
22-3F	-	Reserved
40-42	IO	8253 PIT Counters (0,1,2)
43	I	8253 PIT Mode
44-5F	-	Reserved
60	I	Port A (Keyboard Code/Status 1)
61	IO	Port B
62	I	Port C (Status 2)
63	-	Reserved
64	O	Status 1
65	O	Status 2
66	O	System reset
67-6F	-	Reserved
70	O	HD146818 RTC Address
71	IO	HD146818 RTC Data
72-77	-	Reserved
78	IO	Mouse X-co-ordinate
79	-	Reserved
7A	IO	Mouse Y-co-ordinate
7B-80	-	Reserved
81	O	DMA Page Register Channel 2
82	O	DMA Page Register Channel 3
83	O	DMA Page Register Channels 0,1
84-9F	-	Reserved
A0	O	NMI Mask Control
A1-FF	-	Reserved

Figure 2.2 Internal ports

There are a great many ports, each of which has a unique number by which it is referenced. Some of these are listed in Figures 2.2, 2.3 and 2.4.

Some ports are used for input only, others may only permit output and a few allow data to pass in both directions.

The Amstrad PC System Unit

Standard Device Ports		
Numbers	**I/O**	**Use**
0378	IO	Parallel Printer data
0379	I	Parallel Printer status
037A	IO	Parallel Printer control
037B-037F	IO	Reserved
03B0-037F	IO	Monochrome mode CRTC
03C0-03CF	IO	Video Controller
03D0-03DF	IO	Colour Mode CRTC
03F0-03F1	-	Reserved
03F2	O	Drive selection
03F3	-	Reserved
03F4	I	FDC status
03F5	IO	FDC data
03F6-03F7	-	Reserved
03F8-03FF	IO	UART Tx Data/Control

Figure 2.3 Internal device ports

The higher port numbers (0378h - 03FFh) are used by the standard external devices: parallel printer, monitor and floppy disk controller.

Although most data transfer is done via the ports, most of the time we do not have to concern ourselves with them. This is generally handled by the routines that the internal programs provide for us to use. Indeed, it is unwise to start meddling with the values in the ports without a full understanding of what is likely to happen. Even reading a value from a port, without intentionally changing it, can have an unexpected effect.

In a few instances, described later in the book, direct control of the ports is either desirable or essential. In the main, however, it is far safer and less likely to lead to compatibility problems to stick to the standard routines.

The terminology used here may be somewhat confusing. It is important to make the distinction between these *internal* ports and the *serial and parallel ports* that are physical points

Numbers	Use
0200-020F	External Game Control Interface
0210-0217	External Bus Extension Unit
0220-024F	Reserved
0278-027F	External Printer Port
02F0-02F7	Reserved
02F8-02FF	External Asynchronous RS232C Port
0300-031F	External Prototyping Card
0320-032F	External Hard Disk Controller
0380-038F	External SDLC RS232C Port
03A0-03AF	Reserved
03B0-03BB	External Monochrome Display Controller
03BC-03BF	Printer Port
03C0-03CF	External Graphics Display Controller
03D0-03DF	External Colour/Graphics Display Controller

Figure 2.4 Expansion bus ports

to which external devices are connected. Frequently, the ports are also referred to as *registers*. There is also an important difference between these registers and the segment registers and general registers used in our programs.

Expansion bus ports

In addition to the ports described above a number of ports are allocated for use by the expansion slots. Their precise use depends upon the particular expansion cards that have been attached but the general usage allocated to the individual groups of ports is shown in Figure 2.4.

THE AMSTRAD PC COMPONENTS

The way in which the various components interrelate for the PC1512 and PC1640 is briefly described here.

8087-2 maths co-processor

A socket is provided on the main board for an optional *8087-2 maths co-processor*. This provides additional facilities for floating point arithmetic. The advantage of such a chip is that it provides increased speed and accuracy in numerical calculations. It also has the advantage that such calculations, which take a relatively long time in computer terms, can be farmed out to this additional processor, freeing the 8086 itself for more important work.

The 8087 chip can only be used by programs that have been specifically written to take account of its capabilities. There are many additional machine-language instructions for dealing with the 8087. Since the 8087 is an optional feature neither the chip nor the additional instructions are covered in this book.

Real Time Clock (RTC)

The speed of the system is regulated by an *HD146818 Real Time Clock (RTC)*. This unit provides a programmable periodic pulse: a clock tick, which drives the computer. It is also used as the basis for the current date and time features, and a programmable alarm. Associated with the real time clock is a small piece of battery-backed memory (the non-volatile RAM or NVR).

Direct Memory Access (DMA)

The real time clock is connected to a battery sensor that can tell when the voltage is low. When this happens a single bit in one of the NVR locations is cleared; the next time the mains power is supplied the NVR is reset and its data initialised.

Data transfer between some devices and the memory addresses is controlled by the *8287-4 Direct Memory Access (DMA) Controller*. The 16-bit addresses that can be sent on the bus can only address a total of 64K memory locations (for reasons which are explained later). The DMA controller extends this addressing capability from 64K to 1 megabyte.

The DMA has four channels. One of these is used for memory refresh, the other three are attached to the expansion slots (see Figure 2.5). Channels 1 to 3 are used for transferring 8-bit data.

Associated with each of these additional three channels is a *page register port* that decides which of the 16 possible 64K pages are to be used at any one time. These pages must start at a 64K boundary, so the values sent to the ports must be in the range 00h to 0Fh. Each channel can transfer blocks of data within the selected page. The DMA controller uses ports 81h to 83h for this purpose. It also uses ports 00h to 0Fh for its own purposes.

8287-4 DMA channels		
Channel	Use	Page register port
0	8253 Timer Counter 1	-
1	External SDLC serial port	82h
2	External floppy disk controller	83h
3	External hard disk controller	81h

Figure 2.5 Operation of the DMA Controller

PIT Ports		
Port	Counter	Use
40h	0	General purpose timer
41h	1	Memory refresh (channel 0 of DMA)
42h	2	Sound generation
43h	-	PIT control

Figure 2.6 The PIT ports

Programmable Interval Timer (PIT)

An *8253 Programmable Interval Timer (PIT)* maintains three timers for a variety of purposes. The use of the three timers is as follows:

- Timer 0 is a general purpose timer that can be used in programs.

- Timer 1 is used by channel 0 of the DMA.

- Timer 2 is used when creating sound.

Associated with each of these timers is a count; the counts are read or changed by accessing ports 40h to 42h. Although these ports operate upon word values, they must be read or written a byte at a time. The purpose of these individual bytes is given in Figure 2.6.

The PIT also uses port 43h, which controls the use of the other three ports. The procedure for reading or writing to these ports is generally to send a value first to port 43h; this determines which mode of operation is to be used and which byte is to be accessed. This is then followed by sending or reading either one or two bytes (LSB first) to or from the selected port. This is the process that is used when generating sound (as illustrated later in Figure 14.2).

Programmable Peripheral Interface (PPI)

The IBM PC's, upon which the Amstrad PC's are based, have an *8255 Programmable Peripheral Interface (PPI)*. There is no such device in the Amstrad PC, but its effect is emulated by three ports, named A, B and C. Each of these ports stores specific items of information. Some of this information tells us about the current state of the system; this data is referred to as *Status-1* and *Status-2*. The use of the ports is shown in Figure 2.7. The general uses of these ports is as follows:

- Port B is used for system control and has a port number of 61h. It determines the interpretation of some of the data in ports A and C and also has an effect on the keyboard, the non-maskable interrupt and the speaker.

- Port A is number 60h and is a read-only port. It is used either for the keyboard scan code, or for Status-1 input (its use depending upon bit 7 of port B). Note that setting Port A for Status-1 input temporarily disables the keyboard, so bit 7 of port B must always be cleared after Status-1 has been inspected.

- Port C is also read-only and is numbered 62h. This is used for Status-2 input and the amount of RAM fitted. Only the bottom four bits are used to determine the RAM. However, five bits are used for the RAM code (Figure 2.8). Bit 2 of port B decides which bits can be read at the port.

Two other ports are used in association with these:

- Port 64h is a write-only port that is used in conjunction with port A. Its values are set by the NVR and the main board dip switches.

- Port 65h is a write-only port, used in conjunction with Port C for storing the user memory size.

The Amstrad PC System Unit

Port B: System Control (Port 61h)	
Bit	Meaning when set
7	Port A: Status-1 enabled and keyboard code disabled
6	Keyboard clock enabled
5	External parity errors do not cause NMI
4	Disable user RAM parity checking
3	Not used
2	Port C: Enable LSB and disable MSB
1	Pulse speaker
0	Modulate speaker

Port A: Status-1 (Port 60h)	
Bit	Use
7	0
6	When set indicates second floppy disk drive connected
5	Default display mode (see below)
4	Default display mode (see below)
3	1
2	1
1	When set indicates 8087 installed
0	1

Default display modes (Port 60h, bits 5 & 4)	
Values	Mode
00	IGA or extended adapter on expansion bus
01	Extended CGA (40 x 25 characters) on expansion bus
10	Extended CGA (80 x 25 characters) on expansion bus
11	Extended MDA (80 x 25 characters) on expansion bus

Figure 2.7 The PPI ports

The Amstrad PC System Unit

Port C: Status-2 and RAM size (Port 62h)	
Bit	Use
7	When set, user RAM parity error
6	When set, external parity error
5	8253 PIT output
4	Not used
3	RAM bit 3 (when Port B bit 2 set)
2	RAM bit 2 (when Port B bit 2 set)
1	RAM bit 1 (when Port B bit 2 set)
0	RAM bit 0 (when Port B bit 2 set) or RAM bit 4

Write Status-1 (Port 64h)	
Bit	Use
7	Not used
6	Second floppy disk drive installed
5	Default display mode (as Port 60h)
4	Default display mode (as Port 60h)
3	Not used
2	Not used
1	8087 installed
0	Not used

Write Status-2 (Port 65h)	
Bit	Use
7	Not used
6	Not used
5	Not used
4	RAM bit 4)
3	RAM bit 3)
2	RAM bit 2) As Port 62h
1	RAM bit 1)
0	RAM bit 0)

Figure 2.7 The PPI ports (continued)

RAM size codes (Port C, lower 4 bits)					
	Port B, bit 2				
	Clear	Set			RAM size
RAM bit	4	3	2	1	0	
Port C bit	0	3	2	1	0	
Values	0	1	1	1	0	512K
	0	1	1	1	1	544K
	1	0	0	0	0	576K
	1	0	0	0	1	608K
	1	0	0	1	0	640K

Figure 2.8 User RAM codes

The routine in Figure 2.9 displays some of the current contents of ports A, B and C. The purpose of this routine is only to demonstrate how the ports may be accessed; there are generally easier methods of gaining the same information. Of necessity, the program includes routines that are not fully explained until later in the text.

Programmable Interrupt Controller (PIC) — Whenever a device needs to signal to the CPU that a particular event has occurred (for example, that a key has been pressed) it does so by means of an *interrupt*. The *8259A-2 Programmable Interrupt Controller (PIC)* controls all interrupts apart from one used to signal a fatal error, called the *non-maskable interrupt (NMI)*. There are nine hardware interrupts including the NMI. These interrupts are signals that the computer must act on immediately, unless they have been disabled. All interrupts can be ignored by the use of suitable software.

Floppy Disk Controller (FDC) — The *765A Floppy Disk Controller (FDC)* controls either one or two 5¼" double-sided, double-density disk drives. The controller has a data transfer rate of 250 kilobits per second (approximately 30K per second).

Power supply — Mains power is directed through the monitor in the first instance. From there the transformed power is passed to the

```
PORTABC:                                    ; Display information held by ports
                                            ;   A, B & C

                                            ; Demonstrates calls to ports. Can be
                                            ;   extended to display any of the
                                            ;   available information;
                                            ;   alternatively, the results can be
                                            ;   passed back to a calling routine

                                            ; Calls DISSTR, DISLIN, DISBYT, NEWLIN
                                            ;   (See Figure 13.16)

                                            ; Entry values: None
                                            ; Exit values:  DX changed

                    jmp portst

mess0           db 'Port B (hex): $'
mess1           db 'Keyboard clock enabled$'
mess2           db 'Keyboard clock disabled$'
mess3           db 'External parity errors do not cause NMI$'
mess4           db 'External parity errors cause NMI$'
mess5           db 'RAM parity checking disabled$'
mess6           db 'RAM parity checking enabled$'
mess7           db 'Two floppy drives connected$'
mess8           db 'One floppy drive connected$'

portst:
                push ax
                in al,061                   ; Get Port B
                lea dx, mess0
                call dislin                 ; Display text
                call disbyt                 ; Display Port B byte
                call newlin                 ; Move to next line
                push ax                     ; Message for keyboard
                and al,040                  ; Isolate bit 6
                jz b6zero
                lea dx,mess1
                jmp b6mess

b6zero:
                lea dx,mess2

b6mess:
                call disstr                 ; Display keyboard message
                pop ax
                push ax                     : Message for NMI
                and al,020                  : Isolate bit 5
```

```
            jz  b5zero
                        lea  dx,mess3
                        jmp  b5mess

b5zero:
                        lea  dx,mess4

b5messb:
                        call disstr             ; Display NMI message
                        pop  ax
                        push ax                 ; Message for RAM parity checking
                        and  al,010             ; Isolate bit 4
                        jz   b4zero
                        lea  dx,mess5
                        jmp  b4mess

b4zero:
                        lea  dx,mess6

b4mess:
                        call disstr             ; Display RAM parity message
                        pop  ax
                        or   al,080             ; Set Port A to show Status 1
                        out  061,al
                        in   al,060             ; Get Port A
                        push ax                 ; Message for no. floppy drives
                        and  al,040             ; Isolate bit 6
                        jz   a6zero
                        lea  dx,mess7
                        jmp  a6mess

a6zero:
                        lea  dx,mess8

a6mess:
                        call disstr             ; Display keyboard message
                        pop  ax
                        in   al,061             ; Restore keyboard
                        and  al,061
                        and  al,07f             ; Restore keyboard
                        out  061,al
                        pop  ax
                        int  020
```

Figure 2.9 *Displaying the contents of the PPI ports*

Pin	Use
1	Not used
2	0 Volts (DC)
3	+5 Volts (DC)
4	0 Volts (DC)
5	+5 Volts (DC)
6	Not used
7	-12 Volts (DC)
8	0 Volts (DC)
9	Not used
10	0 Volts (DC)
11	+12 Volts (DC)
12	0 Volts (DC)
13	-5 Volts (DC)
14	Not used

Figure 2.10 The power supply socket

system unit through a 14-way Din socket. The pin arrangement of this socket is shown in Figure 2.10. (This information is for interest only; there is nothing that can be done to affect the way in which power is transmitted.)

The fact that the main power unit is included in the monitor unit makes it difficult to connect any other monitor to the Amstrad PC. It is possible to replace the monitor but only if some other external power supply is connected to the system unit.

MEMORY

Theoretically at least, the 8086 can address up to 1 megabyte of memory. There are basically two different types of memory:

- *Random access memory (RAM)*, which is memory that can be changed at will by a program;

- *Read only memory (ROM)*, which is memory that cannot be changed; its contents have already been fixed when the machine is supplied.

The RAM stores application programs, the operating system and any variable information that is used while the system is running. The RAM is *volatile* memory; it has to be constantly refreshed to maintain its data. When the power is switched off its contents are lost.

The ROM is used for storing permanent routines, such as those to start the computer running and carry out its automatic tests.

The Amstrad PC memory map is shown in Figure 2.11. This memory is automatically divided into a number of separate sections, each of which is described below.

User RAM

The 640K of memory from 00000h to 9FFFFh is allocated to the user RAM. On the PC1512 only the first 512K of this is used, but the additional 128K can be added at any time.

If the PC1512 is upgraded from 512K to 640K RAM, the link LK4 must be moved. The system will then show 640K RAM on power-up. Moving this link on the PC1640 has the effect of temporarily down-grading the memory, the top 128K becoming inaccessible.

The user RAM has *parity checking*. This means that for every byte of RAM there is an additional bit whose value depends on whether the sum of the bits in the byte is even or odd. If, at any time, the parity bit does not match the parity of the byte the system will stop with a memory error message.

Video RAM

The 128K from A0000h to BFFFFh is reserved for the screen. The data here is used by the display adapter to create the current screen display. Although this RAM is actually stored on the adapter board, it is treated as a standard part of memory and the CPU behaves as if it is part of normal RAM. Therefore, we are at liberty to change any values in this part of memory. The PC1640 uses the full 128K of video RAM while the PC1512 uses only 16K, with an additional 4K available for use by an external VDU controller.

Expansion ROM's

The section of memory from C0000h to EFFFFh is allocated to various ROM's.

The Amstrad PC System Unit

```
           PC1512                        PC1640
1M ─┐  ┌──────────────┬──────────┐  ┌──────────────┬─────────────────┐  FFFFF
    │  │   16K ROS    │          │  │   16K ROS    │ ROS             │
    │  ├──────────────┤          │  │  (4 copies)  │ ROS Copy 1      │
    │  │   RESERVED   │          │  │              │ ROS Copy 2      │
    │  │              │ EXPANSION│  │              │ ROS Copy 3      │  F0000
    │  │              │   ROMS   │  │              ├─────────────────┤
    │  │              │          │  │              │ 32K Test Board ROM│ E0000
    │  │              │          │  │  EXPANSION   ├─────────────────┤
    │  ├──────────────┤          │  │    ROM'S     │ 8K HD ROM       │
    │  │  16K HD ROM  │          │  │              ├─────────────────┤
    │  │              │          │  │              │ 24K IGA FONTS   │
    │  ├──────────────┴──────────┤  │              ├─────────────────┤
    │  │                         │  │              │ 8K IGA ROM BIOS │  C0000
    │  │     16K VIDEO RAM       │  ├──────────────┴─────────────────┤  BFFFF
    │  │                         │  │            128K                │
    │  ├─────────────────────────┤  │            VIDEO               │
    │  │ 4K OPTIONAL EXTERNAL VDU│  │            RAM                 │
    │  ├─────────────────────────┤  ├────────────────────────────────┤  A0000
    │  │     OPTIONAL 128K       │  │                                │  9FFFF
    │  │       USER RAM          │  │                                │
512K┤  ├─────────────────────────┤  │                                │
    │  │                         │  │                                │
    │  │                         │  │                                │
    │  │                         │  │                                │
    │  │                         │  │                                │
256K┤  │     512K USER RAM       │  │       640K USER RAM            │
    │  │                         │  │                                │
    │  │                         │  │                                │
    │  │                         │  │                                │
128K┤  │                         │  │                                │
    │  │                         │  │                                │
 64K┤  │                         │  │                                │
    │  ├─────────────────────────┤  ├────────────────────────────────┤
  0K┘  │    2K SYSTEM DATA       │  │      2K SYSTEM DATA            │  00000
       └─────────────────────────┘  └────────────────────────────────┘
```

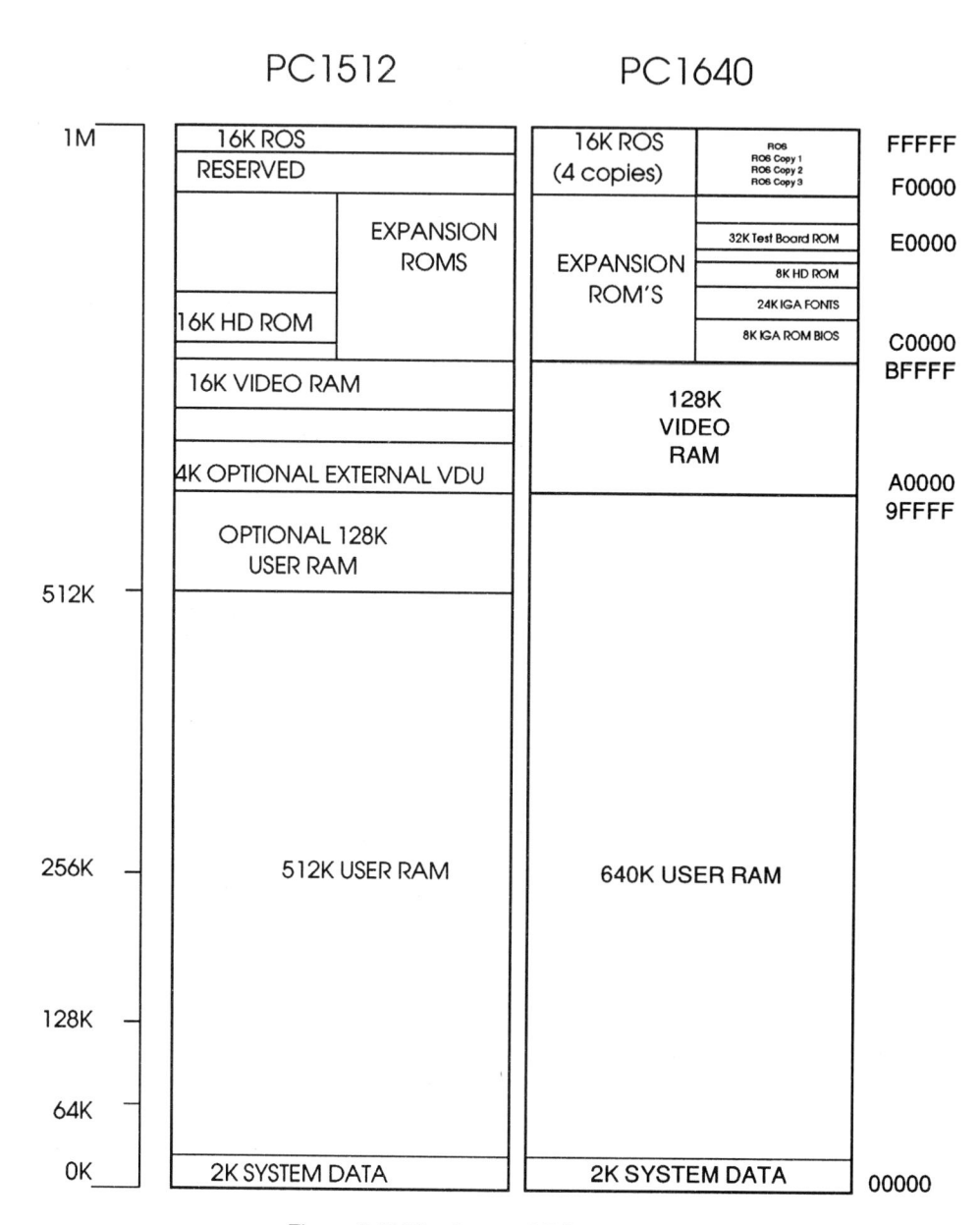

Figure 2.11 The Amstrad PC memory maps

In particular, on the PC1640 the section from C0000h to C7FFFh is used by the Internal Graphics Adapter (IGA). The first 8K of this area contains the IGA routines, while the next 24K is used for the storage of the fonts that make up the displays.

When a hard disk unit is attached this also has its own ROM for holding the hard disk routines. The PC1512 hard disk ROM uses the space from C8000h to CBFFFh. On the PC1640 this ROM is located from C8000h to C9FFFh; other hard disk controllers are allocated the space from CA000h to CCFFFh.

There is a hardware test board available for the PC1640 which has a ROM in the region E0000h to E7FFFh.

Other ROM's can be added as required, as long as they do not interfere with existing ROM's. All ROM's must start at an 8K boundary.

Resident Operating System (ROS)

The last 64K of memory, from F0000h to FFFFFh is reserved for the Amstrad PC's *Resident Operating System (ROS)*. The ROS actually only takes 16K of memory from FC000h onwards, but (on the PC1640) it is repeated three times in the previous 48K.

The resident operating system controls the operation of the computer from the time it is switched on until the disk operating system is loaded into memory and takes over.

SYSTEM RAM VARIABLES

The ROS also contains all the vitally important hardware routines that allow us to control individual parts of the computer system. It is from these small programs that the disk operating system also builds its own routines. The ROS is therefore at the very heart of the computer system.

The first 2K of user RAM is set aside for storing information that needs to be accessed, changed and updated by the computer system while it is running. Most of this information is vital to the operation of the computer so should be changed with care. The specific uses of the main variable storage area, from 0300h to 0500h are shown in Figure 2.12, while the general layout of this part of memory is shown in Figure 2.13.

Each of these individual locations is explained in more detail in the appropriate sections of the book.

The Amstrad PC System Unit

Memory Address	Number of Bytes	Use
0300	100	Stack space during system initialisation
0400	2	Port address of logical serial device 0 (initially the standard serial port)
0402	2	Port address of logical serial device 1 (initially the external asynchronous serial port; 0 if not installed)
0404	4	Reserved
0408	2	Port address of logical parallel device 0 (initially the standard parallel port)
040A	2	Port address of logical parallel device 1 (initially the external parallel port or the external monochrome controller; 0 if neither installed)
040C	2	Port address of logical parallel device 2 (initially the external monochrome controller if the external parallel port is fitted; 0 if only one installed)
040E	2	Reserved
0410	2	System configuration
0412	1	Reserved
0413	2	User RAM size (in kilobytes)
0415	2	Extra RAM size (in kilobytes): User RAM size - 64
0417	1	Keyboard status
0418	1	Keys-pressed status
0419	1	Number being entered with Alt and numeric keypad
041A	2	Pointer to next character in keyboard buffer, as offset from 0400h
041C	2	Pointer to next free space in keyboard buffer, as offset from 0400h
041E	20	Keyboard buffer
043E	1	Floppy disk restore and interrupt flags
043F	1	Floppy drive motor flags
0440	1	Drive motor timeout count
0441	1	Disk status
0442	7	Disk parameters
0449	1	Current video mode
044A	2	Number of columns in current mode

Memory Address	Number of Bytes	Use
044C	2	Current video mode page size (in bytes, including surplus bytes at end of page)
044E	2	Offset of current display page
0450	10	Cursor position (row and column) for each display page
0460	1	Last raster line of cursor
0461	1	First raster line of cursor
0462	1	Current display page
0463	1	Port used for CRTC interface (03B4 for mono, 03D4 for colour)
0465	1	Contents of current video mode control port
0466	1	Contents of EGA colour select port
0467	5	Reserved
046C	4	System clock count
0470	1	Midnight flag (FFh if midnight has been passed)
0471	1	Break status (1234h for system reset; 1235h to skip full hardware reset)
0474	1	Hard disk completion status
0475	1	Number of hard disks connected
0476	2	Reserved (by hard disk BIOS)
0478	3	Parallel printer timeout counts (for printers 0 to 2)
047B	1	Reserved
047C	2	Serial printer timeout counts (for printers 0 and 1)
047E	2	Reserved
0480	2	Offset of absolute start of keyboard buffer, from 0400h
0482	2	Offset of absolute end of keyboard buffer, from 0400h
0484	1	Number of display rows - 1
0485	1	Space used to store each character in character table
0487	1	Adapter status
0488	1	Adapter dip switch settings
0489	77	Not used
0500	1	Print-screen status

Figure 2.12 System RAM variables

The Amstrad PC System Unit

```
              ┌─────────────────────┐
              │   DOS RESIDENT      │
              │      SECTION        │
       00600──┤                     │
              │   DOS DATA AREA     │
       00500──┤                     │
              │ SYSTEM RAM VARIABLES│
       00400──┤                     │
              │  Stack space during │
              │    initialisation   │
       00300──┤ ─ ─ ─ ─ ─ ─ ─ ─ ─ ─ │
              │                     │
              │     INTERRUPT       │
              │      VECTORS        │
              │                     │
       00000──┤                     │
              └─────────────────────┘
```

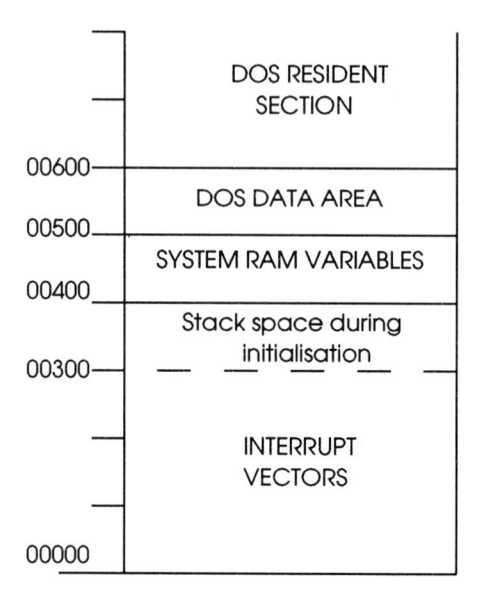

Figure 2.13 Allocation of low memory areas

THE SYSTEM CONFIGURATION

The main board has a number of dip switches and links, used for a variety of purposes, such as the language used for error messages. The states of these switches and links are checked by the system when it is switched on and parts of memory are set accordingly. The current state of the switches and links can be checked in a variety of ways.

THE PC1640 SYSTEM UNIT DIP SWITCHES

A bank of dip switches on the back of the PC1640 system unit are used to set various characteristics of the system. These switches must be set before mains power is switched on; any changes after that have no effect.

The effects of the switches are as follows:

- Switches 1 to 4 indicate the adapter type.

- Switch 5 selects either EGA mode or another mode.

- Switch 8 selects either the ECD or another monitor.

- When switch 10 is OFF, switches 6, 7 and 9 select the character font.

- When both switches 9 and 10 are OFF the English font is automatically selected and the area of ROM used by the foreign fonts (C4000h to C7FFFh) is free for use by any external ROM.

- When switch 10 is ON, the IGA is disabled and switches 6 and 7 indicate the external adapter type. Switches 1 to 5, 8 and 9 have no meaning in this situation.

The values of the switches can be investigated by reading the individual bits of some of the ports. A bit value of 1 represents 'OFF', 0 represents 'ON'. The switches that can be read in this way include:

- Switches 6 and 7 determine the values of bits 6 and 7 respectively of port 037Ah (the parallel printer control port); 0 = OFF and 1 = ON.

- Switch 9 can be determined by reading bit 5 of port 137Ah but only if this immediately follows a read of a particular dummy port (port 0278h is suggested). Interrupts should be disabled during this process.

- Switch 10 is determined by reading bit 5 of port 137Ah but only if this immediately follows a read of another dummy port (a PC1512 port for example). Interrupts should be disabled during this process.

The uses of the dip switches and the corresponding ports are shown in Figure 2.14.

Testing for machine type

If it is necessary to test for the type of Amstrad PC that a program is being run on, this can be done by reading bit 5 of port 037Ah. Before doing so you must read a dummy port, such as one of the PC1512 CGA ports. Bit 5 then returns the following values:

0 PC1640

1 PC1512

Other methods of detecting the machine type are given later.

Switch No.	Port	Switch 9 ON Switch 10 OFF	Switch 9 OFF Switch 10 OFF	Switch 10 ON
1		)	) (English font)	(IGA disabled) Not used
2		) Adapter	) Adapter	Not used
3		) type	) type	Not used
4		)	)	Not used
5		EGA/Other mode	EGA/Other mode	Not used
6	037Ah bit 6	) Character	Not used	) External
7	037Ah bit 7	) font	Not used	) adapter type
8		ECD/Other monitor	ECD/Other monitor	Not used
9	137Ah bit 5	ON	OFF	Not used
10	137Ah bit 5	OFF	OFF	ON

Figure 2.14 The PC1640 dip switches and related ports

Configuration list

It is often essential within a program to find out exactly what is connected to the computer. One method of doing this is to read memory location 0410h. This location stores those items of information from the PPI ports relating to the system configuration.

A far simpler method is to use the ROS interrupt provided for this purpose.

Interrupt: 11h
Service: Get configuration list
Entry values: None
Exit values: AX=configuration list code

The list is encoded in AX using exactly the same format as location 0410h (see Figure 2.15). In effect, this interrupt transfers the memory value into AX. Theoretically, the list can be adjusted but it is unwise to do so unless you have a very good reason. Figure 2.16 provides a routine to display the configuration.

User RAM

The amount of user RAM, given in Port C of the PPI, is also held in location 0413h in memory, a far more accessible

System configuration word (0410h)	
Bit	Use
15	) Number of parallel ports (1 - 3)
14	)
13	Not used
12	Set if games adapter installed
11	0
10	) Number of serial ports (1 - 2)
9	)
8	Not used
7	0
6	Set if second floppy drive installed
5	) Default display mode
4	)
3	1
2	1
1	Set if 8087 maths co-processor installed
0	1

Figure 2.15 The configuration list codes

place. To check the RAM size there is an even better method, using ROS interrupt 12h.

Interrupt: 12h
Service: Get user RAM
Entry values: None
Exit values: AX=user RAM

The hexadecimal value (in terms of kilobytes) is returned in AX. This value is identical to that held in 0413h and 0414h. Figure 2.17 shows how this value may be reported to the user.

The amount of memory above 64K is also held in memory, in the word at 0415h. This 'extra' RAM size is a throwback to the early IBM PC days, when 64K was the standard.

```
CONFIG:                             ; Displays configuration list

                                    ; This program produces similar
                                    ;   information to Figure 2.9 but
                                    ;   accesses memory rather than the
                                    ;   ports

                                    ; The configuratin code is read from
                                    ;   the word at 0410h and converted into
                                    ;   a simple screen display. An enhanced
                                    ;   version of this program provides a
                                    ;   more friendly screen and the chance
                                    ;   to change some of the values.
                                    ; Can be called as routine from another
                                    ;   program

                                    ; Calls DISSTR, DISLIN, DISBYT
                                    ;   (see Figure 13.16)

                                    ; Entry values: None
                                    ; Exit values:  AX,BX,CX,DX,ES changed

            jmp configst            ; Jump to start of program
m1          db '8087 installed$'
m2          db 'No 8087$'
m3          db 'Default display mode = $'
m4          db 'Two floppy drives$'
m5          db 'One floppy drive$'
m6          db 'Number of serial ports = $'
m7          db 'Games adapter installed$'
m8          db 'No games adapter$'
m9          db 'Number of parallel ports = $'
configst:
            lea es,0000h            ; Point to start of memory
            mov bx,0410h            ; BX points to configuration word
            push bx                 ; Save BX
            mov ax,bx
            call diswrd
            and bl,02h              ; Isolate bit 1
            cmp bl,00h              ; Is it 0?
            jz dism2                ; If so, jump
            lea dx,m1               ; Otherwise, point to message 1
            jmp part2
dism2:
            lea dx,m2               ; Point to message 2
part2:
            call dislin             ; Display message
```

```
                pop bx              ; Recover BX
                push bx             ; Save BX
                and bl,30h          ; Isolate bits 5 and 6 of BL   36 3
                lea dx,m3           ; Display message 3
                call disstr
                mov al,bl
                mov cl,04h
                shr al,cl           ; Convert to number (0 - 3)
                call disbyt         ; Display default mode
                call newlin         ; Move to next line
                pop bx
                push bx             ; Save BX
                and bl,40h          ; Isolate bit 6 of BL
                cmp bl,00h          ; Is it 0?
                jz dism5            ; If so, jump
                lea dx,m4           ; Otherwise, point to message 4
                jmp part3
dism5:
                lea dx,m5           ; Point to message 5
part3:
                call dislin         ; Display message
                pop bx
                push bx             ; Save BX
                and bh,30h          ; Isolate bits 1 and 2 of BH
                lea dx,m6           ; Display message 6
                call disstr
                mov al,bh
                call disbyt         ; Display number of serial ports
                call newlin         ; Move to next line
                pop bx
                push bx             ; Save BX
                and bh,10h          ; Isolate bit 4 of BH
                cmp bl,00h          ; Is it 0?
                jz dism8            ; If so, jump
                lea dx,m7           ; Otherwise, point to message 7
                jmp part4
dism8:
                lea dx,m8           ; Point to message 2
part4:
                call dislin         ; Display message
                pop bx              ; Recover BX
                push bx             ; Save BX
                and bh,0C0h         ; Isolate bits 6 and 7 of BH
                lea dx,m9           ; Display message 9
                call disstr
                mov al,bh
                mov cl,06h
                shr al,cl           ; Convert to number (0 - 3)
                call disbyt         ; Display number of parallel ports
```

```
            call newlin             ; Move to next line
            pop bx
            int 20h                 ; End program - change to RET if routine
                                    ;   is to be run from another program
```

Figure 2.16 Displaying the configuration list

```
RAMSIZE:                            ; Displays user RAM size

                                    ; Program uses interrupt 12h to display
                                    ;   the number of 1K blocks

                                    ; Can be called as routine from another
                                    ;   program

                                    ; Limitations - only display hex value.
                                    ;   Call DEL2HEX  (Figure 3.4) to
                                    ;   convert

                                    ; Calls DISSTR, DISBYT, DISLIN
                                    ;   (see Figure 13.6)

                                    ; Entry values: None
                                    ; Exit values:  AX=RAM size
                                    ;               DX changed
            jmp ramst
rammes      db 'User RAM size=$'
rammes2     db ' Kilobytes (in hex)$'
ramst:
            int 12h                 ; Get user RAM size in Kbytes
            lea dx,rammes
            call disstr             ; Display message
            call diswrd             ; Display size
            lea dx,rammes2
            call dislin             ; Display message and start new line
            int 20h                 ; Replace with RET for calls from
                                    ;   another program
```

Figure 2.17 Reporting the RAM size

3. *Programming the 8086*

At the centre of the Amstrad PC is the Intel 8086-2 processor. The entire operation of the computer and the programs that manipulate its various components are dependent on the structure of this chip. This chapter describes the main principles of the 8086, its use of memory and how it is programmed.

DATA TERMINOLOGY

The computer's memory is made up of a massive collection of individual locations, each of which can store only the values 0 or 1. These are the basic building blocks of all computer data, whether it is stored in memory, on disk or being transferred along a cable.

The PC1640 has over five million such locations. To keep things in proportion and make data more manageable a number of terms have been developed to describe various quantities of data. The terms in common use, all of which are used in this book, are described below.

Bits

The basic units of memory are called *bits*, which is short for 'binary digits'. As stated above, each bit may take a value of either 1 or 0.

Sometimes a single bit is used to indicate the state of some part of the system. For example, there is a section of memory that stores information about the current status of the keyboard. One bit indicates whether the Caps Lock function is on or off, another indicates that a Shift key is being pressed, and so on. In such cases, if a bit has the value 1 it is said to be *set*, otherwise it is *clear*. Thus we can set a bit by changing its value to 1, and clear it by changing the value to 0.

Bytes

The main unit of data is the *byte*. This consists of a string of eight bits. Each bit can store two possible values, so the eight bits of a byte can take 256 different combinations (2 to the power 8).

55

When used for storing numeric values a byte can be used in two different ways. A *signed* byte can take either positive or negative values, in the range -128 to 127. An *unsigned* byte can only take positive values and runs from 0 to 255.

Bytes are not always used for storing numbers or instructions. It is often the case that the individual bits of a byte have different meanings. For example, two bytes may be used to store the current time, with bits being grouped together to store the hours, minutes and seconds.

In cases such as this the bits within the byte are numbered from 0 to 7. Bit 0 is the rightmost bit in the byte. It is also known as the *least significant bit (LSB)*, since a change in its value only makes a difference of 1 to the total value of the byte.

Bit 7 is the leftmost bit and is also called the *most significant bit (MSB)*. Changing this bit makes a difference of 128 to a byte's value. In a signed byte, the value of the MSB determines whether the byte is positive (MSB = 0) or negative (MSB = 1). For a signed number the MSB is also known as the *sign bit*.

Words

Although we frequently work in terms of bytes, the Amstrad PC has a 16-bit data bus. That is, 16 bits of data (2 bytes) can be transferred in parallel along the bus. This is essential when dealing with large numbers or when referencing the computer's many memory locations. The combination of two bytes is called a *word*.

In common with bytes, words can be signed or unsigned. A signed word takes values in the range -32768 to 32767. An unsigned word has a maximum of 65535.

The bits in the word are numbered 0 to 15, with bit 15 being the most significant bit and determining whether the word is positive or negative.

Note that 'word' is often a rather loose term, generally used to refer to a collection of bytes. Frequently its definition depends upon the data structures of the computer system under consideration. For example, it is common to have 32-bit words on mainframe computers. In this book a word is always 16 bits long.

Kilobytes and megabytes

While 2-byte words are a convenient form for data transfer the basic unit of data remains the byte. To make life easier, when talking about large quantities the bytes are grouped together into *kilobytes (K)*. One kilobyte (1K) is the equivalent of 1024 bytes.

The PC1512 has a memory of 512K, that of the PC1640 is 640K.

Similarly, larger quantities are referred to in terms of *megabytes (M)*. One megabyte (1M) is the equivalent of 1024K or 1,048,576 bytes.

The PC1640 may be supplied with a 20M hard disk.

Elsewhere, one megabyte may be abbreviated to 1Mb.

Hexadecimal notation

The system of binary used by the computer is impractical for daily use. Our normal decimal system is so far removed from the way in which the computer is structured that it is too confusing for everyday use. There is no easy conversion between our units of 10 and the powers of 2 that are inherent in all computer calculations. Therefore the notation commonly used is that of *hexadecimal (hex)*. This is related to the binary system by taking 16 (2 to the power 4) as its base. This system provides a direct relationship between a hexadecimal digit and a group of four bits (Figure 3.1).

Since there are only ten numeric symbols, the values 10 to 15 are represented by the letters A to F. Thus the decimal numbers 1 to 16 are represented in hexadecimal by the values:

1, 2, 3, 4, 5, 6, 7, 8, 9, A, B, C, D, E, F, 10

It is obviously important to distinguish between hex and decimal when values are written. There are many different conventions but one of the most commonly used - and the one adopted in this book - is to append an 'h' to the number. Thus the decimal value 16 is equivalent to hex 10h. Decimal values of 17 and 27 are represented by 11h and 1Bh respectively.

Each group of four bits is represented by precisely one hex digit. Therefore every byte can be represented by a two-digit

Decimal	Binary	Hexadecimal
0	0000	0
1	0001	1
2	0010	2
3	0011	3
4	0100	4
5	0101	5
6	0110	6
7	0111	7
8	1000	8
9	1001	9
10	1010	A
11	1011	B
12	1100	C
13	1101	D
14	1110	E
15	1111	F

Figure 3.1 Hexadecimal representation of bytes and words

hex number. A word is represented by a four-digit hex number.

As a general rule, any hex values in this book will be padded with 0's where they are representations of fixed-length variables. For example, the number 13 will appear as 0Dh if it is the contents of a byte or 000Dh if it is held in a word. Where the text refers to memory locations, port numbers, interrupt numbers and any other values that are likely to be included in programs the hexadecimal notation is used in preference to decimal. Decimal is only used where it is necessary to relate values to the 'real world'.

Once this system becomes familiar the use of bytes and words also begins to become easier and the conventions begin to make more sense. In particular the following conversions are useful:

■ One byte can store 100h (256) values, in the range 00h to FFh. In a signed byte the values 80h to FFh are negative.

- A word can store 10000h (64K) values, from 0000h to FFFFh. Negative values in a signed word range from 8000h to FFFFh.

- A kilobyte is 400h, a megabyte is 100000h.

Other terms, such as *gigabyte* (1000 M), are not used here.

Conversion tables between decimal and hexadecimal are given in Figures 3.2 and 3.3. The routines in Figure 3.4 provide conversions between these two types of number.

Pages and paragraphs

For convenience, the memory of the computer is divided into 4K sections, or 4096 (1000h) bytes. These sections of memory are known as *pages*. An extension of this terminology is to call each 16 (10h) bytes of memory a *paragraph*. There are 100h paragraphs in each page.

The low-high convention

Just as you think you are beginning to make sense of the numbering system used in the computer world, the way in which data is stored leaps out at you.

For reasons which are not entirely clear, a word is stored in memory with its bytes in reverse order, the low-order byte coming first. (It is probably a relief to learn that each individual byte is stored with its bits the right way round!) Thus if the two words 0B28h and 002Ah are stored as data an inspection of that section of memory reveals the following string of bytes:

```
28 0B 2A 00
```

This convention takes a while to get used to but it comes with practice. Much of the time the way in which data is physically stored is of little importance anyway.

BINARY CALCULATIONS

A complete discussion of the binary system is beyond the scope of this book. However, there are a couple of features of binary numbers when used in calculations that are worthy of note.

Programming the 8086

```
Decimal to Hexadecimal
```

	00	10	20	30	40	50	60	70	80	90
0	00	0A	14	1E	28	32	3C	46	50	5A
1	01	0B	15	1F	29	33	3D	47	51	5B
2	02	0C	16	20	2A	34	3E	48	52	5C
3	03	0D	17	21	2B	35	3F	49	53	5D
4	04	0E	18	22	2C	36	40	4A	54	5E
5	05	0F	19	23	2D	37	41	4B	55	5F
6	06	10	1A	24	2E	38	42	4C	56	60
7	07	11	1B	25	2F	39	43	4D	57	61
8	08	12	1C	26	30	3A	44	4E	58	62
9	09	13	1D	27	31	3B	45	4F	59	63

	100	110	120	130	140	150	160	170	180	190
0	64	6E	78	82	8C	96	A0	AA	B4	BE
1	65	6F	79	83	8D	97	A1	AB	B5	BF
2	66	70	7A	84	8E	98	A2	AC	B6	C0
3	67	71	7B	85	8F	99	A3	AD	B7	C1
4	68	72	7C	86	90	9A	A4	AE	B8	C2
5	69	73	7D	87	91	9B	A5	AF	B9	C3
6	6A	74	7E	88	92	9C	A6	B0	BA	C4
7	6B	75	7F	89	93	9D	A7	B1	BB	C5
8	6C	76	80	8A	94	9E	A8	B2	BC	C6
9	6D	77	81	8B	95	9F	A9	B3	BD	C7

Figure 3.2 Decimal-to-hex conversions

```
Decimal to Hexadecimal

            200   210   220   230   240   250

        0   C8    D2    DC    E6    F0    FA
        1   C9    D3    DD    E7    F1    FB
        2   CA    D4    DE    E8    F2    FC
        3   CB    D5    DF    E9    F3    FD
        4   CC    D6    E0    EA    F4    FE
        5   CD    D7    E1    EB    F5    FF
        6   CE    D8    E2    EC    F6    00
        7   CF    D9    E3    ED    F7    01
        8   D0    DA    E4    EE    F8    02
        9   D1    DB    E5    EF    F9    03
```

Decimal	Hex	Decimal	Hex	Decimal	Hex
100	0168	1000	04EC	10000	2814
200	01CC	2000	08D4	20000	4F24
300	0230	3000	0CBC	30000	7634
400	0294	4000	10A4	40000	9D44
500	02F8	5000	148C	50000	C454
600	035C	6000	1874	60000	EB64
700	03C0	7000	1C5C		
800	0424	8000	2044		
900	0488	9000	242C		

Figure 3.2 Decimal-to-hex conversions (continued)

Hexadecimal to Decimal

	00	10	20	30	40	50	60	70
0	0	16	32	48	64	80	96	112
1	1	17	33	49	65	81	97	113
2	2	18	34	50	66	82	98	114
3	3	19	35	51	67	83	99	115
4	4	20	36	52	68	84	100	116
5	5	21	37	53	69	85	101	117
6	6	22	38	54	70	86	102	118
7	7	23	39	55	71	87	103	119
8	8	24	40	56	72	88	104	120
9	9	25	41	57	73	89	105	121
A	10	26	42	58	74	90	106	122
B	11	27	43	59	75	91	107	123
C	12	28	44	60	76	92	108	124
D	13	29	45	61	77	93	109	125
E	14	30	46	62	78	94	110	126
F	15	31	47	63	79	95	111	127

	80	90	A0	B0	C0	D0	E0	F0
0	128	144	160	176	192	208	224	240
1	129	145	161	177	193	209	225	241
2	130	146	162	178	194	210	226	242
3	131	147	163	179	195	211	227	243
4	132	148	164	180	196	212	228	244
5	133	149	165	181	197	213	229	245
6	134	150	166	182	198	214	230	246
7	135	151	167	183	199	215	231	247
8	136	152	168	184	200	216	232	248
9	137	153	169	185	201	217	233	249
A	138	154	170	186	202	218	234	250
B	139	155	171	187	203	219	235	251
C	140	156	172	188	204	220	236	252
D	141	157	173	189	205	221	237	253
E	142	158	174	190	206	222	238	254
F	143	159	175	191	207	223	239	255

Figure 3.3 Hex-to-decimal conversions

Decimal	Hex	Decimal	Hex
100	256	1000	4096
200	512	2000	8192
300	768	3000	12288
400	1024	4000	16384
500	1280	5000	20480
600	1536	6000	24576
700	1792	7000	28672
800	2048	8000	32768
900	2304	9000	36864
A00	2560	A000	40960
B00	2816	B000	45056
C00	3072	C000	49152
D00	3328	D000	53248
E00	3584	E000	57344
F00	3840	F000	61440
10000	65536		

Figure 3.3 Hex-to-decimal conversions (continued)

Negative numbers   We have already seen that negative numbers are those with the leftmost bit set to 1. This results in a cycle of numbers where -128 follows +127 (Figure 3.5).

From the diagram a symmetry becomes apparent. If all the bits of any binary number on the left-hand side are switched (0's become 1's and vice versa) the result is the same as the corresponding number on the right-hand side. The numbers on the right are the *complement* of those on the left, and vice versa. It can also be seen that the numbers are slightly out of step, forming pairs as follows:

-1,0 -2,1 -3,2 ... -128,127

From this it becomes apparent that a number can be negated by taking the complement and adding 1. The procedure works both ways. For example:

complement(2) + 1 = -3 + 1 = -2

complement(-2) + 1 = 1 + 1 = 2

```
DEC2HEX:                                ; Convert decimal value to hex

                                        ; Entry values: DECIN holds decimal
                                        ;                 value
                                        ; Exit values: AX=hex value
                                        ;              AX,BX,CX,DX,SI changed

              jmp decstart
decin         db '      ',00            ; Decimal value to be converted, as
                                        ;   ASCII string, terminated by null
                                        ;   character. Maximum value 65535.
                                        ;   Routine does not check that number
                                        ;   is valid.

decstart:
              xor ax,ax                 ; Set AX to 0 (AX will hold hex value)
              xor bx,bx                 ; Clear BX
              mov bl,0Ah                ; Move 10 into BX
              xor si,si                 ; Clear SI (pointer to next decimal
                                        ;   digit)

startcon:
              xor cx,cx                 ; Clear CX
              mov cl,decin[si]          ; Get next decimal digit
              cmp cl,00h                ; Check against 0
              jz endcon                 ; If 0, conversion is complete
              mul bx                    ; Otherwise, multiply value in AX by 10
              sub cl,30h                ; Otherwise, subtract 30h to convert
                                        ;   ASCII number to actual value
              add ax,cx                 ; Add new digit
              inc si                    ; Increase SI to point to next digit
              jmp startcon              ; Jump to start of loop
endcon:
              ret

; ------------------------------------------------------------------

D2H:                                    ; Program to convert decimal to hex

                                        ; Value to be converted is included
                                        ;   as command line parameter
                                        ;   (e.g. D2H 12345)

                                        ; Limitations: No checking for validity
                                        ;   of parameter. Maximum 65536.

                                        ; Calls PARSE, NEXTPARM (Figure 6.3),
                                        ;   DISWRD (Figure 13.16), DEC2HEX
```

```
            jmp d2hstart

declen      db ?                    ; Number of digits in decimal parameter

d2hstart:
            call parse               ; Parse the command line
            mov al,[paramlen]        ; Get no. digits and save in DECLEN
            mov [declen],al
            call nextparm            ; Read decimal into PARAMETER
            cld
            xor cx,cx
            mov cl,05h
            mov al,00h
            lea di,decin
            rep stosb                ; Fill DECIN with nulls
            lea si,parameter
            lea di,decin
            mov cl,[declen]          ; Transfer contents of PARAMETER
            rep movsb                ;    to DECIN
            call dec2hex             ; Decimal-to-hex conversion
            call diswrd              ; Display result
            int 20h
```

Figure 3.4 Decimal/hex conversion routines

This process is called *two's complement* and forms the basis of all computer subtraction. Subtraction of a number is the same as the addition of the negative of the number. For example:

10 - 3 = 10 + (-3)

In binary this becomes:

00001010 + 11111101 = 00000111

(The 'carry' bit that is created by the addition is ignored.)

The carry bit and overflows

In any binary calculation there is a possibility that the result will overflow the number of bits that are available for the result. This occurs in two sets of circumstances.

The first case, described above, occurs when a small negative number is added to a large positive value. The result is a

Programming the 8086

```
                        11111111     00000000
               11111110   -1      0   00000001
      11111101    -2                1    00000010
          -3                        2
          .                         .
10111111  -65                      64    01000000
          .                         .
         -126                      125
     10000010  -127            126    01111101
         10000001  -128      127    01111110
             10000000        01111111
```

Figure 3.5 Binary representations

carry bit that can be ignored, since it is merely the side-effect of the way in which negative numbers are stored.

The second case indicates that some sort of error has occurred. At one end of the scale this happens if we subtract 1 from -128, giving a result of 127. In this case the carry bit is also set, indicating that an *overflow* has occurred. In the reverse situation, adding 1 to 127 gives -128 but this time the carry bit is not set even though an overflow has occurred.

The overall result is that we can, to a great extent, ignore the carry bit when doing signed calculations. If the calculation goes over the top of the circle all is well; if it traverses the bottom of the circle then an overflow has occurred.

ASCII

We have seen how numbers are stored in memory. Much of the time we also need to store text. To do this, the same system of bytes is used, for convenience each byte storing a single character.

When text is being stored it is necessary to use a code, so that text characters can be related to the numeric values in memory. The system normally used is that of *ASCII*, an internationally-recognised code for storing up to 128 different characters. This is sufficient for all the letters of the alphabet

Programming the 8086

(upper and lower case), the numeric digits and a large number of mathematical symbols, punctuation marks and other symbols. The order of the codes is not perhaps what we might expect but there is a certain logic to it. 'A' is represented by 40h, 'B' is 41h and so on; the lower case letters start at 60h while the numeric digits 0 to 9 are to be found from 30h to 39h.

Control codes   The first 32 ASCII characters (00h to 1Fh) are reserved for *control codes*. These codes represent operations that perform common computer activities. For example, 0Ah is the line feed character while 0Dh represents a carriage return.

Extended codes   All the characters we need are stored in 128 codes, so it would be feasible to use just 7 bits. However, this is not practical when the computer's memory is divided into 8-bit bytes. The extra bit can be used in several ways.

When transferring data to a printer or another computer it is sometimes used as part of the error-checking procedures.

Some programs that deal wholly with text use the extra bit to signal some specific feature. Use the DOS TYPE command to display the contents of a WordStar document on the screen and you will see that any character that is followed by a space has the MSB set. This saves one character but means that strange characters appear on the screen when the file is accessed outside WordStar.

As a general rule, however, we can make use of the extra bit by extending the number of codes to 256. The extra 128 codes are used to store a variety of extra symbols and graphics characters (in particular all those needed for drawing single and double boxes on the screen). These codes form the *extended ASCII* set. Be warned, however, that standards are not so firm here and variations in codes may occur from one implementation to another.

The standard ASCII characters are shown in Figure 3.6.

Programming the 8086

Decimal	Hex	Char	Decimal	Hex	Char	Decimal	Hex	Char	Decimal	Hex	Char
0	00	NUL	32	20	SPACE	64	40	@	96	60	`
1	01	SOH	33	21	!	65	41	A	97	61	a
2	02	STX	34	22	"	66	42	B	98	62	b
3	03	ETX	35	23	#	67	43	C	99	63	c
4	04	EOT	36	24	$	68	44	D	100	64	d
5	05	ENQ	37	25	%	69	45	E	101	65	e
6	06	ACK	38	26	&	70	46	F	102	66	f
7	07	BEL	39	27	'	71	47	G	103	67	g
8	08	BS	40	28	(	72	48	H	104	68	h
9	09	HT	41	29	)	73	49	I	105	69	i
10	0A	LF	42	2A	*	74	4A	J	106	6A	j
11	0B	VT	43	2B	+	75	4B	K	107	6B	k
12	0C	FF	44	2C	,	76	4C	L	108	6C	l
13	0D	CR	45	2D	-	77	4D	M	109	6D	m
14	0E	SO	46	2E	.	78	4E	N	110	6E	n
15	0F	SI	47	2F	/	79	4F	O	111	6F	o
16	10	DLE	48	30	0	80	50	P	112	70	p
17	11	DC1	49	31	1	81	51	Q	113	71	q
18	12	DC2	50	32	2	82	52	R	114	72	r
19	13	DC3	51	33	3	83	53	S	115	73	s
20	14	DC4	52	34	4	84	54	T	116	74	t
21	15	NAK	53	35	5	85	55	U	117	75	u
22	16	SYN	54	36	6	86	56	V	118	76	v
23	17	ETB	55	37	7	87	57	W	119	77	w
24	18	CAN	56	38	8	88	58	X	120	78	x
25	19	EM	57	39	9	89	59	Y	121	79	y
26	1A	SUB	58	3A	:	90	5A	Z	122	7A	z
27	1B	ESC	59	3B	;	91	5B	[	123	7B	{
28	1C	FS	60	3C	<	92	5C	\	124	7C	|
29	1D	GS	61	3D	=	93	5D	]	125	7D	}
30	1E	RS	62	3E	>	94	5E	^	126	7E	~
31	1F	US	63	3F	?	95	5F	_	127	7F	

Figure 3.6 Standard ASCII characters

\	\	ASCII control codes	\
Dec	Hex	Abbreviation	Meaning
0	00	NVL	Null character
1	01	SOH	Start of header
2	02	STX	Start text
3	03	ETX	End text
4	04	EOT	End of transmission
5	05	ENQ	Enquiry
6	06	ACK	Acknowledge
7	07	BEL	Bell
8	08	BS	Backspace
9	09	HT	Horizontal tab
10	0A	LF	Line feed
11	0B	VT	Vertical tab
12	0C	FF	Form feed
13	0D	CR	Carriage return
14	0E	SO	Shift out
15	0F	SI	Shift in
16	10	DLE	Data line escape
17	11	DC1	Device control 1
18	12	DC2	Device control 2
19	13	DC3	Device control 3
20	14	DC4	Device control 4
21	15	NAK	Negative acknowledge
22	16	SYN	Synchronisation idle
23	17	ETB	End transmission block
24	18	CAN	Cancel
25	19	EM	End of medium
26	1A	SUB	Substitute
27	1B	ESC	Escape
28	1C	FS	File separator
29	1D	GS	Group separator
30	1E	RS	Record separator
31	1F	US	Unit separator

Figure 3.7 ASCII control codes

Programming the 8086

MEMORY ORGANISATION

Each location in memory has a numeric label to identify it. This is the *address* of the location. Every time the computer is given an instruction to store or retrieve information, or carry out some other operation on it, the instruction must include the address of the data.

However, as we have already seen, the 8086 has a 16-bit data bus, along which all this information must pass. The two-byte word that fits on this bus can only take 65536 values (64K). Clearly this is insufficient for the memories of our computers, so the 8086 uses two words to identify an address.

It works rather like the address on a letter, such as '25 South Street'. One part is used to point to the general area while the other identifies a location in that area. 'South Street' on its own is not enough to describe a single house, while there is a '25' in nearly every street; the combination of the two together identifies just one location.

Because of the 64K limit on a word, the 8086 uses one word to point to a general 64K area and the second word to identify a particular byte in that area. The 64K area is called a *segment* and the relative position of a byte in the area is the *offset*.

Of course, it would be feasible to divide the memory into, say, sixteen consecutive, non-overlapping segments, giving one megabyte of addresses. However, as we shall see shortly, this would be rather limiting. In fact, because the 8086 only wants to address one megabyte it allows us to define a segment to start at the beginning of any 16-byte paragraph. As a result segments frequently overlap but this doesn't matter - as long as we keep our wits about us! The effect of this is that the actual location of the start of a segment can be calculated by multiplying the segment by 16 (that is, by adding a zero to its hex value). For example, segment 0B28h begins at the 5-digit location 0B280h.

The offset is always measured from the start of the segment. When describing a location the segment is placed before the offset. For example, the address 0B28:002A is the 42nd byte (002Ah) in the segment that starts at 0B280h. To calculate

Actual address	First segment	Second segment	Third segment
00000	0000:0000		
00001	0000:0001		
...	...		
0000F	0000:000F		
00010	0000:0010	0001:0000	
00011	0000:0011	0001:0001	
...	...	...	
0001F	0000:001F	0001:000F	
00020	0000:0020	0001:0010	0002:0000
00021	0000:0021	0001:0011	0002:0001
...	...	...	...

Figure 3.8 The 8086 segment addressing system

the exact address simply multiply the segment by 16 and add the offset. In this case the exact address is given by:

0B28:002A

= (0B28h x 10h) + 002Ah

= 0B280h + 002Ah

= 0B2AAh

Note that the overlapping of addresses means that 0B28:002A is the same address as 0B29:001A and 0B2A:000A, as well as many others. This addressing system is demonstrated in Figure 3.8.

ELEMENTS OF 8086 PROGRAMMING

There are a few important features that we must examine before proceeding further. These are the basic elements of the 8086's programming capabilities, which are essential for programming. They also provide an insight into the way in which the 8086 operates.

Programming the 8086

THE REGISTERS The 8086 contains a few areas in its work space for storing data and addresses. These are called *registers*. They are the basic variables of the 8086 programming language.

Although we are relatively free to manipulate the contents of the registers as we please, they also have some very specific purposes. In most situations the programmer is constrained to use the registers for storing specific information. Note that the registers are not stored in the user RAM but within the CPU itself.

In the main we will use a part of RAM for storing variable data, rather than the registers. However, the data we use could be anywhere; when we ask the built-in programs of the CPU and the operating system to perform some task they need to know where to look for the data. We also need to know where to look for the results that are returned from such operations.

The main advantage of the registers is that their absolute location is fixed, as are the names by which they are known. They can therefore be used for two purposes:

- As temporary storage places for data and results during calculations

- As places to store addresses when we call a subroutine or move from one program to another

The registers thus form a common area where information can be passed from one program to another, as well as being used extensively as a work area. The full set of registers is shown in Figure 3.9.

THE STACK As we have seen, there are only a limited number of registers available and these are in constant use. The resulting congestion that occurs can lead to disaster if we are not careful about how we use the registers. Problems arise when we need to call a routine to perform some other task.

For example, a register may store the address of our data area but a subroutine may use some other, totally different data area. This means that we must save the original data address before calling the subroutine, so that it can be restored once the subroutine has finished its work.

Programming the 8086

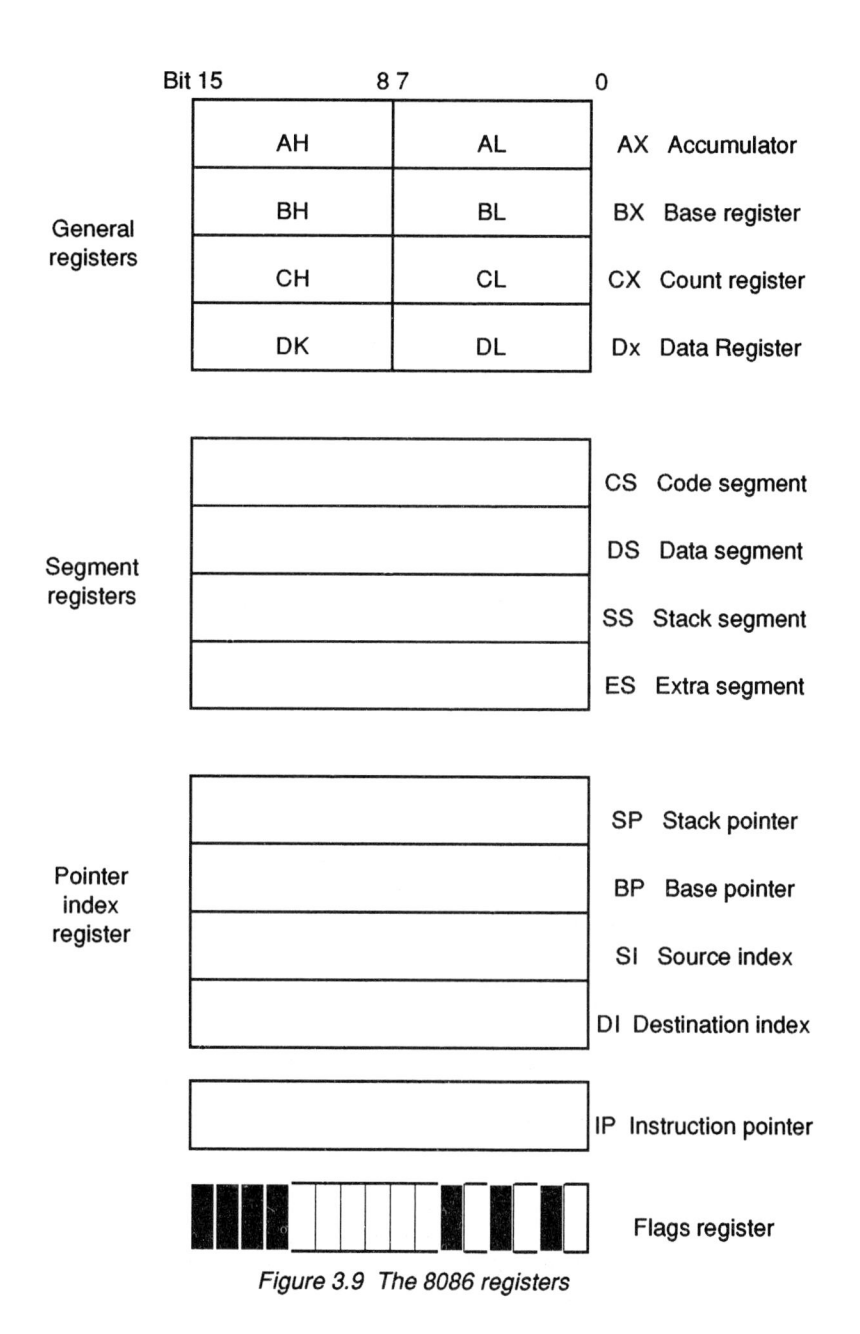

	Bit 15	8 7	0		
	AH	AL		AX	Accumulator
General registers	BH	BL		BX	Base register
	CH	CL		CX	Count register
	DK	DL		Dx	Data Register

Segment registers			
		CS	Code segment
		DS	Data segment
		SS	Stack segment
		ES	Extra segment

Pointer index register			
		SP	Stack pointer
		BP	Base pointer
		SI	Source index
		DI	Destination index

	IP	Instruction pointer
		Flags register

Figure 3.9 The 8086 registers

One way of doing this would be to store the address away in our data area. However, this is a long-winded process (in computer terms). The actual address of the data area would have to be hard-coded into the program; if we don't know where the data area is it is no good using it to store an address!

We get round this problem by using a general-purpose storage area called the *stack*. This is really quite an ingenious idea. Tradition has it that the term 'stack' comes from an analogy with a stack of plates in a cafeteria: not an ordinary stack of plates but one of those that is spring-loaded, so that the plate at the top is always in the same position regardless of how many plates there are. Any new plates are pushed onto the top of the stack and then popped off as needed. The main point to note is that the last plate pushed onto the stack is always the first to pop off it.

Whether or not this simple device provided the inspiration for the originator of the computer stack, the analogy is a good one. This is precisely how the 8086 stack works. Every time we need to temporarily store a piece of data we can *push* it onto the stack. When we need to retrieve it we simply *pop* it off again. The beauty of the system is that we need not concern ourselves with the precise location of any piece of data; all that is taken care of. What we must do, however, is keep very strict control of what is pushed onto the stack and make sure that everything is always popped off the stack in reverse order.

This is usually ensured by placing the 'pops' in the same routine as the corresponding 'pushes'. Thus we might push all the registers onto the stack before calling a subroutine; immediately after the subroutine call there should be a similar set of pop instructions but in reverse order.

The other advantages are that the same stack can be used by any number of subroutines; as long as each one pops everything new off the stack, before it ends, the stack will be in precisely the same state as the calling routine left it. The guiding principle for any routine is always to leave the stack as you found it.

The other major advantage is that we can make the stack almost as large as we like, so any amount of data can be temporarily stored there as long as we are happy to retrieve it in reverse order.

The Stack Pointer   Since the stack is generally self-clearing it is not usual to interfere with the mechanism. However, it is worth noting that one of the registers that is maintained is the *Stack Pointer* *(SP)*.

The Stack Pointer is updated by the system so that it constantly points to the *top of stack*. This is the location of the last item on the stack. In fact, this is perhaps not a very good name since the stack works upside down. The beginning of the stack is actually at the top of memory and the stack increases downwards, so the address of the 'top' of stack actually reduces as more items are pushed onto the stack.

The advantage of this method of filling the stack becomes apparent when trying to devise programs that will fit into a single 64K segment (as is the case with COM programs, for example). The data area can immediately follow the program code at the start of the segment. The stack data automatically starts at the other end of the segment and works down towards the fixed data area. The only problem arises if you run out of stack space while executing the program.

It is feasible to store away the current Stack Pointer at any time, so that an item in the stack can be retrieved by accessing the appropriate part of memory in the usual way. However, it is not generally a good idea to change the Stack Pointer from within a program: if data does not need to be retrieved it should not be put on the stack in the first place. Of course, there are some very good reasons why an experienced programmer may want to tinker with the stack mechanism.

It is important to bear in mind that the processor also makes use of the stack. Every time a subroutine is called the return address is pushed onto the stack; it is popped off again when the subroutine is completed so that the system knows to which instruction it should return. Upsetting the Stack Pointer endangers the whole structure of the program.

An example of how the stack is used is given in Figure 3.10.

Some of the registers are reserved for storing the segment addresses of the parts of memory that are being used by the

Programming the 8086

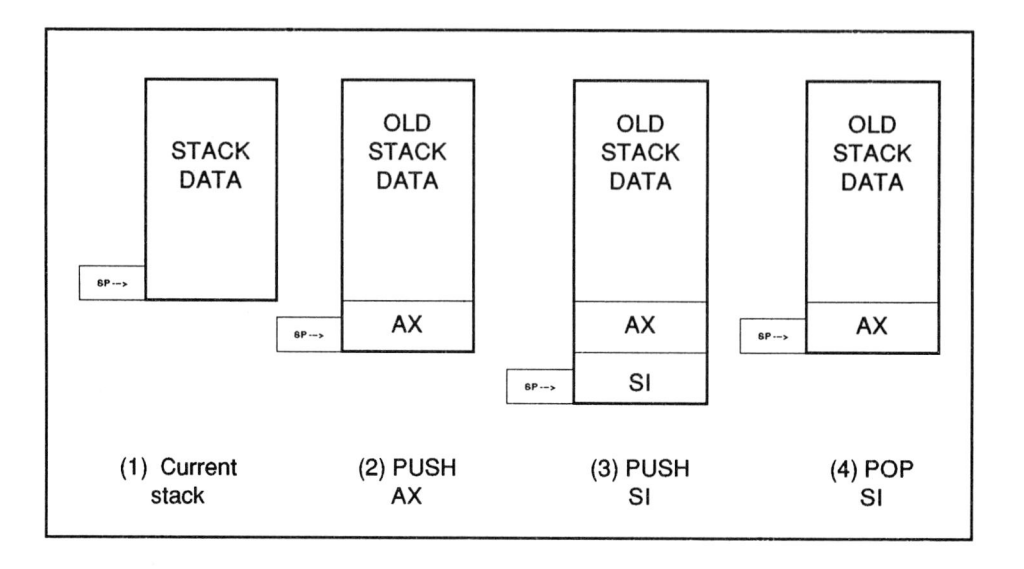

```
┌─────────────────────────────────────────────────────────────┐
│                                                             │
│                                                             │
│              ┌──────┐   ┌──────┐   ┌──────┐                 │
│              │ OLD  │   │ OLD  │   │ OLD  │                 │
│   ┌──────┐   │STACK │   │STACK │   │STACK │                 │
│   │STACK │   │ DATA │   │ DATA │   │ DATA │                 │
│   │ DATA │   │      │   │      │   │      │                 │
│   │      │   │      │   │      │   │      │                 │
│   │      │   ├──────┤   ├──────┤   ├──────┤                 │
│SP→│      │SP→│  AX  │   │  AX  │SP→│  AX  │                 │
│   └──────┘   └──────┘   ├──────┤   └──────┘                 │
│                      SP→│  SI  │                            │
│                         └──────┘                            │
│                                                             │
│   (1) Current  (2) PUSH   (3) PUSH   (4) POP                │
│       stack        AX         SI         SI                 │
│                                                             │
└─────────────────────────────────────────────────────────────┘
```

Figure 3.10 Using the stack

SEGMENT REGISTERS

current program. These are the *segment registers*. There are four of these registers:

- The *Code Segment, CS*, is the part of memory that holds the program code that is being executed.

- The *Data Segment, DS*, is the area reserved for storing data.

- The *Stack Segment, SS*, is the location of the program's stack space. In combination with the Stack Pointer it identifies the current top of stack (SS:SP).

- The *Extra Segment, ES*, is an additional register that is free for the programmer to use when pointing to some other location.

The first three of these need to be maintained at all times if the processor is not to lose its way in the program. In practice these three segment registers often point to the same location in memory, especially for small programs. Alternatively, they may overlap or be in totally different areas of memory.

There is no need to be too concerned about the actual values of CS, DS and SS. This is generally taken care of automatically when the program is executed.

THE GENERAL PURPOSE REGISTERS

Four of the 8086's registers are used as *general purpose registers*. They have a few specific, pre-defined functions but, in general, can be used as we wish. Some 8086 instructions insist that we use particular registers and results are usually found in specific registers. Apart from this we are free to change them in a program, as long as we always bear in mind that certain operations will change their values.

The registers are labelled AX, BX, CX and DX. The AX register is sometimes called the *accumulator* and BX is termed the *base register*. The CX register is frequently used as a counter in loops and may therefore be called the *count* register. DX is sometimes known as the *data* register.

The four registers are primarily word registers but their component bytes can be used independently to give us eight single-byte registers. The high byte of AX is referred to as AH and the low byte is AL. The other six registers are BH, BL, CH, CL, DH and DL.

It is usual to push the values of these registers onto the stack before calling a subroutine and pop them off again on returning. This frees the registers for general-purpose work within the subroutine.

THE POINTER AND INDEX REGISTERS

Four other registers form a group of *pointer registers* and *index registers*. These each have a specific role to play although there is no reason why a program should not use them for another purpose should the need arise.

The Stack Pointer, SP

The *Stack Pointer, SP*, as previously described, is used in conjunction with the Stack Segment to point to the current top of stack. SP gives the offset of this byte in the Stack Segment. Therefore the address of the item at the top of stack is completely defined by the pair of registers SS:SP.

The Base Pointer, BP

Like the Stack Pointer, the *Base Pointer, BP*, is used to identify an offset. Usually it is linked to the base register, BX.

The Source Index, SI

The Source Index, SI is used in conjunction with the Data Segment to identify a position in an array of data. If you are reading a string of bytes to the screen, one character at a

Programming the 8086

time, then SI can be used to point to the next character to be read, incrementing its value each time you go through the loop.

The Destination Index, DI

Similar to the Source Index, the *Destination Index, DI*, is generally used in conjunction with the Data Segment. In this case, however, it is used to identify the point in an array at which data is being written. When data is being modified both SI and DI are used at the same time.

The Instruction Pointer, IP

When a program is being run the computer needs to keep track of the whereabouts of the instruction currently being executed. To do this it uses the *Instruction Pointer, IP*. The IP gives the offset of the current instruction in the Code Segment. Therefore the current instruction is identified absolutely by the register pair CS:IP.

THE FLAGS REGISTER

The last of the 8086's 14 temporary storage locations is the *flags register*. This is different to the other registers in that it does not hold a single value. Instead, most of the 16 bits each have a specific role. Each bit is a *flag*; that is, it can take either the value 0 (*clear*) or 1 (*set*) and the value at any time tells us something about the system. For example, there is a flag to tell us when a calculation has resulted in an overflow and another to indicate that a comparison of two numbers shows that they are identical.

As a general rule the flags register is saved automatically whenever an interrupt is called, and is restored on return from the interrupt. Some of the DOS interrupts do not restore the register; in these cases the flags are used by the interrupts to signal to the program that some sort of error has occurred. After checking the contents of the flags register in these cases we also need to pop the register off the top of the stack, otherwise it will cause problems later.

There are two special instructions that allow us to push the flags register onto the stack and pop it off again later.

The flags and their position in the register are given in the table in Figure 3.11. However, the actual position of a particular flag is not usually of interest. The flags are so important to the operation of most programs that there are a number of instructions that deal with specific flags.

Programming the 8086

Bit	Abbr	Name	DEBUG Clear	DEBUG Set	Meaning if set
0	CF	Carry flag	NC	CY	Result too large or too small for register
1		Unused			
2	PF	Parity flag	PO	PE	Result has even number of bits set to 1
3		Unused			
4	AF	Auxiliary flag	NA	AC	BCD operation requires adjustment
5		Unused			
6	ZF	Zero flag	NZ	ZR	Result of operation was zero
7	SF	Sign flag	PL	NG	Result of operation was negative
8	TF	Trap flag	-	-	Single-step mode
9	IF	Interrupt flag	DI	EI	Interrupts enabled
10	DF	Direction flag	UP	DN	Direction for string operations is negative
11	OF	Overflow flag	NV	OV	Operation resulted in arithmetic overflow
12		Unused			
13		Unused			
14		Unused			
15		Unused			

Figure 3.11 The flags register

When tracing through a program with DEBUG the status of each of these flags is shown on the screen by a series of two-character codes. For example, the Carry Flag is shown as either CY (Carry) when the flag is set or NC (No Carry) when it is clear. The codes for the flags are included in Figure 3.11.

The Overflow Flag

This flag is used to detect operations that result in numbers that are either too large or too small. Generally speaking, the flag is set if the sign of the result is logically incorrect (for example, when 1 + 127 results in -128).

The Direction Flag

Some of the 8086's instructions perform operations that combine moving a value from an array into a register and changing the value of the SI and DI registers. Whether the register is incremented or decremented depends on the value of the direction flag. If the flag is clear the register is increased by 1; if the flag is set it is decreased by 1.

The Interrupt Flag

This flag indicates to the system whether or not it should respond to interrupts. As a general rule the flag is set but

79

Programming the 8086

there are certain circumstances (such as processing the result of a previous interrupt routine) when it may be temporarily cleared. In general it is very unwise to tamper with this flag.

The Trap Flag   This flag is usually clear. It is set by programs such as DEBUG that allow us to trace through a program. If the flag is set the processor only executes one instruction at a time, returning control to the trace program (for example, DEBUG) after each instruction has been executed. This gives us an opportunity to inspect the contents of memory and the registers before continuing with the next instruction.

The Sign Flag   This flag is set when the result of an operation is negative and is cleared when the result is positive.

The Zero Flag   This flag is set or cleared depending on whether or not the outcome of an instruction is zero. For example, when subtracting one number from another the zero flag is set only if the two numbers are the same.

The Carry Flag   Whenever an addition is carried out the value of this flag is either set or cleared, depending on whether or not the result of the operation carried over to the ninth bit (for byte arithmetic) or seventeenth bit (when working with words).

The carry flag can be carried over from one instruction to the next for more complex arithmetic. This flag is also used in some of the instructions that rotate the contents of a byte.

ADDRESSING MODES

The 8086 allows us to provide data for its instructions in a number of forms. For example, when moving an item of data into the AX register we can specify a particular value, the contents of another register, the contents of a location pointed to by a register, and so on. These different ways of identifying data are the *addressing modes*. In all, there are seven addressing modes.

Immediate addressing   The simplest form of addressing is called *immediate addressing* and consists of the actual value to be used. For example, putting a value directly into AX requires a 'move' instruction in the form:

Programming the 8086

```
MOV AX,0432h
```

AX now contains the value 0432h. To put a different value in AX requires a different instruction.

If the label 'DATA' points to location 0432h in the data segment, then this address could be moved into AX with the instruction:

```
MOV AX,DATA
```

AX contains the value 0432h unless the program is changed so that DATA points to a different location.

Direct addressing   The next stage is to specify the contents of a particular memory location. In this case the location is placed in square brackets, indicating 'the contents of'. This is *direct addressing*. For example, suppose that memory location DS:0432 contains the value B3h. This value can be put into AX with the instruction:

```
MOV AX,[0432h]
```

AX now contains the contents of 0432h, which is B3h. If the label 'DATA' had been attached to that location the same effect could be achieved with:

```
MOV AX,[DATA]
```

This is the equivalent of the Pascal instruction AX:=DATA. With direct addressing we can change the contents of a variable without having to change the instruction needed to load the value into memory. However, a different instruction is needed for each memory location.

Register addressing   Frequently we wish to use the contents of a register in the instruction. This is *register addressing* and takes the form:

```
MOV AX,BX
```

The value in BX is copied into AX. If BX originally held the value 0432h, AX would now hold the same value. Any register can be used in one of these instructions (within reason).

Indirect addressing   Sometimes we wish to work with the contents of a location that varies. This is dealt with by *indirect addressing*. For example, if BX holds the value 0432h - as an offset to the data segment - then the contents of location DS:0432h can be loaded into AX with the instruction:

```
MOV AX, [BX]
```

AX takes the contents of the location pointed to by BX (relative to DS). From the previous examples, this would be B3h. Other registers that can be used are SI, DI (both relative to DS) and BP (relative to SS).

Based addressing   The next stage is to use either BX or BP to point to a location in memory, and then select an offset from that point. This is *based addressing*. For example, if DATA points to an array of values starting at 0432h and this location has been stored in BX, then if the fourth word of the array is 0087h it can be loaded into AX with the instruction:

```
MOV AX, [BX + 06h]
```

This instruction loads into AX the value of the location 6 bytes beyond the location pointed to BX, i.e. the contents of 0438h, which is 0087h.

Based addressing can be used with either BX (relative to DS) or BP (relative to SS).

Indexed addressing   Similar to based addressing, *indexed addressing* allows us to identify a variable offset relative to a fixed location. For example, if DATA points to the location 0432h, then the fourth word can be loaded into AX by putting the value 06h into SI and using either of the instructions:

```
MOV AX, [0432h + SI]
```

or:

```
MOV AX, DATA[SI]
```

SI provides an index to the array and AX will again receive the value 00B7h from location DS:0438h.

Either SI or DI can be used for indexed addressing.

Based index addressing   The final addressing mode is *based indexed addressing*. In this case either of the base registers BX or BP are used to point to a base location in either DS or SS respectively; the index registers SI and DI identify an offset relative to these. A further displacement can also be added.

For example, if BX holds the offset 0432h and SI the offset 06h, the fourth and fifth words of the array can be loaded into AX and CX with the instructions:

```
MOV AX,[BX + SI]

MOV AX,[BX + SI + 02h]
```

This is particularly useful for a two-dimensional array, where BX points to the start of a 'row' of data and SI indicates the element to use from that row.

We are now ready to look at the 8086 instruction set.

4. *The 8086 Instruction Set*

The 8086 instruction set consists of over 100 different instructions. These instructions are the basis of all programs and therefore an integral part of the structure of the system as a whole. It is not the purpose of this book to teach you how to program in assembly language but, as an aid to programming, this chapter briefly describes the 8086 instruction set.

THE SYNTAX OF INSTRUCTIONS

Each instruction can be represented by a *mnemonic* - a short abbreviation that indicates the purpose of the instruction. Figure 4.1 lists the instructions in alphabetical order of mnemonics, showing the effect of the instructions on the flags register.

Some instructions require either one or two *operands*. These are items of data that are to be acted upon by the instruction. For example, when performing additions the ADD instruction needs two operands so that it knows which numbers to add.

It is the task of the assembler to convert each mnemonic and operand into a numeric machine code, or *opcode*, that the computer can understand. The actual value that the opcode takes when it is converted to machine code depends on how it is being used (for example, MUL BL has a different code to MUL BX).

Standard operands

The syntax of each instruction is given below. Where instructions may take operands these are represented by *op1* and *op2* (for example, ADD *op1,op2*, which adds the contents of two numbers). The operands may be immediate values or the contents of registers or memory locations. Although there are some variations the majority of instructions use *standard operands* which follow these rules:

- The first operand (op1) can be the contents of a memory location or register (but not a segment register). It can be either a byte or a word in length.

The 8086 Instruction Set

V	Value depends on result and can be used in program
?	Value is changed but cannot be guaranteed
1	Flag is set
0	Flag is clear
-	Flag is unaffected

Mnemonic	Instruction	OF	DF	IF	TF	SF	ZF	AF	PF	CF
AAA	ASCII adjust for addition	?	-	-	-	?	?	V	?	V
AAD	ASCII adjust for division	?	-	-	-	V	V	?	V	V
AAM	ASCII adjust for multiplication	?	-	-	-	V	V	?	V	?
AAS	ASCII adjust for subtraction	?	-	-	-	?	?	V	?	V
ADC	Add with carry	?	-	-	-	?	?	V	?	V
ADD	Add	?	-	-	-	?	?	V	?	V
AND	And	0	-	-	-	V	V	?	V	0
CALL	Call subroutine	-	-	-	-	-	-	-	-	-
CBW	Convert byte to word	-	-	-	-	-	-	-	-	-
CLC	Clear carry flag	-	-	-	-	-	-	-	-	0
CLD	Clear direction flag	-	0	-	-	-	-	-	-	-
CLI	Clear interrupt flag	-	-	0	-	-	-	-	-	-
CMC	Complement carry flag	-	-	-	-	-	-	-	-	V
CMP	Compare	V	-	-	-	V	V	V	V	V
CMPSB	Compare byte string	V	-	-	-	V	V	V	V	V
CMPSW	Compare word string	V	-	-	-	V	V	V	V	V
CWD	Convert word to double word	-	-	-	-	-	-	-	-	-
DAA	Decimal adjust for addition	?	-	-	-	?	?	V	?	V
DAS	Decimal adjust for subtraction	V	-	-	-	V	V	V	V	V
DEC	Decrement	V	-	-	-	V	V	V	V	-

Figure 4.1 The 8086 instruction set and the effect on the flags

Mnemonic	Instruction	Effect on flags
		OF DF IF TF SF ZF AF PF CF
DIV	Divide	? - - - ? ? ? ? ?
ESC	Escape	- - - - - - - - -
HLT	Halt	- - - - - - - - -
IDIV	Integer divide	? - - - ? ? ? ? ?
IMUL	Integer multiply	V - - - ? ? ? ? V
IN	Input	- - - - - - - - -
INC	Increment	V - - - V V V V -
INT	Call interrupt	- - 0 0 - - - - -
INTO	Call interrupt on overflow	- - 0 0 - - - - -
IRET	Interrupt return	V V V V V V V V V
JA	Jump if above	- - - - - - - - -
JAE	Jump if above or equal	- - - - - - - - -
JB	Jump if below	- - - - - - - - -
JBE	Jump if below or equal	- - - - - - - - -
JC	Jump if carry set	- - - - - - - - -
JCXZ	Jump if CX is zero	- - - - - - - - -
JE	Jump if equal	- - - - - - - - -
JG	Jump if greater	- - - - - - - - -
JGE	Jump if greater or equal	- - - - - - - - -
JL	Jump if less	- - - - - - - - -
JLE	Jump if less or equal	- - - - - - - - -
JMP	Jump	- - - - - - - - -
JNA	Jump if not above	- - - - - - - - -
JNAE	Jump if not above or equal	- - - - - - - - -

Figure 4.1 The 8086 instruction set and the effect on the flags (continued)

The 8086 Instruction Set

Mnemonic	Instruction	Effect on flags								
		OF	DF	IF	TF	SF	ZF	AF	PF	CF
JNB	Jump if not below	-	-	-	-	-	-	-	-	-
JNBE	Jump if not below or equal	-	-	-	-	-	-	-	-	-
JNC	Jump if no carry	-	-	-	-	-	-	-	-	-
JNE	Jump if not equal	-	-	-	-	-	-	-	-	-
JNG	Jump if not greater	-	-	-	-	-	-	-	-	-
JNGE	Jump if not greater or equal	-	-	-	-	-	-	-	-	-
JNL	Jump if not less	-	-	-	-	-	-	-	-	-
JNLE	Jump if not less or equal	-	-	-	-	-	-	-	-	-
JNO	Jump if no overflow	-	-	-	-	-	-	-	-	-
JNP	Jump if no parity	-	-	-	-	-	-	-	-	-
JNS	Jump if no sign	-	-	-	-	-	-	-	-	-
JNZ	Jump if not zero	-	-	-	-	-	-	-	-	-
JO	Jump if overflow set	-	-	-	-	-	-	-	-	-
JP	Jump if parity set	-	-	-	-	-	-	-	-	-
JPE	Jump if parity even	-	-	-	-	-	-	-	-	-
JPO	Jump if parity odd	-	-	-	-	-	-	-	-	-
JS	Jump if sign set	-	-	-	-	-	-	-	-	-
JZ	Jump if zero	-	-	-	-	-	-	-	-	-
LAHF	Load AH with flags	-	-	-	-	-	-	-	-	-
LDS	Load pointer into DS	-	-	-	-	-	-	-	-	-
LEA	Load effective address	-	-	-	-	-	-	-	-	-
LES	Load pointer into ES	-	-	-	-	-	-	-	-	-
LOCK	Lock	-	-	-	-	-	-	-	-	-
LODSB	Load byte string	-	-	-	-	-	-	-	-	-

Figure 4.1 The 8086 instruction set and the effect on the flags (continued)

The 8086 Instruction Set

Mnemonic	Instruction	OF	DF	IF	TF	SF	ZF	AF	PF	CF
LODSW	Load word string	-	-	-	-	-	-	-	-	-
LOOP	Loop	-	-	-	-	-	-	-	-	-
LOOPE	Loop if equal	-	-	-	-	-	-	-	-	-
LOOPNE	Loop if not equal	-	-	-	-	-	-	-	-	-
LOOPNZ	Loop if not zero	-	-	-	-	-	-	-	-	-
LOOPZ	Loop if zero	-	-	-	-	-	-	-	-	-
MOV	Move	-	-	-	-	-	-	-	-	-
MOVSB	Move byte string	-	-	-	-	-	-	-	-	-
MOVSW	Move word string	-	-	-	-	-	-	-	-	-
MUL	Multiply	V	-	-	-	?	?	?	?	V
NEG	Negate	V	-	-	-	V	V	V	V	V
NOP	No operation	-	-	-	-	-	-	-	-	-
NOT	Not	-	-	-	-	-	-	-	-	-
OR	Or	0	-	-	-	V	V	?	V	0
OUT	Output	-	-	-	-	-	-	-	-	-
POP	Pop	-	-	-	-	-	-	-	-	-
POPF	Pop flags	V	V	V	V	V	V	V	V	V
PUSH	Push	-	-	-	-	-	-	-	-	-
PUSHF	Push flags	-	-	-	-	-	-	-	-	-
RCL	Rotate with carry left	V	-	-	-	-	-	-	-	V
RCR	Rotate with carry right	V	-	-	-	-	-	-	-	V
REP	Repeat	-	-	-	-	-	-	-	-	-
REPE	Repeat if equal	-	-	-	-	-	-	-	-	-
REPNE	Repeat if not equal	-	-	-	-	-	-	-	-	-

Figure 4.1 The 8086 instruction set and the effect on the flags (continued)

The 8086 Instruction Set

Mnemonic	Instruction	Effect on flags								
		OF	DF	IF	TF	SF	ZF	AF	PF	CF
REPNZ	Repeat if not zero	-	-	-	-	-	-	-	-	-
REPZ	Repeat if zero	-	-	-	-	-	-	-	-	-
RET	Return	-	-	-	-	-	-	-	-	-
ROL	Rotate left	V	-	-	-	-	-	-	-	V
ROR	Rotate right	V	-	-	-	-	-	-	-	V
SAHR	Store AH in flag register	V	V	V	V	V	V	V	V	V
SAL	Shift arithmetic left	V	-	-	-	-	-	-	-	V
SAR	Shift arithmetic right	V	-	-	-	V	V	?	V	V
SBB	Subtract with borrow	V	-	-	-	V	V	V	V	V
SCASB	Scan byte string	-	-	-	-	-	-	-	-	-
SCASW	Scan word string	-	-	-	-	-	-	-	-	-
SHL	Shift left	V	-	-	-	-	-	-	-	V
SHR	Shift right	V	-	-	-	-	-	-	-	V
STC	Set carry flag	-	-	-	-	-	-	-	-	1
STD	Set direction flag	-	1	-	-	-	-	-	-	-
STI	Set interrupt flag	-	-	1	-	-	-	-	-	-
STOSB	Store byte string	-	-	-	-	-	-	-	-	-
STOSW	Store word string	-	-	-	-	-	-	-	-	-
SUB	Subtract	V	-	-	-	V	V	V	V	V
TEST	Test	0	-	-	-	V	V	?	V	0
WAIT	Wait	-	-	-	-	-	-	-	-	-
XCHG	Exchange	-	-	-	-	-	-	-	-	-
XLAT	Translate	-	-	-	-	-	-	-	-	-
XOR	Exclusive or	0	-	-	-	V	V	?	V	0

Figure 4.1 The 8086 instruction set and the effect on the flags (continued)

The 8086 Instruction Set

- The second operand (op2) can be an immediate value or the contents of a memory location or register (but not a segment register). It can also be either a byte or a word.

- If there are two operands, they must be of the same size (either bytes or words).

- The operands cannot both be the contents of memory locations but most other combinations are permissible.

The text indicates where the operands differ from these standard conditions.

Labels Some instructions use *labels*, which represent points in the program to jump to or the names of subroutines. When the program is assembled these labels are replaced by numeric offsets. In general these are *short labels*; that is, the jump must lie in the range +127 to -128.

Duplicate operands Some opcodes have more than one mnemonic associated with them. This can help to make programs more readable and easier to understand. For example, the instructions JGE (Jump if greater or equal) and JNL (Jump if not less) are represented by the same opcode. The logic in these cases is of course the same. Where there are two such identical codes the second option is shown in brackets. Some of the names generally given to these duplicate instructions can be ambiguous, so require careful handling. For example, JNGE (Jump if not greater-or-equal) is the opposite of JGE (Jump if greater or equal).

ARITHMETIC OPERATIONS

The first group of instructions is used to carry out simple arithmetic operations: addition, subtraction, multiplication and division. With addition and subtraction the operation can be performed on values larger than a word by taking account of the carry flag from a previous operation.

Binary addition and subtraction The most commonly-used of the arithmetic instructions are those that carry out straightforward binary addition and subtraction. The instructions assume that the numbers involved have been converted from their decimal format where necessary.

The 8086 Instruction Set

Mnemonic: ADD
Name: Add
Syntax: ADD op1,op2 (Standard operands)
Effect: Adds two items, storing the result in op1.
Flags: OF,SF,IF,AF,PF,CF changed.

Mnemonic: ADC
Name: Add with carry
Syntax: ADC op1,op2 (Standard operands)
Effect: Adds two items, together with the contents of the carry flag, storing the result in op1.
Flags: OF,SF,ZF,AF,PF,CF changed.

Mnemonic: SUB
Name: Subtract
Syntax: SUB op1,op2 (Standard operands)
Effect: Subtracts op2 from op1, placing the result in op1.
Flags: OF,SF,ZF,AF,PF,CF changed.

Mnemonic: SBB
Name: Subtract with borrow
Syntax: SBB op1,op2 (Standard operands)
Effect: Subtracts op2 and the contents of the carry flag from op1, placing the result in op1.
Flags: OF,SF,ZF,AF,PF,CF changed.

Mnemonic: NEG
Name: Negate
Syntax: NEG op1   (Standard operand)
Effect: Subtracts op1 from 0.
Flags: OF,SF,ZF,AF,PF,CF changed.

Incrementing and decrementing — Two instructions are included for incrementing or decrementing a value (adding or subtracting 1 to or from the value).

Mnemonic: INC
Name: Increment
Syntax: INC op1   (Standard operand)
Effect: Increases the value of the operand by 1.
Flags: OF,SF,ZF,AF,PF changed.

Mnemonic: DEC
Name: Decrement
Syntax: DEC op1   (Standard operand)
Effect: Decreases the value of the operand by 1.

The 8086 Instruction Set

Flags: OF,SF,ZF,AF,PF changed.

Binary multiplication and division

For multiplication and division the operands can be either signed or unsigned.

Note that in the case of division, the integer part of the result is placed in either AL or AX (depending on whether you are dividing by a byte or a word). If this part is too large to fit in the register the program will crash with a 'Divide by zero' error. For example, you cannot divide 0200h by the byte 02h; you must divide by the word 0002h.

Mnemonic: MUL
Name: Multiply
Syntax: MUL op1   (Standard operand)
Effect: Performs unsigned multiplication. If the operand is a byte, it is multiplied by the contents of AL and the result is placed in AX. If the operand is a word, it is multiplied by the contents of AX and the result is placed in the pair of registers DX:AX.
Flags: OF,CF changed; SF,ZF,AF,PF undefined.

Mnemonic: IMUL
Name: Integer multiply
Syntax: IMUL op1   (Standard operand)
Effect: Performs signed multiplication. If the operand is a byte, it is multiplied by the contents of AL and the result is placed in AX. If the operand is a word, it is multiplied by the contents of AX and the result is placed in the pair of registers DX:AX.
Flags: OF,CF changed; SF,ZF,AF,PF undefined.

Mnemonic: DIV
Name: Divide
Syntax: DIV op1   (Standard operand)
Effect: Performs unsigned division. If the operand is a byte, AH stores the integer part of AX divided by op1; the remainder from the division is placed in AL. If the operand is a word, AX stores the integer part of DX:AX divided by op1; the remainder from the division is placed in DX.
Flags: OF,SF,ZF,AF,PF,CF undefined.

The 8086 Instruction Set

      Mnemonic: IDIV
      Name: Integer divide
      Syntax: IDIV op1 (Standard operand)
      Effect: Performs signed division. If the operand is a byte, AH stores the integer part of AX divided by op1; the remainder from the division is placed in AL. If the operand is a word, AX stores the integer part of DX:AX divided by op1; the remainder from the division is placed in DX.
      Flags: OF,SF,ZF,AF,PF,CF undefined.

Adjusting for BCD calculations Sometimes it is convenient to work with data in the *binary coded decimal (BCD)* format. In these cases any arithmetic operations that have been carried out will require adjustment so that the results are still in BCD. There are two sets of instructions that carry out these adjustments for both packed BCD and normal, unpacked BCD.

      Mnemonic: AAA
      Name: ASCII adjust for addition
      Syntax: AAA
      Effect: Adjusts contents of AL so that it is correct after the addition of two BCD values.
      Flags: OF,SF,ZF,PF undefined; AF,CF changed.

      Mnemonic: AAS
      Name: ASCII adjust for subtraction
      Syntax: AAS
      Effect: Adjusts contents of AL so that it is correct after the subtraction of one BCD value from another.
      Flags: OF,SF,ZF,PF undefined; AF,CF changed.

      Mnemonic: AAM
      Name: ASCII adjust for multiplication
      Syntax: AAM
      Effect: Adjusts contents of AX so that it is correct after the multiplication of two BCD values.
      Flags: OF,AF,CF undefined; SF,ZF,PF changed.

      Mnemonic: AAD
      Name: ASCII adjust for division
      Syntax: AAD
      Effect: Adjusts contents of AL *before* a division involving two BCD values, so that the result

The 8086 Instruction Set

Flags:	of the division will be the correct BCD value. OF,AF,CF undefined; SF,ZF,PF changed.
Mnemonic:	DAA
Name:	Decimal adjust for addition
Syntax:	DAA
Effect:	Adjusts contents of AL so that it is correct after the addition of two packed BCD values.
Flags:	OF,SF,ZF,PF undefined; AF,CF changed.
Mnemonic:	DAS
Name:	Decimal adjust for subtraction
Syntax:	DAS
Effect:	Adjusts contents of AL so that it is correct after the subtraction of one packed BCD value from another.
Flags:	OF,SF,ZF,AF,PF,ZF changed.

LOGICAL OPERATIONS

Four instructions are used for carrying out the *logical operations* that are at the heart of all computer activities. These operations work on the operands bit by bit, rather than as a whole. For example, the AND operator compares the corresponding bits of the two operands, placing a 1 in the resultant bit only if both bits are 1.

Mnemonic:	AND
Name:	And
Syntax:	AND op1,op2 (Standard operands)
Effect:	Performs logical 'And'. Each bit is set only if the corresponding bits are set in both op1 and op2. The result is placed in op1.
Flags:	OF=0; CF=0; SF,ZF,PF changed; AF undefined.
Mnemonic:	OR
Name:	Or
Syntax:	OR op1,op2 (Standard operands)
Effect:	Performs logical 'Or'. Each bit is set if either of the corresponding bits are set in op1 or op2 (or if the bits are set in both). The result is placed in op1.

95

The 8086 Instruction Set

    Flags: OF=0; CF=0; SF,ZF,PF changed; AF undefined.

    Mnemonic: XOR
    Name: Exclusive or
    Syntax: XOR op1,op2   (Standard operands)
    Effect: Performs logical 'Exclusive or'. Each bit is set if either of the corresponding bits are set in op1 or op2, but not if both bits are set. The result is placed in op1.
    Flags: OF=0; CF=0; SF,ZF,PF changed; AF undefined.

    Mnemonic: NOT
    Name: Not
    Syntax: NOT op1   (Standard operand)
    Effect: Performs logical 'Not', complementing the operand so that all bits with a value 1 become 0, and vice versa.
    Flags: No effect.

FLAG OPERATIONS

A number of instructions are available for manipulating the flags register. Some of these set or clear individual flags (for example, to clear the carry flag before an addition) while others store or retrieve the complete register.

Changing individual flags

Some of the flags can be set or cleared by specific instructions. Most of the flags can also be changed by the results of certain operations (for example, the SUB instruction sets the zero flag when both operands are the same). For those flags where there is no specific instruction the bit can only be cleared by a logical operation involving the entire register.

    Mnemonic: CLC
    Name: Clear carry flag
    Syntax: CLC
    Effect: Clears bit 0 of the flags register (giving it a value of 0).
    Flags: CF=0.

The 8086 Instruction Set

Mnemonic:	CMC
Name:	Complement carry flag
Syntax:	CMC
Effect:	Reverses the value of the carry flag (bit 0 of the flags register). If the value is 1 it becomes 0, and vice versa.
Flags:	CF changed.

Mnemonic:	STC
Name:	Set carry flag
Syntax:	STC
Effect:	Sets bit 0 of the flags register to 1.
Flags:	CF=1.

Mnemonic:	CLD
Name:	Clear direction flag
Syntax:	CLD
Effect:	Clears the value of bit 10 of the flags register (giving it a value of 0).
Flags:	DF=0.

Mnemonic:	STD
Name:	Set direction flag
Syntax:	STD
Effect:	Sets bit 10 of the flags register to 1.
Flags:	DF=1.

Mnemonic:	CLI
Name:	Clear interrupt flag
Syntax:	CLI
Effect:	Clears bit 9 of the flags register. Maskable interrupts are disabled (that is, all subsequent external hardware and software interrupts are ignored).
Flags:	IF=0.

Mnemonic:	STI
Name:	Set interrupt flag
Syntax:	STI
Effect:	Sets bit 9 of the flags register to 1. Interrupts are enabled.
Flags:	IF=1.

Saving and restoring the flags register

There are two basic ways of saving the flags register so that it can be retrieved later on in the program; either the register can be pushed onto the stack or it can be transferred into the

The 8086 Instruction Set

AX register, from where it may be moved to some other location in memory.

Mnemonic: PUSHF
Name: Push flags
Syntax: PUSHF
Effect: Pushes the contents of the flags register onto the stack. The flags themselves are unaffected.
Flags: No effect.

Mnemonic: POPF
Name: Pop flags
Syntax: POPF
Effect: Pops the flags register off the stack. All existing flags are replaced.
Flags: All flags changed.

Mnemonic: LAHF
Name: Load AH with flags register
Syntax: LAHF
Effect: Loads contents of flags register into AH. This is useful if you want to change the value of a flag for which there is no such direct instruction (for example the trap flag).
Flags: No effect.

Mnemonic: SAHR
Name: Store AH in flags register
Syntax: SAHR
Effect: Transfers the contents of AH to the flags register, replacing any existing values.
Flags: All flags changed.

BRANCHING AND LOOPS

There are a large number of instructions for branching from one point in the program to another, or for repeating a series of instructions a number of times. Branching is achieved through the *jump* instructions while repeats can best be achieved using the *loop* instructions.

Comparisons   In all cases except that of the unconditional jump (JMP) and unconditionsl loop (LOOP) the decision on whether or not to

The 8086 Instruction Set

branch depends on the status of the flags register. The flags may have been set by some previous instruction, such as ADD, or they may be set by carrying out a comparison of two values. There are two instructions dedicated to making comparisons between numeric data.

Mnemonic: CMP
Name: Compare
Syntax: CMP op1,op2 (Standard operands; op1 can also be a word register or word memory location when op2 is an immediate byte)
Effect: Compares two values. The flags are set as if op2 had been subtracted from op1 but the values of the operands are unchanged.
Flags: OF,SF,ZF,PF,AF,CF changed.

Mnemonic: TEST
Name: Test
Syntax: TEST op1,op2 (Standard operands)
Effect: Compares two values bit-by-bit. The flags are set as if an AND op1,op2 instruction had been performed but the values of the operands are unchanged.
Flags: OF=0; CF=0; SF,ZF,PF changed; AF undefined.

Branching

There is a jump instruction for almost any occasion! This fine collection of mnemonics provides branches to deal with the status of several of the flags. While the name of the jump instruction provides a common-sense description of what it does, the actual decision on whether or not to jump is made on the basis of the current values of the flags.

Note that many jump opcodes have alternative mnemonics.

The last instruction in the group (JMP) is an unconditional branch.

Mnemonic: JA (JNBE)
Name: Jump if above zero (Jump if not below-or-equal zero)
Syntax: JA short-label
Effect: Jump if the carry flag and zero flag are both 0.
Flags: No effect.

The 8086 Instruction Set

Mnemonic: JAE (JNB)
Name: Jump if above or equal zero (Jump if not below zero)
Syntax: JAE short-label
Effect: Jump if the carry flag is 0.
Flags: No effect.

Mnemonic: JB (JNAE)
Name: Jump if below zero (Jump if not above-or-equal zero)
Syntax: JB short-label
Effect: Jump if the carry flag is 1.
Flags: No effect.

Mnemonic: JBE (JNA)
Name: Jump if below or equal zero (Jump if not above zero)
Syntax: JBE short-label
Effect: Jump if either the carry flag or zero flag is 1.
Flags: No effect.

Mnemonic: JZ (JE)
Name: Jump if zero (Jump if equal)
Syntax: JZ short-label
Effect: Jump if the zero flag is 1.
Flags: No effect.

Mnemonic: JNZ (JNE)
Name: Jump if not zero (Jump if not equal)
Syntax: JNZ short-label
Effect: Jump if the zero flag is 0.
Flags: No effect.

Mnemonic: JG (JNLE)
Name: Jump if greater (Jump if not less-or-equal)
Syntax: JG short-label
Effect: Jump if the sign flag is the same as the overflow flag and the zero flag is 0.
Flags: No effect.

Mnemonic: JGE (JNL)
Name: Jump if greater or equal (Jump if not less)
Syntax: JGE short-label
Effect: Jump if the sign flag is the same as the overflow flag.
Flags: No effect.

The 8086 Instruction Set

Mnemonic: JL (JNGE)
Name: Jump if less (Jump if not greater - or - equal)
Syntax: JL short-label
Effect: Jump if the sign flag and the overflow flag are different.
Flags: No effect.

Mnemonic: JLE (JNG)
Name: Jump if less or equal (Jump if not greater)
Syntax: JLE short-label
Effect: Jump if the sign flag and overflow flag are different or the zero flag is 1.
Flags: No effect.

Mnemonic: JC
Name: Jump if carry set
Syntax: JC short-label
Effect: Jump if the carry flag is 1.
Flags: No effect.

Mnemonic: JNC
Name: Jump if no carry
Syntax: JNC short-label
Effect: Jump if the carry flag is 0.
Flags: No effect.

Mnemonic: JCXZ
Name: Jump if CX is zero
Syntax: JCXZ short-label
Effect: Jump if the CX register is 0.
Flags: No effect.

Mnemonic: JO
Name: Jump if overflow set
Syntax: JO short-label
Effect: Jump if the overflow flag is 1.
Flags: No effect.

Mnemonic: JNO
Name: Jump if no overflow
Syntax: JNO short-label
Effect: Jump if the overflow flag is 0.
Flags: No effect.

The 8086 Instruction Set

Mnemonic: JP (JPE)
Name: Jump if parity set (Jump if parity even)
Syntax: JP short-label
Effect: Jump if the parity flag is 1.
Flags: No effect.

Mnemonic: JNP (JPO)
Name: Jump if no parity (Jump if parity odd)
Syntax: JNP short-label
Effect: Jump if the parity flag is 0.
Flags: No effect.

Mnemonic: JS
Name: Jump if sign set
Syntax: JS short-label
Effect: Jump if the sign flag is 1.
Flags: No effect.

Mnemonic: JNS
Name: Jump if no sign
Syntax: JNS short-label
Effect: Jump if the sign flag is 0.
Flags: No effect.

Mnemonic: JMP
Name: Jump
Syntax: JMP label   (Label can be a short label, a label in this or another segment, a word register or a location in memory.)
Effect: Jump unconditionally to the instruction pointed to by the label.
Flags: No effect.

Loops

Three instructions allow the program to loop round the same set of instructions a number of times. The number of times the loop is executed is given by the value in CX. Each time the loop instruction is encountered CX is decremented; the program then jumps back to the start of the loop if CX is not zero. Therefore CX must be set before the loop is entered. The loop instruction comes at the end of the section to be repeated.

Mnemonic: LOOP
Name: Loop
Syntax: LOOP short-label

The 8086 Instruction Set

Effect:	Decrements CX and jumps to the label if CX is non-zero. The zero flag is not affected when CX reaches 0.
Flags:	No effect.
Mnemonic:	LOOPZ (LOOPE)
Name:	Loop if zero (Loop if equal)
Syntax:	LOOPZ short-label
Effect:	Decrements CX and jumps to the label if CX is non-zero and the zero flag has been set by a previous operation. The program drops out of the loop if the zero flag is clear or in any event when CX becomes 0. The zero flag is not affected when CX reaches 0.
Flags:	No effect.
Mnemonic:	LOOPNZ (LOOPNE)
Name:	Loop if not zero
Syntax:	LOOPNZ short-label
Effect:	Decrements CX and jumps to the label if CX is non-zero and the zero flag has been cleared by a previous operation. The program drops out of the loop if the zero flag is set or in any event when CX becomes 0. The zero flag is not affected when CX reaches 0.
Flags:	No effect.

MOVING DATA

A number of instructions are available for moving data around in memory, without modifying it.

Moving bytes and words

Probably the most commonly-used instruction is that of MOV, a very flexible instruction that will transfer almost any data from any location to any other. In addition, there is a less useful command for swapping the contents of two locations.

Mnemonic:	MOV
Name:	Move
Syntax:	MOV op1,op2 (Standard operands but with the addition that op1 and op2 may also be segment registers; the only additional

The 8086 Instruction Set

	restrictions are that if op1 is a segment register op2 cannot be either a segment register or immediate value)
Effect:	Moves the data or the contents of the location specified by op2 into the location specified by op1.
Flags:	No effect.
Mnemonic:	XCHG
Name:	Exchange
Syntax:	XCHG op1,op2 (op1 and op2 may be registers or memory locations; they may be bytes or words but must be of the same size).
Effect:	Exchanges the contents of the two locations.
Flags:	No effect.
Mnemonic:	XLAT
Name:	Translate
Syntax:	XLAT
Effect:	Loads into AL the contents of the byte at an offset of AL, measured from a base address in BX.
Flags:	No effect.

Loading addresses

Three instructions provide efficient means for loading addresses into registers.

Mnemonic:	LEA
Name:	Load effective address
Syntax:	LEA op1,op2 (op1 is a register; op2 is a word memory location)
Effect:	Moves the effective address of a location into a register.
Flags:	No effect.
Mnemonic:	LDS
Name:	Load pointer into DS
Syntax:	LDS op1,op2 (op1 is a register; op2 is a double-word memory location)
Effect:	Loads DS with the segment address of op2 and register op1 with the offset.
Flags:	No effect.

The 8086 Instruction Set

Mnemonic: LES
Name: Load pointer into ES
Syntax: LES op1,op2 (op1 is a register; op2 is a double-word memory location)
Effect: Loads ES with the segment address of op2 and register op1 with the offset.
Flags: No effect.

THE STACK

Four operations are used purely for manipulating the contents of the stack. Two of these, for pushing and popping the flags register, have already been covered. The two main instructions, for pushing and popping the contents of any other register, are included here.

Mnemonic: PUSH
Name: Push
Syntax: PUSH op1   (op1 may be a segment register, word register or word memory location)
Effect: Stores the contents of the operand on the stack and updates the stack pointer. The contents of the register or memory location are unchanged.
Flags: No effect.

Mnemonic: POP
Name: Pop
Syntax: POP op1   (op1 may be a segment register, word register or word memory location)
Effect: Loads the value at the top of stack into the register or memory location and updates the stack pointer.
Flags: No effect.

The 8086 Instruction Set

ROTATE AND SHIFT

A number of operations shift the contents of a byte to the right or left. One set of instructions shifts the bits, losing one bit in the process. If the shift is to the left then the most significant bit (MSB) is lost; if the shift is to the right the least significant bit (LSB) is lost. The other set rotates the byte so that the bit pushed off at one end of the byte is pushed on again at the other end. Some of the instructions include the carry flag in the operation.

Mnemonic: RCL
Name: Rotate with carry left
Syntax: RCL op1,1   (op1:standard operand)
RCL op1,CL
Effect: The MSB of the first operand replaces the carry flag, all other bits move left one place and the old value of the carry flag replaces the LSB. If the second operand is CL the rotation is carried out CL times.
Flags: OF,CF changed.

Mnemonic: RCR
Name: Rotate with carry right
Syntax: RCR op1,1   (op1:standard operand)
RCR op1,CL
Effect: The LSB of the first operand replaces the carry flag, all other bits move right one place and the old value of the carry flag replaces the MSB. If the second operand is CL the rotation is carried out CL times.
Flags: OF,CF changed.

Mnemonic: ROL
Name: Rotate left
Syntax: ROL op1,1   (op1:standard operand)
ROL op1,CL
Effect: The MSB of the first operand replaces the carry flag, all other bits move left one place and the old value of the MSB replaces the LSB. If the second operand is CL the rotation is carried out CL times.
Flags: OF,CF changed.

Mnemonic:	ROR
Name:	Rotate right
Syntax:	ROR op1,1 (op1:standard operand)
	ROR op1,CL
Effect:	The LSB of the first operand replaces the carry flag, all other bits move right one place and the old value of the LSB replaces the MSB. If the second operand is CL the rotation is carried out CL times.
Flags:	OF,CF changed.
Mnemonic:	SHL (SAL)
Name:	Shift left (Shift arithmetic left)
Syntax:	SHL op1,1 (op1:standard operand)
	SHL op1,CL
Effect:	The MSB of the first operand replaces the carry flag, all other bits move left one place and the LSB becomes 0. If the second operand is CL the shift is carried out CL times.
Flags:	OF,CF changed.
Mnemonic:	SHR
Name:	Shift right
Syntax:	SHR op1,1 (op1:standard operand)
	SHR op1,CL
Effect:	The LSB of the first operand replaces the carry flag, all other bits move right one place and the MSB becomes 0. If the second operand is CL the shift is carried out CL times.
Flags:	OF,CF changed.
Mnemonic:	SAR
Name:	Shift arithmetic right
Syntax:	SAR op1,1 (op1:standard operand)
	SAR op1,CL
Effect:	The LSB of the first operand replaces the carry flag, all other bits move right one place but the MSB is unchanged. If the second operand is CL the shift is carried out CL times.
Flags:	OF,SF,ZF,PF,CF changed; AF undefined.

The 8086 Instruction Set

TYPE CONVERSIONS

Since most double-operand instructions cannot mix data types, there are two instructions that provide a simple method of converting data of one size into data of another size.

Mnemonic: CBW
Name: Convert byte to word
Syntax: CBW
Effect: Converts the byte in AL into a word in AX.
Flags: No effect.

Mnemonic: CWD
Name: Convert word to double word
Syntax: CWD
Effect: Converts the word in AX to a double word in DX:AX.
Flags: No effect.

STRING OPERATIONS

The 8086 includes a number of instructions for handling blocks of data; usually these are applied to text but any block can be manipulated. The same operations could be carried out with the standard instructions but the string instructions are far more efficient. The direction flag should be cleared if the operation is to start at the beginning of the block and work forwards; the direction flag should be set if you want to work backwards through the data.

These instructions can be used on their own or, more usually, in combination with the REP instructions. After the instruction has been executed the DI or SI (or both) end up pointing to the byte or word following the last data item (or the one preceding it if the direction flag was set).

Mnemonic: LODSB
Name: Load string byte
Syntax: LODSB
Effect: Loads the byte pointed to by DS:SI into AL. SI is incremented if the direction flag is

The 8086 Instruction Set

	clear or decremented if the direction flag is set.
Flags:	No effect.
Mnemonic:	LODSW
Name:	Load string word
Syntax:	LODSW
Effect:	Loads the word pointed to by DS:SI into AX. SI is incremented if the direction flag is clear or decremented if the direction flag is set.
Flags:	No effect.
Mnemonic:	STOSB
Name:	Store string byte
Syntax:	STOSB
Effect:	Stores the byte from AL in the location pointed to by ES:DI. DI is incremented if the direction flag is clear or decremented if the direction flag is set.
Flags:	IF=1.
Mnemonic:	STOSW
Name:	Store string word
Syntax:	STOSW
Effect:	Stores the word from AX in the location pointed to by ES:DI. DI is incremented if the direction flag is clear or decremented if the direction flag is set.
Flags:	No effect
Mnemonic:	MOVSB
Name:	Move string byte
Syntax:	MOVSB
Effect:	Moves the byte pointed to by DS:SI to the location pointed to by ES:DI. SI and DI are incremented if the direction flag is clear or decremented if the direction flag is set.
Flags:	No effect.
Mnemonic:	MOVSW
Name:	Move string word
Syntax:	MOVSW
Effect:	Moves the byte pointed to by DS:SI to the location pointed to by ES:DI. SI and DI are incremented if the direction flag is clear or

The 8086 Instruction Set

Flags:	decremented if the direction flag is set. No effect.
Mnemonic:	CMPSB
Name:	Compare string bytes
Syntax:	CMPSB
Effect:	Compares the bytes pointed to by DS:SI and ES:DI. SI and DI are incremented if the direction flag is clear or decremented if the direction flag is set. The flags are set according to the result of the comparison but the data values are unaffected. This instruction is used to search through two strings for differences.
Flags:	OF,SF,ZF,AF,PF,CF changed.
Mnemonic:	CMPSW
Name:	Compare string word
Syntax:	CMPSW
Effect:	Compares the words pointed to by DS:SI and ES:DI. SI and DI are incremented if the direction flag is clear or decremented if the direction flag is set. The flags are set according to the result of the comparison but the data values are unaffected. This instruction is used only occasionally to search through two strings for differences.
Flags:	OF,SF,ZF,AF,PF,CF changed.
Mnemonic:	SCASB
Name:	Scan string byte
Syntax:	SCASB
Effect:	Compares the byte pointed to by ES:DI with AL. DI is incremented if the direction flag is clear or decremented if the direction flag is set. The flags are set according to the result of the comparison but the data values are unaffected. This instruction is used to locate a particular character in a string.
Flags:	OF,SF,ZF,AF,PF,CF changed.
Mnemonic:	SCASW
Name:	Scan string word
Syntax:	SCASW
Effect:	Compares the word pointed to by ES:DI with AX. DI is incremented if the direction

The 8086 Instruction Set

	flag is clear or decremented if the direction flag is set. The flags are set according to the result of the comparison but the data values are unaffected. This instruction is used to locate a particular 2-byte word in a string.
Flags:	OF,SF,ZF,AF,PF,CF changed.
Mnemonic:	REP
Name:	Repeat string instruction
Syntax:	REP
Effect:	Repeats the next string instruction until CX is 0. CX is decremented after the instruction has been executed but the zero flag is unaffected.
Flags:	No effect.
Mnemonic:	REPZ (REPE)
Name:	Repeat string instruction while zero (Repeat while equal)
Syntax:	REPZ
Effect:	Repeats the next string instruction until CX is 0 or the result of a CMPS or SCAS instruction is non-zero. CX is decremented after the instruction has been executed but the zero flag is unaffected when CX reaches 0. The loop ends when a difference is found, or in any event when CX becomes 0. If CX=0 and no difference was found the zero flag will be set.
Flags:	No effect.
Mnemonic:	REPNZ (REPNE)
Name:	Repeat string instruction while not zero (Repeat while not equal)
Syntax:	REPNZ
Effect:	Repeats the next string instruction until CX is 0 or the result of a CMPS or SCAS instruction is zero. CX is decremented after the instruction has been executed but the zero flag is unaffected when CX reaches 0. The loop ends when a match is found between the bytes or words being compared, or in any event when CX becomes 0. If CX=0 and no comparison

The 8086 Instruction Set

produced a match the zero flag will be clear.
Flags: No effect.

COMMUNICATING WITH PORTS

A great deal has to be achieved by sending data to the 8086 ports or by receiving data from them. The 8086 manages this with only two instructions.

Mnemonic: IN
Name: Input
Syntax: IN op1,op2   (op1 is AL or AX; op2 is the port number or DX)
Effect: Input a byte or word from a port, placing the value in AL or AX. The port number can be specified directly (if it is in the range 00h to FFh), or indirectly by placing the number in DX.
Flags: No effect.

Mnemonic: OUT
Name: Output
Syntax: OUT op1,op2 (op1 is the port number or DX; op2 is AL or AX)
Effect: Output the contents of AL or AX to a port. The port number can be specified directly (if it is in the range 00h to FFh), or indirectly by placing the number in DX.
Flags: No effect.

CHANGING THE PROGRAM FLOW

A number of instructions temporarily redirect the flow of the program to some other section of code. These extra sections of code are called *subroutines*. After completing a subroutine the program always continues with the next instruction after the subroutine call.

Mnemonic: CALL
Name: Call subroutine
Syntax: CALL label   (Label can be a short label, a label in this or another segment, a word

The 8086 Instruction Set

	register or a location in memory)
Effect:	Calls the subroutine identified by the name 'label'
Flags:	No effect

Mnemonic:	RET
Name:	Return
Syntax:	RET
	RET op1 (op1 is an immediate value)
Effect:	Ends subroutine. Control is returned to the calling routine, continuing with the next instruction. If there is an operand, that number of entries are popped off the stack.
Flags:	No effect.

Mnemonic:	INT
Name:	Call interrupt
Syntax:	INT op1 (op1 is an immediate value and must be a valid interrupt number)
Effect:	Calls an interrupt. The location of the interrupt routine is held in the interrupt vector table. The flags register is pushed onto the stack; the interrupt and trap flags are cleared.
Flags:	IF=0; TF=0.

Mnemonic:	INTO
Name:	Call interrupt on overflow
Syntax:	INTO
Effect:	Forces an INT 04h call if the overflow flag is set.
Flags:	IF=0; TF=0.

Mnemonic:	IRET
Name:	Interrupt return
Syntax:	IRET
Effect:	Returns control from an interrupt to the instruction immediately following the interrupt call. The flags register is popped off the stack.
Flags:	All flags changed.

The 8086 Instruction Set

PAUSING AND STOPPING

Finally, there are five instructions that disrupt the flow of the program, either by creating a delay or by stopping it altogether.

Mnemonic: NOP
Name: No operation
Syntax: NOP
Effect: Does nothing but takes 3 cycles to do it! This instruction is used to replace an existing, redundant instruction or, more usually, to create a fixed delay in the program.
Flags: No effect.

Mnemonic: ESC
Name: Escape
Syntax: ESC op1,op2 (op1:opcode; op2:operand)
Effect: Passes an instruction to another processor, such as the 8087 maths co-processor.
Flags: No effect.

Mnemonic: LOCK
Name: Lock
Syntax: LOCK
Effect: Prevents another processor from accessing a memory location that is about to be changed, causing the second processor to wait until the operation is complete. LOCK precedes the instruction that is to change the memory.
Flags: No effect.

Mnemonic: WAIT
Name: Wait
Syntax: WAIT
Effect: Stops the program until a hardware interrupt is received or a signal is detected on the TEST pin of the 8086.
Flags: No effect.

Mnemonic: HLT
Name: Halt

The 8086 Instruction Set

Syntax: HLT
Effect: Stops the program until a hardware interrupt is received.
Flags: No effect.

Examples of some of the ways in which many of these instructions can be used will be found throughout the remainder of the book.

5.   *Interrupts*

The previous chapter catalogued the operations that the 8086 processor can perform. However, most of those described were centred around the manipulation of data in memory.

For a process to have real meaning it must be able to do two other things: input data to the program and output results to the user. Therefore an essential component of all programs is the ability to communicate with the real world. The majority of this communication is done through the interrupts. The INT instruction that allows this communication to take place is the subject of this chapter.

INTERRUPTS

An *interrupt* is a signal to the CPU to temporarily suspend whatever action is in progress and perform some other activity. Interrupts are generated either externally by a piece of hardware or internally by a program.

For example, every time a key is pressed the keyboard generates an interrupt. The CPU stops what it is doing and carries out whatever actions may be required by the key press, before resuming its previous task. Similarly, the timer chip generates another type of hardware interrupt 18.2 times a second.

Other interrupts are generated by programs to get the hardware to perform some function. For example, there is an interrupt for setting a pixel on the screen and another for reading a disk sector. In this case we are forcing the processor to temporarily suspend its current activity to carry out our request.

INTERRUPT HANDLERS

There are a large number of interrupts. Associated with each of these is a section of code called an *interrupt handler*. In a sense an interrupt is very like a call to a subroutine. The current activity ceases, the code that has been called is activated and, when the routine is complete, the processing resumes at the next instruction in the main section of code.

The interrupt handlers can be located almost anywhere:

- The ROS interrupts are held in permanent ROM.

Interrupts

- The MS-DOS interrupts are contained in the file IO.SYS.

- Individual applications may contain their own interrupt handlers as replacements for those of the ROS and MS-DOS.

The interrupt handlers can be set to perform virtually any operation but generally they are used to read from and write to the internal ports, relieving the programmer of the tedium of this type of data transfer and ensuring that the operations are carried out safely.

INTERRUPT VECTORS

When an interrupt occurs the CPU needs to know where the interrupt handler is located. It does this through the use of *interrupt vectors*. An interrupt vector is a pointer to an interrupt handler, each handler having its own individual vector. The interrupt vector consists of two words that hold the segment and offset address of the handler.

Since the interrupt could - and does - occur at any time the information relating to these locations is stored in a 'secure' place in memory. This is the very bottom of memory, starting at 0000:0000 for interrupt 00h. The vectors are stored sequentially and, since each vector is four bytes long and space is allocated even when a particular interrupt does not actually exist, it is a simple matter to calculate the vector for any interrupt. For example, the interrupt vector for the keyboard interrupt (09h) is located at 0000:0024; the four bytes at this location point to the start of the keyboard interrupt handler routines.

The advantage of using interrupts is that programs are totally independent of the addresses of the various routines that access the hardware. If there is a new version of MS-DOS or the ROS routines are updated there should be no effect on the applications programs. All that happens is that there is a new interrupt table, containing the address of the new routines. Therefore, a call to an interrupt is just as effective as before. On the other hand, any programs that access DOS or ROS routines directly are inevitably going to encounter compatibility problems when transferred to a different computer or operating system.

The standard interrupt vectors that are available after the Amstrad PC has been started up are shown in Figure 5.1.

Interrupt	Type	Use
00	Hardware	Divide by zero
01	Hardware	Single step
02	Hardware	Non-Maskable Interrupt (NMI)
03	Hardware	Break points
04	Hardware	Overflow
05	Hardware	Print-Screen
06	Hardware	User mouse interrupt
07	Hardware	Reserved
08	Hardware	8259 Timer
09	Hardware	Keyboard
0A-0F	Reserved	
10	ROS	Screen
11	ROS	Equipment list
12	ROS	Memory size
13	ROS	Disk
14	ROS	Serial port
15	ROS	NVR
16	ROS	Not used
17	ROS	Parallel port
18	ROS	System reset
19	ROS	System reset
1A	ROS	Date and time
1B	ROS	Keyboard break
1C	ROS	Clock tick
1D	Address	Video table
1E	Address	Disk table
1F	Address	Graphics character table
20	DOS	Terminate program
21	DOS	DOS functions
22	DOS address	Program termination
23	DOS address	Ctrl-Break address
24	DOS address	Critical error handler
25	DOS	Disk read
26	DOS	Disk write
27	DOS	Terminate and Stay Resident
28-32	DOS	Reserved for DOS
33	DOS	Mouse
34-3F	DOS	Reserved for DOS
40-7F		Available for programmers
80-FF	BASIC	Reserved for BASIC

Figure 5.1 The interrupt vectors

Interrupts

THE INT INSTRUCTION

At the heart of all assembly language programs is the *INT (Interrupt)* instruction. This instruction performs all input and output operations by accessing the computer's and operating system's *interrupts*.

The operand for the INT instruction is the interrupt number. This must be an immediate value; it may not be the contents of a register or memory location.

Before calling the interrupt it may be necessary to supply other information in the registers. For example, to change a pixel on the screen the interrupt finds the pixel location and colour from the registers. The interrupt may also return values in the registers.

When an interrupt is received the flags register is pushed onto the stack, the interrupt and trap flags are cleared and control is passed to the routine pointed to by the relevant entry in the interrupt table.

All interrupts end with an IRET (Interrupt Return) instruction. The effect of this is to pop the flags register off the stack and return control to the calling routine.

THE 8259 INTERRUPT CONTROLLER

All activities with interrupts are overseen by the 8259 Programmable Interrupt Controller. The controller makes use of ports 20h and 21h.

The interrupt lines

The 8086 has two lines which can be used by the hardware to signal interrupts. After each instruction has been completed the CPU checks these two lines. If it detects an interrupt then it immediately proceeds to the relevant interrupt routine.

There are two categories of interrupt, each of which is signalled on a different line:

- Maskable interrupts

- Non-maskable interrupts

Although the activation of the two categories of interrupt is the same, there are some important differences in the way they are handled. The most important difference is that, while the maskable interrupts can be ignored, the non-maskable interrupt cannot be overridden in the normal course of events.

Interrupt types	In addition to whether or not the interrupts are maskable, there are two basic types of interrupt:

- *Hardware interrupts* are created by specific elements of the hardware, as a response to some situation.

- *Software interrupts* are called from within a program.

Although these two types of interrupt are quite different in the way in which they are generated they are both dealt with in the same way.

HARDWARE INTERRUPTS

One type of interrupt is created automatically by the hardware, in response to some physical event. The majority of these are maskable interrupts.

MASKABLE HARDWARE INTERRUPTS	The *maskable interrupts* are signalled on the CPU's *INTR (Interrupt Request)* line, which is supervised by the 8259 Controller.

Whether or not the CPU actually acts upon these interrupts is determined by the state of the interrupt flag (bit 9 in the flags register). If the flag is set then the interrupt is processed; if the flag is clear the interrupt is ignored.

Two special instructions exist to set and clear this flag, STI and CLI respectively. As a general rule it is best to leave the flag set. However, there are occasions when it is necessary to clear the interrupt flag (for example, when processing an interrupt which could not cope with the disruption of a further interrupt). In such cases the flag must be set again as soon as possible. When the interrupts are disabled (that is, the interrupt flag is 0) any key presses or other attempts to input information to the computer are ignored. When a computer hangs it is usually because the interrupts have been disabled but no re-enabled.

NON-MASKABLE INTERRUPT (NMI)	There is a single *non-maskable interrupt (NMI)*. This is a hardware interrupt and is signalled on a different line, the NMI line of the 8086. The CPU is obliged to act on this interrupt regardless of the state of the interrupt flag.

Interrupts

The NMI only occurs in the most extreme of circumstances, such as a memory failure or a reduction in power. It is also connected to the 8087 maths co-processor and the expansion bus. This interrupt signals that some catastrophe has occurred and that processing should not continue.

In fact, the non-maskable interrupt can be disabled by clearing the top bit of port A0h. (The other seven bits of the port are not used, so to disable or enable the NMI the output value should be 00h or 80h respectively.) Disabling the NMI is extremely inadvisable.

INTERRUPTS 00H - 04H

The first five interrupts cannot be called directly from within a program but are issued by the hardware.

Interrupt 00h is invoked when the CPU encounters a 'Divide by zero' situation.

Interrupt 01h is used when tracing through a program and is dependent on the trap flag. When the trap flag is set the CPU generates an interrupt 01h after each individual instruction has been executed. This returns control to the debugging program, which can then inspect the contents of the registers and memory before continuing with the next instruction. The trap flag is set for single-stepping through a program. (This is the procedure used by DEBUG's S command.)

Interrupt 02h is the NMI. When this interrupt is invoked the immediate effect is to clear the screen and display a RAM parity error message. The computer is then completely disabled until it is switched off and back on.

If an 8087 maths co-processor is used within a program then a replacement interrupt 02h must be supplied that also caters for the 8087's NMI's.

Interrupt 03h is used by programs such as DEBUG to set break points within a development program.

Interrupt 04h is used to deal with overflows. This interrupt can also be generated indirectly by software, using the INTO instruction. The INTO instruction checks the overflow flag and, if it is set, generates an interrupt 04h.

A further 8 interrupts (from 08h to 0Fh) are generated by specific devices. All but three of these are dummy routines that may be replaced by new routines.

Stack errors

Due to a software limitation of MS-DOS, programs may tend to crash with the message:

```
Fatal Internal Stack Error - System Halted
```

This occurs when there is insufficient stack space allocated for handling hardware interrupts. DOS versions prior to 3.2 allowed up to 64 stacks but DOS 3.2 provides only 8 stacks as a default (saving 7K of memory).

If this is a problem the STACKS directive can be included in CONFIG.SYS, in the following form:

```
STACKS = 16,128
```

This is the recommended increase, giving 16 stacks each of 128 bytes. (Note that this problem also occasionally occurs on some early PC1512's if a single key is held down for a long period.)

SOFTWARE INTERRUPTS

The second type of interrupt is created from within a program and is totally under the control of the programmer. These interrupts are used to make the hardware perform specific tasks and are generated by an INT instruction. In a sense, they are just another form of subroutine. The main differences are that the address of the subroutine is found from the interrupt vector table, and the interrupt routine ends with an IRET instruction.

All software interrupts are maskable; that is, they are all ignored if the interrupt flag has a value of 0.

Interrupts 05h to 1Fh are all part of the permanent ROS and are all that is needed to make the hardware perform any function that is required.

Interrupts 20h to 2Fh are reserved for use by MS-DOS. These provide alternative means of accessing the hardware and also

Interrupts

give access to all of DOS's file operations. In particular, interrupt 21h is a huge collection of individual services. Each service could have been an interrupt in its own right, since there is no relationship between one service and the next, but the shortage of interrupt numbers would have limited the potential number of services available. As a result, when calling interrupt 21h, it is necessary to specify which service is required by sending the service number in register AH.

Most of the remaining interrupts (30h to FFh) are unused by the ROS and MS-DOS so theoretically are available for the programmer to use.

The interrupts that are available once the Amstrad PC has been booted are listed at the end of the chapter in Figure 5.3.

In the case of the software interrupts it is usual to send the interrupt handler some information in the general registers; the handler generally uses these registers to pass back any results. (This is rather like passing data across to a program via the variables.)

REPLACING INTERRUPTS

The ROS and MS-DOS interrupts provide us with a good range of routines to achieve almost everything we could hope for. Almost, but not quite everything. There is always something we want the computer to do automatically (rather than as a routine that must be called from within a program). For example, we might want the computer to react in a specific way to a particular key combination (as when invoking Sidekick).

As a result, programmers spend a lot of time replacing the standard interrupt handlers with routines of their own. Broadly speaking the principle is to locate a suitable routine somewhere in RAM and then replace the interrupt vector with the address of the new routine.

A well-behaved replacement interrupt handler will end by calling the original routine, whose interrupt vector it has saved.

One way of replacing an interrupt handler would be to calculate the location of the interrupt vector, find the address of the handler and carry out the operation manually. However, DOS provides two interrupt functions of its own to

Interrupts

achieve this end. The methods given below are much safer than any manual method.

The first stage is to save the existing interrupt vector. Interrupt 21h, function 35h returns the interrupt vector, which can then be stored away for future use.

Interrupt: 21h
Function: 35h
Service: Get interrupt vector
Entry values: AH=35h
        AL=interrupt number
Exit values: ES:BX=interrupt vector

The next stage is to replace the vector with the address of the new handler.

Interrupt: 21h
Function: 25h
Service: Set interrupt vector
Entry values: AH=25h
        AL=interrupt number
        DS:DX=pointer to interrupt handler
Exit values: None

If the new interrupt handler is held in the main program its address is fairly easy to calculate (see Figure 5.2). This example shows how the interrupt may perform some additional task before passing control on to the original handler.

Compatibility   As a general rule, it is better to use as high a level of instruction as possible. Therefore, when trying to perform any task the available options should be considered in the following order:

- High-level language instruction

- MS-DOS interrupt

- ROS interrupt

- Direct access to port/memory

The final option, in particular, should be a very last resort, used only when no suitable alternative is available or when

Interrupts

```
REPINT:                                 ; Replace interrupt vector

                                        ; Shell for replacing an interrupt
                                        ;   vector with a new routine
                                        ; First part of program contains
                                        ;   replacement interrupt, second part
                                        ;   is initialisation routine to install
                                        ;   interrupt

                                        ; If this routine is run as it is, it
                                        ;   should have no effect on the
                                        ;   interrupt
                                        ; However, repeated running of the
                                        ;   program will cause a chain of
                                        ;   interrupts to build up in memory.
                                        ;   Extra checks are required to see
                                        ;   whether interrupt vector has already
                                        ;   been changed

            jmp initialise              ; When program is run for first (and
                                        ;   only) time jump to initialisation
                                        ;   section

id          db '(C)1989, SM'            ; Data to identify program later
oldint      label dword                 ; Old interrupt vector
oldoff      dw ?                        ; Offset of vector
oldseg      dw ?                        ; Segment of vector

newint:                                 ; New interrupt vector
            sti                         ; Enable interrupts, where appropriate
            ;                           ; Insert any routines required to be
            ;                           ;   activated before old interrupt
            ;                           ;   called
            pushf                       ; Push flags register
            call oldint                 ; Call old interrupt
            ;                           ; Insert any routines required to be
            ;                           ;   activated after return from old
            ;                           ;   interrupt

            iret                        ; Return to operating system
endint:
            db ' '                      ; Pointer to end of routine to be left
                                        ;   in memory

initialise:                             ; Initialisation routine
            mov al,09h                  ; Get old interrupt vector (e.g.
                                        ;   keyboard)
            mov ah,35h
            int 21h
```

```
            mov oldoff,bx          ; Save offset
            mov oldseg,es          ; Save segment
            lea ds,oldseg
            mov si,offset id       ; Point to where you would expect ID
                                   ;    data to be
            xor cx,cx
            mov cx,0Bh             ; Length of ID data
            mov di,offset id       ; ES:DI points to ID data in this copy
                                   ;    of the program
            repz cmpsb             ; Compare data until difference found
            jnz installed          ; Jump if already installed
                                   ; Otherwise install new interrupt vector
            mov al,09h             ; Set new interrupt vector (e.g.
                                   ;    keyboard)
            mov ah,25h

            ;                      ; Display any messages to user that
            ;                      ;    interrupt has been installed

            mov dx, offset endint; Get offset of end of interrupt
            mov cl, 04h
            shr dx, cl             ; Divide by 16 to get paragraphs
            mov al, 00h            ; Terminate and stay resident
            mov ah, 31h
            int 21h

installed:
            ;                      ; Display message if strings compared OK
            int 20h                ; End program normally
```

Figure 5.2 Replacing an interrupt

speed is critical. Generally speaking, the further down the list you go the more compatibility problems you are likely to encounter.

This book concentrates on the inner workings of the Amstrad PC. As a result there are no high-level language routines included. Most operations are performed with the MS-DOS interrupts but it is worth noting that in some cases the same end can be achieved within a program by the programming language's built-in commands.

Interrupts

Note: All values are hexadecimal

Int-errupt	Func-tion	Service	Entry values	Exit values
05		Print screen		
06		Mouse interrupt	BX=button status CX=X co-ordinate DX=Y co-ordinate	(Defined by programmer)
10	00	Set video mode	AH=00 AL=new video mode	
	01	Set cursor size	AH=01 CH=first raster line (20 for no cursor) CL=last raster line	
	02	Set cursor position	AH=02 BH=page (0 for graphics modes) DH=row DL=column	
	03	Get cursor information	AH=03 BH=page	CH=first raster line CL=last raster line DH=row DL=column
	04	Get light pen information	AH=04	AH= (01h (Switch set) (00h (Switch clear) DH=character row DL=character column CX=pixel row (EGA/Hercules) CH=pixel row (CGA) BX=pixel column
	05	Select active display page	AH=05 AL=page	
	06	Scroll window up	AH=06 AL=number of lines to scroll BH=attribute for new line CH=top row	

Interrupts

Int- errupt	Func- tion	Service	Entry values	Exit values
			CL=left column DH=bottom row DL=right column	
	07	Scroll window down	AH=07 AL=number of lines to scroll BH=attribute for new line CH=top row CL=left column DH=bottom row DL=right column	
	08	Read character	AH=08 BH=page	AH=attribute AL=character
	09	Display character with attribute	AH=09 AL=character BH=page BL=attribute (text modes) CX=repeat count (0 for continuous repeat)	
	0A	Display character	AH=0A AL=character BH=page (text modes) BL=colour CX=repeat count (0 for continuous repeat)	
	0B	Select colour palette	AH=0B BH=palette BL=colour	
	0C	Display pixel	AH=0C AL=colour (add 80 for XOR) CX=pixel column DL=pixel row	
	0D	Read pixel colour	AH=0D CX=pixel column DL=pixel row	AL=colour

Interrupts

Interrupt	Function	Service	Entry values	Exit values
	0E	Display teletype character	AH=0E AL=character BH=page BL=colour (graphics modes)	
	0F	Get video mode	AH=0F	AH=width (characters) AL=video mode BH=page
11		Get configuration list		AX=configuration list code
12		Get user RAM		AX=user RAM code
13	00	Reset disk	AH=00	
	01	Check disk status	AH=01	AH=status code
	02	Read sectors from disk	AH=02 AL=number of sectors to read CH=track CL=sector DH=head DL=drive ES:BX=start of buffer for storing data	AH=error code (if CF=1) AL=number of sectors read (if CF=0) CF= (00 (success) (01 (error)
	03	Write sectors to disk	AH=03 AL=number of sectors to write CH=track CL=sector DH=head DL=drive ES:BX=start of buffer for containing data	AH=error code (if CF=1) AL=number of sectors written (if CF=0) CF= (00 (success) (01 (error)
	04	Verify disk sectors	AH=04 AL=number of sectors to verify CH=track CL=sector	AH=error code (if CF=1) AL=number of sectors verified (if CF=0) CF= (00 (success) (01 (error)

Interrupts

Int- errupt	Func- tion	Service	Entry values	Exit values
			DH=head DL=drive	
	05	Format disk track		

			AH=05
			AL=number of sectors
			    to format
			CH=track
			CL=sector
			DH=head
			DL=drive
			ES:BX=location of list of
			    address marks
				AH=error code (if CF=1)
				CF= (00 (success)
				      (01 (error)

14	00	Initialise serial port		
			AH=00 AL=protocol code DX=port number	AH=main status code AL=modem status code
	01	Send character to serial port		
			AH=01 AL=character to send DX=port number	AH=main status code
	02	Get character from serial port		
			AH=02 DX=port number	AH=main status code AL=character received
	03	Check serial port status		
			AH=03 DX=port number	AH=main status code AL=modem status code
15	00	Read mouse counters (Amstrad-specific)		
			AH=00	CX=X counter DX=Y counter All flags changed
	01	Set NVR value (Amstrad-specific)		

			AH=01
			AL=location to write
			    (00-3F)
			BL=new value
				AH= (0 (success)
				      (1 (address out of range)
				      (2 (write error)
				All flags changed

	02	Read NVR value (Amstrad-specific)		

			AH=02
			AL=location to read
			    (00-3F)
				AH= (0 (success)
				      (1 (address out of range)
				      (2 (checksum error)
				AL=value in NVR
				All flags changed

Interrupts

Int-errupt	Func-tion	Service	Entry values	Exit values
	06	Get ROS version number (Amstrad-specific)	AH=06	BH=major release number BL=minor release number All flags changed
16	00	Read character from keyboard	AH=00	AH=scan code AL=character
	01	Read character if available	AH=01	AH=scan code AL=character ZF= (0 (character available) (1 (buffer empty)
	02	Get keyboard status	AH=02	AL=keyboard status byte
17	00	Send character to parallel port	AH=00 AL=character DX=port number	AH=status code
	01	Initialise parallel port	AH=01 DX=port number	AH=status code
	02	Check parallel port status	AH=02 DX=port number	AH=status code
18		Restart system		
19		Reboot from floppy disk		
1A	00	Get clock count	AH=00	AL= (00 (not yet midnight) (01 (past midnight) CX=clock count (high order word) DX=clock count (low order word)
	01	Set clock count	AH=01 CX=clock count (high order word) DX=clock count (low order word)	
	02	Get RTC time (Amstrad-specific)	AH=02	CH=hours (BCD) CL=minutes (BCD) DH=seconds (BCD)

Interrupts

Int-errupt	Func-tion	Service	Entry values	Exit values

				DL= (0 (GMT only)
				(1 (GMT and BST)
				CF= (00 (RTC functioning)
				(01 (RTC not functioning)
				Other flags changed

	03	Set RTC time (Amstrad-specific)		
			AH=03	CF= (00 (RTC functioning)
			CH=hours (BCD)	(01 (RTC not functioning)
			CL=minutes (BCD)	Other flags changed
			DH=seconds (BCD)	
			DL= (0 (GMT only)	
			(1 (GMT and BST)	

	04	Read date from real time clock (Amstrad-specific)		
			AH=04	CH=century (BCD)
				CL=year (BCD)
				DH=month (BCD)
				DL=day (BCD)
				CF= (00 (RTC functioning)
				(01 (RTC not functioning)
				Other flags changed

	05	Set date of real time clock (Amstrad-specific)		
			AH=05	CF= (00 (RTC functioning)
			CH=century (BCD) (19 or 20)	(01 (RTC not functioning)
			CL=year (BCD)	Other flags changed
			DH=month (BCD)	
			DL=day (BCD)	

	06	Set RTC alarm (Amstrad-specific)		
			AH=06	CF= (00 (alarm now set)
			CH=hours	(01 (alarm was already set)
			CL=minutes	
			DH=seconds	

| | 07 | Reset alarm (Amstrad-specific) | | |

| 1C | | Clock tick | | |

The DOS Interrupts

| 20 | | Terminate program | | |
| | | | CS=PSP address | |

21	00	Terminate program		
			AH=00	
			CS=PSP address	

Interrupts

Int-errupt	Func-tion	Service	Entry values	Exit values
	01	Keyboard input with echo	AH=01	AL=character
	02	Display character	AH=02 DL=character	
	03	Get character from serial port	AH=03	AL=character
	04	Send character to serial port	AH=04 DL=character to send	
	05	Send character to parallel port	AH=05 DL=character to send	
	06	Keyboard input/ screen output	AH=06 DL= (FF(input) (character (output)	AL=Input character ZF= (00 (character available) (01 (buffer empty)
	07	Keyboard input without echo (without break)	AH=07	AL=character
	08	Keyboard input without echo (with break)	AH=08	AL=character
	09	Display string	AH=09 DS:DX=start of string	
	0A	Keyboard string input	AH=0A DS:DX=start of Input buffer	
	0B	Check keyboard buffer	AH=0B	AL= (00 (buffer empty) (01 (character available)
	0C	Clear keyboard buffer, call interrupt 21h function	AH=0C AL=function (01, 06, 07, 08, 0A)	(Various - as for selected function)
	0D	Reset disk	AH=0D	
	0E	Change current drive	AH=0E	AL=drive count

Interrupts

Int-errupt	Func-tion	Service	Entry values	Exit values
			DL=drive number (0=A)	
	0F	Open a file	AH=0F DS:DX=address of FCB	AL= (00 (success) (FF (failure)
	10	Close a file	AH=10 DS:DX=address of FCB	AL= (00 (success) (FF (failure)
	11	Find first matching file	AH=11 DS:DX=address of FCB	AL= (00 (success) (FF (file not found)
	12	Find next matching file	AH=12 DS:DX=address of FCB	AL= (00 (success) (FF (file not found)
	13	Delete a file	AH=13 DS:DX=address of FCB	AL= (00 (success) (FF (file not found)
	14	Read sequential record	AH=14 DS:DX=address of FCB	AL= (00 (success) (01 (nothing read) (02 (DTA too small) (03 (some data read)
	15	Write sequential record	AH=15 DS:DX=address of FCB	AL= (00 (success) (01 (disk full) (02 (DTA too small)
	16	Create a file	AH=16 DS:DX=address of FCB	AL= (00 (success) (FF (directory full)
	17	Rename a file	AH=17 DS:DX=address of FCB	AL= (00 (success) (FF (file not found)
	19	Get current drive	AH=19	AL=default drive (0=A)
	1A	Set disk transfer area addrerss	AH=1A DS:DX=new address of DTA	
	1B	Get FAT information for current drive	AH=1B	AL=sectors in each allocation unit

Interrupts

Int-errupt	Func-tion	Service	Entry values	Exit values
				CX=bytes per sector
				DX=allocation units
				DS:BX=address of ID byte
	1C	Get FAT information for any drive	AH=1C DH=drive (0=default)	AL=sectors in each allocation unit CX=bytes per sector DX=allocation units DS:BX=address of ID byte
	21	Read random record	AH=21 DS:DX=address of FCB	AL= (00 (success) (01 (no data read) (02 (DTA too small) (03 (some data read)
	22	Write random record	AH=22 DS:DX=address of FCB	AL= (00 (success) (01 (disk full) (02 (DTA too small)
	23	Get file size	AH=23 DS:DX=address of FCB	AL= (00 (success) (01h (file not found)
	24	Prepare field for random record	AH=24 DS:DX=address of FCB	AL= (00 (success) (FF (failure)
	25	Set interrupt vector	AH=25 AL=interrupt number DS:DX=address of interrupt handler	
	26	Create PSP	AH=26 DX=segment address	
	27	Read random records	AH=27 CX=number of records to read DS:DX=address of FCB	AL= (00 (success) (01 (no data read) (02 (DTA too small) (03 (some data read) CX=number of records read
	28	Write random records	AH=28 CX=number of records to write DS:DX=address of FCB	AL= (00 (success) (01 (disk full) (02 (DTA too small) CX=number of records written

Interrupts

Interrupt	Function	Service	Entry values	Exit values

	29	Parse filename	AH=29
			AL=parsing code
			DS:SI=address of command line
			ES:DI=address of FCB
				AL= (00 (success)
				     (01 (wildcards found)
				     (FF (invalid drive)
				DS:SI= address of next character in command line
				ES:DI=address of FCB

	2A	Get date	AH=2A	AL=day of week (0=Sunday) CX=year (1980-2099) DH=month (1=January) DL=day
	2B	Set date	AH=2B CX=year (1980-2099) DH=month (1=January) DL=day	AL= (00 (date valid) (FF (date invalid)
	2C	Get time	AH=2C	CH=hours CL=minutes DH=seconds DL=hundredths of seconds
	2D	Set time	AH=2D CH=hours CL=minutes DH=seconds DL=hundredths of seconds	AL= (00 (time valid) (FF (time invalid)
	2E	Disk write verification	AH=2E AL=(00 (verfify off) (01 (verfify on) DL=00	
	2F	Get address of DTA	AH=2F	AX=error code ES:BX=address of DTA
	30	Check DOS version number	AH=30	AH=minor version number AL=major version number BX, CX changed
	31	Terminate and stay resident	AH=31	AX=error code

Interrupts

Int-errupt	Func-tion	Service	Entry values	Exit values
			AL=termination code DX=segment address of memory to free	
	33,00	Get control break	AH=33 AL=00	AX=error code DL=current state
	33,01	Set control break	AH=33 AL=01 DL=code	AX=error code DL=current state
	35	Get interrupt vector	AH=35 AL=interrupt number	ES:BX=Interrupt vector
	36	Check free clusters	AH=36 DL=drive (0=default)	AX= (sectors per cluster) (FFFF (invalid drive) BX=number of available clusters CX=bytes per sector DX=total clusters on disk

	38	Get or set country-dependent information	AH=38
			AL= (00 (standard data, DOS 2)
			     (00 (current country, DOS 3)
			     (01-FE (country code)
			     (FF (code>=255)
			BX=country code (if code>=255)
			DS:DX=address of buffer
				AX=error code (if CF=1)
				
				BX=country code
				DS:DX=address of information

	39	Make directory	AH=39 DS:DX=address of ASCIIZ directory name	AX=error code (if CF=1)
	3A	Remove directory	AH=3A DS:DX=address of ASCIIZ directory name	AX=error code (if CF=1)
	3B	Change directory	AH=3B DS:DX=address of ASCIIZ directory name	AX=error code (if CF=1)
	3C	Create a file	AH=3C CX=file attribute DS:DX=address of ASCIIZ file specification	AX= (file handle (CF=0) (error code (CF=1)

Interrupts

Int-errupt	Func-tion	Service	Entry values	Exit values

	3D	Open a file	AH=3D
			CX=file use code
			DS:DX=address of ASCIIZ
			     file specification
				AX= (file handle (CF=0)
				     (error code (CF=1)

	3E	Close a file	AH=3E BX=file handle	AX=error code (if CF=1)
	3F	Read from file	AH=3F BX=file handle CX=number of bytes to be read DS:DX=address of DTA	AX= (number of bytes read (CF=0) (error code (CF=1)

	40	Write to a file	AH=40
			BX=file handle
			CX=(number of bytes to be written
			   (00 (truncate file at pointer)
			DS:DX=address of DTA
				AX= (number of bytes written (CF=0)
				     (error code (CF=1)

	41	Delete a file	AH=41 DS:DX=address of ASCIIZ file specification	AX=error code (if CF=1)
	42	Move file pointer	AH=42 AL=offset code BX=file handle CX:DX=number of bytes to move pointer	AX=error code (if CF=1) DX:AX=new pointer offset (if CF=0)
	43,00	Get attributes of file	AH=43 AL=00 DS:DX=address of ASCIIZ file specification	AX=error code (if CF=1) CX=attribute byte
	43,01	Set attributes of file	AH=43 AL=01 CX=new attribute byte DS:DX=address of ASCIIZ file specification	AX=error code (if CF=1)
	44	IOCTL functions	AH=44 AL=IOCTL function (Various others)	(Various)

Interrupts

Int- errupt	Func- tion	Service	Entry values	Exit values
	45	Duplicate a file handle	AH=45 BX=file handle	AX= (file handle (CF=0) (error code (CF=1)
	46	Force duplication of handle	AH=46 BX=file handle to copy CX=second file handle	AX=error code (If CF=1) CX=second file handle
	47	Check current directory	AH=47 DL=drive (0=default) DS:SI=address for pathname	AX=error code (If CF=1) DS:SI=address of pathname
	48	Allocate memory	AH=48 BX=memory (paragraphs)	AX=(segment address of allocated memory (error code (If CF=1) BX=largest memory size (If allocation failed)
	49	Free memory	AH=49 ES=segment of block	AX=error code (If CF=1)
	4A	Modify allocated memory	AH=4A BX=memory (paragraphs) ES=segment of block	AX=error code (If CF=1) BX=largest memory size (If allocation failed)
	4B	Load/execute program	AH=4B AL=(00 (Load and run) (03 (Load but do not run) DS:DX=address of ASCIIZ file specification ES:BX=address of control block	AX=error code
	4C	Terminate subprogram	AH=4C AL=return code	
	4D	Get return code of subprogram	AH=4D	AL=return code AH=ending code
	4E	Find first matching file	AH=4E CX=file attribute DS:DX=address of ASCIIZ file specification	AX=error code (If CF=1)
	4F	Find next matching file	AH=4F	AX=error code (If CF=1)

Interrupts

Int-errupt	Func-tion	Service	Entry values	Exit values
			DS:DX=address of Information from last search	
	54	Check verification status	AH=54	AL= (00 (verify off) (01 (verify on)
	56	Rename a file	AH=56 DS:DX=address of old name (ASCIIZ) ES:DI=address of new name (ASCIIZ)	AX=error code (If CF=1)
	57,00	Get date & time stamp	AH=57 AL=00 BX=file handle	AX=error code (If CF=1) CX=time DX=date
	57,01	Set date & time stamp	AH=57 AL=01 BX=file handle CX=time DX=date	AX=error code (If CF=1)
	59	Get extended error code	AH=59 BX=0000	AX=extended error code BH=type of error BL=possible action CH=location of error
	5A	Create a temporary file	AH=5A CX=file attribute DS:DX=address of ASCIIZ pathname	AX=error code (If CF=1) DS:DX=address of pathname (If CF=0)
	5B	Create a new file	AH=5B CX=file attribute DS:DX=address of ASCIIZ pathname	AX= (file handle (CF=0) (error code (CF=1)
	5C,00	Lock file	AH=5C AL=00 BX=file handle CX:DX=offset SI:DI=locked data length	AX=error code (If CF=1)

141

Interrupts

Int-errupt	Func-tion	Service	Entry values	Exit values
	5C,01	Unlock file	AH=5C AL=01 BX=file handle CX:DX=offset SI:DI=locked data length	AX=error code (if CF=1)
	62	Get PSP segment address	AH=62	BX=segment address of PSP
22		Terminate address		
23		Break address		
24		Critical error-handler address		
25		Read sectors from disk	AL=logical drive number (A=0) CX=number of sectors to read DX=first sector (DOS numbering) DS:BX=start of buffer for storing data	AL=DOS error code (if CF=1) AH=ROS error code (if CF=1) CF= (00 (success) (01 (error) Flags register on stack
26		Write sectors to disk	AL=logical drive number (A=0) CX=number of sectors to write DX=first sector (DOS numbering) DS:BX=start of buffer containing data	AL=DOS error code (if CF=1) AH=ROS error code (if CF=1) CF= (00 (success) (01 (error) Flags register on stack
27		Terminate & stay resident		
2F		Access background program	AH=multiplex number (Various) AL=function code	
33	00	Initialise mouse	AH=00h	AL= (FFh (mouse installed) (00h (no mouse found) BL=number of buttons
	01	Show mouse cursor	AH=01	
	02	Hide mouse cursor	AH=02	
	03	Get mouse information	AH=03	BX= (00 (no button pressed) (01 (left button pressed)

Int-errupt	Func-tion	Service	Entry values	Exit values
				(02 (right button pressed)
				(03 (both buttons pressed)
				CX=X co-ordinate
				DX=Y co-ordinate
	04	Set mouse cursor	AH=04 CX=X co-ordinate DX=Y co-ordinate	
	05	Get mouse button press	AH=05 BL=(00 (left button) (01 (right button)	AX= (00 (button not pressed) (01 (button pressed) BX=number of presses since last call CX=X co-ordinate at last press DX=Y co-ordinate at last press
	06	Get mouse button release	AH=00 BL=(00 (left button) (1 (right button)	AX= (00 (button not pressed) (1 (button pressed) BX=number of presses since last call CX=X co-ordinate at last release DX=Y co-ordinate at last release
	07	Set mouse cursor horizontal limits	AH=07 CX=minimum X co-ordinate DX=maximum X co-ordinate	
	08	Set mouse cursor vertical limits	AH=08 CX=minimum Y co-ordinate DX=maximum Y co-ordinate	
	09	Define mouse graphics cursor	AH=09 BX=X co-ordinate offset CX=Y co-ordinate offset ES:DX=address of screen and cursor masks	

	0A	Define mouse text cursor	AH=0A
			BL= (00 (Software cursor)
			    (01 (Hardware cursor)
			CX= (Screen mask (BL=00)
			    (First scan line (BL=01)
			DX= (Cursor mask (BL=00)
			    (Last scan line (BL=01)	

Interrupts

Int-errupt	Func-tion	Service	Entry values	Exit values
	0B	Read mouse counts	AH=0B	CX=X count DX=Y count
	0C	Set mouse interrupt	AH=0C CX=event mask ES:DX=address of new interrupt	
	0D	Turn light pen emulation on	AH=0D	
	0E	Turn light pen emulation off	AH=0E	
	0F	Set mickey:pixel ratio	AH=0F CX=X ratio (per 8 units) DX=Y ratio (per 8 units)	
	10	Hide mouse cursor while updating	AH=10 CX=top left X co-ordinate DX=top left Y co-ordinate SI=bottom right X co-ordinate DI=bottom right Y co-ordinate	
	13	Set threshold for double speed	AH=13 DX=threshold speed (mickeys/second)	

6. *Compiling and Running Programs*

Programs consist of strings of machine-code instructions. Theoretically, these instructions can be placed directly in memory and executed. However, programming directly in machine code is almost impossible, so the usual procedure is to write the program in assembly language, using more intelligible mnemonics and labels. The programs are then assembled into standard machine code. In a similar way, high-level language programs are often compiled into machine code before they are run.

This chapter briefly investigates the principles involved in assembly language programs. It also considers the ways in which programs are started and stopped, and how errors are dealt with.

ASSEMBLERS

The assembly language mnemonics that we use are obviously unintelligible to the CPU. For them to have any meaning, each mnemonic and its associated data must be converted into a form that the CPU can understand. This translation from assembly language into machine code is done by a program called an *assembler*.

The operation of the assembler is fairly straightforward. For our assembly language instructions it is simply a matter of translating each individual opcode and operand into the corresponding machine code equivalent. In addition, however, the assembly language may include further instructions, telling the assembler where each part of the code is to be placed in memory, what format the data is to take and so on. These instruction vary from one assembler to another, though their use is similar for all assemblers.

An original assembly language program is called the *source file*. The first stage is to translate this into an *object file*, which contains machine code. After this a process known as *linking* takes the object file and, using information from external files, produces an *executable file*. The linking process may take in *library files* that contain commonly-used routines. The ex-

Compiling and Running programs

ecutable file is a file with an EXE extension that can be loaded into any part of memory and run. The final stage is frequently to convert this executable file into a binary file, with a COM extension.

Further details of this sequence of events can be found in any good assembly language programming book.

COM AND EXE FILES

As described above, an assembled program can end up in either of two forms, as a COM file or an EXE file. The essential features of a COM file are:

- The code, data and stack must all fit in a single 64K segment.

- The program is loaded into memory at the first available place.

The features of an EXE file are:

- The program can be as large as you like and the data and stack are not confined to the same segment.

- The program has a table of information at the beginning. Only this header is loaded into the first part of memory.

- The program itself can be relocated anywhere in memory.

In addition an EXE program must carry out more initialisation procedures than a corresponding COM file.

EXE files can be converted into COM files using the program EXE2BIN, provided they satisfy the criteria for COM files. Generally, life is much simpler if you stick to COM files whenever possible; all the small programs in this book are suitable for COM files.

THE A86 ASSEMBLER

There are a number of assemblers available for programming the Amstrad, not least Microsoft's own MASM. However, the examples given in this book have all been written with the A86 assembler in mind. The main reason for this is that, in the opinion of the author, A86 is a fast, no-nonsense assembler which cuts out all the unnecessary and unwieldy trimmings that bedevil most assemblers.

Compiling and Running programs

Since all assemblers have the same main purpose - that is, to convert their programs into machine code - and the code produced by each should be more or less the same, the choice of assembler is, to a certain extent, irrelevant. However, by using A86 it has been possible to include a large number of useful routines in a compact manner. These routines can be entered and assembled by anyone who has a copy of A86, without modification. To assist in this process a recent version of A86 is included on the disks associated with this book.

This does not stop those who prefer to use other assemblers from using the routines in this book. However, for those who do so, I regret it will be necessary to add the SEGMENT, ORG and other pseudo-ops that litter these languages. One of the main reasons for using A86 is that it adds its own sensible default values wherever possible, making many pseudo-ops redundant. We only need to use the standard pseudo-ops when we want something not catered for by the defaults.

For compatibility, the extra, non-standard features of A86 (such as its ability to use PUSH statements with multiple operands) have not been used. Apart from this, only a few minor changes need to be made for the listings given here to be used with any other assembler.

A86 is highly recommended for anyone who does not yet use it. Not only is programming simpler, because all the irritating overheads are already taken care of, but compilation is also refined. The production of COM files is a single process and generally takes less time than the production of the half-way house OBJ files generated by other assemblers.

It must be stressed here that A86 is a *shareware* program. Anyone may freely distribute the program for others to use, as long as a few simple rules are followed:

- No charge must be made for the program, apart from a small fee to cover the cost of the disk itself, post and packaging etc.

- Programs produced by A86 can only be sold commercially by registered users.

- Any user who finds A86 useful should become a registered user.

Compiling and Running programs

DEBUG commands

Command Name		Syntax	Effect
A	Assemble	A A address	Assembles code directly
C	Compare	C range, address	Compares memory in range with memory starting at address
D	Dump	D D range	Displays next 128 bytes or range
E	Enter	E address E address, data	Enters data at specified address
F	Fill	F range, data	Fills range with data
G	Go	G	Executes program from start or from address
H	Hexadecimal	H value, value	Adds two hex numbers and also subtracts second from first
I	Input	I port	Inputs value from port
L	Load	L address L address, sectors	Loads a file or disk sectors
M	Move	M range, address	Moves a range of memory to a new address
N	Name	N filename	Names a file to load or save
O	Output	O data,port	Outputs data to a port
P	Proceed		
Q	Quit	Q	Quits DEBUG
R	Register	R R register	Displays contents of registers
S	Search	S range, data	Searches range for data
T	Trace	T T=address T steps	Traces program, optionally from a specified address an/or a number of steps
U	Unassemble	U range	Unassembles a range of code
W	Write	W W address W address, sectors	Writes a section of code to a file or directly to disk

Figure 6.1 DEBUG commands

I strongly urge all A86 users to register. Not only does this help the software writer, but it also gives you the chance to buy a copy of the manual and freedom to sell your software.

DEBUG — Many people will use DEBUG, of course, to assemble and disassemble programs. The use and operation of DEBUG is covered by most assembly language books and will also be found in many other manuals. Therefore, its operation is not covered here, although a full list of the DEBUG commands as implemented on the Amstrad PC is included in Figure 6.1.

THE PROGRAM SEGMENT PREFIX (PSP)

Whenever a program is loaded into memory DOS creates a small block of code that contains vital information about the program. This is called the *Program Segment Prefix (PSP)*.

The PSP is stored in the first 100h (256) bytes of the area allocated to the file. It is for this reason that the program itself always starts at an offset of 100h from the start address of the code segment. The contents of the PSP are shown in Figure 6.2.

The address interrupts — The PSP includes default settings for three interrupt vectors, 22h, 23h and 24h. These interrupts are known as the *address interrupts*. They are not interrupts in the usual sense but pointers to particular sections of code. They store three important addresses: where to go when a program ends, the location of the routine to deal with the Ctrl-Break combination, and the address of the routines that handle certain crucial errors.

DOS always restores the three default interrupt vectors when the program terminates. This means that our programs can change these interrupt addresses - by replacing the interrupt vectors - without fear of doing permanent damage.

It is also feasible to change the defaults by changing the PSP but it is not very good manners to do so. A well-behaved program should always leave the computer as it finds it; there should never be any unpleasant after-effects for the user (though with many well-known programs there are!) The only exception is the Terminate Address (interrupt 22h), which may be changed when one program is run by another.

Compiling and Running programs

	The Program Segment Prefix	
Offset (hex)	Bytes (hex)	Use
00	2	INT 20h instruction
02	2	Top of memory
04	1	Reserved
05	1	Op code (redundant: for CP/M compatibility)
06	4	Number of bytes in segment (CP/M)
0A	4	Terminate address
0E	4	Ctrl-Break address
12	4	Critical error address
16	16	Reserved
2C	2	Environment segment
2E	22	Reserved
50	2	DOS call
52	0A	Reserved
5C	10	File Control Block 1
6C	14	File Control Block 2
80	1	Length of command line
81	7F	Command line parameters

N.B. All segment:offset addresses are stored in reverse order with the low byte of the offset first.

Figure 6.2 The Program Segment Prefix (PSP)

Finding the PSP address

If you want to know where the PSP is, DOS 3 provides a function for locating it.

Interrupt:	21h
Function:	62h
DOS version:	3
Service:	Get PSP segment address
Entry values:	AH=62h
Exit values:	BX=segment address of PSP

The need for this function arises from the fact that a relocatable EXE program could be placed anywhere in memory. It need not necessarily follow the PSP. This interrupt tells us where the PSP starts, so that we can use the information it contains.

Compiling and Running programs

Command line parameters

One of the most important uses for the PSP is to find out what parameters have been passed to the program. The parameters are stored in the 7Fh bytes before the start of the program itself. Thus any of our programs can easily accept additional start-up information from the user, such as the names of files to be operated on.

The length of the command line parameters, stored at offset 80h in the PSP, does not include the program name but does include the space before the parameters; therefore this must be accounted for in determining the length of the parameters. This information is used by the routine in Figure 6.3, which sets up a pointer to the start of the parameters and stores the parameter length in a variable. The following routines select each parameter in turn.

Duplicating the PSP

Early versions of DOS provided a means of copying the current PSP to another location in memory, as the first part of the process to load and run another program.

Interrupt: 21h
Function: 26h
DOS version: 1
Service: Create PSP
Entry values: AH=26h
DX=segment address
Exit values: None

This has now been superseded by function 4Bh (see below) and is rarely used.

ENDING A PROGRAM

DOS uses two identical interrupts to end a program.

Interrupt: 20h
DOS version: 1
Service: Terminate program
Entry values: CS=PSP address
Exit values: None

Interrupt: 21h
Function: 00h
DOS version: 1
Service: Terminate program
Entry values: AH=00h
CS=PSP address
Exit values: None

Compiling and Running programs

```
PARSE:                                  ; Parse the command line

                                        ; Finds the first item of text after
                                        ;   the command and the length of the
                                        ;   command line parameters
                                        ; NEXTPARM will return subsequent
                                        ;   parameters

                                        ; Entry values: None
                                        ; Exit values:  PARAMST=offset address
                                        ;                   of parameters
                                        ;               PARAMLEN=parameters
                                        ;                   total length
                                        ;               BX,CX,DX changed

            jmp parsestart

paramst     db ?                        ; Start of next parameter (offset
                                        ;   from 82h)
paramlen    db ?                        ; Length of remaining parameters

parsestart:
            lea bx,80h                  ; Point to start of command line data
            mov cl,byte ptr [bx]        ; Move parameter length into CX
            cmp cl,00h
            jz noparam                  ; Jump if no parameters
            dec cl                      ; Ignore leading space
noparam:
            mov [paramlen],cl           ; Store parameter length
            mov byte ptr [paramst],00h  ; Store start of parameter
                                        ;   (as offset from 82h)
            ret

; ----------------------------------------------------------------

NEXTPARM:                               ; Get next parameter

                                        ; Routine does not allow for multiple
                                        ;   spaces or for \ characters
                                        ; Limited to 64-character parameters
                                        ; Parameter cannot include $

                                        ; Entry values: None
                                        ; Exit values:  PARAMETER= next parameter
                                        ;
                                        ;               CF=1 if no parameter
                                        ;               AX,BX,CX,SI,DI changed
```

```
                    jmp npstart
parameter           db 64 dup ('&')         ; Parameter to be returned
ends                db '$'                  ; $ to end for string display function

npstart:
                    xor cx,cx               ; Set CL to hold length of remainder
                    mov cl,[paramlen]       ;   of parameters
                    cmp cl,00h
                    jnz getparam            ; Jump if there are more parameters
                    stc
                    jmp nextend
getparam:
                    mov al,' '              ; AL contains search character (space)
                    cld
                    xor bx,bx               ; Point to start of parameter
                    mov bl,[paramst]
                    add bl,82h
                    lea di,bx
                    repnz scasb             ; Search for space or end of parameters
                    jnz endline1            ; Jump if at end of line
                    dec di                  ; Otherwise, move DI back to space at
                                            ;   end of parameter
endline1:
                    sub di,82h              ; Calculate offset of end of parameter
                    xor ax,ax
                    mov al,[paramst]
                    sub di,ax               ; Calculate parameter length
                    mov cx,di
                    push cx                 ; Save parameter length
                    lea di,parameter        ; Point to PARAMETER
                    push cx
                    mov cx,40h
                    mov al,' '
                    rep stosb               ; Clear PARAMETER
                    pop cx
                    xor bx,bx               ; Point to start of parameter for source
                    mov bl,[paramst]
                    add bl,82h
                    lea si,bx
                    lea di,parameter        ; Point to PARAMETER for destination
                    rep movsb               ; Copy parameter out of PSP
                    mov al,[paramst]        ; Calculate start of next parameter
                    pop cx                  ; Recover parameter length
                    add al,cl
                    inc al                  ; Ignore following space
                    mov [paramst],al
```

Compiling and Running programs

```
            mov al,[paramlen]    ; Calculate length of remainder
                    sub al,cl
                    cmp al,00h
                    jz endline2        ; Jump if at end of line
                    dec al             ; Ignore space
endline2:           mov [paramlen],al
nextend:
                    ret

; -------------------------------------------------------------------

PARSTEST:                          ; Program to test parsing routines

                                   ; Prints parameters parsed from
                                   ;    command line

                                   ; Calls PARSE, NEXTPARSE,
                                   ;    DISLIN (Figure 13.16)

                    call parse
getp:
                    call nextparm
                    jc endparse
                    lea dx,parameter
                    call dislin
                    jmp getp
endparse:
                    int 20h
```

Figure 6.3 Locating program parameters

Before calling the interrupt the CS register must contain the segment address of the PSP. Normally this is automatically the case; CS need only be restored if it has been changed within the program (for example, by a FAR call to a subroutine).

Obviously there are no values returned; the program never returns from this interrupt. The interrupt does not close any open files; this should be done before the interrupt is called.

The interrupt restores the Ctrl-Break and critical-error handler addresses to their original values.

Compiling and Running programs

RUNNING A SUBPROGRAM

DOS provides three functions that allow us to run another program, and then continue with the current program.

Interrupt: 21h
Function: 4Bh
DOS version: 2
Service: Load/execute program
Entry values: AH=4Bh
                AL=(00h (Load and run)
                    (03h (Load but do not run)
                DS:DX=address of ASCIIZ file specification
                ES:BX=address of control block
Exit values: AX=return code

This function loads or runs a further program, keeping the current program in memory. The effect of the interrupt depends upon the value placed in AL.

The program may be loaded and run, as a completely separate program (AL=00h); alternatively it may just be loaded into memory, replacing existing code (AL=03h). This is the case for *overlay files*. Certain information needs to be passed to the program:

- The address of the environment to be used by the program.

- The command line, from which the program will get its parameters (these are copied to the new PSP).

- The addresses of the two FCB's.

These parameters are passed across as a control block (Figure 6.4).

When it comes to ending a subprogram a different interrupt is used to those available for the main program.

Interrupt: 21h
Function: 4Ch
DOS version: 2
Service: Terminate subprogram
Entry values: AH=4Ch

Overlays parameter block (Function 4Bh; AL=03h)		
Offset	Bytes	Use
00	2	Overlay address segment
02	2	Relocation factor
Execution parameter block (Function 4Bh; AL=00h)		
Offset (hex)	Bytes	Use
00	2	Environment address segment
02	4	Command line address
06	4	First FCB address
0A	4	Second FCB address

NB: All segment:offset addresses are given in reverse order, with the offset low byte first.

Figure 6.4 Subprogram control block

Exit values: AL=error code

This function ends the subprogram, returning control to the calling program and passing back an error code (which must be determined within the program).

This code can either be accessed within the calling program, or - if the program returns to DOS - can be tested with the DOS ERRORLEVEL batch file function.

Interrupt: 21h
Function: 4Dh
DOS version: 2
Service: Get return code of subprogram
Entry values: AH=4Dh
Exit values: AL=return code

Compiling and Running programs

	Subprogram return codes (Functions 4Ch and 4Dh)
Code	Meaning
00	Normal termination
01	Ended by Ctrl-Break
02	Critical error
03	Ended by interrupt 31h call (TSR)

Figure 6.5 Return codes after ending a subprogram

The third function provides the main program with information about how the subprogram terminated. The return codes are included in Figure 6.5.

The Terminate Address

One of the default interrupt vectors stored in the PSP is the *Terminate Address* (22h). This is not an interrupt in the normal sense of the word; it is never actually invoked. Instead it is used to store the address of the next section of code to be run by DOS when the program terminates.

Normally, the default value is correct and should not be changed. However, if a program runs another program it may want to change the default terminate address to point to a location inside the first program. DOS will then continue running the first program when the second has ended.

ALLOCATING MEMORY

It is sometimes necessary to mark out a block of memory for use by a program. DOS provides three functions that allow us to allocate, change and de-allocate memory.

Interrupt:	21h
Function:	48h
DOS version:	2
Service:	Allocate memory
Entry values:	AH=48h
	BX=memory (in paragraphs)
Exit values:	AX=(segment address of allocated memory
	(error code (if CF=1)
	BX=largest memory size (if allocation failed)

157

Compiling and Running programs

This function sets aside a given number of paragraphs (units of 10h bytes). It returns the address of the start segment of the block in AX. If there is insufficient memory an error code is returned.

Interrupt:	21h
Function:	4Ah
DOS version:	2
Service:	Modify allocated memory
Entry values:	AH=4Ah
	BX=memory (paragraphs)
	ES=segment of block
Exit values:	AX=error code (if CF=1)
	BX=largest memory size (if allocation failed)

In a similar way to the first function, this function changes the size of the block that has been allocated.

Interrupt:	21h
Function:	49h
DOS version:	2
Service:	Free memory
Entry values:	AH=49h
	ES=segment of block to return
Exit values:	AX=error code (if CF=1)

The final memory-allocation function frees a block of memory previously allocated by function 48h. It is important to always tidy up memory by de-allocating space as soon as possible after it is no longer needed.

CRITICAL ERRORS

Inevitably, programs sometimes come across a problem that they just cannot handle, such as a fatal disk error. Such errors are called *critical errors*. In these cases the program terminates early and DOS invokes a special interrupt, 24h, to deal with the situation. The default address of the interrupt is one of those stored by DOS in the PSP. Even if we have replaced the interrupt vector, when the program crashes in this way DOS resorts to the default in the PSP. Change this at your peril!

If the interrupt is left untouched any critical error will result in the familiar DOS error messages appearing on the screen in the middle of the program. If the user is lucky he can rectify the error and continue. In many cases such errors are fatal and final.

Critical error codes	
Code (hex)	Error
00	System files read error
01	System files write error
02	FAT read error
03	FAT write error
04	Directory read error
05	Directory write error
06	Data read error
07	Data write error
80-FF	Non-specific, non-disk error

Figure 6.6 Critical error codes

Our programs can choose to deal with some of these errors themselves, by replacing the interrupt vector (but not the default in the PSP). Any errors not accounted for will still result in a crash but some of the more obvious ones can be handled with friendly and helpful messages to the user.

There is a wealth of information available after a critical error. Bit 7 of register AH tells us in general terms what sort of error it is (Figure 6.6); the low byte of index register DI gives a more detailed error (Figure 6.7); and the stack contains the values of all registers at the point when the function that caused the error was called. The handler must make of all this whatever it can. The best advice is to keep the routines as simple as possible and avoid anything which may compound the problem (any further disk access is out of the question, for example).

After dealing with the error (usually with a suitable message to the user), the interrupt must exit with a value in AL indicating to DOS what action it should take:

    0   Ignore the error and continue

    1   Retry the operation that caused the error

    2   Abort the program

Compiling and Running programs

Detailed error codes	
Code (hex)	Error
00	Disk is write-protected
01	Invalid drive
02	Disk drive not ready
03	Invalid command
04	CRC error
05	Request header invalid
06	Disk seek error
07	Bad media
08	Sector not found
09	Out of paper (printer)
0A	Disk write error
0B	Disk read error
0C	General error

Figure 6.7 Detailed error codes

These options will sound very familiar to regular DOS users! Hopefully our interrupt handlers will couch the options in terms that are rather more helpful than the standard DOS messages. Better still, the handler should give users a simple instruction and ask them to press RETURN (or any key) to continue.

The interrupts covered in this chapter provide all that is needed to run a program but a great deal of programming is required before an application becomes truly user-friendly.

7. Multi-tasking and Resident Programs

Up until this point it has been assumed that there is only one program in memory and only one program at a time running and accessing files. For day-to-day work this is often enough but there are times when two or more programs need to co-exist in the computer.

This chapter looks briefly at two ways in which this can happen: multi-tasking, when two programs are run 'at the same time'; and resident programs, which are kept in memory until needed.

MULTI-TASKING

The Amstrad PC is only able to concentrate on one thing at a time. For example, it cannot read one set of data from disk and write another set to the screen while at the same time sending a file to the printer.

However, using a process called *multi-tasking*, it can give the appearance of doing so. This is achieved by spreading its time around from one activity to another, in an orderly fashion, at such a speed that any delays should pass unnoticed.

An example of how this is done is given by DOS's *PRINT* program, a *print spooler* which prints an ASCII file at the same time as another program is running.

DOS allocates a period of processing to the main program, then switches its attention to PRINT. After another short period it returns control to the main program, and so the cycle continues. This process is also sometimes called *multiplexing*.

Each period is called a *timeslice*. The length of timeslices can be varied and they do not have to be the same for each task being processed. For example, the default timeslice allocated to PRINT is 2 ticks of the system clock for every 8 ticks used by the main program.

The timeslices are all extremely brief, as a result of which the user should never notice that processing time is being used by another program.

The additional program (such as PRINT) is called a *background* program. It runs quietly and independently in the background, the main share of time being allocated to the *foreground* (main) program. Background programs should not require any input from the user once they have been put into effect. Ideally they should be run at the same time as programs that require a great deal of user input. For example, in the time taken to press a key - while the main program waits for something to happen - the background program can be called several times; when word processing, for instance, much of the CPU's time is wasted, since the user can never hope to type fast enough to require more than just a fraction of the processing time. On the other hand, a program that spends most of its time processing - calculating an end-of-year balance sheet, for example - should not be used at the same time as a background program; in such a case the foreground program would be slowed down quite considerably.

The foreground program always takes precedence. For instance, disk access is a process that is comparatively slow and ties up the CPU for relatively long periods. If a foreground program requires a great deal of disk access then the background program will be noticeably slower. Any file being printed in these circumstances will seem to take an eternity to finish.

The reverse of this is that when the background program needs to read data from disk there may be a marked delay in the operation of the main program. In some cases this can make the running of background programs intolerable.

For operations involving the printer in particular, you must take care to keep any waiting times to a minimum. The danger is that the CPU will try to access the printer, discover it is not accepting data and sit around for ages waiting for the printer to give it the signal to continue. Therefore the time that the background program waits while the printer is busy should be kept very small; otherwise the CPU will be tied up for lengthy periods when it could be processing the main program.

Multi-tasking and Resident Programs

Multiplex numbers

Each program that is to run in the background must be given a unique, single-byte *multiplex number*. For example, PRINT has a multiplex number of 01h. DOS reserves numbers 00h to 7Fh for its own use (although background programs are certainly very few and far between).

Even the numbers from 80h to FFh, which are theoretically available to programmers must be used with care. The *APPEND* program has an associated DOS function that checks whether the program has been installed; this function has been allocated number B7h. For this reason it is recommended that only multiplex numbers in the range C0h to FFh should be used.

Accessing the background programs

When a background program is installed it sets up a handler routine; there is a chain of these in memory, each one linked to the next. Whenever a background program is accessed (which is done via interrupt 2Fh) the routine checks through this chain to find the program it wants. (This process is similar to that of device drivers, which are described in Chapter 19.)

Interrupt 2Fh is used to request an action from the background program. It is also used to pass instructions to the background program.

Interrupt: 2Fh
DOS version: 3
Service: Access background program
Entry value: AH=multiplex number
AL=function code
Exit value: Various (depending on program)

The instructions that the handler can accept are determined by the program itself, of course. For example, PRINT uses functions 01h to 05h to add filenames to the print queue, cancel printing and so on.

Function 00h is reserved (in all cases) for finding out the current state of the background program. A return code is passed back in AL as follows:

00h   Handler not yet installed but it is all right to do so

01h   Handler not yet installed; you may not install the handler

163

FFh   Handler installed

Note that code 01h indicates that the interrupt is currently in use for some other purpose but that you may try again later.

TERMINATE AND STAY RESIDENT (TSR) PROGRAMS

It is not often that we can find a use for a background program. There is usually some sort of input required from the user, making them unsuitable for this type of processing.

Far more frequently we need to install a program in memory so that it can be invoked later on. This is the function of a *Terminate and Stay Resident (TSR)* program.

There are many examples of TSR's, the most famous being Borland's Sidekick. This program is installed in memory, usually when the system is booted, and there it sits until required. At any later time a particular key combination brings Sidekick to life, any current application being put temporarily to one side. Sidekick can be used for a variety of purposes, such as editing simple note files, calling up telephone numbers or making an entry in a diary. Once the task has been completed the user escapes from Sidekick and continues with the previous application.

This same general procedure is used by most TSR's. The principles of a TSR are as follows:

1. The TSR is invoked for the first time from the DOS command line (often as part of a batch file).

2. The TSR prepares the method by which it is to be invoked later. To do this it replaces an interrupt handler with one of its own. The most commonly used method is to adapt the keyboard interrupt so that it acts upon a particular combination of key presses.

3. The TSR then terminates in a different way to usual, through interrupt 21h, function 31h. In doing so it tells DOS the size of the code that is to be retained so that DOS can reserve that part of memory.

Multi-tasking and Resident Programs

4. The TSR now lies dormant in memory. DOS ensures that the area used by the TSR remains undisturbed.

5. When the appropriate trigger occurs the TSR is re-activated. Any TSR will generally remain resident until the system is reset.

In most cases a TSR can be invoked more than once. A well-behaved TSR will make sure that the previous application is restored intact when the work of the TSR is done.

TSR replacement interrupts

A TSR can choose almost any interrupt as its method of being re-executed. However, it is important that the new interrupt should end by calling the original interrupt. In this way, more than one TSR can exist in memory at the same time. They can all use the same interrupts and not interfere with each other, as long as they do not use precisely the same method of being invoked; for example, two TSR's cannot be invoked by the same key combination.

The TSR interrupt

As a general rule, TSR's terminate the first time round with interrupt 21h, function 31h.

Interrupt:	21h
Function:	31h
Service:	Terminate and stay resident
Entry value:	AH=31h
	AL=termination code
	DX=segment address of memory to free
Exit value:	AX=error code

The amount of memory required by the TSR must be specified, in paragraphs. This must include the 10h paragraphs of the PSP but it may exclude the code that initialises the TSR, if this is placed at the end of the program.

The shell of a TSR is shown in Figure 7.1 overleaf.

Multi-tasking and Resident Programs

```
TSR:                                    ; Shell for a Terminate and Stay
                                        ;   Resident program

                                        ; Assumes TSR is to be activated by
                                        ;   special key combination

              jmp initialise            ; Jump to initialisation section

int9rec:                                ; Stores old interrupt 09h vector
int9off    dw?
int9seg    dw?
screendata db 200 dup (?)               ; Area to store current screen contents:
                                        ;   size to suit
xcursor    db?                          ; Cursor horizontal position
ycursor    db?                          ; Cursor vertical position

newint9:                                ; New interrupt 09h
              call keycheck             ; Check to see if special key
                                        ;   combination has been pressed
              jc main                   ; If it has, jump to MAIN routine
              pushf                     ; Otherwise call old int 09h
              call int9rec
              iret                      ; Exit

keycheck:                               ; Check key presses
           ;                            ; Requires routine depending
           ;                            ;   on key combination selected
           ;                            ; Set carry flag if correct
           ;                            ;   combination found
              ret

main                                    ; Main routine
              call screensave           ; If any part of the screen is
                                        ;   overwritten call a routine to save
                                        ;   current contents away
              call screenshow           ; Show new screen
           ;                            ; Perform other routines
              call screenrec            ; Recover original screen and display
              iret                      ; Exit

screensave:                             ; Saves current screen
              ret

screenshow:                             ; Show new box or other display
              ret
```

```
screenrec:                      ; Redispalying original screen,
                                ;    including cursor
         ret

initialise:                     ; Initialisation section
                                ; See Figure 5.2 for details
         ret
```

Figure 7.1 The shell of a TSR

8. *Boot Procedures*

This chapter details the procedures that are carried out when the computer is switched on or reset. The early part of this process is beyond our control but nevertheless it provides a useful insight into the mechanics of the Amstrad PC.

TYPES OF BOOT

The term *boot* refers to the situation when the computer is either first started or made to restart. The expression is an abbreviation of *bootstrap*, which is still frequently used (as in 'pulling yourself up by'). It is just one of a number of computer terms that we have had to grit our teeth and learn to live with. When a computer is booted the CPU executes the first program it finds in a particular part of memory. This is the *boot program* that is stored in the ROM.

There are two types of boot:

- *Cold boot*, when the computer is first switched on

- *Warm boot* or *system reset*, usually initiated by the Ctrl-Alt-Del sequence

The effect of these two types of boot is slightly different.

COLD BOOT

When there is a cold boot the computer carries out the following operations:

- Self-testing. The computer memory is cleared. Various checks are carried out on the memory and hardware. Any faults are reported, if possible.

- Initialisation. Information about the system is stored in specific locations.

- Loading of operating system. The programs that form the operating system are read from disk and put into effect.

Boot Procedures

The clearing of memory is not carried out by the warm boot but otherwise the procedure is very similar. The routines that perform the initialisation and self-testing are held in ROM and therefore cannot be changed. These routines are automatically run on power-up and cannot be intercepted, so this part of the computer's operation is totally beyond the control of the programmer. However, knowledge of what occurs at this stage can be useful.

POWER-UP PROCEDURES

The procedures of initialisation and self-testing are described below. All of these procedures are held in the computer's ROM and therfore are permanently fixed.

SELF-TESTS

Before starting on the self-testing procedures the routine disables all interrupts. The video adapter is initialised and the monitor displays the following message:

```
Please wait
```

Below this it prints successive full stops as it begins each of the tests described below. If any of the tests fail, the self-test stops with an appropriate error message and nothing further can be done until the error is corrected.

When the user RAM has been checked (at step 9) the ROS uses the area of memory from 0300h to 03FFh as stack space during the remainder of the initialisation.

The tests are performed as follows:

1. A checksum is carried out on the ROS. All bytes are totalled and should result in a value of 00h in the least significant byte.

2,3,4. The system checks the 8237 DMA Controller, the 8253 Programmable Interval Timer and the 8255 Programmable Peripheral Interface.

5. The speed of the RTC is verified and a hardware test is carried out on the checksum byte of the NVR.

6,7. The serial and parallel ports are checked.

Boot Procedures

8. The mouse registers are cleared and verified.

9. A complete test of all user RAM (512K or 640K) is performed. This involves clearing the contents of RAM. This test is bypassed by a system reset.

10. The 8259 Programmable Interrupt Controller is tested.

11. All disk drives are checked. The heads are moved to track 10 in each case. No data is read from disk so it does not matter if the drives are empty.

12. The final test is carried out by the keyboard controller. If the test is a success the controller returns the value AAh in its port. If any other value is returned then this test is repeated until it is completed satisfactorily. During this test the computer beeps every five seconds.

It is worth nothing that on the PC1512, in certain rare circumstances, one of these messages may appear:

```
Fatal error reading drive C
```

(hard disk machines)

```
Error reading drive A
```

(floppy disk machines)

These errors are not necessarily as fatal as they sound! They can be caused by a corrupt value in the extended RS232 Flow Control parameter of the NVR, and the solution may be simply to replace the batteries.

Language for error messages

Before beginning the self-tests the ROS checks links 1, 2 and 3 on the main circuit board. These determine the language to be used for error messages (Figure 8.1). There is a special case, when all three links are in place, when the system is put into *diagnostic mode*. In this case only the disk and keyboard test are performed, any errors being ignored. The system can then be fully checked using a diagnostic ROM card. Only qualified Amstrad engineers should attempt this sort of diagnostics.

Boot Procedures

LK1	LK2	LK3	Language for Start-up messages
OFF	OFF	OFF	English
OFF	OFF	ON	German
OFF	ON	OFF	French
OFF	ON	ON	Spanish
ON	OFF	OFF	Danish
ON	OFF	ON	Swedish
ON	ON	OFF	Italian
ON	ON	ON	Diagnostics

Figure 8.1 Language links

INITIALISATION The initialisation procedures are as follows:

1. A checksum is performed on the NVR (all bytes are added and checked against the checksum byte). Any error results in the NVR being reset to its default values; a message to check the batteries and set the date and time is displayed.

2. The 8253 Programmable Interval Timer is set to produce an interrupt on counter 0 every 0.0549337 seconds. Counter 1 is set to generate a signal every 15.13 microseconds and counter 2 is disabled.

3. The 8237 DMA controller is set for channel 0 to control the memory refresh; the other channels are disabled.

4. All interrupts are disabled.

5. The settings of the Status-1 and Status-2 registers are determined from the settings of the dip switches, the existence or otherwise of an 8087 chip and the amount of user RAM installed.

6. The system RAM from 0300h to 0500h is set to its initial values.

7. The interrupt vectors for 00h to 1Fh are stored at the bottom of memory. Any vectors above these need to be set by specific application programs. Some of the first 32 vectors

Boot Procedures

point to dummy routines which have no effect; these can be replaced by effective routines as required.

8. Interrupt 13h is invoked to initialise and test the disk interface.

9. The keyboard is tested.

10. The video adapter and ROM are tested.

11. The 8259 Interrupt Controller is initialised; interrupts 00h, 01h and 06h are enabled.

12. If the NVR checksum was correct the time and date when the computer was last used is displayed; otherwise a message to reset the NVR details is shown.

13. The Non-Maskable Interrupt is enabled.

14. Any external ROM's are identified and initialised.

15. The display adaptor ROM is initialised.

16. The boot sector is loaded from disk. The ROS attempts this operation ten times before giving the message to load a system disk.

From this point on the procedures are dependent upon the operating system.

Initialisation of the display adapter ROM

The initialisation of the display adaptor ROM (step 15) includes the following steps:

- The video RAM is tested (but only during a cold boot and not for a reset).

- The video controller is initialised.

- The character fonts are loaded from the tables in ROM.

- The display mode is selected; in the case of the PC1640 this depends on the settings of the system unit dip switches.

- The routine for interrupt 10h (which handles all display output) is installed; again this depends on the type of computer and, for the PC1640, the dip switch settings.

The procedures are somewhat briefer for the PC1512.

WARM BOOT

A warm boot can be activated in a number of ways:

- The user presses Ctrl-Alt-Del. This sequence can also be replaced on the Amstrad PC by the little-known combination Left Shift-Ctrl-Alt-Tab (the advantage being that you can reboot using just one finger!)

- A program forces a warm boot through use of interrupt 19h or by writing to port 66h.

- A fatal error occurs that results in a reboot.

A warm boot is used in a variety of circumstances: to overcome some major error, to load a new operating system (or a different version of the same operating system) or to clear a resident program from memory.

Note that in some cases the computer 'hangs' so completely that a warm boot is ineffective. This is particularly the case when the computer is locked into some loop that involves disk access. In such cases the only alternative left is to switch off and on again.

The warm boot takes place when the computer is already switched on and has performed a cold boot previously. This being the case there is no need for the initialisation of memory. It is assumed that the RAM will not have developed faults. Instead, the warm boot goes directly to the self-testing and the loading of the operating system.

This means that the computer's memory is not actually cleared. All the internal pointers are reset, so that as far as the system is concerned the memory is empty, but the programs and data that were there before the reset are still intact. (This is analogous to the erasing of a file on disk.) This

Boot Procedures

opens the way for a program to rescue the memory contents after a crash.

The Ctrl-Alt-Del sequence in fact activates a particular interrupt.

Interrupt: 18h
Service: Restart system
Entry values: None
Exit values: None

On floppy disk machines the function of this interrupt is simply to call interrupt 19h, which reboots the system from floppy disk.

On hard disk machines the interrupt vector is replaced by one pointing to a new interrupt in the hard disk ROM. This version of the interrupt checks for a floppy disk; if it finds one then it calls interrupt 19h. If there is no floppy disk, the system is loaded from the active partition of the hard disk.

Interrupt: 19h
Service: Reboot from floppy disk
Entry values: None
Exit values: None

No values are returned from these interrupts, of course.

The interrupt handler, whose address is held in the interrupt vector at 0054h, is fully accessible.

It is therefore possible to replace this interrupt with your own version. This can be used to achieve a number of effects:

- You can include an 'Are you sure?' message (Figure 8.2)

- You can 'uncrash' the system

This also opens up the way for inspecting the contents of memory to try and discover the cause of a crash.

Note that any attempt to write to port 66h also causes an immediate system reset. Although it is generally better mannered to leave a program with some suitable message there are occasions when this provides a very effective gesture (for example, when unauthorised access is suspected and the

Boot Procedures

```
RESETQ:                                  ; Prints a query when the computer is
                                         ;   reset with the Ctrl-Alt-Del
                                         ;   combination

                                         ; Limitations: As set up the routine
                                         ;   does not save the current screen
                                         ;   characteristics and display

                                         ; Calls DISSTR (Figure 16.13),
                                         ;   and GETYN (Figure 11.8)

            jmp initialiser              ; First time through, jump to
                                         ; initialisation section

oldvec9     label dword                  ; Address of old int 09h vector
old off     dw ?
Oldseg      dw ?
query       db 'Are you sure?'

checkboot:
            push ax                      ; Checks that reset is required
            push dx
            mov ah,02h                   ; Get keyboard status byte
            int 1bh                      ;   (see Chapter 11)
            and al,0Ch                   ; Filter out all but Alt and Ctrl status
            cmp al,0Ch                   ; Check to see if both are pressed
            jnz notboot                  ; If not, continue as normal
            mov ah,01h                   ; Otherwise, check
            int 16h                      ;   next character in buffer
                                         ;   (see Chapter 11)
            cmp ah,53h                   ; Check to see if Del is pressed
            jnz notboot

                                         ; Ctrl-Alt-Del is being pressed
            lea dx, query                ; Point to message
            ;                            ; Current screen could be saved at this
                                         ;   point
            call disstr                  ; Display message
            call getkey                  ; Get a key press
            cmp al,'Y'                   ; Check to see if user pressed Y
            jnz continue                 ; Jump for any key but Y
            mov al,0FFh
            out 66h,al                   ; Otherwise force a rest
                                         ; Program cannot go beyond this point

notboot:                                 ; If not reset, continue with normal
                                         ;   keyboard routine
            pop dx
            pop ax
```

Boot Procedures

```
                pushf
                call oldrec9        ; Continue with normal keyboard routine
                iret
Continue:
                ;                   ;
                pop dx
                pop ax
                iret

disstr:                             ; This routine will be found in
                ret                 ;    Figure 13.16

getyn:                              ; This routine will be found in
                                    ;    Figure 11.8

initialise:                         ; This routine is similar to that of
                halt                ;    that of Figure 5-2
```

Figure 8.2 Confirming a reset

```
RESET:                              ; Forced system reset

                                    ; This routine should be called whenever
                                    ;   you wish to force a reset of the
                                    ;   system. Since it is not a very
                                    ;   friendly thing to do it should be
                                    ;   reserved for only the most serious
                                    ;   occasions: e.g. when some sort of
                                    ;   unauthorised access is suspected
                                    ; Calls DISSTR (see Figure 13.16)
                jmp resetst

goodbye         db 'Unauthorised access, system resetting$'

resetst:        cli                 ; Clear interrupts to avoid any
                                    ;   evasive action by the user
                lea dx,goodbye      ; Point to exit message
                call dislin         ; Display message
                xor cx,cx
                mov cx,0FFFFh       ; Set CX=65535
delay:          nop                 ; Wait a short time. For a longer
                loop delay          ;   wait call WAITLOOP (Figure 14.2)
                mov al,0FFh
                out 66h,al          ; Forced reset
                int 20h             ; Program now no longer exists
```

Figure 8.3 System reset routine

Boot Procedures

memory contents need to be safeguarded from any replacement to interrupt 19h). This is demonstrated in Figure 8.3.

Reset flags

When a warm boot is requested a value of 1234h is placed in RAM at location 0472h. From this the ROS detects that it must perform a complete reset, with the exception of the user RAM and video RAM initialisation.

As an alternative, the value 1235h can be stored in 0472h. In this case the system testing is carried out in full but the initialisation does not take place.

On successful completion of the tests the value 1234h is placed in location 0488h.

LOADING THE OPERATING SYSTEM

An understanding of the processes that are involved in loading the operating system into memory is beneficial for programmers who wish to modify the way in which the operating system behaves. It is also essential if you wish to replace DOS with an operating system of your own. While it is not suggested that a replacement for DOS is a realistic idea for the casual programmer, a temporary replacement geared to running just one application can be a possibility.

The first few steps are carried out regardless of the operating system that is to be used. After that, however, the procedure is continued with routines that form part of the operating system. The description that follows assumes that the MS-DOS operating system (which is supplied with all Amstrad PC's) is being loaded. For a replacement operating system the process can be as short or as long as you like.

ROM BOOT ROUTINES

After completing the initialisation and self-testing of a cold boot, or on the execution of interrupt 19h, the procedure is as follows:

1. Execution of the boot program begins. This program is located in ROM.

2. The program checks the disk in drive A. If there is no disk and the system has a hard disk, it checks drive C. If there is

Boot Procedures

no disk in drive A and no hard disk the program displays the message:

```
Load a system disk
Press any key to continue
```

The program waits for a key press and the step is repeated. There is no way to make the system boot from any other drive.

3. When a disk is found, the program checks the *boot record*. This is a small piece of code that contains information about the disk and, on system disks, a routine to start loading the operating system.

All disks have a boot record but only system disks have the necessary routines to load the operating system. If this is not a valid boot record the following message is displayed:

```
Non-system disk.
Replace disk. Press any key when ready
```

The program waits for a key press and then starts again at step 2.

4. The boot record is loaded and the routine it contains is executed. The boot record is created by the operating system when the disk is formatted. Therefore it is an integral part of the operating system and, although it must conform to certain standards laid down by the CPU, the procedures from here on are determined by the operating system.

(Note that the concept of files does not really apply to data stored in memory. DOS uses files for its method of storing data and programs on disk (as do most other operating systems). In memory it is quite a different matter. Memory is stacked full of code and data with no real file structure. It is therefore up to you how it is managed. If you design your own operating system there is no reason why you should use files on disk either; all that is needed is some method of accessing data.)

MS-DOS BOOT ROUTINES Assuming that the system is loading MS-DOS, the boot procedures continue as follows:

Boot Procedures

5. The routine checks that the first two files on the disk are *IO.SYS* and *MSDOS.SYS*. IO.SYS contains the routines that deal with input and output. MSDOS.SYS provides an interface between the command processor and the ROS.

On versions prior to DOS 3.3 these files must be in consecutive sectors. If the files are wrong in any way another error message is displayed:

```
Wrong operating system. Change disk
Press any key when ready.
```

Everything stops for a key press and the whole process starts again at step 2.

6. IO.SYS and MSDOS.SYS are loaded into the low end of memory.

7. An initialisation routine in IO.SYS is activated.

8. This routine immediately calls a routine in MSDOS.SYS. MSDOS.SYS has quite a lot of work to do.

9. The routine identifies an area in memory for the disk buffer, followed by an area for storing file control blocks. The precise location will vary depending on which version of the operating system has been loaded.

10. The routine does a check of the equipment that is attached to the system and stores the current status in memory at location 0410h. This equipment list can be found using interrupt 11h.

11. Control is passed back to IO.SYS, which checks to see if the file CONFIG.SYS exists in the root directory of the boot disk. The information contained in CONFIG.SYS is stored in memory.

12. If CONFIG.SYS contains any references to installable device drivers these are loaded into memory (see Chapter 19).

13. The final action of IO.SYS is to load and execute the resident portion of the command processor. The command processor is normally COMMAND.COM but this can be replaced either by using the SHELL instruction or by

Boot Procedures

changing IO.SYS. To load COMMAND.COM the ROS calls MS-DOS interrupt 21h, function 4Bh.

The procedures from this point on depend upon the command processor and can be changed quite easily.

COMMAND.COM BOOT ROUTINES

The command processor now comes into effect. The procedures carried out by the standard command processor, COMMAND.COM, are described below. Any replacement command processor can of course vary these activities.

14. The initialisation portion of COMMAND.COM is loaded immediately above the resident portion and put into effect.

15. This portion checks the root directory of the boot disk for the automatic execution file, AUTOEXEC.BAT. (The name can be changed by altering COMMAND.COM.) If the file does not exist, COMMAND.COM prompts for the date and time.

16. The area of memory occupied by the initialisation portion is then made available for other programs.

17. If the file AUTOEXEC.BAT exists the instructions it contains are executed.

DOS is now fully loaded and the user is in complete control of the system.

9. *Components of MS-DOS*

The heart of the Amstrad PC is its operating system. For the most part this is Microsoft's MS-DOS version 3.2. Although other operating systems can be used - and the PC1512 is supplied with an alternative, DOS Plus - MS-DOS is by far the most widely used system on these machines. It is therefore important that the Amstrad programmer should have a reasonable understanding of how it works.

This chapter details the main components of MS-DOS and how they relate to the operation of the computer. For information on the detailed use of individual DOS file- and disk-handling commands, you should consult a good DOS reference book.

THE DOS BOOT RECORD

The start of every disk, whether a system disk or a data disk, is set aside for some important information. This is termed the *boot record* and is located st the start of every floppy and hard disk.

It contains the following code and information:

- The first four bytes contain a JMP instruction, pointing to a section of *boot code*.

- This is followed by a table of disk information (Figure 9.1).

- Finally there is the boot code which loads IO.SYS and MSDOS.SYS into memory.

This record is loaded into memory every time the computer is booted, following which the boot code is executed.

THE MS-DOS FILES

MS-DOS is comprised of three separate files. Each of these is dedicated to a particular set of operations.

Components of MS-DOS

Offset (hex)	No. Bytes	Use
00	3	Jump instruction (long jump or short jump plus NOP)
03	8	Manufacturer name and DOS version and number
0B	2	Number of bytes per sector
0D	1	Number of sectors per allocation unit
0E	2	Number of reserved sectors
10	1	Number of FAT's
11	2	Number of root directory entries
13	2	Number of sectors on volume
15	1	Media type code
16	2	Number of sectors per FAT
18	2	Number of sectors per track
1A	2	Number of heads
1C	2	Number of hidden sectors
1E	-	Boot routine

Note: Bytes 0Bh - 17h are a copy of the BIOS parameter block (BPB).

Figure 9.1 Boot record disk information

IO.SYS

The first file on an MS-DOS system disk, immediately after the file directory, is called IO.SYS. This file is loaded into memory by the boot code, where it remains until the system is rebooted. It forms the *Basic Input/Output System (BIOS)* and contains all that the operating system needs to communicate with the standard hardware. Any requests to the hardware (such as input from the keyboard and output to the screen or printer) are dealt with by the BIOS, whether the requests are from the operating system or an application program.

Any device may be called on to deal with a range of instructions. First, these instructions must be translated into a form that the device can understand. For each device there is a piece of code which translates every possible instruction into the format required by the device. This piece of code is called a *device driver*.

IO.SYS includes the drivers needed for various standard devices, such as the keyboard, screen and disk drives. Others can be installed in memory when the operating system is being loaded.

Components of MS-DOS

This section of code communicates directly with the hardware and is therefore very dependent upon the Amstrad configuration. Transferring the Amstrad's IO.SYS to another computer system may mean that some of the hardware will not function correctly.

This is one of the reasons that all programs should work through DOS, rather than talking direct to the hardware. An instruction to DOS will be processed correctly, no matter what computer it is on; code that is hardware-specific may have to be changed for every different computer.

MSDOS.SYS   The second system file, MSDOS.SYS, is sometimes termed the *kernel* of MS-DOS. This part of the system receives all requests for hardware operations and for activities with files, such as sending output to the printer or opening a file. These requests are channelled to IO.SYS in a suitable format.

MSDOS.SYS works independently of the hardware. All DOS interrupt functions are sent by MSDOS.SYS to IO.SYS in a format that is identical, regardless of what computer or version of DOS you are using. It is IO.SYS which converts these into machine-specific instructions.

MSDOS.SYS is stored in memory immediately after IO.SYS. MSDOS.SYS is also responsible for loading and executing the command interpreter.

COMMAND.COM   The file COMMAND.COM is the MS-DOS command interpreter. You can replace COMMAND.COM with your own interpreter if you wish to develop your own style of commands or if you have an application with a very limited number of options.

This program forms the interface between the user and the operating system. It is the job of the command interpreter to display messages and prompts to the user, accept commands and process them.

The program is generally located on the root directory of the boot disk. However, it does not need to be here. Using a PATH directive in CONFIG.SYS you can identify a path to the file. Alternatively, the COMSPEC directive indicates the location of COMMAND.COM.

Components of MS-DOS

If the command interpreter is not called COMMAND.COM its name can be given by the SHELL directive in CONFIG.SYS. This has the drawback that if the user changes or overwrites CONFIG.SYS the interpreter will not be loaded. Therefore an alternative is to modify MSDOS.SYS. The file contains the name of the command interpreter, so changing this name results in the operating system automatically searching for a different file. However, tinkering with MSDOS.SYS in this way is not very safe and you may run into problems when different versions of the program are used.

The command interpreter is loaded into memory and executed by DOS interrupt 21h, function 4Bh, which is called by MSDOS.SYS.

COMMAND.COM is comprised of three separate sections:

- The *resident* portion, which stays permanently in memory;

- The *transient* portion, which may be overwritten while an application is running;

- The *initialisation* portion, which is only used when the computer is booted.

Each of these sections has an important role to play. Any new command interpreter should have similar sections.

The resident portion

The resident part of COMMAND.COM is loaded into memory by MSDOS.SYS and remains active until the system is rebooted. Once in memory it cannot be safely overwritten. It is loaded into the low end of memory, immediately above MSDOS.SYS.

Initially, the function of this portion is to load the transient portion and to execute the initialisation portion.

In the normal course of events this portion handles all input/output errors. For example, it is this portion that is invoked during the running of an application when any sort of disk error is encountered and which displays the familiar message:

```
Not ready error reading drive A
Abort, Retry, Ignore?
```

Components of MS-DOS

The resident portion is also responsible for handling interrupts 22h (terminate address), 23h (Ctrl-Break) and 24h (critical error).

Initialisation portion The initialisation part of COMMAND.COM is loaded immediately above the resident portion. It is this section that checks for the existence of AUTOEXEC.BAT and puts it into effect; alternatively it prompts for the date and time. After this first burst of activity this portion is no longer required and will be overwritten by the first application program read into memory.

Transient portion The transient portion is loaded into the top of memory. This part is responsible for displaying the DOS prompt, accepting the DOS commands and processing them. It also holds all the code for the internal commands and loads and executes external commands and other programs.

Because it is in the top of memory it will only be overwritten if you run an application that requires more than the full amount of available memory.

When any application terminates, the resident portion of COMMAND.COM checks to see if the transient portion is still intact. If it is, control is passed to this portion and the DOS prompt is displayed.

If the transient portion has been overwritten, the resident portion attempts to reload it from disk. If it does not exist on the current path, the resident portion displays the familiar message:

```
Insert disk with COMMAND.COM
```

It is also possible to have a second copy of the command interpreter in memory, as we shall see later.

THE ENVIRONMENT

In order to operate successfully MS-DOS needs to know something about the system and the way in which the user wants it to work. This includes information about the hardware, such as the external devices that have been connected (a mouse, for example); it also includes information

Components of MS-DOS

about the way in which the system is to work, such as the country information or the path to be searched for programs. All this information makes up the operating system's *environment*.

CONFIG.SYS

The initial settings for the environment are stored in the file CONFIG.SYS. The information here is read into memory before any other program or batch file is run. It is also loaded before the command processor.

Each line of CONFIG.SYS consists of a variable and the information it is to take, in the form:

```
variable=information
```

The lines are read into memory sequentially and the environment is built up item by item. Therefore the order of items in the list can be important. Consider this example:

```
DEVICE=MOUSE.SYS
PATH=\MSDOS
```

These lines tell the operating system that a device driver for the mouse must be installed and that the path to search for any file is the current directory, followed by \MSDOS. In this case, the file MOUSE.SYS must be in the root directory. If the items were reversed then MOUSE.SYS could be stored in the MSDOS subdirectory.

For the same reason, CONFIG.SYS itself must be in the root directory of the boot disk.

There are a number of items that can be included in the environment. Most of these are optional but for some the operating system has to have a value. If these are not included in CONFIG.SYS (or if there is no CONFIG.SYS in the root directory) then the operating system uses a set of defaults. The main environment variables and their defaults, where applicable, are listed in Figure 9.2.

Country-dependent information

One of the most complex of these commands is the COUNTRY directive, which was introduced with DOS 3. This sets the defaults for a variety of information, including the display format for the date and time, the currency symbol and numeric separators. The country codes used in the directive are shown in Figure 9.3.

Components of MS-DOS

The environment variables		
Directive	Default	Use
COUNTRY	1	Country information
COMSPEC	COMMAND.COM	Command processor
DEVICE	(Standard device)	Installs device drives
BREAK	OFF	Frequency of checks for Break key
BUFFERS	2	Number of sectors for each disk buffer
DRIVPARM	(None)	Disk Drive characteristics
FCBS	4,0	Maximum number of file control blocks
FILES	8	Maximum number of file handles
LASTDRIVE	E	Last drive accessible to DOS
SHELL	COMMAND.COM	Command processor

Figure 9.2 The environment variables

The table also shows the KEYB program that is generally associated with the country. The KEYB programs (such as KEYBUK.COM) are used to set up the keyboard to produce a set of characters relevant to a specific country. However, any combination of COUNTRY information and KEYB program can be used and it is important to make the distinction:

- COUNTRY determines formats for displays (dates, times, etc.)

- KEYB determines the way in which the keyboard operates

Generally you should use the KEYB program that matches the keyboard. Unlike the IBM PC, the Amstrad PC is only delivered with a single KEYB program to match the keyboard that is supplied.

As a further customisation, the links on the main board determine the language to be used for the ROS boot messages and the dip switches decide the display font to be used.

DOS provides an interrupt function for us to use this country-dependent information in our programs.

Components of MS-DOS

Country	Code	KEYB program
Australia	061	
Belgium	032	
Canada	002	
Denmark	045	KEYBDA
Finland	358	
France	033	KEYBFR
Germany	049	KEYBGR
Holland	031	
Israel	972	
Italy	039	
Middle East	785	KEYBIT
Norway	047	KEYBNO
Spain	034	KEYBSP
Sweden	046	KEYBSW
Switzerland	041	KEYBCHF
		KEYBCHG
United Kingdom	044	KEYBUK
USA	001	

Figure 9.3 DOS 3 country codes and keyboard programs

Interrupt: 21h
Function: 38h
DOS version: 2
Service: Get or set country-dependent information
Entry values: AH=38h
AL=(00h (standard data, DOS 2)
  (00h (current country, DOS 3)
  (01h - FEh (country code)
  (FFh (code>=255)
BX=country code (if AL=FFh)
DS:DX=address of 32 byte buffer
Exit values: AX=error code (if CF=1)
BX=country code
DS:DX=address of information

The advantage of this is that the symbols can be incorporated in a program as general variables. By checking to see which country has been selected the correct symbols can be used automatically. This is demonstrated by the program in Figure 9.4, which displays a list of monetary values.

Components of MS-DOS

```
MONEYFMT:                            ; Get monetary symbol format

                                     ; Uses country information to discover
                                     ;   symbol being used for displaying
                                     ;   monetary values

                                     ; Limitations - Assumes DOS 3
                                     ; Entry values: AK=country code
                                     ; Exit values: CSYMBOL=currency symbol
                                     ;              CURLENGTH=length of symbol
                                     ;              CURPOS=position code
                                     ;              CURSPACE=number spaces
                                     ;                between currency and value
                                     ;              BX,CX,DX changed

                jmp moneyst

countryinf:     db 32 dup (?)        ; Buffer to store country information
country         db 44h               ; Country number
csymbol:        db 05h               ; Currency symbol
curlength       db 01h               ; Length of currency symbol
curspace        db ?                 ; Number of spaces after/before symbol
curpos          db ?                 ; Currency position - 0=before, 1=after

moneyst:
                push ax
                push dx
                push es
                mov country,al       ; Save country code for other purposes
                mov ah,38h           ; Set up parameters for interrupt
                lea dx,countryinf
                int 21h
                xor ax,ax
                mov al,02h
                mov di,ax            ; Point to currency symbol
                xor cx,cx
getnul:                              ; Search for null character
                cmp countryinf[di],00h
                jz endloop
                inc cl
                inc di
                jmp getnul
endloop:                             ; Calculate length of symbol
                mov [curlength],cl   ; Store length
                lea es,csymbol       ; ES points to currency symbol
```

191

```
            lea ds,countryinf    ; DS points to country information
            push cx
            mov si,02h           ; Point to symbol in country info
            xor di,di            ; Point to place to store symbol
            cld
            rep movsb            ; Move symbol to CSYMBOL
            pop cx
            inc cl
            mov bx,cx
            mov csymbol[bx],'$'
            mov bh,[countryinf+0Fh] ; Get currency format
            push bx
            and bh,01h           ; Isolate position code
            mov [curpos],bh      ; Save position code
            pop bx
            and bh,06h           ; Isolate value for number of spaces
            mov [curspace],bh    ; Save number of spaces
            pop ax
            ret                  ; End routine

; -----------------------------------------------------------------

MONEYPRN:                        ; Print a monetary value

                                 ; Calls MONEYFMT, DISBYT, DISSTR
                                 ;              (Figure 13.16)

                                 ; Entry values: AL=country code
                                 ;               MONEY=money data
                                 ; Exit values: BX,CX,DX changed

            jmp monprnst

money       db '9999.99$'        ; Money as data string to be displayed

monprnst:
            call moneyfmt        ; Get monetary information
            mov bh,[curpos]      ; Get positions
            jnz after            ; Jump if after value
            call dispsym         ; Display symbol
            call dispspace       ; Display spaces
            call dispmon         ; Display money
            jmp endmon
after:                           ; Symbol is after money
            call dispmon         ; Display money
            call dispspace       ; Display spaces
            call dispsym         ; display symbol
```

```
endmon:
            ret

dispsym:                            ; Display symbol
            lea dx,csymbol          ; Point to symbol
            call disstr             ; Display it
            ret

dispspace:
            mov cl,[curspace]       ; Get number of spaces
            cmp cl,00h
            jz noblank              ; Jump if no blanks
blanks:
            mov al,20h              ; AL=space
            call disbyt             ; Display space
            loop blanks
noblank:
            ret

dispmon:
            lea dx,money
            call disstr             ; Display money
            ret
```

Figure 9.4 Listing monetary values

There is an important difference between the way in which DOS 2 and DOS 3 handle country information. For DOS 3 the complete set of country information is available; the country is set by the COUNTRY directive but our programs can access the information for any country.

For DOS 2, the information is put in place by the relevant KEYB program. There are only three formats, as shown in Figure 9.5.

(It is also worth noting that DOS 3.3 changed the situation yet again, by introducing just a single KEYB.COM program, requiring parameters, and a more complex version of the COUNTRY directive.)

Just in case you are wondering why the DOS 3 COUNTRY codes are such strange values, they correspond to the international telephone codes (padded with leading zeros).

The defaults for each country are shown in Figure 9.6. The structure of the country information is shown in Figure 9.7.

Components of MS-DOS

DOS 2 country-dependent information			
Country code	Area	Date format	Time format
0	America	mm-dd-yy	hh:mm:ss
1	Europe	dd-mm-yy	hh:mm:ss
2	Japan	yy-mm-dd	hh:mm:ss

Figure 9.5 DOS 2 country-dependent information

DOS 3 country-dependent information				
Country Code	Country	Date Format	Hour Format	Currency symbol
1	United States	mm-dd-yy	1 - 12	$
31	Netherlands	dd-mm-yy	0 - 23	
32	Belgium	dd-mm-yy	0 - 23	F
33	France	dd-mm-yy	0 - 23	F
34	Spain	dd-mm-yy	0 - 23	Pt
39	Italy	dd-mm-yy	0 - 23	Lit.
41	Switzerland	dd-mm-yy	0 - 23	Fr
44	United Kingdom	dd-mm-yy	0 - 23	£
45	Denmark	dd-mm-yy	0 - 23	DKR
46	Sweden	yy-mm-dd	0 - 23	SEK
47	Norway	dd-mm-yy	0 - 23	KR
49	Germany	dd-mm-yy	0 - 23	DM
61	Australia	dd-mm-yy	0 - 23	$
358	Finland	dd-mm-yy	0 - 23	MK
972	Israel	dd-mm-yy	0 - 23	

Figure 9.6 DOS 3 country-dependent information

Components of MS-DOS

\	\	DOS 2 country information
Offset (hex)	Bytes (hex)	Use
00	02	Date and time format (see Fig. 9.7)
02	02	Currency symbol
04	02	Thousands separator
06	02	Decimal separator
08	18	Not used
\	\	DOS 3 country information
Offset (hex)	Bytes (hex)	Use
00	02	Date format 0=M,D,Y 1=D,M,Y 2=Y,M,D
02	05	Currency symbol
07	02	Thousands separator
09	02	Decimal separator
0B	02	Date separator
0D	02	Time separator
0F	01	Currency format Bit 0: 0=Before, 1=After Bits 1 and 2: Number spaces between symbol and value
10	01	Currency decimal places
11	01	Time format 0=12-hour 1=24-hour
12	04	Address of routine for defining upper and lower case usage
16	02	Data list separator
18	08	Not used
Note:		The values from the currency symbol to the time separator are all stored as ASCIIZ strings, as is the list separator.

Figure 9.7 Structure of the country information buffer

MODIFYING THE ENVIRONMENT

The environment can be modified from the DOS prompt at any time with the SET command, using the format:

```
SET variable=parameters
```

You can delete any item from the environment with commands in the form:

```
SET variable=
```

This instruction forces the variable to revert back to the default, where there is one.

THE ENVIRONMENT IN MEMORY

Physically, the environment is stored in memory as a block of data. Surprisingly, perhaps, the environment in memory is very similar to the file CONFIG.SYS. It consist of a string of ASCII text, each part of the string identical to a line from the file. Each item is separated from the next by a null character (00h). The last environment item ends with two null characters.

Following this there is a word count and the file specification of the program to which the file relates. (This information appears only for DOS 3.)

OTHER DOS VERSIONS

The Amstrad PC's are supplied with MS-DOS version 3.2 as standard. There is no reason why this should not be updated with other versions of DOS, although there may be problems with the way in which certain aspects of the hardware are accessed.

DOS version number

When DOS is loaded, the version number is displayed at the top of the screen. At any time we can display the version number with the DOS VER command. It is also useful to be able to check on the version number from within a program. This can be done with DOS function 30h.

Interrupt:	21h
Function:	30h
DOS version:	2
Service:	Check DOS version number
Entry values:	AH=30h

Components of MS-DOS

Exit values: AH=minor version number
AL=major version number
BX,CX changed

The minor version number always consists of 2 digits. For example, exit values of AH=03h and AL=20h indicate DOS version 3.2.

The routine in Figure 9.8 can be inserted at the beginning of any program to check that the correct DOS version has been loaded.

A NOTE ABOUT PC-DOS

PC-DOS, the cousin of MS-DOS, works almost identically. The files IO.SYS and MSDOS.SYS are replaced by equivalents called IBMBIO.COM and IBMDOS.COM respectively. Developed specifically for the IBM PC, the main differences are in the way in which PC-DOS communicates with the hardware. The command set for the two variants of DOS is almost identical but some problems will be encountered when trying to run PC-DOS on the Amstrad PC.

Most irritating perhaps is the fact that the operating system is not able to access the Amstrad PC's real-time clock. The clock is maintained by the RTC chip even when PC-DOS is running, so each time you switch on the 'Last used' time will be correct.

However, this time is not transferred to PC-DOS's internal clock, which is set to 00:00 each time you reboot. As a result, all directory entries will show the time since booting rather than time of day, unless you use the TIME command each time the system is started.

Strangely, BACKUP and RESTORE also malfunction and are unusable.

Different versions of MS-DOS should behave themselves although no guarantees can be made.

It is possible to switch from one version of the operating system to another without reformatting the system disk (particularly if you want to change the operating system on a hard disk) provided you bear in mind the following points:

Components of MS-DOS

```
DOSVER:                             ; Check DOS version number
                                    ; Entry values: DX=Minimum DOS version
                                    ;                  number
                                    ; Exit values:  AX=DOS version no.
                                    ;               BX=(0 Version OK
                                    ;                  (1 Version not OK
                                    ; AX,BX,CX,DX changed

              jmp verst

vermess       db 'Program requires minimum DOS version 3.2$'

vesst:
              mov dl,03h            ; Set minimum major version no.
              mov dh,1Eh            ; Set minimum minor version no.
                                    ;   03h,1Eh =3.20
                                    ; (Error message VERMESS may need to
                                    ;    change)
              mov ah,30h
              int 21h
              cmp dl,al
              jl ok                 ; Return if major version OK
              jg notok              ; Display error message if not OK
              cmp dh,ah             ; Otherwise, check minor versions
              jle ok                ; Jump if minor version OK

notok:
              lea dx,vermess
              call disstr           ; Display text
ok:
              ret
```

Figure 9.8 Checking the DOS version number

- The system files must be placed in consecutive blocks, immediately following the file directory.

- Changing IO.SYS will cause hardware problems on some versions.

- Some programs which automatically install themselves assume that the system files are a specific size, so any change may cause problems.

As a general rule, it is not a very good idea to switch operating systems without reformatting the disk.

Components of MS-DOS

COMPATIBILITY CONSIDERATIONS

Programs written for one version of DOS and one IBM-compatible will generally work quite satisfactorily on another version of DOS or a different computer. However, to ensure compatibility you should bear in mind the following points:

- Avoid using the hardware interrupts, as the effect of these may vary between computers. This is particularly true for those interrupts that are Amstrad-specific, such as interrupt 15h, which deals with the NVR.

- Accessing hardware directly can be very unreliable. Avoid it like the plague!

- Avoid using DOS functions that were not available in earlier versions of the operating system, unless you are prepared to accept the limitations that this will cause.

The last point is perhaps the hardest. Before even starting to think about coding a program you must decide what limitations are to be placed on the user:

- If you want the program to run on all implementations of DOS then you will have to ignore all interrupts that were introduced with DOS 2 onwards (which doesn't leave a lot!)

- It is generally regarded as perfectly acceptable to set a condition that the user must have a computer that runs under DOS 2 (a restriction that will be satisfied by all but the oldest PC's). In this case you need only ignore the DOS 3 enhancements (though some of these are very useful).

- If the program is aimed mainly at Amstrad owners a minimum requirement of DOS 3.2 is not unreasonable. Anyone who wants to run your program on another machine may have to update their operating system.

- Keep well clear of any DOS 3.3 enhancements, since these may render your program useless for most Amstrad owners.

This completes our consideration of MS-DOS for the time being. In later chapters we will be looking at the way in which DOS utilises the disks. For the next few chapters we will be looking at the Amstrad hardware; in these chapters a few more of the DOS interrupts are introduced.

10. *The Clock and NVR*

The accurate maintenance of time is an essential feature of many operations within the computer. Indeed, every time the internal clock ticks it sets off a chain reaction throughout the system that results in a single operation being performed. It is only during this period that any processing occurs; the rest of the time the computer lies dormant.

On a more mundane level we need to keep track of the time, if only so that we can tell when individual data files were created. The clock tick also provides the basis for any sound production.

THE CLOCK HARDWARE

The Amstrad PC has an HD146818 real-time clock (RTC). Associated with this is a small amount of static RAM known as the *Non-Volatile RAM (NVR)*. The clock is used to maintain the current date and time of day, as well as a programmable alarm. The NVR stores this information, as well as an additional 50 bytes of system data including the memory size, mouse information, number of disk drives and so on. When the mains power is switched off all this information is retained by the four AA batteries under the base of the monitor unit.

The NVR also records the date and time when the system was last used. This figure is constantly being updated while the mains power is switched on, but remains static when the mains power is switched off. This date and time is shown at the top of the screen whenever the computer is switched on.

The address of the RTC data (as stored in the NVR) is held in port 70h. The RTC also makes use of port 71h.

TIME

The system keeps track of time using the 8253 Programmable Interval Timer (PIT). The system clock (8284A) oscillates at a particular frequency. The frequency of the clock is measured in *MHz*, where 1 MHz is one million cycles per second. The Amstrad PC system clock has a frequency of 1.19318 MHz.

The Clock and NVR

The 8253 Timer counts these pulses from the clock. It uses a single word of memory to do this. Every time the count reaches 65535 (that is, when it is about to overflow to 0 again) the timer issues an interrupt 08h. This is often called a *tick*. The ticks occur roughly every 0.0549 seconds (which is 1,193,180/65,536).

There are therefore approximately 18.2 ticks per second. The ROS routine for interrupt 08h uses these ticks to keep track of the time and date. It also issues an interrupt 1Ch, which is important to many other things that go on inside the computer. A great deal depends upon the interrupt 1Ch signals arriving on time so any program which changes this mechanism should do so with great care.

It is possible to re-program the 8253 so that it produces more frequent ticks. Interrupt 08h can then be changed so that it still issues the interrupt 1Ch on time. For example, if the number of ticks is doubled then interrupt 08h should only call interrupt 1Ch every other tick. Any program that depends on interrupt 1Ch will still work at the right speed.

However, changing interrupt 08h can have a disastrous effect on any program that relies upon it. To keep everyone happy it is sometimes necessary to change the interrupt 08h routine so that it calls the old interrupt 08h routine at the proper time. This only works of course if the number of ticks has been increased; it has no effect when the ticks are slowed down, so this should be avoided.

An example of a program a that is affected in this way is Microsoft's QuickBasic, which speeds up the ticks to three times the normal rate. The result is that the time of day is slowed down to one-third of its normal rate. Therefore you can spend three hours working on a QuickBasic program and discover that, according to the system clock, only an hour has passed! More importantly, the times shown against any changed files in the directory may be incorrect.

Many programs use the ticks in some way: for example, any program that creates sound or real-time movement on the screen, or any sort of timer or clock. The Amstrad's own time-of-day clock is also dependent on these ticks of course.

Checking the clock count

The clock count is stored as a double-word in memory location 046Ch. Next door to this, at 0470h, is a flag that is set to 1 when the clock passes midnight. We can check the current number of ticks using the interrupt 1Ah, rather than by reading these memory locations.

Interrupt:	1Ah
Function:	00h
Service:	Get clock count
Entry values:	AH=00h
Exit values:	AL=(00h (not yet midnight)
	(01h (past midnight)
	CX=clock count (high order word)
	DX=clock count (low order word)

Whenever the count passes midnight (at which stage it would have a value of 001800B0h) it is reset to 0 and the midnight flag is set. If midnight is passed a second time the flag remains set to 1. However, calling interrupt 1Ah clears the midnight flag.

When the machine is switched on, or the current system time is changed, the count is calculated from the current time.

Interrupt 1Ah is useful for timing purposes (Figure 10.1) but of little purpose for calculating the time, since other interrupts achieve this effect.

At any time the clock count can be reset.

Interrupt:	1Ah
Function:	01h
Service:	Set clock count
Entry values:	AH=01h
	CX=clock count (high order word)
	DX=clock count (low order word)
Exit values:	None

The effect of this interrupt is also to reset the time held by the Real Time Clock.

We can use the count to produce a sequence of pseudo-random numbers, as demonstrated in Figure 10.2.

The Clock and NVR

```
            TIMER:                                  ; Time an event in clock ticks
                                                    ; The full version of this routine
                                                    ;   converts the clock ticks into
                                                    ;   seconds

                                                    ; Limitations - this routine is slightly
                                                    ;   inaccurate in that is does not allow
                                                    ;   for the time taken to actually
                                                    ;   perform the calculations

                                                    ; Program does not work if midnight has
                                                    ;   been passed before it starts, and is
                                                    ;   passed again during timing

                                                    ; Calls TIMEROUT, any routine to be
                                                    ;   timed

                                                    ; Exit values: TIMEHI=time high byte
                                                    ;              TIMELO=time low byte
                                                    ;              AX,BX,CX,DX changed

                            jmp timest

            starthi         dw  ?                   ; Start time high word
            startlo         dw  ?                   ; Start time low word
            midflag         db  ?                   ; Midnight flag
            timehi          dw  ?                   ; Time taken high word
            timelo          dw  ?                   ; Time taken low word

            timest:
                            xor ah,ah
                            int 1Ah                 ; Get current clock count
                            mov [starthi],cx        ; Save count
                            mov [startlo],dx
                            mov [midflag],al
                            call timerout           ; Call whatever routine it is to be
                                                    ;   timed
                            xor ah,ah
                            int 1Ah                 ; Get clock count again
                            cmp al,[midflag]        ; Has midnight been passed?
                            jnz aftermid            ; If so, jump
                            sub dx,[startlo]        ; Subtract low word
                            sbb cx,[starthi]        ; Subtract high word
                            mov [timehi],cx         ; Save time taken
                            mov [timelo],dx
                            jmp endtime

            aftermid:
                            sub [startlo],dx        ; Subtract low word
```

204

```
            sub [starthi],cx      ; Subtract high word
            xor bx,bx
            sub bx,[starlo]       ; Subtract from 0
            mov [timelo],bx
            xor bx,bx
            sbb [starthi],cx      ; Subtract from 0
            mov [timelo],bx

endtime:
            ret
```

Figure 10.1 A time routine

```
PSUEDO:                           ; Generates pseudo-random number

                                  ; Extended version of program allows
                                  ;   for the entry of a 'seed' value to
                                  ;   give a unique but repeatable
                                  ;   sequence
                                  ; Routines can be improved to provide
                                  ;   move even distribution of numbers
                                  ; Repeat loop for a sequence
                                  ; Entry values; None
                                  ; Exit values: AL=random byte

            push ax
            push cx
            mov ah,01h
            int 1Ah               ; Get current count
            mov ax,cx
            mov cl,02h
            shr ax,cl             ; Lose last two bits
            xor ah,ah             ; Lose top two bits to give single byte
                                  ;   from middle of CX, now in AX
            not dh                ; Reverse all bits (to avoid DH=00 too
                                  ;   often!)
            mul dh                ; AX=AL x DH
            shr ax,cl             ; Lose bottom two bits
            xor ax,ax
            ret

; - - - - - - - - - - - - - - - - - - - - - - - - - - - - - - -

RNDTEST:                          ; Test pseudo random number generator
```

The Clock and NVR

```
                                ; Call DISBYT, DISSTR (see Ch. 12)
                                ; Entry values: None
                                ; Exit values: CX,DX changed
              jmp rtestst
space         db ' $'           ; Space to print between numbers
rtestst:
              xor cx,cx
              mov cl,64h        ; CL=100
getrnd:
              call pseudo       ; Get random number
              call disbyt       ; Display it
              lea dx, space     ; Point to SPACE
              call disstr       ; Display spaces
                                ; Repeat 100 times to give 5 lines of
                                ;   numbers
              int 20h           ; End
```

Figure 10.2 Generating pseudo-random numbers

DATE AND TIME

The date and time are permanently maintained for us by the system. When the mains power is off this function is still kept going by the battery-backed circuits.

DATE

We can change the date (as set by the system) either using the DOS DATE command or within a program, using one of the DOS interrupt 21h functions.

Interrupt:	21h
Function:	2Bh
DOS version:	1
Service:	Set date
Entry values:	AH=2Bh
	CX=year (1980-2099)
	DH=month (1=January)
	DL=day
Exit values:	AL=(00h (date valid)
	(FFh (date invalid)

The day, date and month must be stored in DL, DH and CX respectively. The system does not carry out any error checks.

The Clock and NVR

Interrupt:	21h
Function:	2Ah
DOS version:	1
Service:	Get date
Entry values:	AH=2Ah
Exit values:	AL=day of week (0=Sunday)
	CX=year (1980-2099)
	DH=month (1=January)
	DL=day

This function is the reverse of function 2Bh, returning the current date. As a useful addition, it also returns, in AL, the day of the week for that date. This day is coded with the numbers 0 to 6, Sunday being 0. (Note that the day of the week is also stored in the NVR, but there the day of the week runs from 1 to 7, starting on Sunday.) Temporarily changing the date, we can find the day of the week for any date from 1980 to the end of the next century.

Interrupt 1Ah provides functions that achieve almost the same effect.

Interrupt:	1Ah
Function:	05h
Service:	Set RTC date
Entry values:	AH=05h (Amstrad-specific)
	CH=century (BCD) (19 or 20)
	CL=year (BCD)
	DH=month (BCD)
	DL=day (BCD)
Exit values:	CF=(0 (RTC functioning)
	(1 (RTC not functioning)
	Other flags changed

Interrupt:	1Ah
Function:	04h
Service:	Get RTC date (Amstrad-specific)
Entry values:	AH=04h
	CH=century (BCD)
	CL=year (BCD)
	DH=month (BCD)
	DL=day (BCD)
Exit values:	CF=(0 (RTC functioning)
	(1 (RTC not functioning)
	Other flags changed

The Clock and NVR

The century in function 05h is overwritten if it is incorrect. For years from 80 to 99 it must be 19, while 00 to 79 implies the next century.

These functions are best avoided. They are specific to the Amstrad PC and may not be found on other PC's (though similar functions are used on IBM PC AT's). Matters are also confused by the use of binary coded decimal (BCD) for storing values. Another complication is that the Amstrad's RTC only provides a 100-year calendar, from 1980, while MS-DOS usually permits 120 years. Any date set between 2080 and 2099 will lose 100 years when the system is reset.

With all the interrupt 1Ah functions that deal with the RTC date and time, if the carry flag is set - indicating a malfunction of the RTC - the values in CX and DX are unchanged (though it is always safest to pop them off the stack anyway).

As a general rule, therefore, it is better to stick to the DOS equivalents.

TIME

In a similar way to the above we can set and read the current time.

Interrupt: 21h
Function: 2Dh
DOS version: 1
Service: Set time
Entry values: AH=2Dh
                   CH=hours
                   CL=minutes
                   DH=seconds
                   DL=hundredths of seconds
Exit values: AL=(00h (time valid)
                   (FFh (time invalid)

The hours, minutes, seconds and hundredths of seconds must be set in the CH, CL, DH and DL registers respectively. Obviously much of the time the DX values will be 0. This function forms the basis of the DOS TIME command.

Interrupt: 21h
Function: 2Ch
DOS version: 1
Service: Get time

The Clock and NVR

Entry values: AH=2C
Exit values: CH=hours
CL=minutes
DH=seconds
DL=hundredths of seconds

This function reverses function 20h and returns the current time. Note that the clock ticks occur every 0.054 seconds, so the current time is only accurate to the nearest $^1/_{10}$th second (approximately). This means that any measure of the passing of time will likewise only be accurate to $^1/_{10}$th second. A timing program should only show values in steps of 0.1. Anything else is likely to be misleading.

Great care should be taken if tampering with the system date and time. A well-behaved program only temporarily changes the values, unless it is made clear that the user is entering new values for the date and time. If the values are being changed for some other purpose (such as finding out the day of the week for a given date) then they should be restored as quickly as possible.

As for the date, the ROS interrupt 1Ah provides two equivalent functions.

Interrupt: 1Ah
Function: 03h
Service: Set RTC time (Amstrad-specific)
Entry values: AH=03h
CH=hours (BCD)
CL=minutes (BCD)
DH=seconds (BCD)
DL=(0 (GMT only)
(1 (GMT and BST)
Exit values: CF=(0 (RTC functioning)
(1 (RTC not functioning)
Other flags changed

Interrupt: 1Ah
Function: 02h
Service: Get RTC time (Amstrad-specific)
Entry values: AH=02h
CH=hours (BCD)
CL=minutes (BCD)
DH=seconds (BCD)

The Clock and NVR

	CF=(0 (RTC functioning)
	(1 (RTC not functioning)
Exit values:	None
	Other flags changed

Again, there is little advantage in using these Amstrad specific functions. The main difference is the option to set up the RTC to allow for the change between GMT and BST in the UK. However, other methods exist to achieve this, as described later.

Accessing date and time directly

We could access the date and time directly by reading or writing the NVR locations where this information is stored. However, this approach is not recommended, since this method of dealing with time can cause a headache for programmers who wish their programs to run on other systems.

If programs are to run elsewhere, then the date and time should only be read and set using the standard DOS interrupts. This will ensure compatibility across systems. Any routine which reads and writes the NVR locations directly will inevitably run into difficulty when run on other systems.

Note that using other operating systems on the Amstrad PC can cause problems with the time because of the use of the NVR for storing the date and time. The memory locations used by the NVR are not standard of course. For example, running PC-DOS 3.3 results in the time being reset each time the system is booted. This is because the system is checking a variable whose value is lost each time the system is started and PC-DOS does not know to check the NVR location to find the time. This is one good reason for sticking to the proper Amstrad PC version of DOS.

The RTC.COM program

It is interesting to note that the early Amstrad PC1512 had a distinct problem with the 24-hour clock. Anyone working past midnight on those machines might have noticed that the clock did not reset itself but continued to increase hour by hour, and likewise the day remained static. Another symptom of this problem is the machine crashing (at midnight) with a 'Divide Overflow' error.

On these machines the RTC.COM program corrects this error, as long as it is run before midnight is reached. However, it is important to note that the RTC.COM program performs its task by complementing the value of one bit in memory; running RTC.COM on a machine that does not have this problem will cause it to get the problem!

THE NON-VOLATILE RAM (NVR)

The Amstrad PC's *Non-Volatile RAM (NVR)* is constantly maintained by the battery backup. It should therefore never lose its contents, though inevitably this will happen. Although the Amstrad PC's batteries are supposed to last a year, in practice the period seems to be shorter. It is possible to swap the batteries with the machine switched on, so as not to lose the contents of the NVR, but only if you catch the batteries in time.

The NVR stores a variety of information but it is broadly divided into two parts. The first fourteen bytes store clock information while the remaining 50 bytes hold a variety of system information.

Writing direct to the NVR

There are two ways to actually insert new values into the NVR. One method is to poke in the values directly by using the two NVR ports. The first stage is to tell the system which location within the NVR is to be accessed. This is done by sending the value to port 70h. Next, the actual value to be written should be sent to port 71h. Alternatively, the current value of any location may be read using the same procedure and ports.

Although this is fairly straightforward, it is not recommended for use, especially when setting values. In general there are suitable interrupts for achieving the same effect, as listed in Figure 10.3.

The NVR interrupts

On the Amstrad PC the NVR has its own special interrupt, interrupt 15h. This interrupt performs a very different action to anything you are likely to find on any other PC. Therefore, it should only be used in programs that are specific to the Amstrad PC range, and no attempt should be made to transfer it across to other compatibles.

Interrupt 15h includes a number of different functions, many of which are described in the appropriate sections. However, there are some general ones which are described here.

The Clock and NVR

Interrupt	Function	Use
15	00	Read mouse counters
	01	Set NVR counters
	02	Read NVR counters
	06	GET ROS version number
1A	02	Get RTC time
	03	Set RTC time
	04	Get RTC date
	05	Set RTC date
	06	Set RTC alarm
	07	Reset alarm
33		Mouse functions

Figure 10.3 Interrupts for changing the NVR

Interrupt: 15h
Function: 01h
Service: Set NVR value (Amstrad-specific)
Entry values: AH=01h
                AL=location to write (00h - 3Fh)
                BL=new value
Exit values: AH=(0 (success)
                     (1 (address out of range)
                     (2 (write error)
                All flags changed

This function writes a new value into a particular NVR location, given as an offset in the range 00h to 3Fh. Because the information in the NVR is so sensitive, the function always checks the value actually written by reading it back and comparing it with the original value, returning an error message if it is incorrect.

The values returned in AH are as follows:

     0   Function successful

     1   Invalid location

     2   Write error

Generally speaking, this function should not be used with the NVR's RTC locations (00h-0Dh), since these are catered for by separate DOS interrupts.

Interrupt: 15h
Function: 02h
Service: Read NVR value (Amstrad-specific)
Entry values: AH=02h
AL=location to read (00h - 3Fh)
Exit values: AH=(0 (success)
(1 (address out of range)
(2 (checksum error)
AL=value in NVR
All flags changed

This function works in a similar way to function 01h, returning the value in AL with an error code in AH (AH=2 indicating that the data in the NVR is incorrect).

Interrupt: 15h
Function: 06h
Service: Get ROS version number (Amstrad-specific)
Entry values: AH=06h
Exit values: BH=major release number
BL=minor release number
All flags changed

This function is used, quite simply, to return the ROS version number, the major part of the number being returned in BH with BL giving the minor part (as a 2-digit number).

If the value of BX is 0 or the carry flag is set, this indicates that the program is running on some machine other than the Amstrad PC. Additional information is available by checking the values of the printer control port.

THE CLOCK INFORMATION

The first section of the NVR stores the current time, the time set for an alarm and the current date; it also has four registers that are used to control the clock. The current time and date are constantly updated, the date being incremented whenever the time passes midnight. The alarm can be set and comes into effect when it matches the current time (regardless of the date). It is not possible to set a date for the alarm directly.

The Clock and NVR

Bytes	Use	Default (hex)
00	RTC seconds	00
01	Alarm seconds	00
02	RTC minutes	00
03	Alarm minutes	00
04	RTC hours	00
05	Alarm hours	00
06	RTC day of week code	00
07	RTC day of month	00
08	RTC month	00
09	RTC year	00
0A	Register A	70
0B	Register B	02
0C	Register C	-
0D	Register D	-

Figure 10.4 The RTC data

The layout of the first fourteen bytes is shown in Figure 10.4. These values can be stored as either standard binary data or as binary coded decimal (BCD). The same type of data must be used for all ten locations but can be determined by the programmer. The range of values for each data mode is shown in Figure 10.5.

The time and date registers

The four time and date registers, rather unimaginatively called A, B, C and D, store various information about the way in which the Real Time Clock is to be used. The potential values of these registers are shown in Figure 10.6. A full description of the square-wave function used in the clock can be found in the Amstrad Technical Reference Manual.

Since much of the information in the registers cannot sensibly be used in most programs, it is beyond the scope of this book. However, the following values are of interest:

- Bit 7 of register A should be set whenever the date and time values are being changed. When it is set no further updates occur. It should be cleared as soon as possible.

- Bit 2 of register B determines the data format; the bit should be cleared for BCD or set for binary data.

The Clock and NVR

Offset	Use	Decimal	Range Binary (hex)	BCD (hex)
00	RTC seconds	0 - 59	00 - 3B	00 - 59
01	Alarm seconds	0 - 59	00 - 3B	00 - 59
02	RTC minutes	0 - 59	00 - 3B	00 - 59
03	Alarm minutes	0 - 59	00 - 3B	00 - 59
04	RTC hours:			
	12-hour	1 - 12	01 - 0C (am)	01 - 12 (am)
			81 - 8C (pm)	81 - 92 (pm)
	24-hour	0 - 23	00 - 17	00 - 23
05	Alarm hours			
	12-hour	1 - 12	01 - 0C (am)	01 - 12 (am)
			81 - 8C (pm)	81 - 92 (pm)
	24-hour	0 - 23	00 -17	00 - 23
06	RTC day of week	1 - 7	1 - 07	01 - 07
07	RTC day of month	1 - 31	01- 1F	01 - 31
08	RTC month	1 - 12	01 - 0C	01 - 12
09	RTC year	0 - 99	00 - 63	00 - 99

Figure 10.5 Range of RTC data

- Bit 1 of register B determines whether the 12- or 24-hour clock is used, the bit being clear for 12-hour and set for 24-hour mode. When the clock is in 12-hour mode, the high bit of the hour byte for both the current time and the alarm is clear for a.m. and set for p.m. times.

- Bit 0 of register B can be set if the machine is to automatically take account of British Summer Time and Greenwich Mean Time.

- Bit 5 of register C is set when the current time becomes the same as the alarm time.

- Bit 7 of register D is usually set but is cleared when the backup power drops below a certain level. This bit is used to test whether the NVR data is liable to be incorrect.

The remainder of the register bits should be left unchanged.

The Clock and NVR

Bit	Register A (NVR offset 0Ah) Use
0	)
1	) Rate selection
2	)
3	)
4	)
5	) Divider code
6	)
7	Set if RTC being updated

Bit	Register B (NVR offset 0Bh) Use
0	Set if BST available, clear for GMT
1	Set for 24-hour mode, clear for 12-hour
2	Set for binary date, clear for BCD
3	Square wave enable
4	End update flag
5	Alarm interrupt enabled
6	Periodic interrupt enabled
7	Set when updates to RTC suspended

Bit	Register C (NVR offset 0Ch) Use
0-3	Always 0
4	Set when RTC update complete
5	Set when alarm time equals RTC time
6	Set when periodic interrupt occurs
7	Interrupt request flag

Bit	Register D (NVR offset 0Dh) Use
0-6	Always 0
7	Set when NVR data valid

Figure 10.6 RTC Registers A - D

GMT and BST   Register B provides a useful option for machines in use in the UK - as long as the system of changing to and from British Summer Time is not altered.

When bit 0 is set the time changes as follows:

- The time advances from 1:59:59 a.m. (GMT) to 3 a.m. (BST) on the last Sunday in April.

- The time jumps back from 1:59:59 a.m. (GMT) to 1 a.m. (BST) on the last Sunday in October.

Unfortunately, this very interesting feature is not actually implemented; as it stands it is up to the user to manually change the time twice a year. Not a massive task perhaps, but neither is the option to use the 12-hour clock available.

THE ALARM   The Amstrad PC incorporates a facility for setting an alarm. The actual time of the alarm is stored in the NVR. The ROS includes a routine that constantly checks to see whether the alarm time has been reached. When the alarm time is reached an Amstrad-specific interrupt, 0Ah, is invoked. This sophisticated procedure is rarely used.

Setting the alarm   Setting the alarm is a simple process. Doing something when the alarm goes off is not quite so straightforward.

Interrupt:	1Ah
Function:	06h
Service:	Set RTC alarm (Amstrad-specific)
Entry values:	AH=06h
	CH=hours (BCD)
	CL=minutes (BCD)
	DH=seconds (BCD)
Exit values:	CF=(0 (alarm now set)
	(1 (alarm was already set)

This function stores the alarm time and activates the process that checks the current time against the alarm.

Although DOS Plus has an *ALARM* program, there is nothing in MS-DOS to make use of this interesting feature. Each time the system is booted the program decides whether or not the alarm should be set for that day. Note that the program will fail if the system is left switched on during the night before an alarm call.

The Clock and NVR

Reacting to the alarm

When the current time and the alarm time match, the system calls interrupt 0Ah, the alarm handler. This is where things get more complex.

Initially, interrupt 0Ah is a dummy routine that does nothing. To be of any use we need to set up our own interrupt routine and put the address into interrupt vector 0Ah.

Clearing the alarm

Any good alarm program must allow the user to switch off the alarm before the time at which it is due to go off. This is done with the last of the interrupt 1Ah functions.

Interrupt:	1Ah
Function:	07h
Service:	Clear RTC alarm
Entry value:	AH=07h
Exit value:	None

The most important point to note is that this type of routine can only be guaranteed to work on Amstrad PC's.

THE NVR SYSTEM DATA

The other information stored in the NVR is listed in Figure 10.7. The various components are explained under the relevant headings, as indicated.

LOSS OF POWER IN NVR

When the mains power is switched on the system checks the high bit of register D to ensure that it is still set, indicating that the NVR has been properly maintained. If this is not the case then the start-up routines issue the messages:

```
Please fit new batteries
Please set date and time
```

The system also resets the NVR to its default values (as previously shown in Figures 10.4 and 10.7).

Note that, theoretically at least, the batteries are not used when the system is switched on.

The Clock and NVR

The NVR data

Bytes	Use	Default (hex)
0E-13	'Last used' time and date	-
14	User RAM checksum	-
15-16	Enter Key translation code	1C0D
17-18	Del(→)	2207
19-1A	Joystick Fire 1 translation code	FFFF
1B-1C	Joystick Fire 2 translation code	FFFF
1D-1E	Mouse button 1 translation code	FFFF
1F-20	Mouse button 2 translation code	FFFF
21	Mouse X co-ordinate scaling factor	0A
22	Mouse Y co-ordinate scaling factor	0A
23	Initial video mode and drive count	20
24	Initial character displays attributes	07
25	Size of RAM disk (x 2K)	00
26	System UART setup	E3
27	External UART setup	E3
28-3F	Not used	-

Figure 10.7 The NVR data

11. *The Keyboard*

The keyboard is one of the main means of getting information into the computer. The Amstrad PC range have a standard keyboard that is completely compatible with the IBM PC keyboard and almost identical in layout.

This chapter looks at the inner workings of the keyboard circuitry and the instructions needed to make use of the information received from the keyboard.

KEYBOARD HARDWARE

The hardware itself consists of a 96-key keyboard and a keyboard controller chip.

The keyboard connects to the system unit through a 6-way female DIN socket (Figure 11.1). Pins 3 and 6 are connected directly to those pins on the mouse connector that correspond to the buttons; as a result the keyboard controller interprets signals from the mouse buttons as if they were from the keyboard.

```
            The keyboard connector
                       ⊔
             5                    1
             o                    o
                      o6
             o                    o
             4         o          2
                       3
```

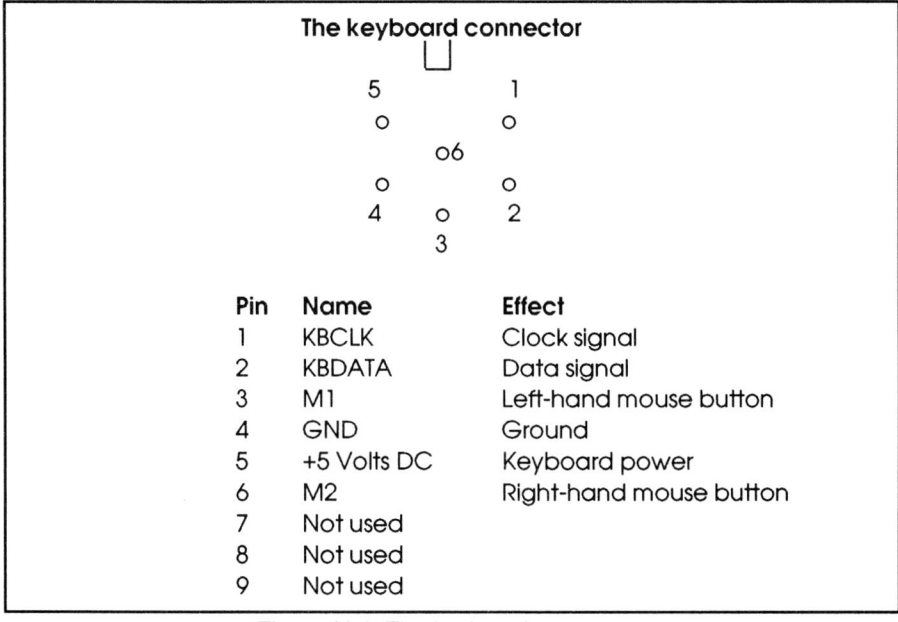

Pin	Name	Effect
1	KBCLK	Clock signal
2	KBDATA	Data signal
3	M1	Left-hand mouse button
4	GND	Ground
5	+5 Volts DC	Keyboard power
6	M2	Right-hand mouse button
7	Not used	
8	Not used	
9	Not used	

Figure 11.1 The keyboard connector

The Keyboard

KEYBOARD TEST

The keyboard controller performs a full test of the keyboard whenever the system is switched on or reset. On completion of a successful test the keyboard sends a code of AAh; if the keyboard is not connected or any other sort of error is found a message is displayed on the screen and the computer beeps. The test is repeated until the error has been corrected.

KEYBOARD LAYOUT

The keyboard is divided into three main sections:

- The central section consists of a standard QWERTY design, including the 26 letters, the numbers 0 to 9 and a range of punctuation marks, mathematical symbols and other characters. It also includes some keys that have a special use.

- The numeric keypad on the right-hand side performs two functions, either as an alternative to the main section for entering numeric data or for controlling cursor movement.

- The function keypad on the left-hand side contains a block of ten programmable function keys.

The keyboard is fully IBM-compatible and almost identical in layout to that of the standard IBM PC, with the following exceptions:

- The keys @ " # ' appear on the UK Amstrad PC as " @ £ #.

- The Alt, PrtSc and Caps Lock keys are in different positions (but act in an identical way).

- The Caps Lock key is fitted with an indicator light.

- There are two additional keys, marked Enter and Del →.

The " @ £ # keys actually behave in the same way as those of the IBM PC, producing the characters @ " # '. To get the characters shown on the UK version of the Amstrad PC you must run the KEYBUK program. This is because the keyboard is in fact a standard US keyboard (like the IBM PC) but with a different set of key caps for the UK version of the machine.

KEYBOARD OPERATION

The use of the individual keys is fairly familiar to most people who have used a computer for any length of time. However, in order to make the most of the keyboard capabilities in a program it is useful to have a full understanding of how the

The Keyboard

keyboard operates and how the operating system software reacts to the various signals it receives.

Whenever a key is pressed the circuits within the keyboard automatically generate a *scan code*. This is a unique single-byte number that identifies which key is being pressed. This code is sent to the keyboard controller chip.

Every key has a scan code and every code is different; even the two Shift keys have different codes so that it is feasible not only to recognise which key has been pressed but also to make the program perform different actions for each key. Most programs do not make any distinction between duplicate keys such as these, of course.

The scan codes that are produced when keys are depressed are in the range 00h to 7Fh (0 to 127).

Similarly, when a key is released the keyboard generates another scan code (or *release code*), which is also sent to the keyboard controller. The release code has a value that is 80h (128) greater than the corresponding scan code for a key press (that is, bit 7 of the code byte is set).

The keyboard controller's main task is to constantly scan the keyboard port for scan codes. As soon as a key press or key release is detected the controller generates an *interrupt 09h* signal and places the scan code in port 60h.

As a general rule the interrupt is dealt with immediately by the CPU and the port is cleared. In certain rare circumstances there is a delay in processing the interrupts. To allow for this the controller has a buffer capable of storing 20 scan codes. (This is different to the main keyboard buffer, which is described below.)

Up to this point the operation of the keyboard is totally beyond the programmer's control. It is not possible to change the scan codes or intercept the codes before they reach port 60h.

INTERRUPT 09H   Interrupt 09h is a hardware interrupt, generated as a matter of routine by the keyboard circuits. As such it cannot be called directly from within a program but the interrupt routine can be changed in order to vary the way in which the keyboard behaves.

The Keyboard

As soon as the interrupt 09h has been generated we can begin to take control of the situation. The interrupt handler is part of the ROS and is stored in ROM. The address of the interrupt 09h routine is stored in RAM in the interrupt table at 0024h. The address can therefore be changed, allowing a program to change the way in which the computer responds to specific key presses.

Before starting to change the keyboard interrupt it is important to realise exactly what goes on in the routine and how much work it does. Perhaps most importantly, any replacement for interrupt 09h may carry out whatever actions it wishes but should end by calling the original interrupt 09h routine so that all eventualities are dealt with.

To start with, the routine reads the scan code from port 60h. Using a lookup table and information about the Shift, Ctrl and Alt keys the scan code is converted into a two-byte code, consisting of the original scan code and the ASCII code for the character that has been pressed. The ASCII code is stored in the low byte of the word. In the case of the special keys (function keys, cursor keys, Ins and Del) the ASCII code is set to 0.

The advantage of this system is that we now have an ASCII value waiting to be dealt with but can also refer to the scan code that originated it should the need arise.

The keyboard buffer

These 2-byte codes are stored in the *keyboard buffer*, where they can be accessed by the program that is currently running. The buffer starts at 041Eh and is large enough to hold the codes for 16 characters. If the buffer is already full the routine issues a further interrupt to make the computer beep and the extra character is discarded.

The offset of the physical start of the buffer (measured from 0400h) is stored at location 0480h; the end of the buffer is at 0482h. The buffer is used on a rotational basis. Each new character is added after the last; when the end of the buffer is reached the next character is stored at the beginning again. Therefore two pointers are needed; one points to the next character to be taken from the buffer, the other points to the next free space. These pointers are stored in low memory at 041Ah and 041Ch respectively. If the two pointers are the same the buffer is empty.

The Keyboard

THE MODIFYING KEYS

Some keys are used to change the way in which the other keys respond. These are the *modifying keys* and they include the following:

- The two *Shift* keys, which convert the letter keys between upper and lower case and provide access to the upper case characters. They are also used to shift the function keys and switch the numeric keypad between its number and cursor functions.

- The *Ctrl* key, which modifies the letter keys to produce a range of *control codes*.

- The *Alt* key, which is used either as an alternative form of control key or, in conjunction with the numeric keypad, to generate the extended ASCII characters.

- The *Caps Lock* key, which toggles the default on the letter keys between upper and lower case.

- The *Num Lock* key, which toggles the default on the numeric keypad between the number and cursor functions.

The effect of all these keys can be changed by suitable routines. A program can detect that a key is still being held down by the fact that it has not yet received a release code. It is also possible to define other modifying keys, since a constant check on the scan codes will reveal whether a release code has been received after the initial scan code has been processed.

Before deciding upon which ASCII code to generate, the interrupt 09h routine first checks the status of the modifying keys.

The keyboard status bytes

Life is much easier if we stick to the standard modifying keys, since the current status of each of these keys is automatically stored in memory and can be accessed at any time. The two bytes at 0417h and 0418h store the keyboard status. The first byte tells us the current state of each key, the second indicates which keys are currently being held down.

Each bit in these two bytes corresponds to a single modifying key (Figure 11.2). The way in which a bit is set depends upon the key involved.

The Keyboard

First keyboard status byte (0417h)		Second keyboard status byte (0418h)	
Bit	Meaning if set	Bit	Meaning if set
7	Insert on	7	Ins pressed
6	Caps Lock on	6	Caps Lock pressed
5	Num Lock on	5	Num Lock pressed
4	Scroll Lock on	4	Scroll Lock pressed
3	Alt pressed	3	Ctrl-Num Lock on
2	Ctrl pressed	2	Not used
1	Left Shift pressed	1	Not used
0	Right Shift pressed	0	Not used

Figure 11.2 The keyboard status bytes

For the keys that are effective only when they are being pressed (Shift, Ctrl and Alt) the bit in 0417h is set when the relevant scan code is received; the bit is cleared as soon as the corresponding release code arrives.

For the keys that have a permanent effect (Caps Lock and Num Lock) the bit in 0417h is changed each time the relevant key press scan code is received. The release codes for these keys are ignored. For example, when the Caps Lock key is pressed for the first time bit 6 is set to 1; no action is taken when the key is released but when the key is pressed a second time bit 6 is cleared.

To discover whether the key is actually being pressed we need to look at the corresponding bits in 0418h. For example, bit 6 is set only while Caps Lock is being physically pressed; it is cleared when the key is released, regardless of the current Caps Lock state.

It is only very rarely that we need to know whether or not one of these keys is being held down. The most important part of 0418h is bit 3, which tells us whether a program has been suspended by pressing Ctrl-Num Lock.

Whenever the routine receives a scan code it has to be able to convert the code into the correct ASCII code. In order to do this it first checks the status bytes to see if any of the modifying keys are effective. For example, if the letter 'A' is

The Keyboard

pressed and one of the Shift keys is also being pressed the routine sends ASCII code 41h ('A'); if the Caps Lock bit is also set then the effects of the two keys cancel each other out and the routine sends ASCII 61h ('a'); if the Ctrl key is being pressed it sends ASCII 01h (Ctrl-A).

This feature of interpreting letters as lower case if both Shift and Caps Lock are on is peculiar to the IBM PC and compatibles and can be somewhat frustrating. The routine in Figure 11.3 gets rid of this irritation by temporarily turning Caps Lock off when either of the Shift keys is on.

Many combinations are ignored by the interrupt 09h routine and require additional programming for them to be effective. For example, Ctrl-Shift-C is simply treated as Ctrl-C. Such combinations can be catered for by checking the status bytes and acting on their values. However, as with anything that works directly with specific memory locations, this sort of activity may damage your ability to run the program on all machines. This is one instance where you should be fairly safe; all good compatibles use the low memory locations for the same purposes and it is likely that any new arrivals will maintain compatibility - but there are no cast-iron guarantees.

Other status keys   In addition to the keys which modify the effect of other keys, there are two keys that have a toggle effect on bits in the status bytes. These are the *Ins* and *Scroll Lock* keys, which are recorded in bits 7 and 4 respectively.

As with Caps Lock and Num Lock, each time one of these keys is pressed the relevant bit is complemented. The Ins key is frequently used to toggle between insert and overwrite modes in word processing and other programs.

The Scroll Lock key is a rather strange key, in that it is rarely used except in combination with Ctrl, and thus opens the way for some interesting effects.

It is important to note that the Ctrl-Break combination does not affect the Scroll Lock bit. Bit 4 should always be cleared at the start of any routine that uses the Scroll Lock key.

Checking the keyboard status   Interrupt 16h provides a means of inspecting the keyboard status byte.

The Keyboard

```
CAPSMOD:                        ; Modify Caps Lock

                                ; This routine should be inserted into
                                ;   the shell for the TSR (Figure 7.2)
                                ;   in place of MAIN
                                ; The effect of the routine is to check
                                ;   for the combination of Caps Lock and
                                ;   a Shift key together; if it finds
                                ;   it, the Shift key is ignored

                                ; Limitations in the effect of this
                                ;   routine is to completely disable the
                                ;   Shift keys when Caps Lock is on,
                                ;   fine for letters but not much good
                                ;   for other characters. Extended
                                ;   version only disables Shift while
                                ;   letter keys are being processed

                                ; Entry values: None
                                ; Exit values:  None

        push bx                 ; Save registers
        push di
        push es
        lea es,0000h            ; ES:DI points to 0417h
        lea di,0417h
        mov bx,[di]             ; Load status bytes
        push bx                 ; Save status
        and bh,40h              ; Isolate Caps Lock bit
        cmp bh,01h              ; Is it set?
        jz                      ; If not, continue as normal
        pop bx                  ; Otherwise, recover status
        and bh,03h              ; Isolate Shift bits
        cmp bh,01h              ; Is either set?
        jz cont                 ; If not, continue as normal
                                ; Otherwise, both are set
        and bh,0FCh             ; Clear Shift bits
        mov [di],bx             ; Store status byte

cont:
        pop es                  ; Restore registers
        pop di
        pop bx
        pushf
        call oldint9            ; Call normal keyboard routine
        iret                    ; Ends
```

Figure 11.3 Modifying the effects of Caps Lock

The Keyboard

Interrupt: 16h
Function: 02h
Service: Get keyboard status
Entry values: AH=02h
Exit values: AL=keyboard status byte

This function returns in AL the first byte of the keyboard status (from memory location 0417h). This is the byte that holds the most useful information about the current status of the keyboard. (It is essential to know whether Caps Lock is on or off but whether or not the key is actually depressed is of little interest.) The routine in Figure 11.4 converts this to usable information.

```
KEYSTAT:                            ; Decode keyboard status

                                    ; Converts main keyboard status byte
                                    ;   into individual characters for use
                                    ;   by other routines
                                    ; Enhanced versions stores characters to
                                    ;   indicate which keys are pressed

                                    ; Entry values: None
                                    ; Exit values:  STATUS=8 bytes of status
                                    ;                      data
            jmp keyst
status      db 8 dup (?)            ; 8 bytes for storing results
keyst:
            mov ah,02h
            int 16h                 ; Get keyboard status
            xor di,di
            xor cx,cx
            mov cl,08h              ; CL=8
getbit:
            rcr al,01h              ; Get next bit
            jc bitset               ; Jump if bit set
            mov status[di],00h      ; Otherwise, store 0
            jmp nextbit
bitset:
            mov status[di],01h      ; Store 1
nextbit:
            inc di                  ; Point to next byte in STATUS
            loop getbit             ; Loop to get next bit
            ret
;------------------------------------------------------------------
```

The Keyboard

```
KEYTEST:                                ; Tests KEYSTAT routine
                                        ; Calls DISSTR, NEWLIN (Figure 13.16),
                                        ;   SCRENCLR (13.11), CUROFF (13.17)
            mov status[08h],'$'         ; Store $ at end of STATUS
            call screnclr               ; Clear the screen
            call curoff                 ; Switch off cursor
endlessloop:
            call keystat                ; Get status
            call disstr                 ; Display status string
            call newlin                 ; Start new line
            call curstop                ; Move cursor to top of screen
            jmp endlessloop             ; Program terminated by Ctrl-Break

curstop:                                ; Move cursor to top of screen
            mov ah,02h
            mov bh,00h
            mov dh,00h
            mov dl,00h
            int 10h                     ; (See Chapter 13 for more details)
            ret
```

Figure 11.4 Inspecting the keyboard status

THE KEYBOARD TRANSLATION TABLE

The keyboard interrupt routine contains a translation table for converting each scan code into a 2-byte code to be sent to the keyboard buffer. The full translation table is given in Figure 11.6.

The following points should be noted:

- Some key combinations are ignored and no codes are sent to the buffer (-).

- Num Lock and Caps Lock have no effect for some keys; in such cases the code is determined by the status of the other modifying keys.

- If either or both Shift keys are pressed when Caps Lock is on, the key is effectively unmodified.

- If Shift is used in combinations with either Ctrl or Alt, the Shift key is ignored and the result can be found in the Ctrl or Alt column.

	Effect for letter key (e.g. A)			
	No lock	Num Lock	Caps Lock	Num Lock + Caps Lock
No Shift	a	a	A	A
Shift	A	A	a	a
Ctrl	^A	^A	^A	^A
Alt	Ignored	Ignored	Ignored	Ignored
Shift+Ctrl	^A	^A	^A	^A
Shift+Alt	Ignored	Ignored	Ignored	Ignored
Ctrl+Alt	Ignored	Ignored	Ignored	Ignored
Shift+Ctrl+Alt	Ignored	Ignored	Ignored	Ignored
	Effect for character key (e.g. 7 &)			
	No Lock	Num Lock	Caps Lock	Num Lock + Caps Lock
No Shift	7	7	7	7
Shift	&	&	&	&
Ctrl	Ignored	Ignored	Ignored	Ignored
Alt	Ignored	Ignored	Ignored	Ignored
Shift+Ctrl	Ignored	Ignored	Ignored	Ignored
Shift+Alt	Ignored	Ignored	Ignored	Ignored
Ctrl+Alt	Ignored	Ignored	Ignored	Ignored
Shift+Ctrl+Alt	Ignored	Ignored	Ignored	Ignored
	Effect for number pad key (e.g. 4 ←)			
	No Lock	Num Lock	Caps Lock	Num Lock + Caps Lock
No Shift	←	4	←	4
Shift	4	←	4	←
Ctrl	Ctrl ←	4	Ctrl ←	4
Alt	Ignored	ASCII 4	Ignored	ASCII 4
Shift+Ctrl	Ctrl ←	4	Ctrl ←	4
Shift+Alt	Ignored	ASCII 4	Ignored	ASCII 4
Ctrl+Alt	Ignored	ASCII 4	Ignored	ASCII 4
Shift+Ctrl+Alt	Ignored	ASCII 4	Ignored	ASCII 4

Figure 11.5 Effect of special key combinations

The Keyboard

Code (UK)	Unmodified	Shift	Caps Lock	Num Lock	Ctrl	Alt
01	Esc	011B	011B	-	011B	-
02	1 !	0231	0221	-	-	7800
03	2 "	0332	0340	-	0300	7900
04	3 #	0433	0423	-	-	7A00
05	4 $	0534	0524	-	-	7B00
06	5 %	0635	0625	-	-	7C00
07	6 '	0736	075E	-	071E	7D00
08	7 &	0837	0826	-	-	7E00
09	8 *	0938	092A	-	-	7F00
0A	9 (	0A39	0A28	-	-	8000
0B	0)	0B30	0B29	-	-	8100
0C	- _	0C2D	0C5F	-	0C1F	8200
0D	= +	0D3D	0D2B	-	-	8300
0E	←Del	0E08	0E08	-	0E7F	-
0F	Tab	0F09	0F00	-	-	-
10	Q	1071	1051	-	1011	1000
11	W	1177	1157	-	1117	1100
12	E	1265	1245	-	1205	1200
13	R	1372	1352	-	1312	1300
14	T	1474	1454	-	1414	1400
15	Y	1579	1559	-	1519	1500
16	U	1675	1655	-	1615	1600
17	I	1769	1749	-	1709	1700
18	O	186F	184F	-	180F	1800
19	P	1970	1950	-	1910	1900
1A	({	1A5B	1A7B	-	1A1B	-
1B	) }	1B5D	1B7D	-	1B1D	-
1C	Return	1C0D	1C0D	-	1C0A	-
1D	Ctrl	-	-	-	-	-
1E	A	1E61	1E41	-	1E01	1E00
1F	S	1F73	1F53	-	1F13	1F00
20	D	2064	2044	-	2004	2000
21	F	2166	2146	-	2106	2100
22	G	2267	2247	-	2207	2200
23	H	2368	2348	-	2308	2300

Figure 11.6 Scan code translation table

Code (UK)	Unmodified	Shift	Caps Lock	Num Lock	Ctrl	Alt
24	J	246A	244A	-	240A	2400
25	K	256B	254B	-	250B	2500
26	L	266C	264C	-	260C	2600
27	; :	273B	273A	-	-	-
28	' @	2827	2822	-	-	-
29	# ~	2960	297E	-	-	-
2A	Left Shift	-	-	-	-	-
2B	\ |	2B5C	2B7C	-	2B1C	-
2C	Z	2C7A	2C5A	-	2C1A	2C00
2D	X	2D78	2D58	-	2D18	2D00
2E	C	2E63	2E43	-	2E0F	2E00
2F	V	2F76	2F56	-	2F16	2F00
30	B	3062	3042	-	3002	3000
31	N	316E	314E	-	310E	3100
32	M	326D	324D	-	320D	3200
33	,	332C	333C	-	-	-
34	.	342E	343E	-	-	-
35	/ ?	352F	353F	-	-	-
36	Right Shift	-	-	-	-	-
37	PrtSc	372A	PrtSc	-	7200	-
38	Alt	-	-	-	-	-
39	Space	3920	3920	-	3920	3920
3A	Caps Lock	-	-	-	-	-
3B	F1	3B00	5400	-	5E00	6800
3C	F2	3C00	5500	-	5F00	6900
3D	F3	3D00	5600	-	6000	6A00
3E	F4	3E00	5700	-	6100	6B00
3F	F5	3F00	5800	-	6200	6C00
40	F6	4000	5900	-	6300	6D00
41	F7	4100	5A00	-	6400	6E00
42	F8	4200	5B00	-	6500	6F00
43	F9	4300	5C00	-	6600	7000
44	F10	4400	5D00	-	6700	7100
45	Num Lock	-	-	-	Pause	-
46	Scroll Lock	-	-	-	Break	-

Figure 11.6 Scan code translation table (continued)

The Keyboard

Code (UK)	Unmodified	Shift	Caps Lock	Num Lock	Ctrl	Alt
47	Key Pad 7	4700	-	4737	7700	-
48	Key Pad 8	4800	-	4838	-	-
49	Key Pad 9	4900	-	4939	8400	-
4A	Key Pad -	4A2D	-	4A2D	-	-
4B	Key Pad 4	4B00	-	4B34	7300	-
4C	Key Pad 5	-	-	4C35	-	-
4D	Key Pad 6	4D00	-	4D36	7400	-
4E	Key Pad +	4E2B	-	4E2B	-	-
4F	Key Pad 1	4F00	-	4F31	7500	-
50	Key Pad 2	5000	-	5032	-	-
51	Key Pad 3	5100	-	5133	7600	-
52	Key Pad 0	5200	-	5230	-	-
53	Key Pad .	5300	-	532E	-	-
54-6F	Not used	-	-	-	-	-
70	Del →	-	-	-	-	-
71-73	Not used	-	-	-	-	-
74	Enter	-	-	-	-	-
75-76	Not used	-	-	-	-	-
77	Joy Fire2	-	-	-	-	-
78	Joy Fire1	-	-	-	-	-
79	Joy Right	4D00	4D00	4D00	4D00	4D00
7A	Joy Left	4B00	4B00	4B00	4B00	4B00
7B	Joy Down	5000	5000	5000	5000	5000
7C	Joy Up	4800	4800	4800	4800	4800
7D	Mouse M2	-	-	-	-	-
7E	Mouse M1	-	-	-	-	-
7F	Not used	-	-	-	-	-

Figure 11.6 Scan code translation table (continued)

- If Ctrl and Alt are pressed together the Alt key takes precedence and the result is to be found in the Alt column.

The effect of the various key combinations is shown in Figure 11.5.

The KEYB programs

As we saw earlier, the character printed on the key does not always match the character that is displayed if the Amstrad PC has anything other than the US version of the keyboard.

The Keyboard

This is because MS-DOS, having originated in the USA, assumes that the machine has a US keyboard.

For any other keyboard we need to interpret the key codes in slightly different ways. The keyboards are all identical, apart from the key caps. So, pressing Shift-2 always produces the scan code 03h. The standard translation table translates this as ASCII 40h (the @ symbol) and not the double-quote (ASCII 22h) that is shown on the UK key cap.

To overcome this problem there is a program for the UK keyboard called *KEYBUK.COM*. (The name is derived from KEYB plus UK.) This program replaces the translation table in memory with one containing the revised codes. For example, scan code 03h is translated as ASCII 22h. Other programs exist for French (FR), German (GR), Spanish (SP), Italian (IT), Swedish (SW), Danish (DA), Portuguese (PO), Greek (GR) and Norwegian (NO) keyboards.

In some cases the interpretation of the ASCII code on the screen is different. This only happens with the extended ASCII characters. For example, ASCII 9Ch produces the £ symbol most of the time but if the internal links have been set so that the Greek font has been loaded it produces an ε.

Therefore, scan code 04h with shift results in ASCII code 9Ch on UK keyboards but ASCII F9h on Greek keyboards; yet in both cases the £ symbol is displayed.

Note that KEYB programs from other computers may work satisfactorily but they will ignore any information from the mouse buttons and joystick, since these codes are specific to the Amstrad. Mouse movement should still be effective, since this duplicates the cursor control keys and is standard.

SPECIAL COMBINATIONS

At an early point in the interrupt 09h routine there is a section that checks for specific key combinations.

The combinations that the routine is seeking are:

- Ctrl-Num Lock, which suspends execution of a program until another key is pressed;

The Keyboard

- Ctrl-Break, the 'break' key, which halts a program and returns control to the operating system;

- Ctrl-Alt-Del, the result of which is to reboot the computer;

- Shift-PrtSc, which sends a screen dump to the printer

- Ctrl-Alt-F1, which cancels the effect of the KEYB programs;

- Ctrl-Alt-F2, which reinstates the KEYB conversion tables.

This check is done before the character is written to the keyboard buffer. As a result the keystrokes never make it to the buffer. Since each of these special routines issues a hardware interrupt and such interrupts are always acted on immediately, the predefined action is executed straight away, regardless of what other keystrokes may be waiting in the buffer.

Any of these special keystrokes can of course be superseded. Many programs overrule the 'break' calls for instance, and a number of programs intercept the Shift-PrtSc combination to vary the way in which the screen dump is performed. The usual method is to replace the relevant interrupt with a new version, rather than to interfere with interrupt 09h.

Ctrl-Num Lock

There is no reason why new 'Special' keys of this type should not be included. Indeed this is one of the steps needed to set up a TSR program so that it can respond to the special key combination that activates it.

The result of pressing the Ctrl key in combination with Num Lock is that all activity within the current program ceases until another key is pressed. This is frequently used with operating system commands such as DIR to temporarily interrupt the listing. Many applications have little use for this operation and bypass it altogether.

When the key combination is enabled, Ctrl-S has an identical effect.

The Ctrl-Num Lock status can be found by testing bit 3 of 0418h, which is set when a program is suspended.

The Keyboard

Ctrl-Break   The 'break' combination is used to halt a program prematurely. The effect of the break is that the interrupt 09h routine issues an interrupt 1Bh. Initially this is just a dummy routine but DOS replaces it with its own routine. DOS also uses its own interrupt 23h vector to store the address of the interrupt handler. Invoking either interrupt 1Bh or 23h will force a break in the program. How it is handled depends on what the program is doing at the time.

As a general rule, DOS uses the Ctrl-Break as a signal that a command or program is to be terminated. When DOS notices a Ctrl-Break it proceeds to close down the program that was running and redisplay the system prompt.

Note that only some operations respond to the Ctrl-Break combination. In particular, the interrupts that accept keyboard input fall into two groups: those that do accept Ctrl-Break and those that don't. Disabling Ctrl-Break altogether can be dangerous as it may leave the user in a situation where they cannot break out of a program. Sometimes this is essential, sometimes infuriating!

A program can quite happily change the interrupt 23h vector. This is one of the three interrupt addresses that DOS stores in the PSP when the program is loaded; when the program ends DOS restores the original interrupt vector. It is feasible to change the vector in the PSP but certainly not recommended.

DOS allows the user to determine the frequency with which it checks for this key combination. This is decided by the *BREAK* directive in CONFIG.SYS. When the directive is set as BREAK=OFF (the default) the check is carried out after input and output but not after disk access; BREAK=ON extends the times at which the check is carried out.

Alternatively, the user can change the Ctrl-Break state at any time with the DOS BREAK command. The Ctrl-Break state can also be changed or inspected within a program, using DOS interrupt 21h, function 33h.

Interrupt:	21h
Function:	33h,01h
Service:	Set or clear Ctrl-Break operation
Entry value:	AH=33h
	AL=01h

The Keyboard

	DL=(00h (Turn Ctrl-Break off)
	(01h (Turn Ctrl-Break on)
Exit value:	AL=FFh (if entry code is invalid)
Interrupt:	21h
Function:	33h,00h
Service:	Get Ctrl-Break status
Entry value:	AH=33
	AL=00
Exit value:	AL=FFh (if entry code is invalid)
	DL=(00h (Ctrl-Break is off)
	(01h (Ctrl-Break is on)

Many programs disable this key combination. If the combination is enabled, then Ctrl-C will generally produce the same effect as Ctrl-Break.

When Ctrl-Break is pressed, bit 7 of memory location 0471h is set. This bit is not automatically cleared. Any program that tests for a break by inspecting this location (which is not used for any other purpose) must clear this byte.

Ctrl-Alt-Del This is the most drastic of the key combinations. In the normal course of events the ROS issues an interrupt 19h to reboot the system. This restores the computer to its original state, as it was at power-up. The system tries to reload COMMAND.COM and frees all of RAM not used by the operating system.

This key combination, and ways in which it may be utilised, were described in Chapter 8.

Shift-PrtSc The combination of Shift and PrtSc results in an interrupt 05h, which in its standard form sends a screen dump to the parallel printer port.

This operation is described in more detail in Chapter 18.

KEY INDICATOR LIGHTS The red indicator lights embedded in the Caps Lock and Num Lock keys themselves are a function of the hardware and not the software. Each time one of these keys is pressed the light alternates between on and off.

Although the light should correspond to the relevant bit in the status byte at all times it is possible to confuse the system and end up with a light that is working 'upside down'. This

The Keyboard

happens if the key is pressed when the interrupts are disabled, in which case the key press is ignored even though the keyboard circuits still respond; in particular this situation can easily arise if the key is pressed while the system is being booted (during its system checks).

Once an indicator light is giving the wrong information it will remain so until the system is rebooted. One of the first functions of the boot programs is to switch these lights off.

THE KEY-REPEAT ACTION

As described earlier, the result of pressing a key is that the keyboard controller despatches the relevant scan code; when the key is released the corresponding release code is sent. In addition to this, the controller keeps track of any key for which it has detected a key press but no key release. It measures the time for which the key has been depressed and after one second it sends a repeat of the original scan code to port 60h. This code is then repeated every 0.083 seconds (about 12 times a second) until a release code is detected.

Although the ROS keyboard routine should perhaps be able to tell that it has received a series of scan codes without corresponding release codes it is not particularly clever in the way in which it handles the situation. However, because the result seems to follow common sense rules the routine appears quite impressive.

The effect is as follows:

■ When a character scan code is received the ROS transmits the relevant codes to the buffer, regardless of whether it is the first key press or a repeat one.

■ Any character key release codes are ignored.

■ If a modifying key scan code is received the relevant bit in the status bytes is set, so repeats have no additional effect.

■ When a modifying key release code is received the relevant bit is cleared.

The result of all this is that when a key is held down it is repeated in the buffer until it is released. Yet when the Shift key is held down, for instance, the keyboard remains in shifted status until the key is released.

239

The Keyboard

An addition to interrupt 09h could detect repeat codes and modify the action accordingly.

The only time the results may be not as expected is when another key is pressed during an automatic repeat; the original key is forgotten and the new key is repeated. For example, pressing Shift in the middle of a sequence results in the Shift code being repeated and no more repeats for the original character.

The repeat action itself is beyond the control of the programmer. The time before a repeat sequence starts and the frequency of the repeat codes are values that are built into the keyboard controller program and therefore cannot be changed.

Keyboard crash

On some early PC1512's this key-repeat action could cause the system to crash. Holding down a key for a long period may result in the message:

```
Fatal Internal Stack Error - System Halted
```

Such machines can be identified by the ROS version number that is shown on the screen when the system is booted. The early versions use a lower case 'v' for the number (v1.0) while later models used capital 'V' (V1.0).

There appears to be no way of overcoming the problem on these older machines, apart from avoiding holding down keys for any length of time.

Note that this message may also be caused by insufficient stack space for handling hardware interrupts.

DUPLICATE KEYS

A number of keys are duplicated on the keyboard. These include the number keys, the Shift keys and a variety of symbols (. + - *). The Return key appears as an Enter key on the numeric keypad. There is also a wealth of Delete keys.

Most programs ignore the distinction between the keys but it is possible to detect the difference and act upon it. This is most frequently used to give a different meaning to Return and Enter but other options can be devised.

Each of these duplicate keys has a different scan code but each pair shares the same ASCII code. Therefore the two-byte codes that are stored in the buffer will be different. The low byte tells the program what character has been selected but determination of the precise key can still be achieved by inspecting the high byte. A program can therefore have different actions for different keys.

Since this information is held in the buffer and the buffer can be accessed by high-level languages, the decision can sometimes be made at quite a high level. (However, some languages - such as BASIC - discard the scan code if a valid ASCII code is detected.) This can only be done with those keys that send a code to the buffer; to determine which Shift key is being pressed, for example, it is still necessary to check the keyboard status bytes. Of course, most high-level languages allow the inspection of individual memory locations.

CONTROL CODES

When the Ctrl key is used in combination with any of the letter keys the program interprets this as an ASCII value between 01h and 1Ah. The combination Ctrl-@ generates the code 00h while the use of Ctrl with the symbols [\ ] ^ _ produces codes 1Bh to 1Fh. These 32 codes are the ASCII *control codes*.

Although their use is open to interpretation by each individual program they form a set of recognised instructions to perform specific operations. Some of these are extremely widely used: for example, 0Dh for a carriage return and 0Ch for a form feed. Sending an 0Dh to the screen routines generally moves the cursor to the left of the screen; most printers interpret this code as an instruction to move the print head to the left-hand side of the carriage. Code 0Ch is recognised by most printers as an instruction to feed the paper to the top of the next sheet.

Each of these codes has a standard name and abbreviation associated with it. The control codes were listed in Figure 3.8.

THE ALT CODES

The Alt key works in a similar way to Ctrl, in that it is used to modify the effect of the character keys. If Alt is being held down the low byte of the translated code is 0 and the high byte holds an adjusted scan code. There are Alt codes for all character keys. If both Alt and Ctrl are being pressed then Alt takes precedence.

There is also a special case when the keys on the numeric keypad are pressed in combination with Alt. The numbers are interpreted as a direct ASCII code. This code is built up in memory, at location 0419h, until the Alt key is released. At this stage the ASCII code is sent to the buffer. There is no limit to the number of keys that can be pressed while Alt is down but only the last three are used; if there are less than three the number is still valid. If the number is greater than 255 then it is converted to a number mod 256.

This action provides a simple method of producing the extended graphics characters in the range 128 to 255, although it works equally well for standard ASCII characters. For example, holding down Alt and then pressing 4 and 6 produces a full stop, while Alt-246 gives the divide symbol and Alt-462 displays the intersection of two double-lines.

The first 32 Alt-codes give the equivalent of the Control codes. Num Lock and the Shift keys have no effect on the result.

In this special case the low byte of the code sent to the keyboard buffer is the calculated ASCII code while the high byte (where the scan code would be expected) is zero, indicating an Alt code.

THE KEYBOARD INTERRUPTS

There is a range of services provided by the ROS and MS-DOS interrupts for accessing the keyboard buffer and status bytes (Figure 11.7).

It is important to note that the DOS functions are effective for the *standard input device*. Although this defaults to the keyboard, any reassignment of the standard input device will affect the outcome.

ACCESSING THE BUFFER

Once the keyboard buffer begins to fill up we can use the codes that are stored there. Access to the buffer is provided through ROS interrupt 16h, which has two functions that allow us to check the buffer. DOS also has similar functions.

Getting a character from the buffer

The first function of interrupt 16h is used whenever a program has to wait for keyboard input.

Interrupt: 16h
Function: 00h

The keyboard interrupts		
Interrupt	Function	Service
16	00	Read character from keyboard
	01	Read character if available
	02	Get keyboard status
21	01	Keyboard input with echo
	06	Keyboard input/screen output
	07	Keyboard input without echo (without break)
	08	Keyboard input without echo (with break)
	0A	Keyboard string input
	0B	Check keyboard buffer
	0C	Clear keyboard buffer, call function

Figure 11.7 The keyboard interrupts

Service: Read character from keyboard
Entry values: AH=00h
Exit values: AH=scan code
AL=character

The function places the ASCII value in AL and scan code in AH, and then removes the character from the buffer. Since we have both parts of the key code we can tell precisely which key was pressed, should that be necessary. We can also test for all the key combinations, such as the control codes and Alt codes. Any ASCII values created through the Alt-keypad combination are also reported, with the scan code set to 0. The only keys not catered for are the special combinations (Ctrl-Break, etc.) which never make it as far as the buffer.

If the keyboard buffer is empty the interrupt waits until there is a valid key press. The only way of interrupting this delay is by using one of the special combinations, such as Ctrl-Break.

A similar effect can be achieved with the DOS keyboard functions, although these provide a wider range of possibilities.

The Keyboard

Interrupt:	21h
Function:	08h
DOS version:	1
Service:	Keyboard input without echo (with break)
Entry values:	AH=08h
Exit values:	AL=character

Interrupt:	21h
Function:	07h
DOS version:	1
Service:	Keyboard input without echo (without break)
Entry values:	AH=07h
Exit values:	AL=character

Interrupt:	21h
Function:	01h
DOS version:	1
Service:	Keyboard input with echo
Entry values:	AH=01h
Exit values:	AL=character

All three of these functions collect a character from the buffer or, if the buffer is empty, wait for a key press. Unlike the ROS service, they do not necessarily return the entire character in one operation. Instead, they initially return the ASCII part of the buffer code in AL. If this is a valid ASCII code (greater than 0) the second byte is removed from the buffer and lost. If the value is 0 (indicating a special key, such as a function key or Ins) the scan code is left in the buffer. It is up to our programs to check for this situation and clear the second code. The second call returns the scan code in AL, which gives us the ASCII code.

The main disadvantage of using the DOS functions rather than those of the ROS is that there is no way of telling which actual key was pressed, unless it is one of the special key combinations. Therefore, you should use the ROS function when the precise key press is critical.

All three of the functions 01h, 07h and 08h wait for a key press if the buffer is empty. Functions 01h and 08h have the added facility that they respond to the break key (Ctrl-Break or Ctrl-C) by issuing interrupt 23h. Function 07h cannot be interrupted by pressing the break key.

```
GETNUMKY:                               ; Get a number from a key press
                                        ; Entry values: CL=max. number (0 - 9)
nexkey:
            mov ah,07h
            int 21h                     ; Get a key press
            cmp al,00h
            jg notspk                   ; Jump if not special code
            int 021                     ; Otherwise, get scan code for special
            jmp nexkey                  ;   and get another key

notspk:
            cmp al,30h                  ; Is key before numbers?
            jl nexkey                   ; Jump if ASCII code  30h ('0')
            sub al,30h                  ; Get key value
            cmp al,cl                   ; Is it less than Ch?
            jg nexkey                   ; If not, get another key
            ret
; ------------------------------------------------------------------
GETYN:                                  ; Get Y or N after prompt

                                        ; Calls DISSTR (Figure 13.16)

                                        ; Entry values: None
                                        ; Exit values:  AL=0 for Y, 1 for N

            jmp ynst

prompt      db 'Are you sure (Y/N)?$'

ynst:
            lea dx,prompt
            call disstr
nexyn:
            mov ah,07h
            int 21h                     ; Get key press
            cmp al,60h                  ; Is it upper case?
            jl ucase                    ; If yes, skip
            sub al,20h                  ; Else, convert to upper case
ucase:
            push ax
            sub al,59h
            jz yes                      ; Is it Y?
            pop ax                      ; Jump if so (in which case AL=0)
            cmp al,4Eh                  ; Is it N?
            jnz nexyn                   ; If not, get another
            mov al,01h                  ; If so, set AL=1
yes:
            ret
```

Figure 11.8 Getting a character

The Keyboard

Function 01h immediately echoes the character to the screen. This can be a useful way of combining two functions in a single operation.

Figure 11.8 uses these functions to return a key press from the user.

Report next character

Sometimes we need to know what the next character is going to be, before deciding how to deal with it.

Interrupt: 16h
Function: 01h
Service: Read character if available
Entry values: AH=01h
Exit values: AH=scan code
AL=character
ZF=(0 (character available)
   (1 (buffer empty)

In this case the function returns the 2-byte code in AX (if there is one), as for function 00h; the zero flag indicates whether or not there is a character in the buffer.

The other feature of the function is that the buffer is left intact; to remove the character you must follow on with a call to function 00h.

The point of this function is that the program is not tied up if the buffer is empty.

The DOS version of this service is function 0Bh.

Interrupt: 21h
Function: 0Bh
DOS version: 1
Service: Check keyboard buffer
Entry values: Ah=0B
Exit values: AL=(00h (buffer empty)
   (FFh (character available)

If there is a character waiting in the buffer, AL contains FFh; if the buffer is empty its value is 00h. Any loop that waits for a key press using this function can be interrupted with Ctrl-Break or Ctrl-C.

This function leaves the buffer unchanged.

The Keyboard

The final option in this group of services is one of the options of DOS function 06h.

Interrupt:	21h
Function:	06h
DOS version:	1
Service:	Keyboard input/screen output
Entry values:	AH=06h
	DL=(FFh (input)
	(character (output)
Exit values:	AL=input character
	ZF=(0 (character available)
	(1 (buffer empty)

This rather unusual function is used for both keyboard input and screen output. For keyboard input DL must be set to FFh before the interrupt is called. Again, the zero flag is used to indicate whether or not there is a character waiting.

This function has an advantage over its ROS counterpart in that the ASCII value is returned in AL. For a special key, AL is 0 and the function must be repeated to get the scan code.

Clearing the buffer

Sometimes it is useful to let the user choose a series of options by quickly typing them in; on other occasions we may want the program to display some message in full before allowing the user to proceed. In this latter case, any key presses stored up in the buffer must be discarded. Interrupt 16h, functions 00h and 01h provide us with a simple means of clearing the keyboard buffer, an essential procedure when we want to make sure that any extraneous key presses are not going to upset the flow of the program. Clearly this cannot be achieved with function 00h alone, since this function always waits for a key press. Therefore we need to repeat a loop in which the program checks the buffer and reads a character if there is one, continuing until the buffer is empty (Figure 11.9).

An alternative is to clear the buffer using DOS function 0Ch.

Interrupt:	21
Function:	0Ch
DOS version:	1
Service:	Clear keyboard buffer, call interrupt 21h function
Entry values:	AH=0Ch

247

The Keyboard

```
BUFRCLR:                        ; Clear the buffer

                                ; Entry values: None
                                ; Exit values: Flags changed
nextchar:
        mov  ah,01h
        int  16h                ; Check buffer
        jnz  empty              ; Jump if no character available
        mov  al, 00h            ; Otherwise, read character
        int  16h
        jmp  nextchar           ; and repeat loop

empty:
        ret
```

Figure 11.9 Clearing the buffer

                    AL=function (01h, 06h, 07h, 08h, 0Ah)
Exit values: (Various - as for selected function)

The function reads and discards each character in turn. It then continues with one of the other interrupt 21h functions (01h, 06h, 07h, 08h or 0Ah), depending on the value in AL. The effect of this function is therefore as follows:

AL=01h	Clear buffer, wait for key press and display character (responds to break)
AL=06h, DL=FFh	Clear buffer, do nothing else
AL=06h, DL=char.	Clear buffer, display character
AL=07h	Clear buffer, wait for key press (no break)
AL=08h	Clear buffer, wait for key press (responds to break)
AL=0Ah	Clear buffer, input string (see below)

The only option that requires further explanation is when AL=06h and DL=FFh. In the normal course of events, function 06h checks whether the buffer is empty and returns a character if there is one. Since the buffer is empty, the function cannot return a character in this instance.

The Keyboard

Interrupting a program

Either interrupt 16h, function 01h or interrupt 21h, function 0Bh can be used when a program is to be interrupted by a keystroke. At regular intervals the program can test to see if the buffer is still empty, acting upon the key press as soon as it is received.

String inputs

Much of the time we want to get a whole string of data from the keyboard, rather than just a single character. This can require some complicated programming. One option would be to program a loop that accepts a series of characters until Return is pressed, allowing for the Del keys to rub out unwanted characters. However, DOS provides an interrupt function that takes a lot of the hassle out of reading a string of characters from the keyboard.

Interrupt:	21h
Function:	0Ah
Service:	Keyboard string input
Entry values:	AH=0Ah
	DS:DX=start of input buffer
Exit values:	None

This function allows the user to input a string of text, up to a maximum length determined by the programmer. It takes care of all the usual editing facilities.

The program must identify the area in memory where the text is to be stored, which is pointed to by DS:DX. The first byte at this location (which must be set before the interrupt is called) is the maximum number of characters to be input, up to 253 (including the Return).

DOS uses the second byte to return the number of characters in the string (excluding the Return character). The string itself starts at the third byte and ends with a Return character (0Dh). When setting aside space in memory for the input buffer remember to allow two characters for the information passed to and from the interrupt routine and one for the Return character.

For example, if we want to get an eight-character filename the space needed in all is 11 (0Bh) characters. After the user has typed the name 'CONFIG' the space will look like this:

```
0B 06 43 4F 4E 46 49 47 0D ?? ??
```

The Keyboard

(The last two, unused bytes will still contain whatever values were originally stored in that part of memory.)

Since DOS tells us how many characters there are there is no need to search for the Return character. The routine in Figure 11.10 allows the entry of a filename and extension.

Once the interrupt has been called the programmer loses control until the user presses either Return or Ctrl-Break.

This function is particularly useful when any single line of input is required and the DOS editing facilities are deemed to be adequate. Where any sort of error checking is required during input (for example, to ensure that only numbers are typed in numeric input) this function will not suffice.

It is this function that is used by most high-level languages for input, although these do not usually restrict input length. Thus, accessing the function directly provides added flexibility and sophistication to our routines.

The following keys can be used during the input:

← Del	Delete last character
←	Delete last character
Return	Complete entry
Ctrl-Break	Abandon entry

If the maximum number of non-Return characters have been typed and the next character is not Return, DOS makes the computer beep and the extra character is ignored.

Parsing the command line

Many DOS commands allow the user to include filenames and parameters in the command line. To make use of this extra information DOS must extract each separate piece of text. It locates filenames by searching for spaces in the command line; parameters are identified by checking for '/' characters. This process is called *parsing*.

```
GETFNAME:                           ; Get a filename

                                    ; Limitations - no error checking

                                    ; Calls DISSTR (Figure 13.16)

                                    ; Entry values: None
                                    ; Exit values:  FNAME=filename
                                    ;               AX,DX,DI changed
                jmp getfnamest

entry:
inlen           db 0d
rtlen           db ?
fname           db ? dup 0d
fnmes           db 'Enter file name: $'

getfnamest:
                lea dx,fnmes        ; Point to FNMES
                call disstr         ; Display prompt
                lea dx,entry        ; Point to ENTRY
                mov ah,0a
                int 21h             ; Get name from user
                ret
; - - - - - - - - - - - - - - - - - - - - - - - - - - - - - - - -

FNAMETEST:                          ; Test routine to get filename

                                    ; Calls GETFNAME, DISSTR, NEWLIN
                                    ;              (Figure 13.16)

                call getfname
                mov al,[rtlen]      ; Get length of name
                xor ah,ah
                mov di,ax
                mov fname[di],24h   ; Add '$' to name
                lea dx,fname        ; Point to name
                call newlin
                call disstr         ; Display name
                int 20h
```

Figure 11.10 Entering a filename and extension

12. *The Mouse, Light Pen and Joystick*

Most of the time, the keyboard provides our main means of inputting information into the computer. The Amstrad PC has provision for a number of other methods for getting data into the machine. Three other devices are allowed for: the mouse, an optional joystick and light pen. These three devices are the subject of this chapter. The other forms of input - the disk drives and serial port - are covered in later chapters.

THE MOUSE

All Amstrad PC's are supplied with a *mouse* as standard. This mouse plugs into the system unit through a 9-way female DIN socket, located next to the keyboard connector (Figure 12.1). This socket will not accept any other type of mouse and any attempt to do so may be damaging to both the mouse and the PC. Any other mouse (such as the Microsoft mouse) should be connected via the expansion slots.

There are two ways of getting information from the mouse:

- By reading and writing the appropriate ports

- By running the MOUSE.COM program which provides access to the MS-DOS mouse interrupts

By far the simplest - and safest - method is that provided by MOUSE.SYS but the ports are worth considering since they provide an insight into the workings of the mouse.

There are a large number of interrupts and functions relating to the mouse (Figure 12.2).

MOUSE OPERATION

The mouse sends input to the computer in two different ways. The output from the two buttons is connected directly to two pins on the keyboard connector. These produce scan codes 7Dh (right) and 7Eh (left), and release codes FDh and FEh respectively.

When these scan codes are being translated into 2-byte codes to be put in the keyboard buffer the routine uses the two

The Mouse, Light Pen and Joystick

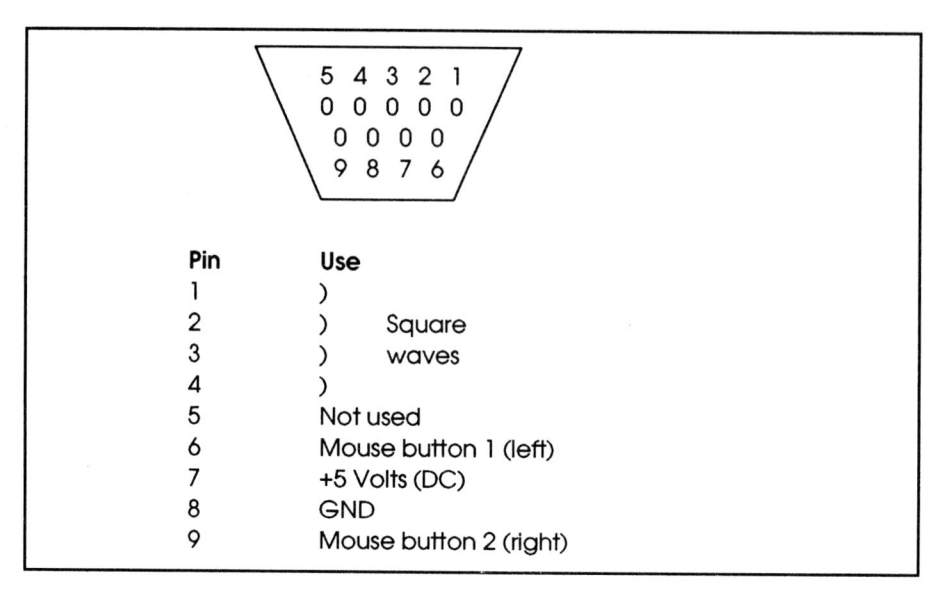

```
      5 4 3 2 1
      0 0 0 0 0
       0 0 0 0
       9 8 7 6
```

Pin	Use
1	)
2	) Square
3	) waves
4	)
5	Not used
6	Mouse button 1 (left)
7	+5 Volts (DC)
8	GND
9	Mouse button 2 (right)

Figure 12.1 The mouse connector

Interrupt	Function	Use
06		User-defined interrupt
33	00	Initialise mouse
	01	Show mouse cursor
	02	Hide mouse cursor
	03	Get mouse information
	04	Set mouse cursor
	05	Get mouse button press
	06	Get mouse button release
	07	Set mouse cursor horizontal limits
	08	Set mouse cursor vertical limits
	09	Define mouse graphics cursor
	0A	Define mouse text cursor
	0B	Read mouse counts
	0C	Set mouse interrupt
	0D	Turn light pen emulation on
	0E	Turn light pen emulation off
	0F	Set mickey:pixel ratio
	10	Hide mouse cursor while updating
	13	Set threshold for double speed

Figure 12.2 The mouse interrupts

The Mouse, Light Pen and Joystick

special values in the NVR (at bytes 1Dh - 20h) for the translation. The default is for both buttons to produce scan codes and ASCII codes of FFh.

Any other values can be put into the NVR. To make the buttons replicate other keys all that is necessary is to put the relevant ASCII code into the low byte. For example, to make the buttons act as Return and Esc the translation codes could be FF0Dh and FF1Bh. The scan code of FFh can be used by a program to distinguish between the mouse and the real Return or Esc key.

The internal mouse circuits maintain a pair of (X,Y) counters. They indicate the movement of the mouse since the values were last checked; they do not provide co-ordinates relative to the screen, since the mouse has no way of knowing where the pointer is on the screen. These counters are increased or decreased by any movement of the roller as follows:

Right	Increase X counter
Left	Decrease X counter
Forwards	Increase Y counter
Backwards	Decrease Y counter

Every movement of $\frac{1}{8}$mm ($\frac{1}{200}$th inch) changes the counters by 1.

The values of the counters can be read from ports 78h and 7Ah. Reading these ports also clears the values. Each counter can take values in the range -32768 to 32767. If these values are not read frequently enough then they can overflow.

An alternative, more straightforward method is provided by one of the NVR interrupt functions.

Interrupt: 15h
Function: 00h
Service: Read mouse counters
Entry value: AH=00h
Exit value: CX=X counter
DX=Y counter
All flags changed

255

The Mouse, Light Pen and Joystick

This returns the X and Y counter values and then clears their contents. The function reads the registers twice, to make sure the mouse is not still moving; if it is moving, it repeats the process until the counts are the same twice in succession.

A similar service is provided by the mouse interrupt (interrupt 33h, function 0Bh - see below).

MOUSE.COM AND MOUSE.SYS

To use the mouse two files are needed:

- MOUSE.COM - the program which installs the mouse and sets up the mouse interrupts

- MOUSE.SYS - the mouse device driver

The version of MS-DOS 3.2 that is provided with the Amstrad PC includes a set of services (in interrupt 33h) that controls the operation of the mouse. Before they can be used you must run the MOUSE.COM program; this is usually done by including the 'MOUSE' command in AUTOEXEC.BAT.

These interrupt functions are totally compatible with those provided by the industry-standard Microsoft Bus Mouse. Therefore any program written to take advantage of interrupt 33h should work satisfactorily on other computers that have the Microsoft Mouse or a compatible mouse.

The device driver must be loaded when the system is booted. Therefore CONFIG.SYS must include an instruction in the form:

```
DEVICE = MOUSE.SYS
```

Once you have run MOUSE.COM, the mouse remains installed until the system is reset.

Installing the mouse

When the MOUSE program is run it displays the message to tell you that it is installing the MOUSE. Two error messages may be displayed:

```
MOUSE: Mouse Driver already installed
```

This message is displayed if you run MOUSE.COM a second time. It may also indicate that some other program is obstructing the routine that installs the mouse.

```
              MOUSE: Amstrad Mouse not found
```

This indicates that there is a fault with the mouse or that it is not connected. This message will also be displayed if you try to run the Amstrad version of MOUSE.COM on another type of computer.

MOUSE.COM replaces two of the standard interrupts with versions of its own:

- Interrupt 08h, which produces clock ticks every 0.054 seconds, is replaced by an interrupt that speeds this up to three times the normal rate, with a tick every 0.018 seconds. The purpose of this is to produce smoother movement of the mouse pointer.

- Interrupt 06h becomes the Mouse Button interrupt routine.

The 8253 Interrupt Controller is also programmed so that Counter 0 produces an interrupt every 0.018 seconds (instead of 0.054 seconds).

Various defaults are set:

- The X and Y counters are set to 0

- The scaling factors for movement are read from the NVR (see below)

- The mouse is assumed to be in text mode

- The mouse cursor position is set to the middle of the screen

All these values are stored as a set of parameters. These are listed, with their defaults, in Figure 12.3.

At any time the mouse can be re-initialised using the first of the interrupt 33h functions.

Interrupt: 33h
Function: 00h
Service: Initialise mouse
Entry value: AH=00h

The Mouse, Light Pen and Joystick

Parameter	Default
X counter	0
Y counter	0
Mickey:pixel ratios:	
Horizontal	8:8
Vertical	16:8
Mode	Text
Text cursor	Reverse character
Cursor position	Centre of screen
Graphics cursor	Arrow
Cursor visibility	Hidden
Focal point	-1,-1
Screen Mask	0000
Horizontal limits	0,639
Vertical limits	0,199
Light pen emulation	On

Figure 12.3 The mouse defaults

    Exit value: AL=(FFh (mouse installed)
                          (00h (no mouse found)
                      BL=number of buttons

All parameters are reset to their defaults.

Side effects of MOUSE.COM

The fact that MOUSE.COM changes the tick rate can cause problems when working with some applications. Microsoft programs, for example, notice that the clock has been speeded up and automatically allow for this by slowing it down again. Thus we get the effect that after spending three hours in QuickBasic, only an hour appears to have passed. This is only a temporary problem. The time stored in the NVR is not affected, so when the system is rebooted the time will have corrected itself.

The problem can be overcome in a number of ways:

- Do not run MOUSE.COM unless you really need to use the mouse.

- Install a Microsoft serial mouse.

The Mouse, Light Pen and Joystick

- Get hold of a doctored MOUSE.COM; there are several versions around but they do give the pointer a jerkier movement.

Apart from this minor difficulty, MOUSE.COM does not appear to cause any problems when installed with other software.

THE MOUSE CURSOR

When the mouse is installed it is represented on the screen by a cursor. The form of this cursor depends on the current display mode:

- In text modes, the cursor moves from character to character and takes the form of an inverse character.

- In graphics modes, the cursor moves a pixel at a time and is represented by an arrow.

As the mouse is moved the cursor moves correspondingly on the screen. All movement and the appearance of the cursor are automatically taken care of by the mouse driver. The way in which the mouse works can be varied.

Moving the mouse cursor

The mouse cursor can be moved to a new position on the screen with function 04h of interrupt 33h.

```
Interrupt:      33h
Function:       04h
Service:        Set mouse cursor
Entry value:    AH=04h
                CX=X co-ordinate
                DX=Y co-ordinate
Exit value:     None
```

The X co-ordinate (horizontal position) must be in the range 0 to 639 while the Y co-ordinate (vertical position) has a range of 0 to 199. The full range is always used, even in text modes; for example, the rightmost position is always 639, regardless of display mode. Therefore a calculation is needed to determine the co-ordinates in those modes where the number of available pixels (graphics modes) or characters (text modes) differs from 640 x 200.

For example, in 80-column, 25-row text modes, the co-ordinates for a particular character position are calculated from:

The Mouse, Light Pen and Joystick

$$X \text{ co-ordinate} = \text{column} \times 8 \quad (\text{Column} = 0,...,79)$$

$$Y \text{ co-ordinate} = \text{row} \times 8 \quad (\text{Row} = 0,...,24)$$

Graphics mode positions are scaled in a similar way.

Cursor limits

Initially, the cursor can move anywhere on the screen. However, you can restrict the area in which the cursor moves.

Interrupt: 33h
Function: 07h
Service: Set mouse cursor horizontal limits
Entry value: AH=07h
CX=minimum X co-ordinate
DX=maximum X co-ordinate
Exit value: None

Interrupt: 33h
Function: 08h
Service: Set mouse cursor vertical limits
Entry value: AH=08h
CX=minimum Y co-ordinate
DX=maximum Y co-ordinate
Exit value: None

These two functions set the minimum and maximum values for the X and Y co-ordinates respectively, effectively marking a rectangle on the screen to contain the cursor.

Cursor appearance

The default appearance of the cursor, in both text and graphics modes, can be changed. The cursor is affected by two factors:

■ The *screen mask* determines the shape of the cursor

■ The *cursor mask* sets the relative attributes of the cursor

These masks are binary values that determine the appearance of the cursor.

In text modes each mask is a word in length. A logical AND operation is performed between the bytes storing the screen data (attribute and character) and the screen mask; there is then a logical XOR between the result and the cursor mask. The way in which the screen data is stored is explained in full in the next chapter.

The Mouse, Light Pen and Joystick

There is a limit to the number of 'sensible' values that can be given to the masks.

One service sets the mouse cursor in text modes.

Interrupt: 33h
Function: 0Ah
Service: Define mouse text cursor
Entry value: AH=0Ah
BL=(0 (Software cursor)
    (1 (Hardware cursor)
CX=(Screen mask(BL=0)
    (First scan line(BL=1)
DX=(Cursor mask (BL=0)
    (Last scan line(BL=1)
Exit value: None

If the software option is selected (BL=0) the cursor is determined in the manner described above.

For a hardware cursor (BL=1) the cursor mimics the standard screen cursor, consisting of a set of raster lines (as described in the next chapter).

In graphics modes we have far more control over the cursor. The graphics cursor consists of a 16 x 16 pixel block. Each of the two masks consists of 16 words, where each word corresponds to a row of 16 pixels. The first word relates to the top row of the cursor, the last corresponds to the bottom row. The bits in each word are mapped onto the bits in the row, bit 15 being the leftmost pixel.

The shape of the cursor is determined by the screen mask. A 0 bit includes the pixel in the shape, a 1 excludes it. The colour is set by the cursor mask. Within the cursor the colour can be either of the logical colours 0 or 1; outside the cursor (in the 16 x 16 block) the colour either stays the same as the background or is inverted. The precise appearance of the cursor at any position is determined in the same way as for the text cursor; the driver carries out a logical AND between the existing display and the screen mask, followed by an XOR with the cursor mask.

As well as setting the shape and colour of the graphics cursor, we also need to specify the *focal point*. This is the pixel that is to be used to determine the position of the cursor on the screen. For example, the focal point of the default graphics cursor is the tip of the arrow; if the cursor is defined as a cross then the focal point will be the centre of the cross, since this is the point the user will manoeuvre on the screen.

Unless we specify otherwise the focal point is the top left-hand corner of the cursor block. Any other point is calculated as an offset relative to this point, up to a maximum of 16 pixels in any direction.

The masks and focal point are all defined with a single function.

Interrupt: 33h
Function: 09h
Service: Define mouse graphics cursor
Entry value: AH=09h
    BX=X co-ordinate offset
    CX=Y co-ordinate offset
    ES:DX=address of screen and cursor masks
Exit value: None

Once the cursor has been defined it can be moved around on the screen with function 04h.

Hiding the mouse cursor

Both types of cursor (the normal screen cursor and the mouse cursor) can be displayed on the screen at the same time. However, it makes sense to turn the screen cursor off when using the mouse, and vice versa.

Two functions are provided to hide and show the mouse cursor.

Interrupt: 33h
Function: 02h
Service: Hide mouse cursor
Entry value: AH=02h
Exit value: None

Interrupt: 33h
Function: 01h
Service: Show mouse cursor
Entry value: AH=01h
Exit value: None

In the first case the mouse cursor is no longer displayed (though its logical position is retained); the second function redisplays the cursor. The normal screen cursor can be turned on and off with the functions described in the next chapter.

Function 10h provides a more complicated method of hiding the screen.

Interrupt: 33h
Function: 10h
Service: Hide mouse cursor while updating
Entry value: AH=10h
CX=top left X co-ordinate
DX=top left Y co-ordinate
SI=bottom right X co-ordinate
DI=bottom right Y co-ordinate
Exit value: None

This function hides the mouse cursor while the screen is being updated and defines a rectangle where the update is to occur. This function is used for much faster updates than can be achieved with function 02h. As with that function, the cursor can only be redisplayed with function 01h.

Relative movement

In its default setting, each increment of the X and Y counters represents physical movement of the mouse of $^1/_8$mm (approximately 0.005 inches). This is translated into a single unit in the screen co-ordinates (i.e. one pixel for high resolution displays). This ratio can be changed.

Almost unbelievably, the unit of mouse movement for each unit on the screen is called the *mickey*. Thus 1 mickey = 0.005 inches and the default mickey:pixel ratio is 1:1. The ratio is changed with function 0Fh.

Interrupt: 33h
Function: 0Fh
Service: Set mickey:pixel ratio
Entry value: AH=0Fh
CX=X ratio (per 8 units)
DX=Y ratio (per 8 units)
Exit value: None

Each ratio is given in terms of the number of mickeys for each 8 units on the screen. The default values are 8 and 16 (giving a 1:1 ratio horizontally and 2:1 ratio vertically). Reducing the ratio value to 1 moves the cursor faster, each mickey moving the cursor eight pixels (i.e. one full character in most text modes). Increasing the value to, say, 32 results in much slower movement, with 4 mickeys needed for each pixel on high resolution screens. The physical distances moved by the mouse to move the cursor across the full screen width in these examples are 0.4" and 12.8" respectively (compared with the default 3.2").

To make a permanent change in the default mickey:pixel ratios we can change the values stored in the NVR. (These are the defaults adopted by the mouse each time MOUSE.COM is run.) To do so, use the NVR interrupt 15h, function 01h with AL set to 21h (X ratio) or 22h (Y ratio) and the new ratio in BL.

Mouse speed

A further refinement allows us to double the speed of the pointer when the mouse is moved quickly.

Interrupt:	33h
Function:	13h
Service:	Set threshold for double speed
Entry value:	AH=13h
	DX=threshold speed (mickeys/second)
Exit value:	None

The mouse driver is able to calculate the speed of the mouse movement (in terms of mickeys/second). This function sets a threshold; when the mouse speed reaches this threshold its relative movement on the screen is doubled.

The default is 64 mickeys/second. This is also the threshold that is set for the special case when DX is 0. To keep the cursor at normal speed set a high threshold. (The maximum value is 32767.)

Mouse movement

Function 0Bh returns the total movement since the last call.

Interrupt:	33h
Function:	0Bh
Service:	Read mouse counts
Entry value:	AH=0Bh
Exit value:	CX=X count
	DX=Y count

This count is reset each time the function is called but is unaffected by calls to any other function.

MOUSE BUTTONS AND POSITION

Having selected a point on the screen with the mouse the user must be able to indicate some course of action. This could be done via the keyboard; however, mixing mouse and keyboard operations is not very successful and therefore the usual procedure is to do everything with the mouse, using the two buttons to select an activity.

The advantages of using the mouse buttons are that the user does not need to take his hand off the mouse and also that the buttons can be used in a surprising number of ways: double-clicking, shift-clicking, dragging and so on.

One method of getting mouse button information is through the relevant keyboard scan codes. However, for applications where a specific type of button-press is required this can be rather cumbersome, so functions 05h and 06h provide a far more efficient method.

Interrupt: 33h
Function: 05h
Service: Get mouse button press
Entry value: AH=05h
　　　　　　　BL=(0 (left button)
　　　　　　　　　(1 (right button)
Exit value: AX=(0 (button not pressed)
　　　　　　　　(1 (button pressed)
　　　　　　　BX=number of presses since last call
　　　　　　　CX=X co-ordinate at last press
　　　　　　　DX=Y co-ordinate at last press

This function can be used to test each button in turn, to decide which one is currently being pressed. It also tells us how many times the button has been pressed since we last checked and the position of the cursor on the screen the last time the button was pressed.

Interrupt: 33h
Function: 06h
Service: Get mouse button release
Entry value: AH=00h
　　　　　　　BL=(0 (left button)
　　　　　　　　　(1 (right button)
Exit value: AX=(0 (button not pressed)

The Mouse, Light Pen and Joystick

        (1 (button pressed)
        BX=number of presses since last call
        CX=X co-ordinate at last release
        DX=Y co-ordinate at last release

This function is very similar to function 05h, but gives the number of button releases.

A simpler method for checking the button is given by function 03h.

Interrupt:	33h
Function:	03h
Service:	Get mouse information
Entry value:	AH=03h
Exit value:	BX=button status
	CX=X co-ordinate
	DX=Y co-ordinate

Note that in this case the button status is given in BX (rather than AX) and is defined as follows:

0   No button pressed

1   Left button pressed

2   Right button pressed

3   Both buttons pressed

CX and DX give the current cursor position.

Interrupt 06h   Interrupt 06h is reserved for a programmable mouse interrupt. Initially there is only a dummy interrupt, which has no effect. it is sometimes useful to install an interrupt that is activated every time the mouse moves or a button is pressed. We can do this using interrupt 33h function 0Ch.

Interrupt:	33h
Function:	0Ch
Service:	Set mouse interrupt
Entry value:	AH=0Ch
	CX=event mask
	ES:DX=address of new interrupt
Exit value:	None

The segment and offset addresses of the new interrupt 06h are placed in ES and DX respectively. CX determines the conditions under which this interrupt is called (the *event mask*). The value of CX is determined by setting individual bits as follows:

01h	(bit 0)	Act when cursor position changed
02h	(bit 1)	Act when left button pressed
04h	(bit 2)	Act when left button released
08h	(bit 3)	Act when right button pressed
10h	(bit 4)	Act when right button released

Once the new interrupt 06h has been installed it is called whenever one of the required events occurs. For example, if the new routine is to be called when either button is pressed, but in no other event, the value of CX should be set to 0Ah.

The mouse information passed to the interrupt includes the current button status (defined as for interrupt 33h, function 03h) and the current screen co-ordinates of the mouse cursor.

Interrupt: 06h
Service: Mouse interrupt
Entry value: BX=button status
CX=X co-ordinate
DX=Y co-ordinate
Exit value: (Defined by programmer)

The mouse is checked for events at each clock tick (every 0.018 seconds).

LIGHT PEN EMULATION

The mouse can be made to emulate the light pen. Functions 0Dh and 0Eh of interrupt 33h turn this emulation on and off respectively.

Interrupt: 33h
Function: 0Dh
Service: Turn light pen emulation on
Entry value: AH=0Dh
Exit value: None

Interrupt: 33h
Function: 0Eh
Service: Turn light pen emulation off
Entry value: AH=0Eh
Exit value: None

When the emulation is turned on, any calls to interrupt 10h, function 04h return the screen co-ordinates of the mouse cursor (see below).

THE LIGHT PEN

Although a light pen is not supplied with the Amstrad PC, the system board does allow for the addition of such a device. The 6-pin light pen connector is adjacent to the expansion slots. The pins are shown in Figure 12.4.

A light pen is a fairly simple device and can be constructed quite cheaply.

The operation of the light pen is fairly basic, allowing the pen to be pointed at a location on the screen which is then translated into a pair of co-ordinates.

Interrupt: 10h
Function: 04h
Service: Get light pen information
Entry value: AH=04h
Exit value: AH=(01h (Switch set)
                    (00h (Switch clear)
                 DH=character row
                 DL=character code
                 CX=pixel row (EGA/Hercules)
                 CH=pixel row (CGA)
                 DX=pixel column

When the light pen is switched on (indicated by AH=1), this function returns its position on the screen. The screen hardware senses the position. The co-ordinates are returned in two ways, as character row and column numbers and as pixel co-ordinates. The pixel row is returned in either CX or CH, depending on whether or not the screen is in EGA mode.

The Mouse, Light Pen and Joystick

The light pen connector	
	0 0 0 0 0 0
	1 2 3 4 5 6
Pin	**Use**
1	- (Light pen input)
2	Keyway
3	- (Switch)
4	GND
5	+5 volts (DC)
6	+12 volts (DC)

Figure 12.4 The light pen connector

Note that the mouse can be made to emulate the light pen, using interrupt 33h, function 0Dh (as described above).

THE JOYSTICK

The third device to provide an alternative to keyboard input is the optional joystick. The device connects into a 9-way male D-type connector on the back of the keyboard.

The joystick is even simpler to accommodate in programs than the light pen. It has two buttons, marked 'Fire 1' and 'Fire 2', and the joystick handle can be moved up, down, left and right. Whenever it is moved a signal is sent continuously until it is released. The effect is similar to that of holding down a key. If the joystick is moved diagonally two signals are sent.

The 9-way cable has a wire for each button and each direction, as shown in Figure 12.5.

The Mouse, Light Pen and Joystick

The joystick connector

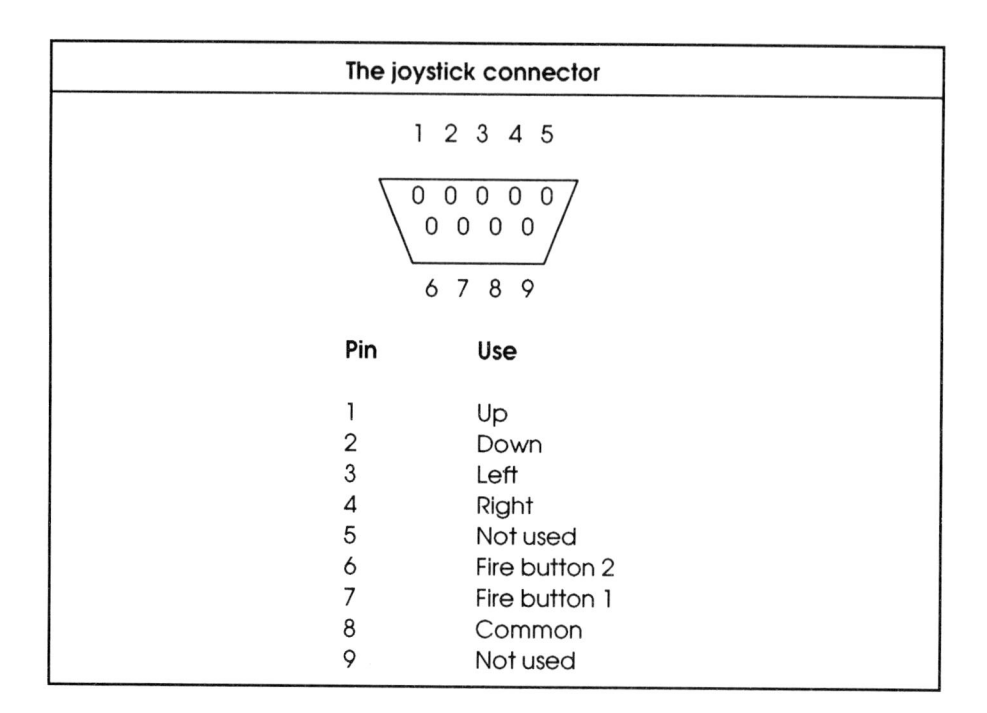

```
    1 2 3 4 5
   ╲ o o o o o ╱
    ╲ o o o o ╱
       6 7 8 9
```

Pin	Use
1	Up
2	Down
3	Left
4	Right
5	Not used
6	Fire button 2
7	Fire button 1
8	Common
9	Not used

Figure 12.5 The joystick connector

The joystick connector will accept any industry-standard joystick. Attempting to connect any device other than a joystick could be damaging to the computer's circuits.

Since the joystick is connected directly into the keyboard the signals it sends are received by the keyboard controller as scan codes; the range of codes is from 77h to 7Ch.

When the scan codes for the fire buttons are translated into ASCII codes two values in the NVR are used (bytes 19h - 1Ch). The default for both of these is FFFFh, as for the mouse buttons, but they can be changed with interrupt 15h, function 01h. The movement codes are put into the buffers as scan codes with an ASCII code of 00h.

If these additional devices are attached to the Amstrad PC, the machine becomes much more flexible as far as the user is concerned. For an even greater range of input possibilities use the serial port (see Chapter 18).

13. *The Screen*

This chapter looks at the Amstrad display options: the operation of the Amstrad display, the monitors that are available and how programs can use them to their best effect.

DISPLAY HARDWARE

The screen is probably the most complex of the Amstrad's devices. It is in constant use and the display is continually changing. Its operation depends upon the carefully-controlled interaction of a number of separate components, as well as some fairly sophisticated programming.

The main items of hardware include:

- The monitor, which actually produces the display.

- The video RAM, where the information to be displayed is stored.

- The display adapter, a card in the Amstrad that converts the information in RAM into a form that the monitor hardware can understand.

The various alternatives are described below.

Video connectors There are two connections between the monitor and the system unit. One of these carries mains power from the monitor to the system unit; the other takes information to be displayed in the other direction. This video connection on the system unit takes the form of a 9-way female D-type socket, the details of which are shown in Figure 13.1.

PIXELS AND RESOLUTION

All screen displays are made up of a rectangular grid of tiny dots called *pixels* (which, we are led to believe, is short for 'picture elements'). Each pixel can be set to any single colour. A character is generated by switching on a particular pattern of pixels. Similarly, any drawing is created by setting the colour of the pixels in the relevant positions.

The Screen

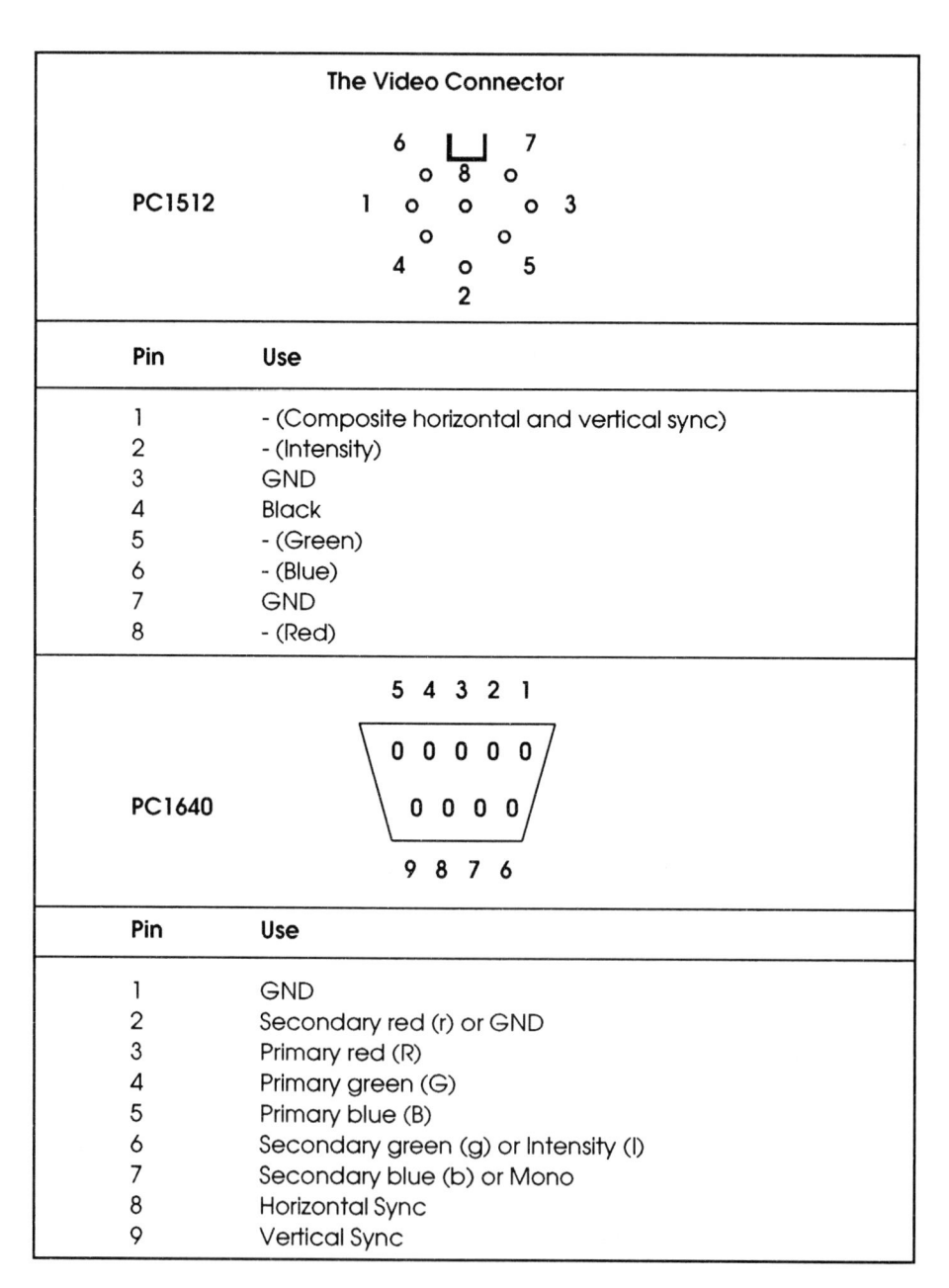

The Video Connector		
PC1512	6 ⊔ 7 ○ 8 ○ 1 ○ ○ ○ 3 ○ ○ 4 ○ 5 2	
Pin	Use	
1	- (Composite horizontal and vertical sync)	
2	- (Intensity)	
3	GND	
4	Black	
5	- (Green)	
6	- (Blue)	
7	GND	
8	- (Red)	
PC1640	5 4 3 2 1 ╱ 0 0 0 0 0 ╲ │ 0 0 0 0 │ 9 8 7 6	
Pin	Use	
1	GND	
2	Secondary red (r) or GND	
3	Primary red (R)	
4	Primary green (G)	
5	Primary blue (B)	
6	Secondary green (g) or Intensity (I)	
7	Secondary blue (b) or Mono	
8	Horizontal Sync	
9	Vertical Sync	

Figure 13.1 The video connector

The Screen

The more pixels there are, the better the picture and the more detailed it can be. The *resolution* of the screen is a qualitative measure of the density of pixels.

For Amstrad PC monitors, the number of pixels along each row is either 640 or 720, while the number in any vertical column is 200 or 350.

As with any other part of the computer system there is a variety of settings for the hardware, and trade-offs inevitably have to be made. For example, the limitations of memory mean that it is not possible to use the full resolution and the complete range of colours at the same time. If a program uses the full colour range the resolution suffers, and vice versa.

MONITORS

The Amstrad PC is supplied with a range of monitors for both the PC1512 and PC1640. The monitors for the PC1512 are different to those of the PC1640. Any monitor may be attached to any system unit of the correct type but it is not possible to switch monitors between different types of system unit (that is, a PC1512 monitor cannot be connected to a PC1640 system unit and vice versa).

There are two monitors for the PC1512, the Monochrome Monitor (MM) and the Colour Monitor (CM). The PC1640 has three monitors, referred to as the Monochrome Display (MD), the Colour Display (CD) and the Enhanced Colour Display (ECD). Two of these (the MD and ECD) are totally different in all respects to the PC1512 monitors.

The PC1512 Monochrome Monitor (MM)

This monitor has a medium resolution screen and, although technically monochrome, is actually able to display up to 16 different shades of grey. This provides it with a certain degree of graphics capability.

The resolution of the MM is 640 pixel columns across the screen by 200 rows.

The PC1512 Colour Monitor (CM)

This monitor also has a medium resolution display and is capable of displaying up to 16 colours (including black and white). The monitor can produce graphics although they are not particularly exciting.

273

The Screen

The resolution of the CM is also 640 x 200.

In fact, the CM is identical in construction to the MM, with the only exception that each colour on the CM appears on the MM as a shade of grey. The CPU and display adapter do not need to know which monitor is actually attached. The adapter believes it is sending colour signals to the monitor but these just appear on the MM screen as shades of grey. The obvious advantage of this is that any program that runs satisfactorily on the CM will run identically on the MM and vice versa. For most business applications, where colour is helpful but not essential, the MM is adequate. Text displays that are enhanced by colour will still be distinctive, if a little bland, on the MM.

The PC1640 Monochrome Display (MD)

This monitor is very different to the PC1512 MM. It is monochrome in every sense of the word, in that it can only display either black or white at each point on the screen. There are no variations in colour, no shades of grey. The only brightness in this rather dull black and white landscape is the ability to display each white dot as either high or low intensity.

When text is displayed this can appear as normal, inverse, underlined or high intensity, or any combination of these.

The trade-off is that this monitor has a high resolution of 720 x 350 pixels.

The PC1640 Colour Display (CD)

The Colour Display on the PC1640 is identical in resolution, colour and operation to the PC1512's Colour Monitor. It is medium resolution (640 x 200), displaying up to 16 colours.

The PC1640 Enhanced Colour Display (ECD)

This monitor is high resolution, capable of displaying up to 16 colours at any time from a selection of 64. The monitor can display some fairly intricate graphics. However, the disadvantage for the programmer is that a program written specifically to take advantage of the ECD's graphics capabilities will not run without modification on a lower-resolution monitor. The result is that each program requiring high resolution graphics must either be capable of switching between displays or must include overlay files for each type of monitor.

Many programmers overcome these restrictions by devising programs for the lowest possible resolution, ignoring the enhancements offered by screens such as the ECD. In fact, as

The Screen

we shall see, with a little forethought it is possible to devise generalised display routines that bypass these compatibility difficulties.

The resolution of the ECD is 640 x 350 pixels.

ADAPTER MODES

The types of display we can use depend upon the physical constraints of the monitor hardware; the way in which we use the monitor is constrained by the adapter in the system unit.

The Amstrad PC1512 has a CGA-compatible adapter, which has a single mode of operation, acting in exactly the same way as the standard CGA adapters found on many other machines.

The Amstrad PC1640 provides far more options. It has a single adapter, regardless of monitor type, called the *Internal Graphics Adapter (IGA)*. This adapter is unique to Amstrad but provides compatibility with all of the following:

- Colour Graphics Adapter (CGA)

- Extended Graphics Adapter (EGA)

- Monochrome Display Adapter (MDA)

- Hercules Monochrome Adapter (HMA)

- Plantronics Colour Adapter (PCA)

The adapter can be set to emulate any of these standard adapters. The type of emulation must be set before the computer is switched on. This is determined by the dip switches on the back of the PC1640 system unit. The first four switches are used for this purpose (Figure 13.2). The settings also determine the type of any secondary adapter that may be attached to the system (though these are only an indication to the system of what may be attached and do not imply that an adapter has actually been fitted).

If two adapters are installed then the additional, non-standard adapter can be set to be the primary adapter, as

The Screen

Switch 1	2	3	4	Adapter
OFF	OFF	ON	OFF	MD (Internal)
ON	OFF	ON	OFF	MD (Internal)
OFF	ON	ON	OFF	ECD350 (Internal)
ON	ON	ON	OFF	ECD200 (Internal)
OFF	OFF	OFF	ON	CD (Internal)
ON	OFF	OFF	ON	CD (Internal)
OFF	ON	OFF	ON	CGA (External)
ON	ON	OFF	ON	CGA (External)
OFF	OFF	ON	ON	MDA/HERC (External)
ON	OFF	ON	ON	MDA/HERC (External)
OFF	ON	ON	ON	MDA/HERC (External)
ON	ON	ON	ON	MDA/HERC (External)

Figure 13.2 The adapter dip switches

shown in the second set of switch settings. In these cases the second adapter *must* be fitted. When two adapters are fitted the user can switch output between them with the DOS MODE command.

The ECD 200-line mode gives an identical display to the standard CD display in most cases. However, some programs check the dip switch settings and assume that 350 lines can be achieved; if the monitor is, in fact, a colour display the programs will fail to produce a readable display.

Switch 5 should be OFF for EGA mode or ON for any other mode.

Switch 8 should be ON for ECD monitors or OFF for CD or MD monitors.

Although the emulation mode for the adapter can be set for different modes for any monitor, its effect is obviously limited. (An ECD monitor can emulate CGA but a CD monitor cannot display EGA screens.)

When switch 10 is OFF, switches 6, 7 and 9 select the language font (Figure 13.3); this also determines the language to

The Screen

Switch			Language
6	7	9	
Any	Any	OFF	English (diagnostic mode)
ON	ON	ON	English
OFF	OFF	ON	Danish
ON	OFF	ON	Portuguese
ON	ON	OFF	Greek

N.B. Switch 10 OFF

Figure 13.3 The language dip switches

be used by power-up error messages. All of these switches can be overridden by selecting a different country file when DOS is loaded but it is important to make the distinction:

- The dip switches select the language for hardware and ROS messages.

- The links determine the font to be used.

- The DOS KEYB programs and COUNTRY.SYS file select the key translation tables and time/date formats for any messages; these are also used by DOS or programs that run under DOS.

- If a particular application program needs to use different languages then it must sort it out itself!

When switch 10 is ON the system ignores the setting of the first four switches and assumes that an external adapter has been installed. In that case the adapter type is determined by switches 6 and 7 (Figure 13.4).

Information about the adapter is stored at 0487h in memory. The next byte stores the settings of switches 1 to 4, as shown in Figure 13.5.

The Screen

Switch		Adapter
6	7	
OFF	OFF	EGA
ON	OFF	CGA 40-column
OFF	ON	CGA 80-column
ON	ON	MDA/Hercules
N.B. Switch 10 ON		

Figure 13.4 The external adapter dip switches

Adaptor switch settings byte (0488h)	
Bit	Meaning if set
0	Dip Switch 1 OFF
1	Dip Switch 2 OFF
2	Dip Switch 3 OFF
3	Dip Switch 4 OFF
4	Always 1
5	Always 1
6	Always 1
7	Always 1

Figure 13.5 Adaptor switch settings byte (0488h)

VIDEO RAM

The PC sets aside a 128K block of memory from A0000h to BFFFFh for storing the current contents of the screen. This is called the *video RAM*. On the Amstrad PC1512 range only 16K of this memory is actually used by the standard adapters. This memory is additional to the 512K or 640K user RAM. The video RAM is physically located on the graphics adapter board.

The Screen

The PC's display is said to be *memory-mapped*. That is, for each location on the screen there is a corresponding location in memory that stores the data to be displayed.

For text displays there are generally two bytes of memory for each character position on the screen; one stores the character itself, the other its display attributes (such as the colour).

For graphics screens the situation is somewhat more confusing. The bit pattern in memory corresponds exactly to the pixel display, so there are no conversions to be made. However, the data in memory is not in the same order as the data on screen. The way in which graphics displays are stored is described later.

CREATING THE SCREEN DISPLAY

The data in memory is read by the CRT (Cathode Ray Tube) controller, which converts the bit pattern in memory into the pattern needed to create the screen display. The way in which the data is translated depends upon the type of display (text or graphics).

This new pattern is in turn translated into corresponding spots of light on the screen by turning an electron beam on and off. The beam scans the phosphorescent surface of the CRT. When a bit is set (with a value 1) the beam is turned on and the corresponding pixel is lit; when the bit is clear the beam is turned off.

Each line across the screen is called a *raster line*. The beam scans a raster line from left to right lighting up the pixels as required. The beam is then switched off while it moves back across the screen and down to the start of the next line. This is called the *horizontal retrace*. When the beam reaches the bottom right-hand corner of the screen it is turned off for a longer period so that it can return to the top left-hand corner and start again. This is the *vertical retrace* and can be an important period for enhancing the quality of the display.

Screen refresh rate

The screen is refreshed 60 times a second. That is, every one-sixtieth of a second the entire contents of the relevant portion of video RAM are read and the screen is updated accordingly. This is the time taken for the electron beam to work from top to bottom and back again. Theoretically this means that we could have a whole new display sixty times a second, providing very realistic movement for our graphics. In practice of course it doesn't work quite like this!

The Screen

The spanner in the works is the fact that the CPU cannot operate fast enough to do all the calculations that are needed and rewrite the video RAM in such a short space of time. Even filling a simple text screen with the same character at every location takes several seconds on the Amstrad PC. However, small amounts of movement can be achieved quite smoothly. The less there is to change, the faster the apparent movement on the screen.

Taking advantage of the vertical retrace

The principle of mapping memory to the physical display is a convenient one for the programmer and is also highly efficient. However, it does have its drawbacks. The main difficulty arises from the fact that the same piece of memory is being used for two things at once. On the one hand a program is filling the memory with data, updating the contents of memory every time the display is to be changed; on the other hand the memory is being constantly read to create the display.

Problems arise when the program writes to a memory location at the same time that it is being read. The resultant confusion over the contents of memory, when repeated many times over, results in a 'snow' effect.

If this becomes a problem it can be overcome by making use of the vertical retrace period. During this time nothing is being read from memory, so we can happily write the video RAM without fear of snow. This period is quite long in computer terms (1250 microseconds) and sufficient to write quite a few bytes to memory. Many programs write to the video RAM only during the vertical retrace, thus eliminating snow. This is not usually necessary on the Amstrad PC.

The trick is achieved by checking the value of the *vertical synchronisation signal*. This is a single bit that forms part of the adapter I/O port. The bit is set during vertical retrace and then cleared while the screen is actually being written. Therefore to eliminate snow a program checks the value of this bit at regular intervals and writes to memory only when the bit is set.

CHANGING THE SCREEN DISPLAY

There are four ways to change the contents of the current screen display:

- Use high level language commands

- Use the DOS interrupts to write characters, strings or pixels

- Use the ROS interrupts to write individual characters or pixels

- Write the data directly to the video RAM

Each of these is progressively faster but the trade-off is that the higher up the list you go the more assured you can be of compatibility from one system to another.

While the usual advice is to use as high a level as possible when programming, in this case the dangers are not so great. If at all possible it is advisable to use the DOS interrupts or, failing that, the ROS interrupts; if necessary, however, it is quite permissible to resort to direct writing to memory in order to increase speed or flexibility. Indeed, it is largely accepted by many programmers that the only way to get really efficient screen-handling is to program directly at the memory level.

The memory locations that are used for screen text are consistent throughout most PC's and display adapters and it is unlikely that new generations of PC's will introduce any incompatibility, unless they take a radically different approach to screen-handling. However, it is worth remembering that any time you go outside DOS to perform some activity you may be setting yourself up for future compatibility problems.

Another drawback of writing directly to memory is that any program that is created in this way may only run on a limited number of adapters. However, with a little care even this may be overcome. All monitors in the Amstrad PC range are able to use all the text modes, so the only potential problem is with graphics; and there, as we shall see later, programming the memory directly is unlikely to be a sensible option anyway.

Screen interrupts Most of the features of the screen are accessed through hardware interrupt 10h. DOS also has some screen output interrupts. As with the keyboard, the DOS interrupts all affect the standard output device. Normally this is the screen but the effect is the same on any output device.

The screen interrupts are listed in Figure 13.6.

The Screen

COLOUR
Each of the individual pixels on the screen consists of more than one component. Variations in which of these components are 'turned on' affects the colour of the pixel. The number of pixel components and their effect depends upon the monitor type.

PC1640 MD
The PC1640's Monochrome Display has only one component for each pixel, so the pixel can be either on or off. However, the component has two intensities, so that when the pixel is on there is a choice of normal white and intense white.

PC1512 CM and PC1640 CD
The standard colour displays for the PC1512 and PC1640 are identical in their structure. Each pixel on the screen is made up from a combination of three separate colour components. These colours are red, green and blue, from which the term *RGB* is derived.

However, unlike some RGB monitors, the Amstrad colour screens also have a single *intensity* component for each pixel. These are sometimes referred to as *IRGB* monitors.

The three basic RGB colours yield eight possible combinations, ranging from black (when all three are off) to white (when all are on). For each of these combinations the intensity component can be either on or off, resulting in a total of 16 colours. (If the intensity component is on then all the colours are intensified.) When the intensity component is switched on the colours are lighter, as well as brighter.

The colours are represented by a four-bit code when stored in memory. Each bit represents one component (intensity, red, green, blue); the bit is set if the component is to be on, otherwise it is cleared. For example, 0000 represents black, 0010 is green and 1111 is intense white. The decimal or hexadecimal interpretations of these codes are the numbers that are frequently used in high-level programming languages and all the ROS and MS-DOS interrupts. Once the system is understood the numbering of the colours appears more logical. The colours and their interpretations are listed in Figure 13.7.

The advantage of this system is that when a colour is stored in video RAM the CRT controller can make a direct map from the bit pattern in memory to the pixel components to achieve the desired effect.

The Screen

The Screen Interrupts		
Interrupt	Function	Service
10	00	Set video mode
	01	Set cursor size
	02	Set cursor position
	03	Get cursor information
	05	Select active display page
	06	Scroll window up
	07	Scroll window down
	08	Read character
	09	Display character with attribute
	0A	Display character
	0B	Select colour palette
	0C	Display pixel
	0D	Read pixel colour
	0E	Display teletype character
	0F	Get video mode
21	02	Display character
	06	Keyboard input/screen output
	09	Display string
	0C	Clear keyboard buffer, call function

Figure 13.6 The screen interrupts

PC1512 MM   The construction of the PC1512's monochrome monitor is similar to that of the colour monitors. The difference is that the three 'colour' components are actually different intensities of white. With the addition of the main intensity component this still gives 16 variations. These range from black to bright white but the 14 options in between are all shades of grey.

PC1640 ECD   The ECD screen of the top-of-the-range PC1640 also has three colours for each pixel. In this case, however, each colour is comprised of two components: low intensity and high intensity. Either of these may be on or off independently of the intensity of the other two colours. Thus each colour is available in four different intensities: off, low, high, or

The Screen

The IRGB colours					
No.	Colour	Intensity	Red	Green	Blue
0	Black	0	0	0	0
1	Blue	0	0	0	1
2	Green	0	0	1	0
3	Cyan	0	0	1	1
4	Red	0	1	0	0
5	Magenta	0	1	0	1
6	Brown	0	1	1	0
7	White	0	1	1	1
8	Grey	1	0	0	0
9	Light Blue	1	0	0	1
10	Light Green	1	0	1	0
11	Light Cyan	1	0	1	1
12	Light Red	1	1	0	0
13	Light Magenta	1	1	0	1
14	Yellow	1	1	1	0
15	Intense White	1	1	1	1

Figure 13.7 The IRGB colours

low-plus-high. The highest intensity occurs when both components are on.

Since any of the three colours can be independently set to any of the four intensities this results in a potential of 64 (4x4x4) different colour combinations.

The low intensity components are frequently referred to as *rgb* so that the complete system becomes *rgbRGB*.

These various components are transmitted to the monitor along separate lines, as previously shown in Figure 13.1. The precise way in which the signals are interpreted depends on which monitor is fitted. The use of pin 2, in particular, is determined by the setting of dip switch 8.

THE VIDEO STATE

Whatever monitor you have, it can be used in a number of different ways. It is possible to vary the number of pixels per row and the number of colours used, as well as selecting the basic type of data to be displayed.

The way in which the monitor operates at any one time is called the *video state*. The video state includes the following parameters:

- The display mode

- The number of characters per line

- The number of active display pages

- The number of colours available

DOS provides several alternatives in the MODE command for changing the video state. In addition there are a number of DOS functions and a ROS interrupt dedicated to changing the video state.

Each of these features is described below.

DISPLAY MODES

The *display mode* determines the sort of data the screen can display. The number of modes available varies depending on the adapter but in all cases these fall into two basic groups:

- *Text modes.* In these modes only text and predefined graphics characters can be displayed.

- *Graphics modes.* In these modes each pixel can be individually set to be any of the available colours.

The modes are numbered from 0 to 15.

TEXT MODES

The essential feature of the text modes is that they are character-based. Each character on the screen can be individually set but it is not possible to go to any greater detail than this.

Text modes cannot display lines or other shapes unless these are made up from recognised graphics characters. In a text

The Screen

mode the screen is divided into a grid of rectangles, each of which can display an individual character. We have complete control over the colour of the character and its background. These colours can vary from one character to the next.

The advantage of the text modes is that they only use a small portion of memory. Each character on the screen is stored in two bytes of memory. Therefore a screen of 25 rows by 80 columns only requires 2000 bytes of memory. (The mode is allocated a full 2K of memory, the 48 extra bytes at the end being left unused.) This provides some interesting opportunities for any programmer who does not need to work with graphics displays.

The first of the two bytes stores the ASCII code of the character, while the second holds the character's *attribute*.

The character can be any of the extended ASCII codes, so the various predefined graphics characters can be displayed. Although this creates an illusion of graphics the standard box-drawing characters are as far as we can go to enhance the text display.

Stored in ROM is a table of data corresponding to the 256 ASCII values. For each value there is a set of bytes that hold the bit pattern needed to represent that particular character on the screen. When a character is to be displayed the ASCII code is used as an offset into this table to find the corresponding bit pattern.

The data for text displays is stored from B8000h onwards.

The routine in Figure 13.8 draws a single- and double-line box on the screen.

The attribute byte stores the colour of the character and its background. The attribute byte is split into either two or three parts. The way the byte is used depends upon the adapter type that has been selected.

In all cases the low four bits are used for the foreground colour (the colour of the character itself). The high four bits are used in CGA modes for two purposes. Bits 6, 5 and 4 select the background colour; since only three bits are used only the first eight colours (0 to 7) can be specified for the background.

The Screen

```
OUTLIN:                           ; Draw single- or double-box

                                  ; Calls CUROFF (Figure 13.17)

                                  ; Entry values: BOXDTA=pointer to
                                  ;                      box data
                                  ; Exit values:  None

            jmp boxst

boxdta      db 05h,1ah,12h,44h,02h,03h,01h ; Top left row,col, bottom
                                  ;     right row,col,
                                  ; Background colour, line colour
                                  ; Line thickness (1 or 2)

numrow      db ?                  ; Number of rows in box

numcol      db ?                  ; Number of cols in box
attrib      db 00                 ; Colour attributes for box
boxch       db 0da,0c5,0bf,0b3,0c0,0c5,0d9 ; Box characters: single
boxch2:     db 0c9,0cd,0bb,0ba,0c8,0cd,0bc ;                 double
                                  ; top left, horizontal, top right,
                                  ;   vertical, bottom left, horizontal
                                  ;   bottom right

            push ax
            push bx
            push cx
            push dx
            push si
            push di
            call curoff
            xor cx,cx
            mov cl,boxdta[02h]    ; Get last row number
            sub cl,[boxdta]       ; Difference from first to last
            inc cl                ; Number of rows = difference + 1
            mov [numrow],cl       ; Store number of rows
            xor cx,cx
            mov cl,boxdta[03h]    ; Calculate line length
            sub cl,boxdta[01h]
            inc cl
            mov [numcol],cl       ; Store number of cols
            xor di,di
            mov [attrib],01h
                                  ; Call attrib
            mov al,[boxdta]       ; Get first row number
            cbw
```

287

The Screen

```
        mov si,ax           ; SI=first row number
repcol:
            mov dx,si           ; Set up cursor at start of current row
            mov dh,dl
            mov dl,boxdta[01h]
            cmp cl,[numrow]     ; First time through?
            jz toplin           ; If yes, draw top line
            cmp cl,01h          ; Last time through?
            jz btmlin           ; If yes, draw bottom line
            mov al,boxch[di]    ; If no, select vertical line
            call dis1           ; Draw line
            mov dl,boxdta[03h]  ; Set cursor to end of row
            call dis1           ; Draw line

toplin:
            call disrow
            add di,02h          ; Point to vertical line character
            jmp nexrow

btmlin:
            inc di              ; Point to next characters
            call disrow
            jmp nexrow

nexrow:
            inc si
            loop repcol
            call curon
            pop dx
            pop cx
            pop bx
            pop ax
            int 20h

dis1:                           ; Display 1 character on current page

                                ; Entry values: AL=character to display
                                ;               DH=row
                                ;               DL=column
                                ;               ATTRIB=pointer to colour
                                ;                       attribute
            push ax
            push bx
            push cx
            xor bx,bx
            mov ah,02h
```

```
                int 10h             ; Move cursor to display position
                mov bl,[attrib]     ; Set attributes
                mov cx,01h          ; Count = 1
                mov ah,09h
                int 10h
                pop cx
                pop bx
                pop ax
                ret

dismany:                            ; Display many characters on current
page
                                    ; Entry values: AL=character to display
                                    ;               CX=number of times to
                                    ;                   display
                                    ;               DH=row
                                    ;               DL=column
                                    ;               ATTRIB=pointer to colour
                                    ;                   attributes
                push ax
                push bx
                xor bx,bx
                mov ah,02h
                int 10h             ; Move cursor to display position
                mov bl,[attrib]     ; Set attributes
                mov ah,09h
                int 010h
                pop bx
                pop ax
                ret

disrow:                             ; Display a row
                mov al,boxch[di]    ; Select first character
                call dis1           ; Display first character
                mov cl,[numcol]     ; CL = width of box
                sub cl,02h          ; Allow for ends of line
                mov al,boxch[di+1]  ; Select middle character
                call dismany        ; Display middle of row
                mov al,boxch[di+2]  ; Select last character
                call dis1           ; Display last character
                ret
```

Figure 13.8 Drawing boxes

The Screen

```
                    Encoding character attributes

    Bit    7    6    5    4    3    2    1    0
               ─────────────        ─────────────
              Blink Background        Foreground
                     colour            colour
                     (0-7)             (0-15)

    CGA Modes
    Examples:

    17h    0    0    0    1    0    1    1    1    White on blue
    CFh    1    1    0    0    1    1    1    1    Bright white on
                                                    red, blinking

    Monochrome modes
    Sensible values

    07h    0    0    0    0    0    1    1    1    White on black
    70h    0    1    1    1    0    0    0    0    Reverse
    01h    0    0    0    0    0    0    0    1    Underline
    00h    0    0    0    0    0    0    0    0    No character

    (Add blink (bit 7) and/or intensity (bit 3) to any of these combinations.)
```

Figure 13.9 Encoding character attributes

The highest bit determines whether the character is to blink. If the bit is set, the character blinks. This is achieved by alternately displaying the character and a blank background. Each cycle of the blink takes roughly 0.25 seconds to complete. The blink speed is a feature of the hardware and cannot be changed.

This process of encoding the data is illustrated in Figure 13.9.

The routine in Figure 13.10 demonstrates how a block of text may be written to the screen. It uses embedded commands to change the text attributes.

GRAPHICS MODES

Theoretically at least, graphics modes provide much more scope for the programmer, since each individual pixel can be set independently of the rest. In practice, this is fine for any sort of drawing work but provides problems whenever we want to display some ordinary text. Since most displays involve a mixture of both text and graphics this results in the inevitable trade-offs.

Graphics programming is limited by the expanse of memory needed to contain just a single screen. The memory-hungry graphics modes soon eat up our video RAM, especially if many different colours are needed.

Graphics modes have the advantage over text modes that they provide the option to set the colour of each pixel independently of the rest. There is no need to concern ourselves here with foreground and background. Clearing the screen is effected of filling the entire screen with a single 'background' colour. Once this has been done each pixel can be set to whatever colour we choose.

When displaying characters in graphics mode the situation is somewhat different, and turns out to be far less flexible than the text modes. Although the instructions that print characters in text modes can be used with equal ease in graphics modes they can only specify the foreground colour. The background colour is fixed as the universal background colour for the screen.

If you do want to vary the background colour, two options exist:

- Design your own character set, put a block on the screen in the required background colour and overlay it with the character bit pattern in the foreground colour.

- Use the character drawing functions to display the character and then replace all pixels in the block that have the background colour with the new background colour.

The first suggestion requires a great deal of effort and is of little practical use; the second option, however, is perfectly feasible, if a little slow.

The graphics display data is stored from B0000h onwards.

The Screen

```
WRITETEXT:                              ; Write a block of text to the screen

                                        ; Takes text from memory
                                        ; Attributes defined by specail codes
                                        ;   embedded in text. Special codes
                                        ;   consist of 01h followed by
                                        ;   attribute byte. Text terminated by
                                        ;   null character.

                                        ; Entry values: TEXT=text to be
                                        ;   displayed
                                        ; Entry values: AX,BX,DX,SI,DI changed

            jmp writest

                                        ; Insure text here. Use 0Dh for CR-LF
                                        ;   sequence. Make sure attribute is
                                        ;   returned to normal at end of text.

text        db 01h,07h,'Text is placed here',0Dh
            db 'with',01h,70h,'attributes',01h,70h
            db 'inserted in the text',0Dh
            db 'as',01h,3Dh,'required',01h,07h,00h
attrib      db ?                        ; Current attribute
linestart   db ?

writest:
            lea dx, text                ; DX points to TEXT
            lea bx,0b800h               ; BX points to display RAM
            xor ax,ax
            int 10h                     ; Set mode 0 and clear screen
            mov [attrib],07h            ; Initialise attribute (white on black)
            mov [linestart],00h         ; Point to top left-corner of string
            xor si,si                   ; SI is offset to TEXT
            xor di,di                   ; DI is offset to display RAM
next char:
            mov al,text[si]             ; Get byte
            cmp al,01h                  ; Is it attribute?
            jz attribute                ; Jump if it is
            cmp al,0Dh                  ; Is it CR?
            jz creturn                  ; Jump if so
            cmp al,00h                  ; Is it end of text?
            jz endwrite                 ; If so, jump
            mov bx[di],al               ; Otherwise, display character
            mov bx[di+1],attrib         ; Store current attribute in next byte
            add di,02h                  ; and character
            jmp endloop                 ; Point to next screen location
```

```
attribute:
            inc si
            mov al,text[si]        ; Get attribute
            mov [attrib],al        ; Save attribute
            inc si
            inc di
            jmp endloop
Creturn:
            mov si,[linestart]     ; SI points to start of line
            add si,10h             ; Add 160 to SI; i.e. point to start of
                                   ;    next line
            mov [linestart],si     ; Save start of new line
            inc di
andloop:
            jmp nextchar
endwrite:
            ret                    ; End routine (replace with INT 20h for
                                   ;    standalone program

; - - - - - - - - - - - - - - - - - - - - - - - - - - - - - - - -

WRITEST:                           ; Test block writing program

                                   ; Calls WRITETEST

            jmp testst

testdata    db 64h dup (?)         ; Allow for 100 bytes
dataend     db ?                   ; End of data marker

            lea es,text
            lea ds,testdata
            xor si,si
            xor di,di
            mov cx,dataend         ; Calculate length of text
            sub cx,testdata
            cld
            rep movsb              ; Move TESTDATA into TEXT
            call writetext
            int 20h
```

Figure 13.10 Writing a block of text of text to the screen

The Screen

Changing modes Two ROS interrupts are supplied for changing the current video mode and for reporting the current mode.

Interrupt:	10h
Function:	00h
Service:	Set video mode
Entry values:	AH=00h
	AL=new video mode
Exit values:	None

The new mode is placed in AL before calling the interrupt. This interrupt clears the screen before clearing the appropriate section of video RAM, even if the new mode number is the same as the current mode. Thus we have a simple screen-clearing operation; this method is fast on the Amstrad PC but may be slower on other compatibles.

Interrupt:	10h
Function:	0Fh
Service:	Get video mode
Entry values:	AH=0Fh
Exit values:	AH=width (characters)
	AL=video mode
	BH=page

This interrupt returns the current mode in AL. By combining the two functions we can devise an alternative to DOS's CLS command (Figure 13.11).

The current mode can also be found in memory at 0449h. The next byte (044Ah) stores the number of columns in the screen display (either 40 or 80). The number of rows, less 1, is stored at 0484h; this is usually 24 (18h), indicating 25 rows.

DISPLAY PAGES The low memory usage in text modes means that it is possible to store the information for more than one screen at a time. In modes 0 and 1 the video RAM can be divided into 2K sections, each of which is called a *display page*. The interrupt functions allow us to decide which display page is going to be used at any time. There is always an *active display page* and this is used for the current display. When the active display page is changed the display circuits immediately start displaying the contents of the new page so that the screen changes almost instantly.

```
SCRENCLR:                           ; Clears the screen
                                    ; Can be called from any routine
                                    ; All registers preserved
            push ax
            push bx
            mov ah,0fh
            int 10h                 ; Get current mode
            mov ah,00h
            int 10h                 ; Set mode, same as before
            pop bx
            pop ax
            ret
```

Figure 13.11 Clearing the screen

This means that we can build up a picture in a non-active display page and - only when it is complete - switch from the current page. In this way the user does not have to sit through the distracting process of watching a display being updated, though of course the time taken to prepare the display is the same. Concerns about 'snow' disappear as well.

Since every page must start at a 2K boundary there is a small amount of wasted space at the end of each page. The amount of space taken up by a single page in the current mode (including the wasted space) is stored at location 044Ch. This varies between 2K and 32K.

The start address of the current page can be found from location 044Eh, where it is stored as an offset from the start of the video RAM.

Multiple work areas

Perhaps the most effective use for the display pages occurs when the programmer wishes to provide two complete work areas for the user. For example, the menu options may be displayed on one page while the actual work area may be on another. By pressing a single key the user can instantly switch to the menu page while another key takes you directly back to the work area.

Alternatively, two or more different files may be worked on at one time, providing facilities for cutting and pasting.

The Screen

A similar approach is adopted by memory-resident programs, which can be made to spring instantly to life when invoked, later disappearing with equal rapidity. There is also potential for some very sophisticated programming; as long as you know which display pages are being used, a memory-resident program can read the memory associated with a non-active display page to find out what was on the screen when the program was called.

The active display page is selected through a ROS interrupt. The contents of any page can be changed at any time. All instructions relating to the screen require you to specify the page that is to be affected. Thus any new data can be displayed immediately on the active page or stored for a future display on a non-active page.

The text modes use the 16K of memory from B8000h to BBFFFh. The number of pages depends upon the number of characters to be displayed and the number of colours and palettes that can be selected. This provides a number of pages between 1 and 8.

Display pages are numbered from 0. The number of pages for each mode is given in Figure 13.12.

Selecting the active display page

A change of page is achieved through function 05h of interrupt 10h. When the interrupt is called AL should contain the new display page.

Interrupt: 10h
Function: 05h
Service: Select active display page
Entry values: AH=05h
　　　　　　　AL=page
Exit values: None

The new page is displayed as soon as the interrupt has been executed. Figure 13.13 provides the shell of a routine to switch between three work areas and a menu page.

The current active display page number is stored in memory at 0462h.

The Screen

Video mode statistics

Video modes

Display mode	Display type	Text cols or horizontal pixels	Text rows or vertical pixels	Colour
0	Text	40	25	Black & white
1	Text	40	25	Colour
2	Text	80	25	Black & white
3	Text	80	25	Colour
4	Graphics	320	200	Colour
5	Graphics	320	200	Black & white
6	Graphics	640	200	Black & white
7	Text	80	25	MDA

Maximum values for text modes

Mode	Characters Rows	Characters Columns	Colours Foreground	Colours Background	Blink?	Palettes	Page
0	40	25	16*	16*	No	1	8
1	40	25	16	8	Yes	1	8
2	80	25	16*	16*	No	1	4
3	80	25	16	8	Yes	1	4
7	80	25	3**	2**	No	1	1

* Colour suppressed modes: the 'colours' are shades of grey
** Monochrome styles: only 4 combinations allowed

Memory requirements for characters and pages in text modes

Mode	Bytes Per Char.	Char size page	Page Memory	Allocated Pages	Page locations (paragraphs) 0	1	2	3	4	etc...
0	2	1000	2K	16K	8	B800	B880	B900	B980	BA00 etc...
1	2	1000	2K	16K	8	B800	B880	B900	B980	BA00 etc...
2	2	2000	4K	16K	4	B800	B900	BA00	BB00	
3	2	2000	4K	16K	4	B800	B900	BA00	BB00	
7	2	2000	4K	4K	1	B800				

Figure 13.12 Video mode statistics

The Screen

Maximum values for graphics modes

Mode	Pixels Rows	Columns	Colours	Palettes	Pages	Allocated Memory
4	200	320	4	2	1	16K
5	200	320	4*	2	1	16K
6	200	640	2	1	1	16K
13	200	320	16	1	1	32K
14	200	640	16	1	1	64K
15	350	640	2	1	1	28K
16	350	640	16/64	1	1	112K

* Colour suppressed modes: the 'colours' are shades of grey.

Memory requirements for characters and pages in graphics modes

Mode	Colours byte	Pixels/row	Pixels/row	Bytes/size	Rows	Page	Pixels	Location
4	4	4	320	80	200	16K	64000	B8000
5	4	4	320	80	200	16K	64000	B8000
6	2	8	640	80	200	16K	128000	B8000
13	16	2	320	160	200	32K	64000	A0000
14	16	2	640	320	200	64K	128000	A0000
15	2	8	640	80	350	28K	224000	A0000
16	16	2	640	320	350	112K	224000	A0000

Figure 13.12 Video mode statistics

PALETTES

The variety of colours on monitors such as the ECD creates severe problems because of the vast amount of memory needed to store a screenful of data with this number of possible options.

Each pixel has six components, so if all the colours were to be available three bytes would be needed for every four pixels. Given the high resolution of the ECD (640 by 350 pixels) a single display would need 168,000 bytes of memory (164K).

The Screen

```
MENUPAGE:                       ; Displays a menu on the screen and gets
                                ;    a key press

                                ; Calls DISMESGS (Figure 13.16),
                                ;    GETNUMKY (Figure 11.9)

                                ; Entry values: None
                                ; Exit values:  All registers preserved

            push ax
            push bx
            push cx
            mov bx,coords       ; BX points to coordinates and text
            mov al,[nummes]     ; CX=number of messages
            cbw
            mov cx,ax
            call dismesgs       ; Display options and prompt
            mov cx,ax
            call getnumky
            pop cx
            pop bx
            pop ax
            int 20h             ; Replace with RET for call from another
                                ;    routine

nummes:                         ; Sample data
            db 04h              ; Number of messages
coords:     db 08h,20h,0ch,0ah,20h,1ch,0ch,20h,2ch,0fh,1ch,3ch
                                ; row,col,offset;row,col,offset,....
            db "Option 1       $" ; Options
            db "Option 2       $"
            db "Option 3       $"
            db "Select option (1,2 or 3)$" ; Prompt
```

Figure 13.13 Switching between work areas

Clearly this is out of the question, so the system limits the number of colours that can be used. A subset of the colours are made available; this set of colours is called a *palette*.

The colours in the palette are given *logical* numbers starting from 0. For example in a 16-colour palette the colours are numbered from 0 to 15. These are different to the *physical* colours which tell us exactly which components of the pixel are to be turned on. The display equipment has to translate each logical colour into a physical colour. It is the logical number that is stored in video RAM.

The Screen

Mode(s) Palette		Logical No.	Colour	Bit pattern
4/5	0	0	Black	00
		1	Green	01
		2	Red	10
		3	Brown	11
	1	0	Black	00
		1	Cyan	01
		2	Magenta	10
		3	White	11
6	0	0	Black	0
		1	White	1
10	0	0	Black	00
		1	Cyan	01
		2	Magenta	10
		3	White	11

Figure 13.14 Video mode palettes

In those cases where the full colour set is available (most colour modes of the CM and CD, for example) the logical colour numbers correspond to the physical numbers.

In some modes more than one palette is available, in which case the palettes are numbered from 0 and can be selected by a suitable instruction.

In other cases there is only one palette but you can select which colours are to be included in it; you can choose the physical colour that is to be mapped onto each logical colour. Any order of colours is permissible and a colour may be re-used (so that two different logical colours are mapped onto the same physical colour). The standard palettes are listed in Figure 13.14.

Modes 4 and 5 permit four colours and two palettes. The two bits that determine the colour in memory represent the red and green components in palette 0 and all-but-green for palette 1. An added complication is that logical colour 0,

The Screen

Logical No.	Colour	Low Red	Low Green	Low Blue	High Red	High Green	High Blue	Physical No.
0	Black	0	0	0	0	0	0	0
1	Blue	0	0	0	0	0	1	1
2	Green	0	0	0	0	1	0	2
3	Cyan	0	0	0	0	1	1	3
4	Red	0	0	0	1	0	0	4
5	Magenta	0	0	0	1	0	1	5
6	Brown	0	0	0	1	1	0	6
7	White	0	0	0	1	1	1	7
8	Grey	1	1	1	0	0	0	56
9	Light Blue	1	1	1	0	0	1	57
10	Light Green	1	1	1	0	1	0	58
11	Light Cyan	1	1	1	0	1	1	59
12	Light Red	1	1	1	1	0	0	60
13	Light Magenta	1	1	1	1	0	1	61
14	Yellow	1	1	1	1	1	0	62
15	Intense White	1	1	1	1	1	1	63

Figure 13.15 The default EGA palette (rgbRGB)

which is normally black, can be set to any physical colour. When writing text in these modes, logical colour 0 is used for the background and logical colour 3 for the character in the foreground. This is the same for both palettes.

Mode 6 has only two colours, black and white. The bit value determines whether all colour components are on or off.

Mode 10 has a single four-colour palette, identical to palette 1 of mode 4.

Modes 13 and 14 (the EGA modes) provide a default palette of 16 colours. These colours are chosen by switching all the low intensity components on or off at the same time. The high intensity components vary in the same way as the CGA colours. Thus the logical colours from 8 to 15 are those with all the low intensity bits set. The default EGA palette is shown in Figure 13.15.

The Screen

Selecting a palette

Function 0Bh of interrupt 10h is used to choose the palette for Modes 4 and 5.

Interrupt: 10h
Function: 0Bh
Service: Select colour palette
Entry values: AH=0Bh
BH=palette
BL=colour
Exit values: None

The interrupt is used in two ways. The palette is selected by setting BH to 1 and BL to the palette number (either 0 or 1). Having chosen the palette we can choose the border or background colour. When BH is 0, BL gives the border colour by declaring it as logical colour 0. This can be any of the full 16-colour set.

In text modes logical colour 0 is also used for the border; the background of each individual character can be set independently. In graphics modes, logical colour 0 is used both for the border and the background colour, so the selected colour will spread across the entire screen.

DISPLAYING CHARACTERS

There are a number of functions of interrupt 10h dedicated to displaying characters. All displays start from the current cursor position.

Interrupt: 10h
Function: 0Ah
Service: Display character
Entry values: AH=0Ah
AL=character
BH=page (text modes)
BL=colour (graphics modes)
CX=repeat count (0 for continuous repeat)
Exit values: None

This function displays the character from AL at the current cursor position, in the page whose number is BH. (The page number need only be specified in text modes.)

The Screen

The characters are written along the current line. The effect when the end of the line is reached depends on the mode:

- In text modes the next character is printed at the start of the next line; when the bottom of the screen is reached the screen scrolls up one line to make room.

- In graphics modes any additional characters are ignored.

If the count, CX, is set to 0 the characters repeat until Ctrl-Break is pressed.

The attribute of the character in text modes is the same as that of the previous character. The default is white on black. In graphics modes the colour must be specified in BL.

For most applications the main disadvantage with this function is that the cursor remains at its original position.

Interrupt: 10h
Function: 09h
Service: Display character
Entry values: AH=09
AL=character
BH=page
BL=attribute (text modes)
CX=repeat count (0 for continuous repeat)
Exit values: None

This function is almost identical to function 0Ah. The only difference is that in text modes the attribute of the character must be specified; that is, the foreground and background colours and whether or not the character should blink. The attribute byte is calculated as follows:

Attribute = Foreground + (Background * 10h) + Blink

where 'Blink' is 80h if the character is to flash, otherwise 00h.

Interrupt: 10h
Function: 0Eh
Service: Display teletype character
Entry values: AH=0E
AL=character
BH=page
BL=colour (graphics modes)

The Screen

Exit values: None

Again, this function is similar to function 0Ah. As with function 0Ah there is no control over the attribute; the colour and blink attribute are the same as the last character printed. For graphics modes the colour must still be specified. There are two main differences:

- The function is used to display just one character at a time.

- The cursor moves forward one place each time.

This is known as *teletype (TTY) mode* because the principle is similar to that of the original teletype terminals. When the end of a line is reached the cursor moves to the start of the next line; when the bottom of the screen is reached the screen scrolls up to create a new blank line.

There is a slight disadvantage when displaying a screenful of text, in that when a character is written to the last character of the last line the screen scrolls. This function is therefore no good for drawing a box right around the screen, for example.

Function 0Eh usually prints the ASCII character specified but there are some characters that produce special effects:

- ASCII 07h makes the computer beep (*bell*)

- ASCII 08h moves the cursor back one place and deletes the previous character (*backspace*)

- ASCII 0Ah moves the cursor down one line but leaves it in the same column (*line feed*)

- ASCII 0DL moves the cursor back to the first column and down one line (*carriage return*)

Function 0Eh is the equivalent of function 0Ah followed by function 01h (see below).

MS-DOS has two interrupt 21h functions that perform similar tasks.

The Screen

Interrupt: 21h
Function: 02h
DOS version: 1
Service: Display character
Entry values: AH=02h
DL=character
Exit values: None

This is almost identical to interrupt 10h function 0Eh. The only difference is the way in which the function deals with the backspace character (ASCII 08h); with the DOS function the character is not deleted but the cursor moves back so that the original character may be overwritten.

DOS checks for the break-key combination after this interrupt.

Interrupt: 21h
Function: 06h
DOS version: 1
Service: Display character (see also Chapter 11)
Entry values: AH=06h
DL=character other than FFh
Exit values: None

This function may also be used for keyboard input (as described earlier). If any character other than ASCII FFh is placed in DL then the character is output to the screen in an identical way to function 02h.

Displaying a string

It is possible to display a string on the screen by some sort of loop, using the functions described above. This can be rather tedious when the string is straightforward with no change in attributes. Interrupt 21h provides a function to simplify this process.

Interrupt: 21h
Function: 09h
DOS version: 1
Service: Display string
Entry values: AH=09h
DS:DX=start of string
Exit values: None

The cursor is advanced to the space after the last character. This function has an identical effect to the loop in Figure

The Screen

```
                                ; This listing includes a selection of
                                ;   routines for displaying results and
                                ;   values on the screen

DISBYT:                         ; Display byte in AL as hex
                                ; All registers preserved
            push ax
            push cx
            push ax
            mov cl,04h
            shr al,cl           ; Get first 4 bits
            call dis4           ; Display as character
            pop ax
            and al,0fh          ; Get last 4 bits
            call dis4           ; Display as character
            pop cx
            pop ax
            ret

dis4:                           ; Display single hex character
            cmp al,0ah          ; Check for value = 0Ah
            jge letter
            add al,30h          ; Convert to ASCII code for 0 to 9
            jmp disch

letter:
            add al,37h          ; Convert to ASCII code for A to F

disch:
            mov ah,0eh
            int 10h
            ret

; -------------------------------------------------------------------

DISWRD:                         ; Display word in AX as hex

                                ; Entry values: None
                                ; Exit values: All registers preserved
            push ax
            mov al,ah
            call disbyt         ; Display high byte
            pop ax
            call disbyt         ; Display low byte
            ret

; -------------------------------------------------------------------
```

The Screen

```
DISSTR:                             ; Display string

                                    ; Entry values: DX=offset address of
                                    ;                      message
                                    ; Exit values: All registers preserved

        push ax
        mov ah,09h                  ; Call interrupt to display text at DX
        int 21h
        pop ax
        ret

; ----------------------------------------------------------------

NEWLIN:                             ; Print CR,LF to start new line
        push ax
        mov al,0Dh                  ; AL=Carriage Return (0Dh)

                                    ; Entry values: None
                                    ; Exit values:  All registers preserved

        mov ah,0Eh                  ; Print CR
        int 10h
        mov al,0Ah                  ; AL=Line Feed (0Ah)
        mov ah,0Eh                  ; Print LF
        int 10h
        pop ax
        ret

; ----------------------------------------------------------------

DISLIN:                             ; Display a line of text

                                    ; Entry values: DX offset address of
                                    ;                      message
                                    ; Exit values:  All registers preserved

        call disstr                 ; Displaying string
        call newlin                 ; Move to new line
        ret

; ----------------------------------------------------------------

DISMESGS:                           ; Display a set of screen messages

                                    ; Data can be stored as part of calling
                                    ;   routine

                                    ; Limitations - each item must end with
```

The Screen

```
                                ;    $ and length must be calculated as
                                ;    an offset from start of data area

                                ; Calls SCRENCLR (Figure 13.11)

                                ; Entry values: BX=ptr to coords &
                                ;                   offsets
                                ;               CX=no. messages
        push ax
        push cx
        push dx
        push di
        push si
        xor di,di
        call screnclr           ; Clear the screen

nexmes:
        mov dh,[bx+di]          ; Get row number
        inc di
        mov dl,[bx+di]          ; Get column number
        inc di
        push bx
        xor bx,bx
        mov ah,02h
        int 10h                 ; Move cursor to position
        pop bx
        mov al,[bx+di]          ; Get offset of string from start of
                                ;   data area
        cbw
        mov si,ax
        lea dx,[bx+si]          ; Point to string
        call disstr             ; Display text
        inc di                  ; Point to next item
        loop nexmes             ; Get next message
        pop si
        pop di
        pop dx
        pop cx
        pop ax
        ret

                                ; Data in form: row,col,offset,row,col,
                                ;               offset,....
                                ;               "First message$"
                                ;               "Second message$"
                                ;               ....
```

Figure 13.16 Display routines

The Screen

13.10, except that the end of the string is signified by a $ (ASCII 24h) rather than the null character (ASCII 00h). The main disadvantage of this service is the $ character that terminates the string. This service is fine for many types of output but fails wherever the string could possibly contain a $ character as part of the output text.

Reading a character from the display

There are some occasions when it is useful to know what is already on the screen. Obviously, most programs should know exactly what the screen looks like at any time, since they have complete control over the display and can inspect characters as they are written.

However, sometimes the current contents of the screen is a complete mystery to the program or it is simpler to read a character from the screen than to perform complicated search routines.

The first situation is particularly prevalent with memory resident programs where we wish to find out exactly what the user was doing when the program was invoked.

The ROS provides a function to read the contents of any screen location.

Interrupt: 10h
Function: 08h
Service: Read character
Entry values: AH=08h
BH=page
Exit values: AH=attribute
AL=character

In text modes the character and its attribute are returned in AL and AH respectively. This function even works in graphics modes where the character is obtained by matching the pattern in the character block against the ASCII character table in memory.

The function could be duplicated for text modes simply by reading the contents of the video RAM at the appropriate point, of course. However, it is not practical to try and do likewise with graphics modes, so this function is extremely useful for any graphics screens.

The Screen

If the character is unrecognised or distorted (for example, by having a line drawn across a corner of the character block) the value in AL is 00h.

Figure 13.16 uses these services to create a number of routines for displaying text of various lengths, moving to a new line and so on. These routines have been used extensively throughout the book.

THE CURSOR

Most people are familiar with the *cursor*, a flashing line or block that indicates the point at which the next character will appear when typed.

The 8086 speeds up programming quite considerably by automatically providing a cursor for every display page. The system keeps track of the position of the cursor in terms of its row and column numbers. In text mode 0, for example, the system maintains the positions of eight independent cursors, one for each page. These positions are stored in memory at locations 0450h to 045Fh.

Note that whenever there is a change of mode (even if the mode number is unchanged) the cursor is automatically reset to its original position in the top left-hand corner of the screen (row 0, column 0).

CURSOR TYPES There are cursors for both text and graphics modes but the way in which the system deals with them is slightly different.

The text cursor In text modes the cursor defaults to a small flashing block that is the same width as the character block and two pixels deep. We can change this cursor in a very limited way, by specifying which raster lines in the block are to be used. The raster lines are numbered from 0 at the top to either 7 (CGA) or 13 (MDA/EGA) at the bottom of the block. The default size is a flashing block from lines 6 to 7 for the CGA or 11 to 12 for the MDA and EGA. We can set the first and last lines and all lines in between are used (as described below). We have no control over the width of the cursor (which is the width of a character block), nor its colour or flashing attribute.

The Screen

The graphics cursor

The computer maintains a record of the current cursor position in graphics modes as well as text modes. However, the cursor is not displayed in this case, so although we can move the cursor and read its position using appropriate interrupts, we need some extra programming if we are to physically display the cursor.

CHANGING THE CURSOR

The screen position of the cursor is measured from (0,0) in the top left-hand corner to (24,39) or (24,79) in the bottom right, depending on mode. Initially, whenever there is a change of display mode, the cursor is set to the top left-hand corner of the screen.

Interrupt 10h includes three functions that relate to the cursor.

Moving the cursor

Recall that interrupt 10h function 0Eh automatically moves the cursor after each character has been displayed. If we use any of the other character-displaying functions or want to move the cursor to a different part of the screen than we must use function 02h.

Interrupt: 10h
Function: 02h
Service: Set cursor position
Entry values: AH=02h
BH=page (0 for graphics modes)
DH=row
DL=column
Exit values: None

The cursor position is entirely specified by the row, column and page numbers. The page number must always be given, even in those modes where there is only one page (in which case its value must be 0). Figure 13.17 demonstrates how the cursor may be used.

Changing the cursor size

The second of the three interrupt functions that affect the cursor allows you to change the size of the cursor. This is done by specifying the first and last raster lines, counting from 0 on the top line to a maximum of either 7 or 13, depending on adapter type.

Interrupt: 10h
Function: 01h
Service: Set cursor size

The Screen

```
                           ; This listing includes two routines -
                           ;    one to turn the cursor off and
                           ;    one to turn it on again. These
                           ;    routines should be used as a pair

CUROFF:                    ; Turn cursor off

                           ; AX and CX must be pushed onto stack
                           ;    before call, and popped after CURON
            jump curst
cursz       dw ?           ; cursor size
curst:
            mov ah,03h
            int 10h        ; Get current cursor characteristics
            mov [cursz],cx ; Save cursor size
            mov ch,20h
            xor cl,cl
            mov ah,01h
            int 10h        ; turn cursor off
            ret

; ---------------------------------------------------------------

CURON:                     ; Turn cursor on

            mov cx,[cursz] ; Recover cursor size
            mov ah,01h
            int 10h        ; Restore cursor
            ret
```

Figure 13.17 Cursor routines

Entry values: AH=01h
CH=first raster line (20h for no cursor)
CL=last raster line
Exit values: None

Apart from setting a cursor that takes up part of the block the following options are available:

- Set CH=0 and CL to the maximum (7 or 13) to create a complete block cursor.

The Screen

- Set CH and CL to be the same for just a single flashing line.

- Set CL less than CH to get a cursor that appears at both top and bottom of the block.

- Set CH=20h for a special case that makes the cursor disappear.

This service can be combined with function 02h to completely define the cursor.

The size of the cursor that is selected applies to all display pages, so if you need a different type of cursor in each page you must change the size when you choose the mode. The first and last raster lines of the current cursor are stored in memory at 0461h and 0460h respectively.

To vary the width or flashing features of the cursor, use some of the possibilities described below.

Get cursor information

While it is usually possible to calculate where the cursor ought to be, it is generally far simpler to use function 03h to get the information.

Interrupt: 10h
Function: 03h
Service: Get cursor information
Entry values: AH=03h
BH=page
Exit values: CH=first raster line
CL=last raster line
DH=row
DL=column

This function allows us to discover both the character position and the extent of the cursor in terms of raster lines.

Custom-built cursors

To use any other type of cursor in text modes, such as a solid block or one which flashes at a different rate, we need to turn the cursor off and supply our own cursor. This can be done quite easily by reversing the colours of the character at the cursor.

Alternatively, a cursor with a different flashing speed can be achieved by constantly switching the block on and off while

The Screen

waiting for input; a different-shaped flashing cursor can be displayed by alternating the character with a graphics character. The disadvantages here are that the program is completely tied up whenever it is waiting for input and it is also necessary to devise a complete routine for data input. This is only really worthwhile if the application needs to carry out any sort of data validation as the entry is being typed. Much of the time we can get away with validating the data only when the user presses Return.

We can display a graphics cursor in a similar way to that described above for text modes. In this case, however, we have the added advantage that the cursor can be created by using logical operations on the pixels in the character block. For example, you can invert the block at the cursor by replacing each colour by its logical inverse.

WINDOWS

The current fashion is to make great use of windows on the screen. A *window* is simply a rectangle on the screen in which all activity is to take place. The general principle is that whenever the user selects an option a new window is overlaid on the screen, replacing everything in the window but leaving the remainder of the display outside unchanged; when the operation is complete the part of the screen that was overlaid is redrawn.

In even simpler applications the new windows are just stacked one on top of another, with the entire screen being redrawn when required. The logical approach would be to make all windows non-overlapping but this principle is rarely applied. This craze for windows is a little strange, given the untidy nature of many applications and the unreadability of much of the background text. However, the fad seems likely to continue unabated for some years, so it is worth investigating the methods that can be adopted for windowing.

Placing a window on the screen

Displaying the window in the first place is a fairly straightforward operation:

1. Save the current contents of the window, using the character-reading service to get each character in turn and store it in memory.

The Screen

2. Fill the window with a rectangle of the required colour.

3. Draw an outline inside the window, using a single- or double-line box.

Filling the window

Any text that is needed can be placed in the window. It is up to the programmer to take care of the details of keeping all activity within the confines of the window. Here we can make use of the cursor-reading service, moving the cursor to the start of the next line as required.

SCROLLING

The principles of controlling windows are not as complex as they may appear at first sight. However, the procedures are greatly enhanced by two Interrupt 10h functions that *scroll* a window (that is, move it all up or down by one or more lines).

Interrupt: 10h
Function: 06h
Service: Scroll window up
Entry values: AH=06h
AL=number of lines to scroll
BH=attribute for new line
CH=top row
CL=left column
DH=bottom row
DL=right column
Exit values: None

This is an extremely useful service. Not only does it move everything within a window up one line but it also allows us to determine the colour of the new blank lines that are added at the bottom. Usually we only need to scroll one line at a time but any number of lines can be specified.

It is up to us what we do with the line that is scrolled off the top of the window; it can be stored in memory or on file, or just ignored altogether.

Similarly any new text at the bottom can come from wherever we like: memory, a disk file or user input.

Interrupt: 10h
Function: 07h
Service: Scroll window down
Entry values: AH=07h

The Screen

                                AL=number of lines to scroll
                                BH=for new line filler attribute
                                CH=top row
                                CL=left column
                                DH=bottom row
                                DL=right column
Exit values: None

The associated function, 07h, scrolls the window down one or more lines. The two scrolling functions together give us complete vertical control over the window. The arrow keys can be used to move around the window.

GRAPHICS DISPLAYS IN MEMORY

The data that makes up the displays for graphics mode is somewhat different to that for text modes. There is a direct correspondence between the bits in memory and the pixels on the display.

The amount of space needed to store the logical colour depends on the number of colours in the palette; the numbers of bits for each pixel for 2-, 4- and 16-colour modes are 1, 2 and 4 respectively. Therefore the numbers of pixels represented by each byte are 8, 4 and 2 respectively. From the number of pixels per row it is a simple calculation to obtain the number of bytes to store in a single row, and hence the number of bytes for the complete display.

The way in which the data is stored is not perhaps as simple as might be supposed. The available memory is sub-divided into a number of 8K *banks*. The first row of data is stored sequentially at the start of the first bank; however, the second row is stored at the start of the second bank. For 16K modes (with two banks), the third row is stored in the first bank again, immediately following the first row's data; the fourth bank goes in the second bank and so on. Thus bank 1 holds the data for rows 0,2,4,6,... while bank 2 holds rows 1,3,5,7,.... The data is written sequentially for each bank in turn, so all the even rows are written first and then the odd rows are filled in.

For 32K modes there are four banks; bank 1 holds rows 0,4,8,..., bank 2 holds 1,5,9,... and so on.

The Screen

The way in which we can use this information is limited. For modes 4 to 6 we can access the data directly through memory. The location of any pixel in memory is calculated from:

Even rows:

Offset byte= 50h x (Row/2) + Int(Column/n)

Offset bit= (Column mod n) x (8/n)

Odd rows:

Offset byte= 2000h + 50h x Int(Row/2) + Int(Column/n)

Offset bit= (Column mod n) x (8/n)

where n is the number of pixels per byte. Note that the offset bit is measured from the left of the byte.

In fact it is far simpler to use the interrupts.

For EGA modes the situation is rather different. Although the display memory theoretically begins at A0000h it is rather cunningly disguised. The display memory cannot be directly accessed, nor does it make sense to try.

WORKING WITH PIXELS

When displaying any sort of graphics it is necessary to set one or more pixels to a given colour. For example, to draw a line all the pixels between two points must be set to the same colour. The ROS interrupts do not provide any sophisticated services for this sort of operation; all we have is the most basic of instructions to set any pixel to any colour.

All other operations must be built up from this single activity. A line can be drawn by changing all pixels between two points; a box is a combination of lines, and so on. Circles are a little more tricky but can be generalised without too much difficulty.

The position of any pixel is defined by its raster line (or row number from 0 at the top to 199 or 349 at the bottom, and its column from 0 on the left to 319, 639 or 719 (depending on mode). When referring to a pixel position it is usual to abbreviate it to a pair of co-ordinates in the form (x,y), where x is the column and y is the row. Thus (0,0) is at the top-left hand corner and the bottom left is either (0,199) or (0,349), depending on mode.

The pixel operations can only be used in graphics modes, of course.

Writing a pixel   Function 0Ch of ROS interrupt 10h allows us to set the colour of any individual pixel.

Interrupt:	10h
Function:	0Ch
Service:	Display pixel
Entry values:	AH=0Ch
	AL=colour (add 80h for XOR)
	CX=pixel column
	DL=pixel row
Exit values:	None

There are two options for the colour. The first is to specify a logical colour from 0 to 15. The pixel is set to this colour, regardless of the background colour or what was there before.

The second option is to add 80h to the logical colour. In this case the system carries out an XOR operation between the existing pixel colour and the colour specified in AL, to determine the actual colour that will be displayed.

This has a number of advantages:

- The object does not disappear if we use the background colour on an empty screen.

- If an object is placed on another object of the same colour it will still be visible (though the colour will change).

- If a line passes across an object it will never disappear though its colour may change several times.

The disadvantage is that it becomes quite difficult to predict in advance what colours are actually going to be displayed.

The Screen

This option is no good if you want one object to completely obscure another but it does provide a sort of transparency which can be useful at times.

Note that the XOR operation is always applied to the *logical* colour, not the physical colour. Therefore, no matter what physical colours may be attached to logical colours 5 and 9, they will always produce the colour attached to logical colour 12.

Reading a pixel Since the ability to XOR colours and the procedures for geometric shapes produce some complex patterns on the screen it is obviously impractical to keep track of the colour of each individual pixel. This is especially the case in graphics modes where the contents of memory are not easily decoded.

Therefore, any time we need to know the colour of a pixel we can use function 0Dh.

Interrupt: 10h
Function: 0Dh
Service: Read pixel colour
Entry values: AH=0Dh
                 CX=pixel column
                 DL=pixel row
Exit values: AL=colour

This service is particularly useful when we want to store away a screenful of information.

Note that there are no equivalent pixel-based operations in the DOS interrupts; DOS is very much character-orientated.

THE VIDEO PORTS

Through the interrupts we have a great deal of control over all sorts of display information: the cursor size and position, background colour, mode and so on. Of course, all this information has to be stored somewhere; this is the purpose of the *video ports*. These are where the CPU keeps track of what is going on with the display. The video ports are numbered from 03B0h to 03DFh.

Theoretically, it is possible to change the contents of all these registers. However, there are only a very few that are considered safe to use. Even in these cases, the improvements in efficiency are minimal.

Indeed, in some cases it is very dangerous to do so and can have a fatal effect on the monitor. This is one of the very few occasions when a software error can actually result in physical damage to the hardware. Inexperienced programmers are therefore strongly advised to keep to the ROS interrupts and avoid direct programming of the ports.

The contents of some of these ports are duplicated in memory locations 0463h to 0466h.

CONCLUSION

There are a number of different ways of writing to the screen:

- In text modes writing directly to memory is often most efficient.

- In graphics modes it is more sensible to use the interrupts.

- The video registers should be avoided at all costs.

14. Sound

The Amstrad PC has a single speaker, which is capable of producing sound of any frequency within a specific range. Although it is a fairly unsophisticated sound system it can be used to create some interesting tones. It may not be particularly melodic but then you are not buying the PC as a synthesiser.

This chapter considers the components that are used to create sound and the programming that they require.

THE PRODUCTION OF SOUND

The production of sound is even more basic than the other parts of the system that have been considered so far. There are in fact only two things we can do with the speaker: push the speaker out and pull the speaker in.

When a voltage is passed through the speaker the result is that the speaker moves outwards; when there is no voltage the speaker returns to its original position. The movement of the speaker shunts the air particles that surround it; these in turn knock into the adjacent particles and the wave that this creates ripples outwards. We hear this as a sound; in the case of a single pulse of the speaker it is a single click.

If the speaker is pulsed a number of times in quick succession the clicks blend into a musical note. The *frequency* of the sound is determined by the rate at which the clicks are generated. The closer the sounds are together the higher the frequency of the sound that we hear.

Each complete pulse of the speaker in and out is called a *cycle*. The frequency of the sound is measured in cycles per second, or *herz (Hz)*. By varying the number of pulses per second the frequency of the note can be determined.

Although we can set the frequency of the sounds, we have no control over the volume of the individual notes. The speaker in the Amstrad PC is not very sophisticated so there is a tendency for the volume to vary depending on the frequency.

PROGRAMMING THE 8253 TIMER

One way of creating sound is to program the timer chip to emit pulses at a given frequency and then direct these pulses to the speaker.

The timer has a register in which it stores the number of ticks after which it is to generate a pulse. Any value can be placed in this register, which is two bytes long and can therefore store an unsigned integer up to 65535. The timer counts the clock ticks and when the number reaches the value stored in its register it emits a pulse and resets the counter to 0.

The higher the value in the register, the lower the number of pulses per second and the lower the frequency of the sound. To get a high note the number in the register should be reduced. The number to be placed in the register for a particular sound can be calculated as follows:

Register value = CPU frequency / sound frequency

To produce middle C requires a frequency of 261.63 so the count is calculated as follows:

Register value = 1193180 / 261.6

= 4561.09

Therefore putting the value 4561 in the register is the closest we can get to middle C.

Similarly the frequency of the sound can be calculated by rearranging the formula:

Sound frequency = CPU frequency / register value

For example, if the register is set to its maximum value the frequency is calculated as follows:

Sound frequency = 1193180 / 65536

= 18.206

This is the lowest note the Amstrad PC can produce and is slightly higher than the A three octaves below middle C.

Sound

	Sound frequencies (Hz)						
			Octave				
Note	1	2	3	4	5	6	7
C	16.4	32.7	65.4	130.8	261.6*	523.3	1046.5
C#	17.3	34.7	69.3	138.6	277.2	554.4	1108.7
D	18.4	36.7	73.4	146.8	293.7	587.3	1174.7
D#	19.5	38.9	77.8	155.6	311.1	622.3	1244.5
E	20.6	41.2	82.4	164.8	329.6	659.3	1328.5
E#	21.8	43.7	87.3	174.6	349.2	698.5	1396.9
F	23.1	46.3	92.5	185.0	367.0	740.0	1480.0
G	24.5	49.0	98.0	196.0	392.0	784.0	1568.0
G#	26.0	51.9	103.8	207.7	415.3	830.6	1661.2
A	27.5	55.0	110.0	220.0	440.0	880.0	1760.0
A#	29.1	58.3	116.5	223.1	466.2	932.3	1864.7
B	30.9	61.7	123.5	246.9	493.9	987.8	1975.5

* Middle-C

Figure 14.1 Sound frequencies

A table of the frequencies of standard notes is given in Figure 14.1.

Sound generation procedures

The production of sound using the timer requires two separate stages: programming the timer and setting the PPI port.

The 8253 Timer's register needs to be set in two parts, by sending values to its ports. The timer's ports are numbered 42h and 43h. The timer register is set as follows:

1. Instruct the timer to expect a value for the register, by sending the value B6h to port 43h.

2. Send the register value to port 42h as two separate bytes, with the low byte followed by the high byte.

As soon as the timer receives the second byte it starts to send out pulses. However, these pulses are emitted to any part of the system that cares to listen. There is no audible sound until the speaker is switched on.

The speaker is just one of the devices controlled by the Programmable Peripheral Interface (PPI) chip. Instructions are sent to this chip by sending values to its port, number 61h.

The chip is constantly checking this port and acting upon its value. Only bits 0 and 1 effect the speaker; the other bits are used to control other devices and therefore they must be left unchanged.

When bit 0 of port 61h is cleared to 0 the speaker is turned on and ready to receive further instructions directly; in this state the speaker is pushed out when bit 1 is set to 1 and is pulled in when bit 1 is cleared.

When bit 0 of port 61h is set to 1 the speaker is ready to be controlled by the timer. Whether or not it sounds depends upon whether bit 1 is set or clear.

Thus we can determine the method of generating sound with bit 0 and the movement of the speaker with bit 1.

To make the speaker respond to the pulses of the timer both of these bits must be set to 1. This is done quite simply by the formula:

New port value = Old port value OR 03h

(Remember that the original values of bits 3 to 7 must not be altered.)

Once the speaker has been switched on the value in the timer register can be varied to change the note that is being played. The frequencies and duration of the notes can be determined from a string of data values (Figure 14.2) or by key presses.

The advantage of this method is that most of the work is done by the timer chip and therefore the CPU is free to carry on with other tasks while any particular note is playing. The disadvantage is that the sound produced is somewhat 'tinny' and has little scope for enhancement.

Sound

```
                        ; Three routines to generate sound:
                        ;   by displaying the BEL character;
                        ;   by programming to the Timer;
                        ;   and by writing direct to the ports

BEEP1:                  ; Sound the speaker once

                        ; Uses the standard DOS interrupt to
                        ;   display a character - in this case
                        ;   Chr$(7) (BEL)

                        ; Entry values: None
                        ; Exit values:  All register preserved

            push ax
            push dx
            mov dl,07h      ; DL = BEL
            mov ah,02h
            int 21h         ; Display character
            pop ax
            pop dx

; ----------------------------------------------------------------

TUNE:                   ; Plays a tune

                        ; Entry values: MUSIC=string of data
                        ; Exit values:  AX, CX, SX, SI changed

            jmp timest
freq        dd 1843200          ; Timer frequency
music       dw 294,2000h,330,2000h,262,2000h,131,2000h,196,4000h,0000h
                        ; Music data: frequency,duration
                        ;   terminated by nulls
timest:
            in al,61h
            push ax
            or al,03h           ; Set bits 0 and 1
            out 61h,al          ; Send value to port 61h
            xor si,si
note:
            mov ax,word ptr [freq]      ; Move Timer frequency into DX:AX
            mov dx,word ptr [freq+2]
            cmp byte ptr tune[si],0000h ; Is next note 0?
            jz endtune              ; If so, end
            div music[si]           ; Divide Timer frequency by note
            add si,02h              ; Point to duration
```

Sound

```
                push ax
                mov al,0B6h
                out 43h,al              ; Tell Timer to expect value
                pop ax
                out 42h,al              ; Send low byte
                mov al,ah
                out 42h,al              ; Send high byte
                mov cx,music[si]        ; Put duration in CX
                add si,02h
                call waitloop           ; Call delay loop
                jmp note                ; Repeat
endtune:
                pop ax
                out 61h,al              ; Switch speaker off
                int 20h


waitloop:                               ; Delay loop
                                        ; Delay value should be placed in CX

                push cx                 ; Save current CX
                xor cx,cx
                mov cl,20h              ; Loop 32 times
noploop:
                nop                     ; Loop to do nothing
                loop noploop
                pop cx                  ; Get CX back
                loop waitloop           ;    decrement and loop
                ret

; -----------------------------------------------------------------

SOUND:                                  ; Generate sound by direct write to port

                jmp soundst

portin:         db ?                    ; Port value on entry


soundst:
                cli                     ; Disable interrupts
                xor cx,cx
soundloop:
                in al,97                ; Get port 97h value
                mov [portin],al         ; Save value
                mov al,79
                out 97,al               ; output to port
                mov bx,cx
wait2:                                  ; Wait for shorter time each time
```

```
        dec bx
        jnz wait2
        mov al,[portin]     ; Get original port value
        out 97,al           ; Send to port
        inc cx
        cmp cx,0300h
        jnz soundloop
        sti                 ; Enable interrupts
        int 20h
```

Figure 14.2 Generating sound

DIRECT CONTROL OF THE SPEAKER

The alternative method for creating sound is to control the speaker directly. Again this is done through the PPI chip but this time bit 0 of port 61h is cleared. The speaker is then switched on and will pulse either in or out every time bit 1 changes between 0 and 1.

The speaker is switched on by the instruction:

New port value = Old port value AND FCh

This clears bits 0 and 1. To make a continuous tone the program must instruct the speaker to pulse in and out at a regular rate, by alternately setting and clearing bit 1. The instruction takes the form:

New port value = Old port value XOR 02h

Each time this instruction is issued the speaker changes its status.

The disadvantage of creating sound in this way is that it requires the constant attention of the program. It is also difficult to calculate the number of times the loop must be executed each second to create the required frequency. Finally, there is the very large problem that a different computer, working at a different speed, will produce a note of a completely different pitch.

However, there is one very big advantage to this direct programming. The programmer has complete control not only

Sound

over the pitch of the sound but also over the type of sound that is created. By varying the amount of time between pulses all sorts of different sounds can be created. With a great deal of work it is possible to really make the Amstrad 'sing'!

15. Disks and Disk Drives

The Amstrad PC uses two types of disk as its standard means of permanent data storage; these may be floppy disks or hard disks. This chapter describes the way in which the disk drives operate and how data is organised on the disks.

The chapter also looks at ways in which disks can be prepared for use, and how data can be copied onto and off disks. All these operations are carried out by the disk interrupts, which are listed in Figure 15.1.

FLOPPY DISK HARDWARE

The operation of the floppy disk drives is controlled by the uPD765A Floppy Disk Controller (FDC). This controller supports up to two $5\frac{1}{4}"$ drives. The system is able to discover the number of floppy drives installed by checking links LK1 and LK2 on the main board. LK1 is ignored; LK2 selects either one or two drives (Figure 15.2).

All data transfer is done via the DMA controller. The data transfer rate is 250 Kilobits/sec (approximately 30K per second). The clock frequency for the FDC is 4 MHz.

The operation of the drives is determined by port 03F2h, the use of which is shown in Figure 15.3. Bits 0 and 1 are used to select the drive; theoretically the FDC can cope with up to four floppy drives but the limit on the Amstrad PC is two. Therefore bit 1 is always 0, with bit 0 selecting the drive (0 for A, 1 for B). To switch the motor on bits 0 and 1 must be correctly set, after which either bit 4 (for drive A) or 5 (drive B) must be set.

When the drive motor is on the drive indicator light comes on. Data is read or written almost immediately. To test whether a drive motor is running, check location 043Fh. Bit 0 represents drive A and bit 1 is for drive B. A bit is set if the corresponding drive motor is on. After the data transfer is complete the drive stays on for a while as it slows down.

Disks and Disk Drives

Interrupt	Function	Effect
13	00	Reset disk
13	01	Read disk status
13	02	Read sectors
13	03	Write sectors
13	04	Verify sectors
13	05	Format tracks
21	0D	Reset disk
21	1A	Set disk transfer area address
21	2E	Disk write verification
21	2F	Get address of DTA
21	54	Check verification status
25	-	Read sectors from disk
26	-	Write sectors to disk

Figure 15.1 The disk interrupts

Link	Meaning if set
1	Drive A
2	Drive B
3	Not used
4	Not used

Figure 15.2 The floppy drive links

Bit	Use
7	Not used
6	Not used
5	Switch on drive 1 motor and enable selection of drive
4	Switch on drive 0 motor and enable selection of drive
3	Set to enable request to DMA
2	Reset Controller (by clearing, waiting, then setting bit)
1	) Select drive (00=drive A)
0	) (01=drive B

Figure 15.3 The effect of port 03F2h

Disks and Disk Drives

When a disk operation is complete the timeout value in the disk parameter table is loaded into location 0440h. This value is decremented at each clock tick. The default value is 64h; with 18.2 ticks per second this gives a timeout period of about 5.4 seconds. When the value is 0 the relevant bit at 043Fh is cleared and the drive light goes out.

The drive motor does not have to stop before another disk access can take place; when data is transferred from one drive to another both drives will be running. The drive light stays on either until the other drive is accessed or the motor stops. Only one floppy drive light can be on at a time.

The floppy disk interrupt The hardware interrupt for the FDC uses bit 7 of 043Eh. This bit is set by interrupt 0Eh.

The disk parameter table The ROM associated with the floppy disk controller contains a set of data relating to the operation of the drives. This is held in the *disk parameter table*. The location of the table is stored as interrupt vector 14h. This interrupt cannot be called from within a program. However, it is possible to change the vector to point to a different table, should this be necessary.

The values stored in the table are given in Figure 15.4.

Disk rattle On some PC1640's there is a tendency for the floppy disk drive to rattle. This only happens if a hard disk is also

Byte	Use	Value (hex)
00	2nd byte of disk controller command	DF
01	3rd byte of disk controller command	02
02	Motor timeout	64
03	Sector size code (default = 512 bytes)	02
04	Last sector or track	09
05	Gap length for read and write	2A
06	Data length	FF
07	Gap length for formatting	50
08	'Blank' character for formatting	F6
09	Head settling delay	0F
0A	Motor on delay	04

Figure 15.4 The disk parameter table

Disks and Disk Drives

installed. The problem can be overcome by running the program FDQUIET.COM, supplied on original disk 1.

DISKS

The Amstrad PC may be supplied with drives for two types of disk:

- Floppy disks (also referred to as 'minidisks' or 'diskettes')

- Hard disks (also known as 'fixed disks' or 'Winchesters')

In this book the two types of disk will be referred to as *floppy disks* and *hard disks*; any reference to the term *disks* can be taken to apply to both types of disk.

As well as the standard types of disk supplied as an integral part of the Amstrad PC, other types of disk can be added.

The Amstrad PC is supplied with either 1 or 2 5¼" drives. It can also be fitted with a 3½" drive, either internally or as an external device. Although other disk formats can theoretically be used and are mentioned below, these alternative, non-standard forms are not covered in detail.

FLOPPY DISKS Floppy disks consist of a circular disk coated with a magnetic substance. The disk is held loosely inside a square plastic case for protection. In the centre of the disk is a hub that is gripped by the disk drive; the drive can then spin the disk at very high speeds.

Cut into the disk case is an oval slot and the disk drive's read and write heads are positioned over this slot. As the disk spins it passes beneath the heads and they are able to write to the disk or read data previously written there.

The case has a square notch cut in one side. This is the *write-protect notch*. This is physically checked by the drive every time it performs a write operation. When the tab is covered the drive is physically restricted from changing the contents of the disk in any way.

The *index hole* at the hub of the disk is used by the drive to locate the 'start' of the tracks when formatting.

Disks and Disk Drives

```
DRIVEPARM d /F:f /H:L /S:s /T:t /NONREMOVABLE /CHECKDOOR

    where:

    d               Drive number (0=A, 1=B, etc.)
    f               Disk format (see below)
    h               Number of heads
    s               Number of sectors
    t               Number of tracks
    /CHECKDOOR      Checks to be carried out on door look before any access
    /NONREMOVABLE   Non-removable device

        N.B.  Only the drive number must be specified.
              All other parameters optional.
```

Figure 15.5 The DRIVPARM directive

HARD DISKS

Although the principles of hard disk operation are identical to those of floppies, the physical construction is very different.

Firstly, the disks are 3½" rather than 5¼". They are encased in a sealed unit, where a vacuum allows data to be stored much more compactly. They are spun at much higher speed than the floppies, providing faster access to data. These features need not particularly concern the programmer.

The major difference, of which we do need to be aware, is that the 'disk' actually consists of two physical disks, one above the other on a central spindle. As a result the hard disk has four 'sides'.

NON-STANDARD DEVICES

If you install a non-standard disk unit in the Amstrad PC then DOS needs to know the details. This is done via the DRIVPARM directive in CONFIG.SYS. The details to be specified are given in Figure 15.5.

The number of hard disks that have been installed is stored in memory location 0475h.

DISK ARCHITECTURE

The way in which disks are used is pretty much the same regardless of type; their actual construction - or *architecture* - is very different of course. A number of terms are used to describe the different parts of the disk. These are all used in the various ROS and MS-DOS interrupts, in the directories and so on, so a full understanding of their meaning is essential before we can consider how the disk is used.

The terminology used to define the organisation of the disks is as follows:

- *Platters.* Each hard disk unit consists of two or more physical disks, called platters, each of which has two sides. A floppy disk is analogous to a single platter.

- *Sides.* Each floppy disk has two sides, numbered 0 and 1.

- *Heads.* On hard disks the sides are frequently referred to as heads. These are numbered from 0 to 3.

- *Tracks.* Each side is marked out with a number of concentric circles, called tracks, along which the data is to be written. The tracks are numbered from 0 on the outside to either 39 or 79 on the inside. The maximum number of tracks per disk is limited by the disk drive.

- *Cylinders.* The tracks are grouped into cylinders, all the tracks with the same number forming a single cylinder. For example, cylinder 5 on a hard disk consists of the four tracks labelled 5 on sides 0 to 3.

- *Partitions.* Each hard disk is divided into one or more partitions, each partition consisting of a group of consecutive cylinders.

- *Sectors.* Each track is divided into a number of sectors, numbered from 1. The size and number of sectors is determined by the operating system or programmer. However, the capacity of each track is limited by the drive.

- *Clusters.* For the convenience of the operating system one or more sectors are sometimes grouped into clusters. Typically, there are two sectors per cluster.

Disks and Disk Drives

- *Density*. The number of tracks that each disk may hold and the capacity of each track is determined by the drive. These may be *double-density* or *quad-density*. Quad-density drives are also called 'high density'.

This method of organisation means that any part of a disk can be identified by a 3-dimensional reference:

- For a hard disk this is the head, cylinder and sector numbers.

- For a floppy disk it is the side, track and sector numbers.

The other terms will be explained in more detail as required.

HOW THE DISK IS USED

The reason for grouping tracks into cylinders becomes apparent when the method of accessing the disk is considered. The disk drive has a number of reading and writing heads; in the case of the Amstrad PC there is one head for each side. Thus a 20M hard disk with two platters has four heads; a floppy disk has two heads. All heads are moved at the same time and are at the same position relative to the centre of the disk. As the disk spins in the drive each head is able to read the data from a single track as it passes.

To make disk access as fast as possible the disk is filled a cylinder at a time; that is, data is first written to track 0 on side 0, then track 1 on side 1 and so on. When all tracks in a cylinder have been written the heads are advanced to the next cylinder, and the process is repeated. Thus a disk is filled cylinder by cylinder rather than side by side; this means that movement of the heads is kept to a minimum. Switching from one head to another merely involves accessing a different data channel and can be achieved under the control of the software; to access a different cylinder the heads must be physically moved. This takes a comparatively long time.

Since floppy disk drives also have two heads and the same method of writing data is employed (writing sides 0 and 1 alternately) it is obviously impossible to put a disk in upside down and expect to make sense of it (even if it is of the variety with write-protect notches on two edges), unless the disk has been formatted a side at a time.

Disks and Disk Drives

FORMATTING

A new disk contains no tracks or sectors, it is merely covered evenly with a substance that can store data. In order to recognise where to store data the drive must mark out the tracks on the disk, and on each track the start of the first sector must be identified. The drive does this by writing a string of data along the complete length of each track.

This process is called *formatting*. Because the drive physically writes to every byte of every track any existing data on a disk that is reformatted is irrecoverably lost.

Bad sectors

As it formats the disk the drive also verifies that every sector is usable. It does this by writing a string of 0's along the track, reading the track, re-writing the track with 1's and re-reading it. In this way every bit is written and read with both possible data values; any particular bit that cannot be read back correctly is incapable of being used to store data.

Since MS-DOS always works with complete sectors, any fault immediately results in the complete sector being marked as a *bad sector*. This sector is then ignored by the operating system. It takes only a single bad bit or byte for a complete sector to be unusable.

Bad sectors need not necessarily cause a problem. It is more common than not for any new hard disk to contain some bad sectors, though floppy disks that are formatted and repeatedly show bad sectors should be discarded. Bad sectors that develop after data has been stored can be identified with the CHKDSK command, though any data in them will be lost.

Note that the DOS DISKCOPY program, when used with a source disk that has bad sectors, will not copy any bad sectors to the target disk. This provides one useful means of copy protection: store some data on a sector, mark it as bad and read in the sector at the start of the program. The bad sector will not appear in directory listings and does not belong to a file so is not copied; DISKCOPY only copies across good sectors, ignoring any bad sectors.

Disks and Disk Drives

FLOPPY DISK TYPES

Floppy disks, disk formats and drives are catalogued according to their capacities as follows:

- Single- or double-sided

- Double- or quad-density

- Tracks per inch (tpi)

Floppy disks can actually be used for formats other than those intended by the manufacturer. For example, a single-sided disk can be formatted as double-sided quite easily. In fact the only difference between single- and double-sided floppy disks is that in the case of single-sided disks only one side is guaranteed by the manufacturer. It is perfectly possible to use a single-sided disk in a double-sided drive and many people do this; however, this is not recommended since the disk may develop faults and the slight saving in costs is surely far outweighed by the potential loss of valuable data.

Double-density floppy disks can also be used in quad-density drives but this practice is not advised for the same reasons.

Note also that problems can be encountered with double-density floppy disks that have been used in quad-density drives. It is not unusual to discover that after a disk has been formatted as double-density and then written by a quad-density drive (e.g. in an IBM PC-AT), the files cannot be read by some double-density drives. However, although many computers suffer from this difficulty this is not usually a problem with Amstrad PC's, which seem well able to cope with such disks.

Floppy disk organisation

The standard Amstrad PC is supplied with either one or two floppy disk drives. Each of these is double-sided (i.e. there are two heads, one for each side) and double-density.

DOS 3.2 formats floppy disks with 2 sides, 40 tracks per side and 9 sectors per track, each track containing 512 bytes. The capacity of a standard floppy disk is therefore:

2 x 40 x 9 x 512 = 368,640 bytes = 360K

Disk format codes

Disk code	Format
0	320K or 360K
1	1.2 Mb
2	720K
3	8-inch single density
4	8-inch double density
5	Hard disk
6	Tape drive
7	Other

Figure 15.6 Disk formats

DOS 1 used only 8 sectors per track and some early drives were only single-sided. While these earlier formats can be handled by later DOS versions, the reverse is not true: DOS 1 cannot cope with 9-sector tracks. Also, double-sided drives can read single-sided disks but double-sided disks cannot be read in a single-sided drive.

This does not cause a problem for the Amstrad PC's. If floppy disks are to be read by other machines with either DOS 1 or single-sided drives, the disks must be formatted with the /8 and /1 parameters respectively. Most programs these days take little notice of the earlier formats and there is no real need to ensure compatibility. However, if all disk access is done through the built-in commands, rather than through direct commands to the drives, the potential compatibility problem is already catered for.

DOS 3 is also capable of handling 3½" floppy disks and quad-density disks of both sizes; to utilise these formats a non-standard drive must have been fitted to the Amstrad PC. The disk formats that can be accommodated by DOS are summarised in Figure 15.6.

Hard disk organisation

The hard disk version of the PC1512 was originally supplied with either a 10M or 20M hard disk. The PC1640 and later versions of the PC1512 and PC1640 were supplied with 20M hard disks only. Other hard disks can be attached, of varying capacities.

Disks and Disk Drives

A 10M hard disk has just one platter (and therefore two sides or heads); a 20M hard disk has two platters (four sides).

The standard 20M hard disk has 306 cylinders. MS-DOS reserves one cylinder for its own use when the disk is partitioned. It also reserves four sectors on each of the other cylinders for storing information of its own.

Each track on a cylinder contains in the region of 30 sectors, each of 512 bytes.

PREPARING A HARD DISK

The preparation of a hard disk to store data is rather more complicated than the simple formatting required by a floppy and consists of three stages:

- HDFORMAT formats the entire hard disk

- FDISK divides the hard disk into partitions

- FORMAT prepares a DOS partition

Each of these operations must be carried out once only, and in the right order.

HDFORMAT

The hard disk format program, HDFORMAT.COM, is part of DOS. It performs a complete format of the hard disk, marking out the 306 cylinders. Since it does not know which operating systems are to be used, and therefore how many sectors per track, it does not mark out the sectors.

In the process it destroys any partitions and all data. HDFORMAT does not identify any bad sectors.

This process should only ever have to be carried out once. Any subsequent reformatting can be achieved by changing the partitions and/or reformatting individual partitions.

Note that performing HDFORMAT more than once may have an adverse effect on the hard disk.

FDISK

The DOS FDISK program marks out partitions on the hard disk. One cylinder is used by DOS to store information about the hard disk, leaving 305 for the partitions themselves. Each partition consists of a group of consecutive cylinders on the disk. The program allows you to define the first cylinder of the partition and the number of cylinders in the partition.

Disks and Disk Drives

The hard disk may contain up to four partitions. The maximum size of any partition under DOS 3 is 32Mb. DOS 2 only allowed one DOS partition but under DOS 3 there may be up to four DOS partitions; each of these is allocated its own drive letter.

DOS 3.3 provides a further variation, allowing any of these to be defined as the *primary* partition. A second partition may be defined as the *extended* partition and may also be active at the same time as the primary partition. There is no limit to the size of the extended partition, since it is divided into one or more sub-partitions, each of which has its own drive letter; each sub-partition may not exceed 32Mb. This effectively removes any limit on the number of DOS partitions and the amount of space allocated to DOS.

While this is not important for the standard Amstrad PC, which does not have enough hard disk space to worry about such considerations, if a high capacity hard disk is attached then it may well be worth installing DOS 3.3 to allow this form of partitioning.

Not all of the hard disk has to be divided into partitions, even if all four partitions are created. Although DOS warns you that deleting a partition will destroy its data, all that happens is that the information relating to the partition in the reserved cylinder is deleted; the cylinders used by the partition are made available for any new partitions. This means that defining a new partition with the same size, start cylinder and operating system recovers all the data, providing a useful means of hiding files on the disk. However, this sort of operation is extremely risky and no guarantees can be made.

Unlike some computers, the Amstrad PC does not require the installation of a device driver for the partitions.

FORMAT

A hard disk cannot be used by DOS until it has been partitioned. Each partition must then be prepared for data. We now have a disk with the tracks all marked but without a directory or file allocation table (which stores vital information about the location of files on disk). The DOS FORMAT program adds this information by writing certain data to specific sectors. In the case of hard disks, however, it does not need to carry out the low-level format that is included in floppy formatting; this has already been done by HDFORMAT.

Disks and Disk Drives

This is well worth knowing. All that FORMAT C: does is destroy the directory and file allocation table. The data remains intact and can therefore be recovered (theoretically at least!) by rebuilding the directory and file allocation table.

The spin-off from this is that is we want to destroy information altogether a FORMAT is insufficient; nothing less than HDFORMAT will do. (Alternatively, use FORMAT C: and then write sufficient new data to completely fill the hard disk; or write a blank sector of data to each sector in turn.)

Format Summary The various level of format are as follows:

- HDFORMAT performs a low-level format on hard disks, marking tracks only.

- FORMAT C: performs a high-level format on hard disks, writing directory sectors.

- FORMAT A: performs both a high-level and low-level format on floppy disks, marking tracks and writing sectors.

FORMATTING A DISK TRACK

The 8086 provides only one instruction for formatting a disk.

Interrupt:	13h
Function:	05h
Service:	Format disk track
Entry values:	AH=05h
	AL=number of sectors to format
	CH=track
	CL=sector
	DH=head
	DL=drive
	ES:BX=location of list of address marks
Exit values:	AH=error code (if CF=1)
	CF=(0 (success)
	(1 (error)

Only one track can be formatted at a time. Thus to format an entire disk it is necessary to set up a loop to format each track in turn.

341

This single instruction provides us with surprising flexibility. Obviously we must specify the drive, head and track number to format. In addition we must give the number of sectors per track and the layout of each individual sector.

The formatting process identifies the index hole on floppy disks and uses this to locate the first sector on the track. Each sector is then marked by placing an *address mark* at the start of the sector followed by the required number of bytes of blank data.

The address mark uniquely identifies the sector and completely defines its characteristics. It consists of four bytes that specify the following:

- Track (or cylinder) number

- Side (or head) number

- Sector number

- Code for the number of bytes per sector

As a general rule the track and side numbers match the values given in CH and DH; the sector numbers usually start from 1 and work through sequentially to the number given in AL; the number of bytes per sector is generally the same for each sector. However, any of these values can be changed at will; this causes chaos if we try to use the disk in ordinary circumstances but, used carefully, can provide some interesting copy-protection methods.

The address marks are used by the other services when reading, writing and verifying sectors; that is, the services search the given track number for a sector whose address mark matches the values given in the registers, so the order of the sectors is irrelevant. Reading or writing a sector that is marked with the wrong track or side number becomes impossible under these circumstances.

The data written to each track fills the track, without gaps, starting from the index hole on floppy disks; there is usually an unused area at the end of each track.

Disks and Disk Drives

Byte	Meaning	Normal Range	
		Hard disk	Floppy disk
1	Track/cylinder	0 - ??	0 - 39
2	Side/Head	0 - 3	0 - 1
3	Sector	1 - ??	1 - 9
4	Number bytes (code)	0 - 3	0 - 3
	N.B ?? = Number varies		
Byte 4: number of bytes code			
	Code	Bytes/sector	
	0	128	
	1	256	
	2	512	
	3	1024	

Figure 15.7 Sector address marks

The address marks must be stored in memory at ES:BX; there must be one 4-byte mark for each sector. The information relating to sector address marks is given in Figure 15.7.

Interleaving

The fact that logical sectors can appear in any physical order on the track means that hard disks can use a method called *interleaving*. Here the sectors are stored using a regular sequence. For example, with 2:1 interleaving the order of sectors is 1, 41, 2, 42, 3, 43, ... while 3:1 interleaving results in 1, 31, 61, 2, 32, 62, ...

The reason for this method is that the disk passes the head so quickly it cannot read and store all the information in one cycle. It reads one sector into a buffer but by the time this has been stored to memory the next sector has already passed. Therefore with 1:1 interleaving the disk has to rotate a full revolution before the next sector can be read. With 2:1 or 3:1 interleaving the time taken to pass the next one or two sectors is sufficient to store the first set of data away. So with 2:1 interleaving - if the CPU is fast enough - a complete track can

Disks and Disk Drives

be read in two revolutions; 3:1 interleaving takes 3 revolutions.

Obviously the disk is used most efficiently when the interleave ratio is as small as possible; this depends on the CPU speed and disk drive speed.

For the Amstrad PC hard disks the ratio is 3:1.

Varying the format

Different formats can be applied for different purposes. As a general rule, if our disks are to be used with DOS in a normal fashion then we should stick to the DOS FORMAT command and incorporate calls to this command in our programs.

However, there are good reasons for occasionally varying this procedure. In particular, we may want to make changes for copy-protection purposes.

Note that the largest number of bytes a floppy disk will take on one sector is in the region of 5120 for the inner track (track 39); that is, 10 sectors of 512 bytes, 20 of 256 bytes, etc. However, the drive head moves at constant speed so the outer tracks will take considerably more. When a track is formatted there is generally an unused area at the end of each track. If too many sectors are specified the head overruns and passes the index hole before the last sector has been completed; this results in a format failure.

Any errors in formatting are reported in the AH register, when the carry flag is set. The error numbers are listed in Figure 15.8.

ACCESSING A DISK

Whenever DOS needs to access a disk it first issues a Command 01h (Media check) to the device driver. (These commands are discussed in more detail in Chapter 19.) The purpose of this command is to test whether or not the disk has been replaced since the last access. The result is as follows:

- If the disk has not been changed then DOS assumes that the FAT and directory stored in memory are still an accurate copy of the disk's FAT and directory.

- If the disk has been changed DOS re-reads the FAT and directory.

Disks and Disk Drives

- If the response from the device driver is that it doesn't know whether the disk has changed, DOS checks the drive's file buffers. If these still contain information that has not been written to disk DOS assumes that the disk has not changed and writes the changed data to disk. (Should the disk have been replaced in fact, then the result is a corruption of the new disk and incomplete data on the old disk.) On the other hand, if the file buffers are empty, DOS assumes that the disk is different and reads the FAT and directory, as well as issuing a Command 02h (Build BPB) to the driver.

WORKING WITH SECTORS

Most of the time, when we want to access information on the disk, we will use the DOS file services. MS-DOS is, after all, a *disk* operating system and as such has been designed with the prime aim of transferring data to and from disk. Indeed, most of the time the way in which data is stored on disk makes it impractical to work with individual sectors.

However, there are some occasions when it becomes necessary to work with a single sector, in particular when we want to look at the disk directory and associated information, which is the only data on the disk whose position is fixed.

The ROS provides interrupts for reading, writing and verifying sectors.

The DOS sector-based interrupts

The ROS reading and writing options are duplicated by the MS-DOS interrupts.

The two MS-DOS interrupts (25h and 26h) are rather curious, in that they are the only DOS functions that work directly with the disk, rather than the DOS disk and file structures. In general, it seems a pointless exercise to use these interrupts when we could use the more efficient ROS interrupts.

Note also that the DOS interrupts do not pop the flags register off the stack; this must be done by the calling routine.

DOS sector numbers

The DOS routines are very similar to those of the ROS, with the exception that they use different registers and, more importantly, a different numbering system for the sectors of the disk. Rather than locating a sector by giving the side, track and sector number the sectors are numbered sequentially from the first sector, which is DOS sector 0.

Disks and Disk Drives

If a standard numbering system has been used (that is, the same number of sectors per track and all numbered sequentially from 1) then the following formula can be used to convert from ROS's Side:Track:Sector system to DOS sector numbers:

DOS sector = (Side x Sector per track)
 + (Track x Sectors per track x Number of sides)
 + Sector - 1

To convert from DOS sector numbers to the ROS system use the formulae:

Side = Int((DOS sector)/(Sectors per track))
 mod (Number sides)

Track = Int((DOS sector) /
 (Number sides x Sectors per track))

Sector = ((DOS sector) mod (Sectors per track)) + 1

where Int(x) represents the integer part of x.

For example, with a two-sided disk and 9 sectors per track, the fifth sector on side 1, track 3 can be translated as follows:

DOS sector = (1 x 9) + (3 x 9 x 2) + 5 = 68

or:

ROS Side = Int((68 - 1) / 9) mod 2 = 7 mod 2 = 1

ROS Track = Int((68 - 1) / (2 x 9)) = Int (67 / 18) = 3

ROS Sector = ((68 - 1) mod 9 + 1 = 4 + 1 = 5

Reading sectors Interrupt 13h, function 02h is used to read a sector into memory.

Interrupt: 13h
Function: 02h
Service: Read sectors from disk
Entry values: AH=02h
AL=number of sectors to read
CH=track
CL=sector

Disks and Disk Drives

	DH=head
	DL=drive
	ES:BX=start of buffer for storing data
Exit values:	AH=error code (if CF=1)
	AL=number of sectors read (if CF=0)
	CF=(0 (success)
	(1 (error)

The service reads one or more sectors into an area of memory pointed to by ES:BX. If you are writing a general routine to read in a sector from any disk make sure you allow enough space in memory for sectors of 1024 bytes.

When more than one sector is read they must all be on the same track and side.

Usually, you will be working with one sector at a time. It is only when copying an entire disk or some similar operation that it is necessary to read all the sectors in one track at the same time.

You may also want to read an entire track when comparing the contents of the two disks (as in the DOS DISKCOMP program).

DOS provides an almost identical interrupt to the above.

Interrupt:	25h
DOS version:	1
Service:	Read sectors from disk
Entry values:	AL=logical drive number (A=0)
	CX=number of sectors to read
	DX=first sector (DOS numbering)
	DS:BX=start of buffer for storing data
Exit values:	AH=DOS error code (if CF=1)
	AL=ROS error code (if CF=1)
	CF=(0 (success)
	(1 (error)
	Flags register on stack

This interrupt requires conversions between the ROS Side:Track:Sector numbering system and DOS's own rather strange sector numbering.

Writing sectors   The converse of the above function writes one or more sectors from memory to disk.

347

Disks and Disk Drives

```
Interrupt:       13h
Function:        03h
Service:         Write sectors to disk
Entry values:    AH=03h
                 AL=number of sectors to write
                 CH=track
                 CL=sector
                 DH=head
                 DL=drive
                 ES:BX=start of buffer containing data
Exit values:     AH=error code (if CF=1)
                 AL=number of sectors written (if CF=0)
                 CF=(0 (success)
                     (1 (error)
```

This function works in a similar manner to function 02h.

The DOS equivalent is interrupt 26h.

```
Interrupt:       26h
DOS version:     1
Service:         Write sectors to disk
Entry values:    AL=logical drive number (A=0)
                 CX=number of sectors to write
                 DX=first sector (DOS numbering)
                 DS:BX=start of buffer containing data
Exit values:     AH=DOS error code (if CF=1)
                 AL=ROS error code (if CF=1)
                 CF=(0 (success)
                     (1 (error)
                 Flags register on stack
```

A copy of a disk can be made by repeating the functions to read and write a sector. The DOS DISKCOPY program also incorporates the function to format a track, as necessary. One problem with DISKCOPY on single-drive machines is that there is no way of telling when the disks are put in in the wrong order.

Verifying sectors   The verify function checks that sectors are not damaged.

```
Interrupt:       13h
Function:        04h
Service:         Verify disk sectors
Entry values:    AH=04h
                 AL=number of sectors to verify
```

	CH=track
	CL=sector
	DH=head
	DL=drive
Exit values:	AH=error code (if CF=1)
	AL=number of sectors verified (if CF=0)
	CF=(0 (success)
	(1 (error)

The operation of this function is similar to that of the read and write functions. It checks the address of each sector and performs a CRC check on the data.

The service does not check that data has been written correctly. If you want to check that a write operation transferred data accurately the most effective method is to read the sector back into memory, alongside the original data, and then compare the two sets of data.

However, this sort of operation is not really necessary, unless you think there may be a fault in the drive. Most data errors can be detected by the verify option but this, again, is very rarely needed.

DOS provides a service to verify all sectors as they are written.

Interrupt:	21h
Function:	2Eh
DOS version:	1
Service:	Disk write verification
Entry values:	AH=2Eh
	AL=(00 (verify off)
	(01 (verify on)
	DL=00h
Exit values:	None

This service can be used to either turn verification off (the default when the system is started) or on. It forms the basis of the DOS VERIFY command.

Again, this is not a verification that the data has been accurately transferred but a check on the sector parity. Verification makes all disk access much slower.

Yet another DOS function tells us the current verification status.

Disks and Disk Drives

Interrupt:	21h
Function:	54h
DOS version:	2
Service:	Check verification status
Entry values:	AH=54h
Exit values:	AL=(00 (verify off)
	(01 (verify on)

There certainly do seem to be a lot of functions for such a worthless operation!

DISK BUFFERS For each open file DOS maintains a disk buffer in memory. The purpose of these buffers is to minimise the frequency of disk accesses (since any operation involving the disks is slow in comparison to operations in memory).

When any instruction is given to write data to disk, DOS actually places it in the disk buffer. It is only when the buffer is full that it actually writes the data away. Similarly, when requested to read data from disk DOS first checks the buffer to see if the required data is already there. If it is not, DOS writes away all changed data and reads in enough data to completely fill the buffer.

The size of the buffer is measured in terms of sectors (since DOS must always read and write whole sectors). The default is 2 sectors but this can be changed with the BUFFERS directive in CONFIG.SYS.

The number of sectors allocated needs to be quite finely tuned. Too small a buffer slows down the program while too large a buffer takes up valuable memory; a large buffer also takes longer to read and write. Generally speaking, a program that uses sequential files should have small buffers, since the entire file is being read anyway; for random access files the number can be determined by the amount of chopping and changing from one part of the file to another.

Each sector in the buffer takes up to 528 bytes of memory: 16 bytes for a header and 512 bytes for the data itself.

The buffers are only finally written away when the file is closed. This explains the reason that data may be lost if a program is not exited properly.

Disks and Disk Drives

ROS disk status codes	
Code (hex)	Meaning
01	Bad command
02	Missing address mark
03	Disk write-protected
04	Sector not found
05	Reset failure
06	Drive empty/drive door open
07	Hard disk parameter table invalid
08	DMA error
09	DMA boundary error
0A	Bad hard disk sector mark
10	CRC error
11	Hard disk CSC error
20	Controller error
40	Seek failure
80	Time-out error
AA	Hard disk not ready
BB	General hard disk error
CC	Hard disk write error
E0	Hard disk status error

Figure 15.8 The disk status

Disk buffers are a feature of MS-DOS; they need not be a concern if using the ROS interrupts to read and write sectors.

THE DISK STATUS

All disk-based operations return a single byte in AH called the *disk status*. This byte is set to 0 if the operation was completed successfully. If any sort of error occurred the carry flag is set and the type of error is indicated by the disk status. The errors are the same for all disk operations, although obviously some of them apply only to one or two operations (see Figure 15.8).

The disk status remains the same until the next disk operation. The status can be checked at any time.

Disks and Disk Drives

Interrupt: 13h
Function: 01h
Service: Check disk status
Entry values: AH=01h
Exit values: AH=status code

This service returns in AH the disk status derived from the last disk operation, no matter how long ago it may have been.

The value in AX is identical to that stored in memory location 0441h for floppy disk operations. The next seven bytes are used to store return information after a floppy disk operation; these bytes are also used for hard disk parameters. Further on in memory, at 0474h, the hard disk BIOS stores its disk status.

The floppy disk status can also be affected through input to port 034Fh. Port 03F5h is used for other FDC information.

The usual procedure is to deal with disk errors with a single routine that is called after every disk operation. As a general rule every operation should be tried 2 or 3 times before the error routine is invoked. This is for a variety of reasons; the speed of the drive may not be sufficient the first time the routine is called, the user may be in the process of shutting the drive door, and so on.

The DOS functions return the same error codes in AH but also set their own errors in AL. These errors add very little to those of the ROS (Figure 15.9).

Resetting the disk After any error it is usual to *reset* the disk drive.

Interrupt: 13h
Function: 00h
Service: Reset disk
Entry values: AH=00h
Exit values: None

This operation merely repositions the drive head over a particular track, ready for the next disk operation.

DOS also provides a function to reset the disk.

Interrupt: 21h
Function: 0Dh

DOS disk error codes (AL)	
Code (hex)	Meaning
00	Disk write-protected
01	Bad drive number
02	Drive not ready
04	CRC error
06	Seek error
07	Unknown disk format
08	Sector not found
0A	Write error
0B	Read error
0C	General error

Figure 15.9 DOS disk error codes

DOS version: 1
Service: Reset disk
Entry values: AH=0Dh
Exit values: None

This function writes away any information still held in its disk buffers, as well as resetting the disk. However, this is not the recommended method for clearing the buffers. If a file is extended the new length is not stored in the directory, which will cause problems later. To make sure this does not happen, all files should be properly closed.

16. *The Disk Directory*

Once a disk has been formatted, all information is stored on disk as a file, whether it is a program, data or information needed by the system. This chapter describes the directories used by MS-DOS for recording details of the files stored on a disk.

The interrupts detailed in this chapter are all peculiar to MS-DOS; different operating systems will use different interrupts. The information given here all relates to the DOS system of organising disks and files. The interrupts that relate to the disk directory are listed in Figure 16.1. Note that the interrupt 21h functions from 2Fh onwards are not available on DOS 1. Those from 59h onwards are only available on DOS 3. Therefore all these functions are usable on the Amstrad PC but may restrict portability to other PC's (those above 57h in particular).

ASCIIZ strings DOS 1 used various characters to indicate the end of text, such as Ctrl-Z to mark the end of files, '$' for the end of input strings and carriage return (0Dh) for other items.

DOS 2 moved closer to the Unix style by adopting the null character (00h) as a standard terminator. In particular, it is used to terminate strings applied as input for interrupts; all DOS 2 functions expect file specifications to be terminated by the null character. This form of input, consisting of standard ASCII characters ending with 00h is generally referred to as *ASCIIZ* (ASCII with zero).

DISK STRUCTURE INFORMATION

When we use the DOS FORMAT command on a floppy disk two things happen; there is a low-level format of the disk - using ROS interrupt 13h function 05h - and the data that determines the disk structure is placed on the disk. The FORMAT command when used on a hard disk ignores the low-level formatting, merely placing the disk structure information on the disk. In either case the operating system files may also be transferred.

The disk structure information falls into three parts:

The Disk Directory

Interrupt	Function	Effect
21	0E	Change current drive
	19	Get current drive
	1B	Get FAT information for current drive
	1C	Get FAT information for any drive
	29	Parse filename
	36	Check free clusters
	39	Make directory
	3A	Remove directory
	3B	Change directory
	47	Check current directory
	57,00	Get date and time stamp
	57,01	Set date and time

Figure 16.1 Directory interrupts

- The *boot record*, which holds information about the disk and can be used to load the operating system if it is on the disk.

- The *file allocation table (FAT)*, which holds information about how space is allocated to files on the disk.

- The *disk directory*, which stores information about the files on the disk.

Each of these three components is discussed below.

HOW DIRECTORIES ARE CREATED

After the FORMAT command has marked the tracks on the surface of the disk it performs the following operations:

1. The *boot record* is placed in Side 0, Track 0, Sector 1.

2. Two copies of the File Allocation Table (FAT) are stored immediately after the boot record.

3. A blank directory is created, immediately after the second FAT.

4. If the /S parameter has been specified the two system files (IO.SYS and MSDOS.SYS) are placed after the directory,

followed by COMMAND.COM. The FAT and file directory are updated accordingly.

5. An option is provided to give the disk an 11-character volume label.

THE FILE DIRECTORY

A file directory is simply a list of the files that are stored on the disk. The main directory on the disk (which has its physical location immediately after the FAT) is called the *root directory*. The directory has a finite size and therefore can only store a limited number of files. Since we need to store many hundreds of files on a hard disk the root directory alone is clearly not enough. For this reason DOS 2 introduced the concept of *sub-directories*.

A sub-directory is simply a file that has a structure identical to that of the root directory. Therefore, it may be used for storing details of more files. Any sub-directory may hold other sub-directories, and so on for as many levels as are needed.

Because a sub-directory is a file and any file can be any reasonable length, there is effectively no limit to the number of entries in a sub-directory. The important difference is that a root directory is restricted to a specific fixed-length location on the disk while a sub-directory can be extended as often as we like. However, common sense suggests that we should keep sub-directories small for them to be manageable. These conditions are, of course, left to the end-user but it is the task of the programmer (or his documenter) to advise on usage.

DOS uses the directory and the FAT to locate a file and to find blank areas for storing new data. Therefore if data is placed on the disk and not recorded in the directory and FAT, the data does not exist as far as DOS is concerned. This means that it is in danger of being overwritten whenever any DOS file operations are performed.

This is particularly likely to happens if you use the ROS interrupts to store data directly onto sectors. For this reason, you should always use the DOS interrupts wherever possible and let DOS worry about where data is stored. If you do write

357

The Disk Directory

direct to blank areas of the disk make sure you update the FAT accordingly.

The only reasons for working directly with sectors are:

- When a different operating system is being used or there is no disk operating system at all

- When inspecting or changing the disk structure information

- As a means of copy-protection

Perhaps most importantly, it is unwise to start mixing DOS operations and ROS sector interrupts on the same disk because of the confusion that can arise.

DIRECTORY STRUCTURE

It is important to stress that, apart from the disk-structure information, everything DOS places on the disk is recorded in the directory and allocated space on disk. This includes sub-directories and the disk's volume label.

The file directory consists of a number of entries, one for each file. Each entry is 32 bytes long, so there are 16 entries per 512 byte sector. For the root directory, the number of entries is limited by the number of sectors allocated by the operating system, and this depends on the type of disk. The number of entries for a variety of disk formats is given in Figure 16.2. The Amstrad PC's 360K floppy disks have 7-sector directories, allowing up to 112 root directory entries. There is no limit to the size of sub-directories.

The structure of each directory entry is given in Figure 16.3. The use of each parameter is described below.

Filename

Every file must have a *filename*, up to a maximum of eight characters long, consisting of letters, numbers and the symbols shown in Figure 16.4. There must be no spaces in the name. Upper and lower case letters are treated as being the same, the lower case letters being converted to capitals before being stored in the directory. The filename is padded with trailing spaces to fill it out to eight characters.

Directory code

If the first character of the filename is not a legal filename character then it must be one of the following:

The Disk Directory

Space allocations for FAT & root directory (5.25")							
		Size in sectors FAT	Root directory	Total (Boot + FATx2 + directory)	Entries in root directory	Cluster size	Data clusters
8 sector	SS DD	1	4	7	64	1	323
	DS DD	1	7	10	112	2	351
9 sector	SS DD	2	4	13	64	1	630
	DS DD	2	7	12	112	2	708
	QD	7	14	29	224	1	2371

Figure 16.2 Root directory entries

Contents of file directory entries	
Bytes	Meaning
0-7	Filename of entry code
8-10	Extension
11	Attributes
12-21	Reserved (unused)
22-23	Time stamp
24-25	Date stamp
26-27	Start cluster
28-31	File size

Figure 16.3 Directory structure

- 00h (the null character). The directory entry has not yet been used

- 2Eh (full stop). Indicates information relating to a sub-directory

- E5h (σ). Deleted file

These special cases are described later.

359

The Disk Directory

Character	Hex	Explanation
!	21	Exclamation
#	23	Hash
$	24	Dollar
%	25	Percent
&	26	Ampersand
'	27	Apostrophe
(	28	Open bracket
)	29	Close bracket
-	2D	Minus
0 - 9	30 - 39	Decimal numbers
A - Z	41 - 5A	Upper case letters
_	5F	Underscore
a - z	61 - 6A*	Lower case letters
{	7B	Open brace
}	7D	Close brace
~	7E	Tilde

* Lower case letters converted to upper case (41h - 5Ah)

Figure 16.4 Valid filename characters

Extension

Most files are given an *extension* to indicate what sort of files they are.

The file extension is padded with blanks (32h) if it is less than three characters long. (The period that separates the filename and extension in file specifications is not stored in the directory of course; this is filtered out by the DOS commands.) The rules for the extension are the same as those for the filename.

The COM, EXE and BAT extensions have special meanings for DOS and must be used in certain circumstances. Apart from these, there are some commonly-applied conventions but actual usage is entirely up to the user. Application programs usually suggest default extensions for certain purposes and use other extensions for specific files but it is not usual to force users to adopt any specific extensions.

The Disk Directory

Bit	Meaning (if set)
0	Read-only file
1	Hidden file
2	System file
3	Volume label
4	Subdirectory
5	Archive
6-7	Not used

NB Under DOS 1 only bits 1 and 2 were used

Figure 16.5 The file attribute byte

Attribute A single *attribute byte* stores information about what sort of file it is. Each bit in the attribute byte indicates some feature of the file (Figure 16.5). The attributes are as follows:

- *Read-only.* The file cannot be changed. Its contents may be displayed or printed only. If this attribute is not set then the file can be changed and the file is said to be a *Read/Write* file.

- *Hidden file.* The file is not included in DIR directory listings, and is therefore ignored by any program that uses this command to get a list of files. It is also ignored by DOS commands such as COPY and TYPE.

- *System file.* Indicates this is one of the files read into memory when the system is booted, before the command processor is executed. (Usually IO.SYS and MSDOS.SYS.)

- *Volume label.* This entry is not a file but is used purely to hold the name of the disk.

- *Sub-directory.* This file is a sub-directory, storing details of further files.

- *Archive.* The file has not been copied by the BACKUP or XCOPY commands since it was created or last modified. The /M parameter in the BACKUP and XCOPY commands checks this attribute and only backs up those files for which it is set. Whenever DOS stores a file or updates its

The Disk Directory

Code (hex)	Read-only	Hidden	System	Volume	Subd.	Archive
00						
01	X					
02		X				
03	X	X				
04			X			
05	X		X			
06		X	X			
07	X	X	X			
08				X		
10					X	
12		X			X	
20						X
21	X					X
22		X				X
23	X	X				X
24			X			X
25	X		X			X
26		X	X			X
27	X	X	X			X

Figure 16.6 Valid file attributes

directory entry in any way this bit is set; only BACKUP and XCOPY are used to clear the bit though there is no reason why other routines should not be made to do so.

Theoretically any combination of attributes could be set but many are meaningless or have no effect. For example, setting bits 6 and 7 does not affect the way in which the file is treated by the operating system; similarly, the archive attribute has no meaning when applied to a sub-directory. However, there is no reason why these unusual combinations should not be set by a program for a special purpose: for example, a program might set the archive attribute on the volume label entry to indicate that the disk has been backed up at some stage.

The combinations likely to be encountered (assuming no tampering with the system) are illustrated in Figure 16.6.

The Disk Directory

The file attributes can be read or changed with DOS function 43h. In both cases, the file specification must be supplied as an ASCIIZ string.

Interrupt:	21h
Function:	43,00h
DOS version:	2
Service:	Get attributes of file
Entry values:	AH=43h
	AL=00h
	DS:DX=address of ASCIIZ file specification
Exit values:	AX=error code (if CF=1)
	DX:AX=attribute byte

This function returns the current attributes as a byte in CL.

Interrupt:	21h
Function:	43,01h
DOS version:	2
Service:	Set attributes of file
Entry values:	AH=43h
	AL=01h
	CX=new attribute byte
	DS:DX=address of ASCIIZ file specification
Exit values:	AX=error code (if CF=1)

This function sets the attributes for a file. The new attribute byte is placed in CL; CH must be zero.

The DOS ATTRIB command changes the read-only and archive attributes of a file. It can also be used to list all files with their attributes.

Time stamp

Two bytes are used to store the time at which the file was created or last modified. This is called a *time stamp*. Whenever a change is made to the file this value is updated. However, the time stamp is not changed when the file is copied or renamed. Thus, the time should always give an accurate representation of when the last changes were made.

The time-stamp word is stored in the traditional manner with the low byte first. For example, the two bytes in the directory may appear as 'D943'. The actual value is 43D9h.

Within this word the data is packed quite tightly to give the full range of values:

363

The Disk Directory

- The top five bits store the hour, in the range 0 to 23.

- The next six bits represent the minutes, from 0 to 59.

- The last five bits give the number of seconds, divided by 2.

There is insufficient space in the word to store the seconds exactly. Therefore the last part yields a number in the range 0 to 29 which, when doubled, gives the seconds from 0 to 58.

Date stamp   The next two-byte word stores the date when the file was created or changed, again with the low byte first (the *date stamp*). The date is packed into the word as follows:

- The top seven bits store the number of years since 1980; the range is 0 to 119 representing the years from 1980 to 2099.

- The next four bits store the month, from 1 to 12.

- The last five bits give the day of the month, from 1 to 31.

These items are only any use if the date and time are correctly maintained in the system of course.

Note that when the values are being stored by the interrupt there is no error checking; for example, putting in a date of 31/2/2088 and a time of 30:63:63 does not make the system jump up and down with rage; however it will mean that the directory listing looks a little strange!

DOS function 57h (described in the next chapter) also updates the time and date for an open file.

Start cluster   This item points to the location on disk of the first cluster of the file.

File size   This is the actual size of the file in bytes. Divide by the cluster size and round up to calculate the number of clusters allocated to the file

Even though most files do not use whole numbers of clusters, the complete cluster is always allocated to them and is therefore unavailable for other files. As a result, even a file of only ten bytes in length reduces the free space on directory

The Disk Directory

listings by 1024 bytes, even though the file size may be listed as 10.

Some programs read and write data to disk a block at a time, so the size may always be shown as a multiple of 128 bytes, for example, even though the true end of the file comes earlier.

The size is stored as a double-word. Following the usual convention, the value is stored with the least significant byte first, so the four bytes are in reverse order.

DISPLAYING THE DIRECTORY

By using all this information about the directory entries and combining it with the interrupts to read disk sectors, we can inspect the directory of any disk.

VOLUME LABELS

Volume labels are merely names attached to disks for ease of identification. Although they have little effect on the operation of the system they can be a useful safeguard, for example to identify different versions of programs or data.

The volume label is held in the filename and extension parts of the directory entry and may therefore be up to 11 characters long. The date and time stamps are used to store the date and time when the volume was created, or the time when the volume label was added or changed if this is different.

The volume label can be changed with the LABEL command (DOS 3 only) and can be displayed with the VOL command.

The routine in Figure 16.7 provides the opportunity to enter or change the label of any disk.

SUB-DIRECTORIES

As we have seen above, a directory is only a collection of fixed-length records, each one containing information about a particular file stored on the disk.

The Disk Directory

```
FINDVOL:                            ; Displays a disk's volume label
                                    ; This is a totally self-contained
                                    ;   program which could be converted
                                    ;   into a routine

                                    ; Entry values: None
                                    ; Exit values:  AX, BX, CX, DX changed

              jmp volst
fname         db '*.*',00h
volst:
              mov cx,08h            ; CX=Volume attribute
              lea dx,fname          ; Point to filename
              mov ah,4eh
              int 21h               ; Find first matching file
              lea dx,9eh            ; Point to filename
              mov bx,9eh
              mov byte ptr [bx+08h],'$'  ; Add a $
              mov ah,09h
              int 21h               ; Display volume name
              lea dx,0a7h
              mov byte ptr [bx+0ch],'$'
              int 21h
              int 20h
```

Figure 16.7 Displaying the disk label

A sub-directory is merely an extension of this idea. In the same way as for the root directory it is, in effect, a random access file whose records contain information about files on the disk.

SUB-DIRECTORY STRUCTURE The size and layout of sub-directory entries is identical to that of the root directory. The main difference is that a sub-directory is not restricted to a particular location on the disk. Since it is a normal file - in most senses - it is not restricted in size either and can be extended as much as you wish. Therefore there is no artificial limit to the number of entries in the sub-directory.

The first two entries in the sub-directory have the following values and meanings in the filename field:

. (2Eh) Sub-directory

.. (2E2Eh) Parent directory

The first indicates to DOS that this is a sub-directory. The date and time stamps contain the date and time at which the sub-directory was created. The size field indicates the amount of space taken up by the sub-directory. The start cluster number is the start cluster of the sub-directory itself.

The second entry refers to the *parent directory*, the only relevant part being the start cluster number which is the start position of the parent directory. If this value is 0000h the parent is the root directory.

The cluster number here and that of the sub-directory's entry in the parent directory provide an important link between the directories. The main entry points to the start of the sub-directory; the entry in the sub-directory points back to the main directory. These values allow us to move with ease up and down the directory tree; without them we would be able to move in only one direction.

THE CURRENT DRIVE AND DIRECTORY

Whenever a command or instruction refers to a disk drive or a directory there are two ways of specifying its name:

- The full specification can be given, to avoid any ambiguity.

- The drive, directory or both can be ignored, in which case the current defaults are used.

There are a number of ways of changing the defaults.

Current drive

Unless we specify otherwise, any operations that are carried out refer to the *current drive*. This is the default drive that is searched by DOS whenever it needs to find a file or perform some action on an entire disk.

Initially the current drive is the one from which the operating system was booted. At the DOS command line the current drive is changed by entering the drive letter and a colon.

DOS provides two interrupts for finding out which is the current drive and for changing the drive. The drive is always referred to with a numeric code, where 0 represents drive A, 1 is drive B and so on.

The Disk Directory

Interrupt:	21h
Function:	19h
DOS version:	1
Service:	Get current drive
Entry values:	AH=19h
Exit values:	AL=default drive code (0=A, 1=B, etc.)

This is a very simple interrupt, returning the current drive code in AL.

There is also a DOS function whose main purpose is to change the current drive.

Interrupt:	21h
Function:	0Eh
DOS version:	1
Service:	Change current drive
Entry values:	AH=0Eh
	DL=drive number (0=A, 1=B, etc.)
Exit values:	AL=drive count

This is a rather curious service. The new drive number is placed in DL, but the service returns the number of available drives in AL. This has the disadvantage that we can use the function to discover the number of drives but only after we have found out the current drive; otherwise, this function on its own will reset the current drive.

This function is used by DOS commands such as 'A:' to change to drive B.

Remember that the number of drives will include the RAM disk (if there is one). It will also include a logical drive B for single-floppy systems (i.e. an Amstrad PC1640 HD20 with one floppy and a RAM disk will report four drives).

The current drive can also be checked by inspecting port 03F2h.

The current directory

In the same way as there is a current drive, so there is a *current directory*. This is the directory in which DOS will search for a file unless we specify otherwise. Initially the current directory is the root directory of the current drive. Unlike the current drive, of which there is only one, there is a current directory for each drive.

The Disk Directory

Any of the current directories can be changed. One way to do this is through the DOS CD (CHDIR) command. Another way is via the DOS interrupts.

Interrupt: 21h
Function: 47h
DOS version: 2
Service: Check current directory
Entry values: AH=47h
DL=drive (0=default)
DS:SI=address for pathname
Exit values: AX=error code (if CF=1)
DS:SI=address of pathname

Function 47h returns the current directory for the drive number specified in DL. The directory consists of the path from the root directory, excluding the drive specifier and the initial backslash; the result is an ASCIIZ string, so is terminated by the null character. If the current directory is the root directory, then this is reported simply as the null character.

Interrupt: 21h
Function: 3Bh
DOS version: 2
Service: Change directory
Entry values: AH=3B
DS:DX=address of ASCIIZ directory name
Exit values: AX=error code (if CF=1)

This function is very simple to use and is the equivalent of the CD (CHDIR) command. The drive is specified in DL and the ASCIIZ string containing the pathname is pointed to by DS:DX. The drive specifier and root directory backslash need not be included in the path name.

Paths

As a general rule any command that is entered refers to the current directory or, if the path begins with a backslash, the root directory. DOS makes life a little easier with the PATH and APPEND commands, which allow us to provide a list of paths that are searched for programs and data files respectively when DOS cannot find them in the current directory. There is no simple interrupt-based alternative to these high-level commands.

369

The Disk Directory

Creating a sub-directory

Sub-directories are created through DOS with the MD (MKDIR) command. This is based on DOS function 39h.

Interrupt:	21h
Function:	39h
DOS version:	2
Service:	Make directory
Entry values:	AH=39
	DS:DX=address of ASCIIZ directory name
Exit values:	AX=error code (if CF=1)

The service is very straightforward. The ASCIIZ string gives the directory path and name of the new directory. If no drive is specified it is assumed to be on the current drive; if no backslash is given at the start of the path it is assumed to be a path from the current directory.

The effect of the function is to add the sub-directory name to the directory list and allocate one cluster to the sub-directory. This will be expanded as needed.

Deleting a sub-directory

To delete a sub-directory DOS provides the RD (RMDIR) command, which is based on DOS function 3Ah.

Interrupt:	21h
Function:	3Ah
DOS version:	2
Service:	Remove directory
Entry values:	AH=3Ah
	DS:DX=address of ASCIIZ directory name
Exit values:	AX=error code (if CF=1)

This function is set up in exactly the same way as that to change the current directory (3Bh). The directory to be deleted must be completely empty and must not be the current directory.

These limitations can be somewhat annoying, although they do provide safeguards.

Renaming a sub-directory

Rather surprisingly, perhaps, there is no direct facility in DOS for the renaming of sub-directories. It can only be done by creating a new directory, copying the contents of the old directory, deleting the original files and renaming the old directory. If the directory has sub-directories of its own the task can become almost impossible.

The Disk Directory

It is surprising, then, that DOS does not have a command for this fairly simple task. It is quite easy to devise a routine to achieve this aim. Be careful about renaming sub-directories though, especially if they may be included in path names in batch files.

The directory tree It is useful to be able to display the directory structure on the screen, in terms of the nesting of sub-directories and the location of files.

This is done in a fairly rudimentary form by the DOS TREE command.

THE FILE ALLOCATION TABLE (FAT)

Although the computer has interrupts for reading and writing sectors, for convenience (as we shall see below) DOS always allocates space to files in terms of *clusters*. The size of a cluster varies from one disk format to another but it is always a whole number of sectors, and varies from 1 to 8 sectors in length, depending on the size of the disk.

The obvious way to store files on disk would be to start at the beginning and add files consecutively, one after the other, with each file using an unbroken series of consecutive clusters. This DOS does, to start with at least. However, difficulties begin to arise when files are deleted or extended. Rather than try and find a space big enough for any new file DOS adopts a principle of always filling the first available gap; if this is not large enough to hold the file then the file is split into two or more parts, filling the available gaps in strict order. Similarly, when a file is extended the new section is slotted into the first gap DOS finds, wherever this may be on the disk. Such files are said to be *fragmented*.

The result of this is that any well-used disk - in particular a hard disk - is covered with fragments of files in no particular order. Obviously DOS has to be very careful about how it stores the data and has to have a method for recovering the fragments and reconstituting the files.

All the information about where the fragments are located is stored in the *File Allocation Table (FAT)*. Each cluster on the disk has a corresponding entry in the FAT. The start cluster

The Disk Directory

number in the directory entry indicates the location of the first cluster in the file. The entry in the FAT for this cluster is the number of the next cluster of the file; the FAT entry for the second cluster points to the third, and so on until a special code is encountered indicating that the cluster contains the end of the file.

Within a fragment each cluster will simply point to the next consecutive cluster. A group of fragments that can be traced from one end to the other is called a *chain*. In general a chain contains a complete file, running from the first cluster, as specified in the file directory, to the cluster containing the end-of-file marker.

However, when a disk becomes corrupt (for example, if the machine is switched off in the middle of a disk operation) the result may be that there are *lost clusters*. In these cases chains exist that do not have a proper start point in the directory. Programs such as CHKDSK check the FAT for lost chains and have an option to convert them to proper files, with an entry in the directory. The CHKDSK message when it locates problems such as these is in the form:

```
nnn lost clusters found in nnn chains
```

The other problem that may occur is that the FAT entries for two clusters may contain the same cluster number; in this case a chain exists that appears to belong to two files. When CHKDSK encounters this problem it gives a message of the form:

```
Files cross-linked at cluster nnn
```

In this case the ambiguous part of the chain is converted to a file since it is impossible to tell to which file it should belong.

Fragmentation   When a disk becomes fragmented it can cause the system to slow down considerably. Eventually it will lead to noticeable delays in applications whenever the disk is accessed. To overcome this problem it is necessary to re-arrange all the file fragments so that they are consecutive on the disk. You can devise a routine that does just this but be warned: you *must* make a backup copy of the disk before you start in case the process is interrupted for any reason.

The Disk Directory

Disk type, as indicated by first byte of FAT			
		1st byte (Hex)	
5.25" 8 sector	SS DD	FE	
	DS DD	FF	
9 sector	SS DD	FC	
	DS DD	FD	
	QD	F9	
3.5"	SS	FC	
	DS	FD	
	QD	F9	
Hard disks	10Mb	F8	
	20Mb	F8	
Meaning of first byte of FAT			
1st byte (Hex)	Disk type		
F8	Hard disk		
F9	DS 15 sectors		
FA	Not used		
FB	Not used		
FC	SS 9 sectors		
FD	DS 9 sectors		
FE	SS 8 sectors		
FF	DS 8 sectors		

Figure 16.8 FAT disk codes

STRUCTURE OF THE FAT

DOS stores two identical copies of the FAT on each disk, ostensibly in case the first copy gets corrupted. In fact, DOS apparently never uses the second copy. It does provide the programmer with an opportunity for recovering a damaged FAT, though its use is limited by the fact that the two copies are stored consecutively on the first track so any physical damage to the disk is likely to affect both FAT's at the same time.

373

The Disk Directory

If problems arise when a file operation is interrupted, then the second copy of the FAT will contain the disk information as it was before the operation began. It therefore indicates the place to put any lost or ambiguous clusters.

If one of the sectors in the FAT is unreadable then the second FAT can be copied to a new disk and the disk reconstructed.

The FAT is stored immediately after the directory. The first byte of the FAT contains a code indicating the type of disk, as shown in Figure 16.8. The next two bytes are always FFh (three bytes for 20M disks). The remainder of the FAT contains the map of the disk.

The numbering of the clusters on the disk starts with the first cluster after the directory. Rather oddly, this is cluster number 2. The number of data clusters for each type of disk is given in Figure 16.2.

Any mention of Cluster 0 refers to the root directory. This occurs as the start cluster number in the directory entry of a sub-directory, where the parent is the root directory. Cluster 1 is never used.

The size of each FAT entry depends upon the disk capacity, as follows:

- Disks of capacity less than 20M have 12-bit entries.

- Disks of capacity of 20M or more have 2-byte (16-bit) entries.

The 12-bit entries can store cluster numbers up to 4096. 20M disks contain more clusters so this is insufficient. Presumably the original intention of the 12-bit entries was to save disk space; in fact the only real savings are on 10M and quad density disks, and even there the savings are minimal when compared to the overall capacity.

The 2-byte entries are much easier to handle since they can be easily read by programs such as DEBUG. The 12-bit entries are not so simple, since each group of 3 bytes in the FAT is packed with two entries and to identify their values these need to be unpacked.

The Disk Directory

2-byte FAT entries

First of all we will look at the most straightforward type of FAT, with 2 bytes allocated to each entry. To unpack an entry from the FAT of a hard disk with capacity 20M or more the procedure is quite simple. The bytes in the FAT are numbered from 0, with two bytes per entry. The first four bytes are not used for this purpose, so the entry for cluster 2 is in bytes 4 and 5, cluster 3 uses bytes 6 and 7, and so on.

In general, the entry for cluster n can be found in bytes $(n \times 2)$ and $(n \times 2)+1$. Remember that the two bytes are stored with the low byte first.

12-bit FAT entries

Here the procedures are somewhat more complicated and require more patience. The entry for cluster 2 is stored in byte 3 and half of byte 4; cluster 3 uses the other half of byte 4 and all of cluster 5, and so on. The complexity is further increased by the fact that the high four bits are stored after the low byte, and any split bytes are stored low byte first. For example, byte 4 contains the middle 4 bits of cluster 3 followed by the high 4 bits of cluster 2.

In general, the entry for cluster n can be found in bytes:

$Int((n \times 3)/2))$ and $Int((n \times 3)/2+1)$.

If the cluster number is odd, ignore the last four bits of the word; otherwise, ignore the first four bits. (Remember that the entry is stored low byte first.)

FAT AND DISK INFORMATION

Three functions of interrupt 21h return information about the FAT.

Interrupt: 21h
Function: 1Bh
DOS version: 1
Service: Get FAT information for current drive
Entry values: AH=1Bh
Exit values: AL=sectors in each allocation unit
CX=bytes per sector
DX=allocation units
DS:BX=address of ID byte

In this case the function returns the information relating to the disk in the current drive, including the following:

- The number of sectors per cluster

375

The Disk Directory

- The number of bytes per sector
- The number of clusters on the disk
- A pointer to the start of the FAT in memory

Although a part of the FAT is kept in memory it is not safe to assume that the whole FAT is there. Usually this part of the function is used to obtain the first byte, which tells you what sort of disk it is.

Interrupt: 21h
Function: 1Ch
DOS version: 1
Service: Get FAT information for any drive
Entry values: AH=1Ch
     DL=drive (0=default, 1=A, 2=B, etc.)
Exit values: AL=sectors in each allocation unit
     CX=bytes per sector
     DX=allocation units
     DS:BX=address of ID byte

This function is almost identical to 1Bh, except that we must specify the drive in DL before calling the routine. Here we have a rather annoying quirk. Instead of using the normal numeric codes we have to shift all the drives up one; thus 1 represents A, 2 is B, and so on. Code 0 is used to represent the current drive, whatever it may be. This change seems rather pointless, since we can use function 1Bh if we want the information for the current drive.

The type of data returned is the same in each case.

Interrupt: 21h
Function: 36h
DOS version: 1
Service: Get free clusters
Entry values: AH=36h
     DL=drive (0=default, 1=A, 2=B, etc.)
Exit values: AX=(sectors per cluster
         (FFFFh (invalid drive)
     BX=number of free clusters
     CX=bytes per sector
     DX=total clusters on disk

The Disk Directory

The third function, added for DOS 2, works in the same way as 1Ch and with the same drive-numbering scheme. However, it returns one extra item, the number of unused clusters, which can be found in BX. This value can be used to calculate the amount of free space in bytes (as is the case at the bottom of a standard directory string).

Note that when the amount of space recorded against each file is added to the free space the total is likely to fall short of the total disk space. This is because space is allocated a cluster at a time (making it no longer available) but the directory records the true length of the file, which will usually be less than a precise number of clusters.

CHANGING THE DIRECTORY AND FAT

Any time that an operation is carried out using any of the DOS commands or DOS interrupts, DOS automatically updates the file directory and both copies of the FAT. Any changes our programs make to the directory and FAT should be carried out with extreme caution; further DOS operations may have unexpected results, unless the likely knock-on effects are thought through very carefully.

Some fairly safe operations include:

■ Undeleting a file

■ Changing a file's attributes, in particular its read-only, hidden, system or archived status

■ Changing the date and time stamps

Changing features such as the file length or start cluster may be useful for copy-protection purposes but can result in files being overwritten by DOS unless extra precautions are taken.

DELETED FILES

When a file is 'deleted' the first character of the filename in the directory entry is changed to the hex value E5h (usually represented by the extended ASCII character σ).

(Note that DOS 1 may also use the code E5h to indicate an entry that has not yet been used.)

This is the only action that DOS takes. The remainder of the directory entry is intact, as is the file itself. However, as far as DOS is concerned the file no longer exists. The next new file to be created re-uses any available deleted entry in preference

377

The Disk Directory

to one of the unused entries. Thus deleting a file and creating a new one results in the new file taking the position of the old in any directory listing.

The last root directory entry will only ever be used when the directory is full. (Likewise, the last cluster on the disk is only ever used when the disk is full. Thus the most secure place to store any data is on the innermost track. However, bear in mind that some hard disk parking routines move the head over this last track, on the assumption that it is extremely unlikely to contain any data.)

The relevant entries in the FAT are also marked as relating to deleted files and will be re-used as soon as possible. DOS always searches for a vacant directory entry from the beginning of the directory, and searches for an available cluster from cluster 2 onwards.

In this way DOS is rather unkind to its users. While holding out the hope that a deleted file can be recovered, any chance of doing so is immediately crushed as soon as any new file is created or an existing file significantly extended. Life would have been much simpler had DOS used all directory entries and blank clusters in rotation.

A file can be recovered - if you are fast enough - by changing the first byte of the directory entry to a suitable character. The user must supply this character since it has been permanently lost, having been overwritten by E5h.

If no changes have been made to the disk since the file was deleted no other action need be taken. However, if changes have been made it may be that some of the clusters have been re-used, so any rescue program must check through the chain to see how much of the file can be recovered. Because of the way DOS re-uses space from the first available cluster onwards, the chances are that if any cluster has been re-used it will be the first one and hence the file will be totally unrecoverable.

If this happens - or if the data is largely or wholly intact but the directory entry has been overwritten - then it is possible to convert some of the chains into files. This is the process carried out by CHKDSK on a corrupt disk when the /F parameter is specified.

The Disk Directory

The rescue process need not end here however. This is all very well but anyone who has tried this sort of activity will know that unless the chains form the start of a file or are in ASCII format they may be totally useless. This is because they do not contain the necessary header data for the file, as is the case for word-processor files such as those created by WordStar. The files cannot be read in as ASCII files because they contain illegal characters and they cannot be read in as proper files because the lack of header data makes them unrecognisable to the program.

The third part of a comprehensive rescue process is therefore to add a suitable header to the data. The exact procedure varies depending on the nature of the files created by a program, and knowledge of the header must be gained.

The processes used to recover a WordStar file illustrate the general procedure to be adopted:

1. Create a dummy header containing general information, by creating a new file within the application program. (Details such as page numbering that relate to the file as a whole can be easily added when the file has been read into the program.)

2. Pad the header with blank data (e.g. spaces for a word processor - or text to tell the user how to complete the recovery process). The header should fill a complete cluster. This dummy header can exist as data in the rescue program if you want to include this part of the process within the routine.

3. Recover or create the directory entry, with the start cluster number being the location of the dummy header. If the dummy file was created by the application program this will have been done already; otherwise our routine must take care of it.

4. Change the FAT entry for the dummy header's cluster so that it points to the start of the rescued data.

5. Calculate the length of the rescued data, add the length of the dummy header and store this in the directory entry as the file length.

It is then up to the user to go into the file in the usual way and complete the job.

The Disk Directory

Note that confusion can be caused by the fact that there may be more than one copy of a file in the directory and the data may appear several times. Most programs, when saving a new version of a file, first rename the existing file, then save the new file and finally 'delete' the original file. Thus a rescue session may end up with a number of chains in which the data is repeated. The final stage for the unfortunate user is to look at each new file and decide how to mix and match to get as much as possible of the recent data.

An alternative to the creation of dummy headers is to strip out all special codes and convert the file to ASCII. The disadvantage here is that any page formatting and typeface information is lost. The advantage is that such a file can be easily imported into most good application programs.

17. Files

We have already seen how details of files are stored in directories and that their locations are kept in the FAT. But what is a file? A file is simply a collection of information, stored sequentially, in a series of clusters. How we put that information together is entirely up to us. We can store it as a long string of data, adding all new information to the end and extending as necessary; or we can store the data in records of fixed length, and allocate enough space in the file to hold all the records that are needed.

Before we start on the detail it is worth noting that there are two methods within DOS for handling files. The first method, which was included in DOS version 1, involves the setting up of a block of data (a 'File Control Block') that gives details such as the file's name, date when modified and so on. This was later superseded, in DOS 2, by a far simpler method, under which DOS simply allocates a number to each file as it is opened (a 'File Handle').

Since the only real purpose in using the original method is to provide compatibility in programs with DOS 1 - and it is now considered unlikely that many people are still using purely DOS 1 - the main consideration below is given to the newer of the two methods.

This chapter discusses the various types of file and how they are handled; it also looks at the instructions for manipulating files. Most of the file handling is done by the file interrupts, which are listed in Figure 17.1.

FILE SPECIFICATIONS

Whenever a file is referred to in a command we need to give enough information to uniquely identify the file. This *file specification* consists of up to four items that point to the file. These items must be strung together, with no spaces separating the component parts.

Drive specifier The first thing to be done is to identify which drive the disk is in. The drives are labelled as follows:

    A   Left-hand drive on dual drive systems or the only drive on single-floppy drive systems

Files

	File interrupts	
Interrupt	Function	Effect
21	0F	Open a file
21	10	Close a file
21	11	Find first matching file
21	12	Find next matching file
21	13	Delete a file
21	14	Read sequential record
21	15	Write sequential record
21	16	Create a file
21	17	Rename a file
21	21	Read random record
21	22	Write random record
21	23	Get file size
21	24	Prepare field for random record
21	27	Read random records
21	28	Write random records
21	3C	Create a file
21	3D	Open a file
21	3E	Close a file
21	3F	Read from file
21	40	Write to a file
21	41	Delete a file
21	42	Move file pointer
21	43,00	Get attributes of file
21	43,01	Set attributes of file
21	44	IOCTL functions
21	45	Duplicate a file handle
21	46	Force duplication of handle
21	4E	Find first matching file
21	4F	Find next matching file
21	56	Rename a file
21	5A	Create a temporary file
21	5B	Create a new file
21	5C,00	Lock file
21	5C,01	Unlock file

Figure 17.1 File interrupts

Files

B	Right-hand drive (dual-floppy drive systems) or logical second drive (single-drive systems)
C	Hard disk, or RAM drive on floppy disk systems
D	RAM drive on hard disk systems

Directory path

The drive letter is followed by a colon (:). These labels are attached to the drives when the system is booted; they are not permanently fixed. DOS always allocates the drives sequentially. If there is no physical floppy drive B then DOS creates logical drive B. Any commands relating to drive B then result in a message to put in the disk for that drive.

The *directory path* gives a set of instructions on how to find the file and in which directory it is located. The path consists of the string of directories that must be traversed to reach the file.

Directory names must end with the backslash (\). The root directory has no name as such, and is therefore represented by the backslash on its own.

Filename and extension

Finally, the name of the file itself must be specified. These last two items must be separated by a period (.). The filename is the only part of the specification that cannot be omitted. If there is an extension then it must be included.

HOW DOS INTERPRETS FILE SPECIFICATIONS

If a file specification begins with a backslash (\) DOS searches for the first matching name in the root directory; otherwise it searches in the current directory. If the name is a sub-directory it checks that the next character is '\' and, if it is, searches that directory for the next name.

If the name is '..' it automatically locates the parent directory from the start cluster number and identifies it as a directory. If the name is '.' then it locates the same sub-directory again, without realising it has not got anywhere. Therefore no special rules are needed for dealing with the '.' or '..' options.

Files

FILE TYPES

There are essentially two different types of files. The type of file that is used in any particular circumstance depends on the nature of the data that is to be stored.

SEQUENTIAL FILES

In some cases it is necessary to store just a long string of unstructure data. In these case we use *sequential files*. A sequential file consists of a string of data, of no fixed length, and with no fixed record length. All new data is simply added at the end of the file and the file is extended as required.

This sort of file is ideal for any sort of text data or any situation where the data that is stored cannot be defined in the standard database way (using fixed-format records and fields).

The advantage of using sequential files is that we need have no concern about where any data is going to be stored. Anything new is simply added to the end. The main disadvantages arise when we wish to retrieve the data. Since there is no record number attached to any particular part of the data there is generally no alternative but to read the file from the beginning until we can locate the particular items of data that we need. However, with careful programming it is generally possible to place a few markers within the file and to jump to those points to make reading files faster.

The file pointer

DOS maintains our current position within a sequential file using a *file pointer*. This pointer gives us the offset of the current position from the beginning of the file. Various options exist for moving this pointer within the file. Normally, as each item of data is read from the file, the file pointer is moved along the file accordingly. Similarly, the file pointer is increased as new data is added to the file.

As a general rule, when reading data from a sequential file, it is necessary to set the pointer to zero (that is, at the beginning of the file) and read from that point onwards. However, if you have set markers within the file and the location of these is stored away - perhaps at the very beginning of the file - then we can jump directly to a specific point within the file to start a search or overwrite.

Files

End-of-file markers

In most circumstances DOS uses the Ctrl-Z character (ASCII 1Ah) to denote the end of a sequential file. All DOS commands (such as TYPE) continue until they encounter this character. There is no reason why we should stick to this convention, although it generally makes life easier if we do so.

More modern operating systems (such as Unix) use the null character (ASCII 00h) as an end-of-file marker. The recent DOS functions are turning towards this convention and use the null character to terminate strings and other text items (ASCIIZ).

ASCII FILES

For many purposes it is essential to produce files that can be used in any situation without fear of disrupting a program. This is particularly the case when transferring data files between two different programs (with compatible formats) or when using DOS commands such as TYPE.

In these circumstances, the usual procedure is to convert the existing data files into *ASCII files*. The rules for ASCII files are as follows:

- Most of the text should consist of the standard ASCII characters, in the range 20h to 7Fh.

- There must be no extended ASCII characters (80h to FFh).

- The only control characters allowed are the line feed (0Ah), form feed (0Ch) and carriage return (0Dh).

RANDOM ACCESS FILES

The second type of files used by DOS are called *random access files*. These differ considerably from sequential files in that they consist of a number of consecutive but independent *records*. Each record is generally used to store one set of data. However, the restriction here is that the records are of fixed length; each record in the file must contain the same number of bytes.

This does not mean that we have use the same structure for each record in the file, but if we do use different structures then the record length must be large enough to take the largest type of structure; any data items that do not fill the record must be padded out to fill the entire record. The advantage is that we can jump directly to any set of data within the file simply by specifying the record number.

Files

It is worth noting that, in a sense, sequential files are simply random access files with a record length of one byte. This means that by keeping track of what is stored at each location within the sequential file we can devise a means of jumping to a specific section of data. In a similar sort of way, a random access file is merely a form of sequential file where the usual jump is calculated in specific units defined by the record length. This corespondence between the two types of files is used to good effect by DOS in its more recent interrupt functions, where the distinction between file types becomes blurred.

DATA TRANSFER AREAS (DTA)

Most of the DOS file functions have to either read data in from a file or write data from memory out to a file. In most of these cases the data which is being read or written is stored in memory in a special area called the *data transfer area (DTA)*. This is the main area for input and output of data. As a rule any data that we wish to output to the file is stored in this area and it is here that we collect any data that has been read in from a file.

The default size for the DTA is 128 bytes and its default location is in the Program Segment Prefix (PSP). We do not have to stick to this particular location, however.

Interrupt: 21h
Function: 1Ah
DOS version: 1
Service: Set disk transfer area address
Entry values: AH=1Ah
                    DS:DX=new address of DTA
Exit values: None

This is a very straightforward interrupt which simply identifies a new area of memory as the DTA.

Interrupt: 21h
Function: 2Fh
DOS version: 2
Service: Get address of DTA
Entry values: AH=2Fh
Exit values: AX=error code

Files

    ES:BX=address of DTA

This function is used to discover the current position of the DTA. It is far simpler to use this function early on in the program to find out the whereabouts of the DTA than to try and calculate the address from its position within the PSP.

STANDARD ERROR MESSAGES

The DOS functions from 38h onwards use a set of standard error mesesages. These are listed in Figure 17.2. The fact that an error has occurred is generally indicated by the carry flag being set. In these cases the error is returned in AH. Sometimes, however, the carry flag is not set, so it is always worth checking the value of AH and perhaps bypassing the carry flag altogether; if no error has occurred AH will be 0.

In DOS 3 there is additional error information available after certain functions have resulted in failure. The extra error codes are accessed by calling function 59h immediately after the original interrupt has been shown to be in error.

Interrupt: 21h
Function: 59h
DOS version: 3
Service: Get error codes
Entry value: AH=59h
        BX=0000h
Exit value: AX=extended error code
        BH=type of error
        BL=possible action
        CH=location of error

This information is available in the following circumstances:

- When the carry flag is set.

- When an operation on a file that was opened with an FCB returns the value FFh in AH.

- When returning from a critical error interrupt handler.

In these cases four extra pieces of information are returned: an extended error code, a code for the type of error, where the

Files

DOS 2 error codes	
Code (hex)	Error
01	Bad functions number
02	File not found
03	Path not found
04	All handles in use
05	Access denied
06	Invalid handle number
07	Memory blocks corrupt
08	Insufficient memory
09	Address for memory block invalid
0A	Invalid environment
0B	Bad format
0C	Access code invalid
0D	Data error
0E	Not used
0F	Drive specification invalid
10	Cannot delete current directory
11	Wrong device
12	No more matching files

Figure 17.2 Standard error messages for DOS functions 38h onwards

error occurred and even how to handle the error. These various pieces of information are shown in Figure 17.3. Obviously, only large programs can afford to deal with all these options, or even need to.

AMBIGUOUS FILENAMES

All versions of DOS allow us to specify *ambiguous filenames* in commands, using the two wildcards * and ?. These wildcards are also available for use with some of the DOS interrupts. The ? replaces any single letter and the asterisk is placed at the end of either the filename, extension or both to indicate that we don't care what value the name takes from this point on. When DOS comes across an ambiguous filename that

Files

DOS 3 error codes (AX)	
Code (hex)	Error
01	Function number invalid
02	File not found
03	Path not found
04	All file handles in use
05	Access denied
06	File handle invalid
07	Memory blocks invalid
08	Insufficient memory
09	Memory address invalid
0A	Environment command invalid
0B	Format invalid
0C	File use code invalid
0D	Data invalid
0E	Not used
0F	Drive specifier invalid
10	Cannot remove current directory
11	Different device
12	No more matching files
13	Disk write-protected
14	Disk identifier invalid
15	Drive not ready
16	Bad command
17	Data error on disk
18	Request header invalid
19	Seek error
1A	Bad media
1B	Sector not found
1C	Out of paper (printer)
1D	Write error
1E	Read error
1F	General failure
20	File sharing error
21	File locking error
22	Disk change error
23	No free FCB's
50	File exists
51	Not used
52	Unable to create directory
53	Critical error

Files

Type of error (BH)	
Code (hex)	Meaning
01	Lack of resources
02	Temporary problem
03	Unauthorised access
04	Internal DOS error
05	Hardware fault
06	DOS software error
07	Application software error
08	Not found
09	Bad format
0A	Locked
0B	Media error
0C	Exists already
0D	General

Possible action (BL)	
Code	Meaning
01	Try again
02	Try again later
03	User can solve problem
04	Close files, end program
05	End program immediately
06	Ignore error
07	User action, then retry

Location of error (CH)	
Code	Meaning
01	Unknown
02	Disk drive
03	Not used
04	Serial device
05	Memory

Figure 17.3 DOS 3 extended error codes

Files

Default DOS file handles		
Handle	Device Name	Device
0	CON:	Keyboard
1	CON:	Screen
2	CON:	Screen error
3	AUX:	First connected serial device
4	PRN:	First connected parallel device

Figure 17.4 Reserved DOS file handles

includes an asterisk it always expands the asterisk to the relevant number of question marks. When comparing a filename against an ambiguous name, DOS always assumes that the filename and extension are padded with blanks where necessary and accepts these as being an acceptable match.

DOS has a number of functions that deal with ambiguous filenames (those to rename and delete groups of files, for example). In such cases the ambiguous file specification can be used directly. In other cases, when we want to repeat a command for all files within a group, we need to use some of the DOS interrupts for finding matching files, looping round the routine until no further matches are found.

FILE HANDLES

As noted at the start of this chapter, there are two distinct ways of referrring to files. The simplest and by far the most effective method of referencing files is that of *file handles*. This method was developed in DOS 2 in order to be able to deal with sub-directories and pathnames; the earlier methods in DOS 1 could not cope with these concepts.

The principle is that when a new file is created or an existing file is opened all the program has to do is to tell DOS which file is to be used. The method by which this is done is to specify the standard drive, path and file specification. DOS

Files

then allocates a file handle to this file. This simply consists of a number. As long as the file remains open any references to that file can simply be made by quoting the number. The file-handle number is fixed for that particular file until the file is closed. After the file has been closed the file handle can be re-used with another file.

The file handle that is given to each file is fully under the control of DOS and it is unwise to tamper with this system. However, the programmer must keep track of all file handles at all stages of the program. It is up to the programmer to ensure that he knows which files are open and what their file handles are at any stage.

As a matter of interest, DOS reserves the first five handles for its own use (see Figure 17.4). Other file handles are allocated as and when needed. In DOS 2 there is a maximum of 20 file handles at any one time. DOS 3 allows this to be extended, but provides a default of 20. In fact, 20 should be quite sufficient for most purposes. The number of files that can be open at any one time can be changed with the FILES directive in CONFIG.SYS, when the system is booted up.

When file handles are used DOS treats sequential and random files as being the same. In other words, it treats all files as being random access files with record length 1. It is up to the programmer to keep track of locations in any random files, which will be based upon the record length. In fact this can make life much simpler.

FINDING A FILE

Frequently we wish to carry out an operation upon more than one file at a time, by specifying wildcards within the file specification. The functions in this section can be used with individual files of course, but in general they are used for a group of more than one file. The file specification is given as an ASCIIZ string, pointed to by the register pair DS:DX, and may include the ? and * symbols.

Interrupt: 21h
Function: 4Eh
DOS version: 2
Service: Find first matching file
Entry values: AH=4Eh
CX=file attribute
DS:DX=address of ASCIIZ file specification
Exit values: AX=error code (if CF=1)

DOS returns the name of the first file it finds that matches the string that we have given, the name being placed in the DTA.

We can also specify certain atrributes, in particular whether the file is a hidden, system or directory file. In these cases the search also checks that the file it finds specifies the criteria given.

Alternatively, the file can be specified as having a volume label attribute. In this case the filename is ignored and the program simply selects the one and only file (if there is one) which has this attribute.

Interrupt:	21h
Function:	4Fh
DOS version:	2
Service:	Find next matching file
Entry values:	AH=4Fh
	DS:DX=address of information from previous search
Exit values:	AX=error code (if CF=1)

This function merely continues the search that was begun with the previous function. It uses the same ambiguous filename and returns the name of the next file in the DTA. Note that the first 21 bytes of data in the DTA are used by DOS to decide which is the next file and these should therefore be left undisturbed by the program. The layout of the DTA after a file has been found are shown in Figure 17.5.

The routine in Figure 17.6 demonstrates how we may locate all files that match a particular name and display them on the screen.

CREATING AND OPENING FILES

No operations can be carried out with a file until it has either been created or, if it already exists, re-opened. As soon as a file has been opened in one of these ways it is allocated a file handle. DOS provides four ways of opening files. In each case DS:DX points to the ASCIIZ file specification, and the new file handle is returned in AX. Errors are signalled by the carry flag being set. Any error code is returned in AX.

Interrupt:	21h
Function:	5Bh

Files

	DTA after file found	
Offset (hex)	Bytes (hex)	Use
0	15	'Next file' information
15	1	File attribute
16	2	Time stamp
18	2	Date stamp
1A	4	File size
1E	0D	Filename, period, extension (ASCIIZ)

Figure 17.5 The DTA after finding a file

```
SEARCH:                                  ; Searches for all files that match a
                                         ;   given specification and prints
                                         ;   them in a list (Demonstration Prog)

            jmp searchst

fnamea      db '\*.*',00h                ; Put file specification here, or get it
                                         ;   by parsing the command line

searchst:
            push ax
            push bx
            push cx
            push dx
            push di
            mov cx,16h
            lea dx,fnamea                ; Point to file specification
            mov ah,4eh
            int 21h                      ; Find first match
            jc quit                      ; Exit if not found
show:
            lea dx,9eh
            mov bx,9eh
            mov byte ptr [bx+0ch],'$'    ; Add $ to name in PSP
            mov ah,09h
            int 21h                      ; Print name
            call blank                   ; Blank name in PSP
            lea dx,fnamea
```

```
            mov ah,4fh
                    int 21h             ; Get mext match
                    jnc show            ; Repeat if found
quit:
                    pop di
                    pop dx
                    pop cx
                    pop bx
                    pop ax
                    int 20h             ; To make into routine put RET here
blank:                                  ; Fill area to be used by filename
                                        ;    with balnks
                    push cx
                    mov cx,0ch          ; Repeat 12 times
                    xor di,di
put:
                    mov byte ptr [bx+di],20h  ; Store space
                    inc di
                    loop put
                    pop cx
                    ret
```

Figure 17.6 Finding matching files

DOS version: 3
Service: Create a new file
Entry values: AH=5Bh
                CX=file attribute
                DS:DX=address of ASCIIZ pathname
Exit values: AX=(file handle (CF=0)
                (error code (CF=1)

This function, which is available in DOS 3 only, is used for creating totally new files. Generally, it is used for names that have been designated by the user. It can also be used on all other occasions when you do not want to overwrite an existing file. The function checks to see if the file already exists and, if it does, the attempt fails. Of course, it may be that the user intends to overwrite an existing file, in which case this can be allowed for by using error messages to warn the user that the file exists; if they decide to continue use function 3Ch (described below) to open the file.

Files

Interrupt:	21h
Function:	5Ah
DOS version:	3
Service:	Create a temporary file
Entry values:	AH=5Ah
	CX=file attribute
	DS:DX=address of ASCIIZ pathname
Exit values:	AX=error code (if CF=1)
	DS:DX=address of ASCIIZ file specification (if CF=0)

This rather curious function is also only available in DOS 3. The difference here is that the filename is allocated by DOS. The ASCIIZ path must end with 12 spaces, in which DOS will place its own filename. If the file is to be in the current directory, and therefore no path is given, then the ASCIIZ string must just consist of 12 spaces. DOS has its own method of ensuring that the name it gives is unique and therefore that no existing file is going to be overwritten.

A possible use of this function is for creating temporary files, though function 3Ch below is generally a far better option since it gives the programmer full control over the filename.

It is important to note that files created with this function are not automatically deleted by DOS when they are closed; the program must ensure that these temporary files are deleted once their use is complete, otherwise there is likely to be a build-up of temporary files with names which will be meaningless to both the user and programmer.

Interrupt:	21h
Function:	3Ch
DOS version:	2
Service:	Create a file
Entry values:	AH=3Ch
	CX=file attribute
	DS:DX=address of ASCIIZ file specification
Exit values:	AX=(file handle (CF=0)
	(error code (CF=1)

This function is far more useful for creating temporary files and was available from DOS 2 onwards. The function automatically overwrites any existing file that has the name given. If the file does not exist then the file is created. Therefore, it is ideal for temporary data storage where the

File use codes	
Bit	Meaning
7	Set if file cannot be used by subprogram
6	)
5	) Disk share mode (see below)
4	)
3	Reserved
2	) (000 Read only
1	) Access type (001 Write only
0	) (010 Read/write

N.B. Only bits 0,1,2 are available for DOS 2.

Disk share modes (bits 0,1,2)	
Bit 2 1 0	Meaning
0 0 0	Compatible mode
0 0 1	No read/write
0 1 0	No write
0 1 1	No read
1 0 0	'Deny none' mode

Figure 17.7 File use codes

program can specify the same name each time it is run. There is no need to worry about the file having to be deleted. All that will happen is that there will be one temporary file with this name in permanent existence on the disk. It is also useful for those occasions where the user specifies a filename that already exists and wishes the existing file to be overwritten.

The only real problem that can occur with this function is when a file is chosen that has a read-only attribute. In this case - or the more unlikely event of the directory being full - then an 'access denied' error code will be returned. Errors

Files

also arise if the program specifies a bad pathname, or when all file handles have been used.

Interrupt:	21h
Function:	3Dh
DOS version:	2
Service:	Open a file
Entry values:	AH=3Dh
	AL=file use code
	DS:DX=address of ASCIIZ file specification
Exit values:	AX=(file handle (CF=0)
	(error code (CF=1)

This is the only function that is used purely to open an existing file. Its use is slightly more complex than those above because it must take account of the fact that the file may be being shared by some other program. The way in which the file is to be used must be specified in AL (see Figure 17.7).

In DOS 2 only the bottom three bits are used, in which case the only options are to set the file as read-only, write-only or read/write.

Under DOS 3 it is necessary to set the other bits as well. The top bit indicates whether or not this file can be used by a subprogram executed by the main program, without being re-opened. The next three bits indicate what actions should be taken when a second program attempts to open the same file. Bit 3 should always be 0.

File buffers

Every time a file is opened (whether it is newly created or an existing file) DOS allocates an area of memory for that particular file's data; this is the *file buffer*. Whenever any data is written to a file DOS actually stores the data in this buffer, rather than sending it to disk. The buffer cannot hold the entire contents of a large file, so when the file pointer is moved to a new section of the file DOS saves away the current contents of the buffer and reads in the new part.

This means that some of the data which we believe to have been written to file has actually only been stored in memory and is therefore not secure. Our data is saved only when a new section is read into the buffer or when the file is finally closed.

Files

Note that any complications with the file pointer are dealt wiht by DOS. The programmer can always treat the pointer as if the entire file is on disk.

MOVING THE FILE POINTER

When a file is opened or created the file pointer is set to point to the current end of file. In the case of a new file it will be set to the start of the file. As data is added, so the file pointer will move to the new end of the file each time the file is opened. In order to read data from a file that already exists, it is necessary to move the pointer to the position from which we wish to start reading.

Interrupt: 21h
Function: 42h
DOS version: 2
Service: Move file pointer
Entry values: AH=42h
AL=offset code
BX=file handle
CX:DX=number of bytes to move pointer
Exit values: AX=error code (if CF=1)
DX:AX=new pointer offset (if CF=0)

Using this function we must give the start point and a positive offset from that point. The value that is given is an unsigned integer and can therefore never be negative. The way in which we choose the start point is given by the value of AL as follows:

- AL=0   Offset from beginning of file

- AL=1   Offset from current pointer position

- AL=2   End of file (in which case the offset must always be 0)

This function can be used in some of the following ways:

- To start reading from the beginning of the file set AL=0 and the offset to 0. To skip the first few items in the file, set a positive offset.

- To continue from current file pointer set AL=1 and an offset of 0, or give a positive offset if you wish to skip a few items.

399

Files

- To determine the current file size, set AL=2 and an offset of 0. The value returned by the function will then be the current length in bytes.

It is up to us to keep track of where the file pointer is within the file. If we want to move back through the file then we must use a value of AL=0 and calculate the offset. For example, if the current file pointer is on byte 95h and we want to re-read the previous five characters then we must set AL=0 and the offset to 90h.

For random access files, the offset can be calculated by:

offset=(record number - 1) x record size

WRITING TO A FILE

Before a file can be written to, it must be opened. DOS automatically sets the file pointer to add to the end of the file unless otherwise specified. Should we wish to write to the middle of the file (for example when using random access files) then we must use the function above to set the file pointer before invoking this function.

Interrupt:	21h
Function:	40h
DOS version:	2
Service:	Write to a file
Entry values:	AH=40h
	BX=file handle
	CX=(number of bytes to be written
	(00h (to truncate file at pointer)
	DS:DX=address of DTA
Exit values:	AX=(number of bytes written (CF=0)
	(error code (CF=1)

Most errors can be tested for by checking the value of the carry flag. In some circumstances - for example when we run out of disk space - the carry flag may not be set. This error can be tested for by checking to see whether the bytes that have been written match the bytes that were supposed to be written. Note that the file pointer is automatically updated by this function.

READING FILES

This function works in a similar way to the service above, retrieving data from the file. The only difference is that we must specify where in memory we wish to put the data that is to be read.

Files

Interrupt:	21h
Function:	3Fh
DOS version:	2
Service:	Read from a file
Entry values:	AH=3Fh
	BX=file handle
	CX=number of bytes to be read
	DS:DX=address of DTA
Exit values:	AX=(number of bytes read (CF=0)
	(return code (CF=1)

The data is returned to the area specified and the pointer is automatically updated.

CLOSING FILES Once we have finished with a file there is a single, simple-to-use interrupt to close the file.

Interrupt:	21h
Function:	3Eh
DOS version:	2
Service:	Close a file
Entry values:	AH=3Eh
	BX=file handle
Exit values:	AX=error code (if CF=1)

When this function is invoked any data which is still in the file buffer that has not yet been written away will be automatically written to the file. The buffers are then cleared. The handle can now be re-used. Remember that it is very important to keep track of which files are open at any time. Ending a program without closing all files may result in the last sections of data intended for those files being lost. For particularly important data it can be useful to close a file each time a user has written the data, and then re-open it ready for the next piece of data. This may require more disk accesses but it will ensure the security of the data.

Note that function 3Eh does not unlock any files that have been locked (see below).

Displaying a file DOS uses the TYPE command to display the contents of an ASCII file on the screen.

Comparing files The DOS COMP command compares two files for differences.

Files

LOCKING AND UNLOCKING FILES

DOS 3 introduced several new functions for dealing with shared access to a file, for use when networking. Obviously it is essential to make sure that two people using the same or different programs are not writing to the same part of the same file at the same time. Surprisingly, this is quite simple to achieve.

Interrupt: 21h
Function: 5C,00h
DOS version: 3
Service: Lock file
Entry values: AH=5Ch
                 AL=00h
                 BX=file handle
                 CX:DX=offset
                 SI:DI=locked data length
Exit values: AX=error code (if CF=1)

Interrupt: 21h
Function: 5C,01h
DOS version: 3
Service: Unlock file
Entry values: AH=5Ch
                 AL=01h
                 BX=file handle
                 CX:DX=offset
                 SI:DI=locked data length
Exit values: AX=error code (if CF=1)

When AL is set to 0 the file is locked. Before invoking the function you must specify the file handle, the offset (from the beginning of the file) of the area of file that is to be locked and the length of data that is to be locked. The program that locks the file in this way will then be able to write to that section of the file but all other programs will be excluded from changing that section of data. Having written to this part of the file, it should be unlocked as quickly as possible. This is done by repeating exactly the same command, using the same parameters, but this time with AL=1.

As a matter of good practice the file should be unlocked as soon as possible. There should be an unlock statement to match each lock statement and all unlocking should be done before the file is closed. If a file is closed before it is unlocked, or if the program terminates before this happens, then the results may be unpredictable.

Files

DUPLICATION OF FILE HANDLES

If we want to perform two operations at once on the same file (for example to move records from one part of the file to another) then matters can be simplified by having two file handles that refer to the same file. In this case we can duplicate the file handle but it is important to keep track of which handles refer to which files.

Interrupt: 21h
Function: 45h
DOS version: 2
Service: Duplicate a file handle
Entry values: AH=45h
BX=file handle
Exit values: AX=(file handle (CF=0)
(return code (CF=1)

This function simply allocates a new file handle to an existing open file.

Interrupt: 21h
Function: 46h
DOS version: 2
Service: Force duplication of handle
Entry values: AH=46h
BX=file handle to copy
CX=second file handle
Exit values: AX=error code (if CF=1)
CX=second file handle

This function differs from the one above in that it uses an existing file handle rather than allocating a new one. The file to which the handle was previously allocated is automatically closed.

FILE CONTROL BLOCKS (FCB'S)

The file handles described above are fairly easy to use. DOS 1 used a much more complex method of controlling the number of open files. Each file that is opened is allocated a block of data in memory, which tells DOS various information about the file. These sets of data are referred to as *file control blocks (FCB's)*.

Files

Each block is divided into a number of records, as shown in Figure 17.8. The programmer must specify the drive, filename and extension; DOS fills in the rest. The programmer is also free to change the size of the record, the current block of data to be considered and the position in that block. Before invoking any file operation, the location of the file control block must be specified in DS:DX.

There are two main disadvantages to using file control blocks. The first is that it requires a lot more work on the part of the programmer. The second is that the file control blocks cannot cope with directory paths in any form. Although these FCB's may be used in programs that store data in sub-directories, before accessing any file you must use the more advanced commands to set the current directory.

The only real advantage of using FCB's is if you want to write programs that will be compatible with DOS 1. For most applications, this is now unnecessary, since very few machines still operate solely under DOS 1. It is not generally regarded as a serious drawback to have to specify that a program requires DOS 2 or later versions. (When it comes to deciding whether or not to use the DOS 3 functions, of course, then this is a slightly different matter.)

CREATING AND OPENING FILES

Two functions are supplied for opening files using FCB's, depending on whether or not the file already exists.

Interrupt: 21h
Function: 16h
DOS version: 1
Service: Create a file
Entry values: AH=16h
 DS:DX=address of FCB
Exit values: AL=(00h (success)
 (FFh (directory full)

This function creates a file if it does not already exist. If the file does exist then it sets the size to 0, in effect deleting the existing contents. In both cases the files are left open.

Interrupt: 21h
Function: 0Fh
DOS version: 1
Service: Open a file
Entry values: AH=0Fh

Files

The File Control Block (FCB)		
Offset (hex)	Bytes (hex)	Use
00	01	Drive
01	08	Filename
09	03	Extension
0C	02	Current block number
0E	02	Record size
10	04	File size
14	02	Date created
16	0A	Reserved
20	01	Current record number
21	01	Relative record number

N.B. The block starting at 16h stores the new filename and extension during renaming.

Figure 17.8 Structure of File Control Blocks

Exit values: DS:DX=address of FCB
AL=(00h (success)
(FFh (failure)

This function opens an existing file. Once opened, the programmer is free to change the current block number and the byte number within the block (for sequential files) or the record size and random record number for random access files. Note that the record size defaults to 80h.

FINDING FILES   A similar option to that for file handles exist for locating a series of files using ambiguous filenames that include the wildcards. In this case the ambiguous name must be placed in the appropriate position in the FCB.

Interrupt: 21h
Function: 11h
DOS version: 1
Service: Find first matching file
Entry values: AH=11h
DS:DX=address of FCB
Exit values: AL=(00h (file found)
(FFh (file not found)

Files

This function finds the first matching name and places it in the FCB. It also creates a second FCB in the data transfer area. As for the file handle functions, you can specify attributes, including a new volume label. (Note that the volume label was not used in DOS 1.)

Interrupt: 21h
Function: 12h
DOS version: 1
Service: Find next matching file
Entry values: AH=12h
DS:DX=address of FCB
Exit values: AL=(00h (file found)
(FFh (file not found)

This function continues the search, returning a value of FFh in AL if no file was found.

Parsing a filename from a command line

The FCB has one advantage in that it provides an opportunity to parse a filename from within a command line.

Interrupt: 21h
Function: 29h
DOS version: 1
Service: Parse filename
Entry values: AH=29h
AL=parsing code
DS:SI=address of command line
ES:DI=address of FCB
Exit values: AL=(00h (success)
(01h (wildcards found)
(FFh (invalid drive)
DS:SI=address of next character in command line
ES:DI=address of FCB

The value of AL determines exactly how this function works (see Figure 17.9). The function also returns a flag indicating whether the filename that it has located is unique or ambiguous. If ambiguous, all asterisks are converted to question marks.

SEQUENTIAL FILES

When using FCB's, there are different functions for dealing with sequential and random files. In the case of sequential files, there is one function for writing data to the file and another for reading it. After each file access, DOS

Parsing codes (Interrupt 21h, function 29h)		
Bit	Meaning if clear	Meaning if set
7-4	Always 0	
3	Do not change extension	Change extension in FCB to extension in command line
2	Do not change filename	Change filename in FCB to extension in command line
1	Do not change drive specifier	Change drive specifier in FCB to extension in command line
0	File specification starts at first byte	Skip blanks and other separators to find file specification

Figure 17.9 Parsing control bits

automatically updates the current block and offset in the FCB, but this can be easily changed.

Interrupt: 21h
Function: 15h
DOS version: 1
Service: Write sequential record
Entry values: AH=15h
DS:DX=address of FCB
Exit values: AL=(00h (success)
(01h (disk full; nothing written)
(02h (DTA too small)

This function writes data that has been placed in the DTA to the disk file buffer. If the buffer is full then its contents are transferred to the disk file. Remember that the file pointer always acts as if all data had been written to the file and is able to keep track itself of which data has been written and which not.

Interrupt: 21h
Function: 14h
DOS version: 1
Service: Read sequential record
Entry values: AH=14
DS:DX=address of FCB
Exit values: AL=00h (success)

Files

          (01h (end of file; no data read)
          (02h (DTA too small)
          (03h (end of file; some data read)

In a similar way to the above, this function reads data from the disk buffer and places it in the DTA. If the appropriate section of data is not already in the buffer, then the buffer is filled from the relevant section of the file from disk.

RANDOM FILES   A number of functions exist for accessing random files that have been set up with FCB's. Since the record size is fixed the position in the file must be set before we read or write one or more records.

Interrupt:	21h
Function:	24h
DOS version:	1
Service:	Prepare field for random record
Entry values:	AH=24h
	DS:DX=address of FCB
Exit values:	AL=(00h (success)
	(FFh (failure)

Although this function is technically for random files, there is no reason why we should not use the record size, current block and offset to calculate a sequential record number. Therefore, we can use the file interchangeably as either a sequential or random file.

Interrupt:	21h
Function:	22h
DOS version:	1
Service:	Write random record
Entry values:	AH=22h
	DS:DX=address of FCB
Exit values:	AL=(00h (success)
	(01h (disk full; nothing written)
	(02h (DTA too small)

This function writes a single record to the file. The record number must have been set first, on all occasions. It is not automatically updated.

Interrupt:	21h
Function:	28h
DOS version:	1

Service:	Write random records
Entry values:	AH=28h
	CX=number of records to write
	DS:DX=address of FCB
Exit values:	AL=(00h (success)
	(01h (disk full; nothing written)
	(02h (DTA too small)
	CX=number of records written

This function operates in a similar way to function 22h, but allows more than one record to be written at a time. Note that it also has the advantage that the record number is automatically updated to point to the next record in line. The DTA must be large enough to contain all the records that are to be written.

There is a special case, when the number of records is set to 0, under which DOS truncates the file after the record that has been specified. This is a useful way to shorten a file after any sort of housekeeping operation but must be used with extreme caution.

Interrupt:	21h
Function:	21h
DOS version:	1
Service:	Read random record
Entry values:	AH=21h
	AS:DX=address of FCB
Exit values:	AL=00h (success)
	(01h (end of file; no data read)
	(02h (DTA too small)
	(03h (end of file; some data read)

This function reads a single record. The record number must have been set before the function was invoked.

Interrupt:	21h
Function:	27h
DOS version:	1
Service:	Read random records
Entry values:	AH=27h
	CX=number of records to read
	DS:DX=address of FCB
Exit values:	AL=00h (success)
	(01h (end of file; no data read)

Files

        (02h (DTA too small)
        (03h (end of file; some data read)
      CX=number of records read

In a similar way to function 21h, this service reads more than one record at a time, automatically updating the record number in the FCB. The DTA must be large enough to take all the data.

CLOSING FILES Closing a file that has been opened with an FCB is fairly straightforward.

Interrupt: 21h
Function: 10h
DOS version: 1
Service: Close a file
Entry values: AH=10h
                DS:DX=address of FCB
Exit values: AL=00h (success)
                (FFh (failure)

Before closing the file DOS compares the directory with the details in the FCB in an attempt to ensure that it is closing the same file that was originally opened. This goes some way to reducing the chance of creating havoc in the file if the user swaps the disk.

DETERMINING THE FILE SIZE One useful function of files opened with FCB's is that to allow us to discover the size of the file.

Interrupt: 21h
Function: 23h
DOS version: 1
Service: Get size of file
Entry values: AH=23h
                DS:DX=address of FCB
Exit values: AL=00h (success)
                (01h (file not found)

Before invoking this function, the FCB must have been set with the current record size. To determine the length of the file in bytes, rather than in records, set the record size to 1.

SWAPPING DISKS

Unfortunately DOS has no way of telling when a disk is changed. If we do not take great care this can cause chaos. Much of this can be avoided if we ensure that the user has as little opportunity as possible to swap a disk without permission. Many commercial programs do not take such precautions and the result can be either that the program crashes or, in some cases, that there is a complete disaster and all data is lost. It is not unusual to discover that having swapped a disk without thinking about it a complete file (even one that has been saved regularly) is apparently lost because DOS scrambles the directory.

A good program should guard against this in whatever way it can. One method is to write some sort of signature to the disk when a file is opened and check this whenever any file operation is carried out, deleting the signature when the file has been closed. Another way is to create a signature file on the directory. Since it is possible that the user may swap a disk, close down the program and then start it up again with the same disk, this signature should include the date and time. A copy of the disk signature is then held in memory and then comparisons are carried out for any file operation.

RENAMING FILES

There are two ways of renaming a file using DOS interrupt 21h. The first method, which is often preferable, actually allows us to move a file within a disk, from one directory to another as well as renaming it. The second uses the FCB.

Interrupt: 21h
Function: 56h
DOS version: 2
Service: Rename a file
Entry values: AH=56h
DS:DX=address of old name (ASCIIZ)
ES:DI=address of new name (ASCIIZ)
Exit values: AX=error code (if CF=1)

This function only renames a single file at a time and does not allow the use of wildcards. However, we can overcome this by using the file-matching functions and a suitable loop.

The file specification must be given at DS:DX, and the new name at ES:DI. The great advantage of this function is that we can specify a different drive as well as a different name. The file is then moved. All that happens is that DOS moves the directory entry from one directory to another and changes the filename as it does so. The file itself is not physically affected on the disk. For this reason we cannot use this function to move files from one drive to another. To do so, we would need to use a copy function.

Interrupt:	21h
Function:	17h
DOS version:	1
Service:	Rename a file
Entry values:	AH=17h
	DS:DX=address of FCB
Exit values:	AL=(00h (success)
	(01h (file not found)

This is an earlier version of the Rename option. The new name is placed at a different location in the FCB, at offset 16h. No path is specified, of course, so the file to be renamed must be in the default directory. This is the basis of DOS's RENAME command.

The advantage of this method is that it allows us, in a single function, to rename a group of files using an ambiguous specification. All files that match the specification are found and renamed. Any ambiguity in the new name is expanded out to question marks, and in those places where there is a question mark the character is left the same in the name. In all other places it is changed.

DELETING FILES

Two simple commands exist to delete files from disk.

Interrupt:	21h
Function:	41h
DOS version:	2

Files

Service:	Delete a file
Entry values:	AH=41h
	DS:DX=address of ASCIIZ file specification
Exit values:	AX=error code (if CF=1)

This function deletes a single file, pointed to by DS:DX. It will only delete files that have a read/write attribute.

Interrupt:	21h
Function:	13h
DOS version:	1
Service:	Delete a file
Entry values:	AH=13h
	DS:DX=address of FCB
Exit values:	AL=(00h (success)
	(FFh (file not found)

This function deletes several files at a time, using an ambiguous file specification. DOS uses this function for its DEL (ERASE) command. The 'Are you sure (Y/N)?' message that is displayed when the ambiguous filename is '*.*' is not a part of the function's standard facilities.

Note that in both cases, all that happens is that the files are deleted from the directory. The physical files on disk are left unchanged, until they are overwritten by a new file.

CHANGING THE TIME AND DATE STAMPS

Function 57h provides opportunities for both discovering the date and time stamp on a file and for changing it.

Interrupt:	21h
Function:	57,00h
DOS version:	2
Service:	Get date and time stamp
Entry values:	AH=57h
	AL=00h
	BX=file handle
Exit values:	AX=error code (if CF=1)
	CX=time
	DX=date

413

Files

In order to use this service the file must have been opened with a file handle. The date and time are returned in CX and DX.

Interrupt: 21h
Function: 57,01h
DOS version: 2
Service: Set date and time stamp
Entry values: AH=57h
AL=01h
BX=file handle
CX=time
DX=date
Exit values: AX=error code (if CF=1)

In this case the new date and time in CX are prepared to go into the directory. The new time and date stamp are only actually written to the directory when the file is closed.

REDIRECTION, PIPES AND FILTERS

So far we have considered only the standard operations of files and devices. This section considers ways in which we can vary the behavious of our standard routines.

FILTERS

The previous sections have considered simple operations that have created or modified files in various standard ways. Generally these operations are carried out within an application. For example, a word-processor program modifies text while a database program allows the user to change individual records.

Sometimes we need to modify a complete file, creating a new file in the process. For example, we might want to convert a WordStar file to ASCII format or expand the tabs in a file, replacing this with spaces.

This is all done with programs called *filters*. The distinguishing feature of a filter is that it takes the contents of a complete file, modifies it and writes the result to another file. The most famous DOS filter is SORT, which sorts the lines of an ASCII file into alphabetical order. There are even simpler filters, including MORE, which reads in a file and

Files

displays it a screenful at a time, and FIND, which searches a file for a particular section of text.

The basic operations to be carried out by any filter are:

1. Open the existing file and create a new file.

2. Read in part of the data.

3. Process the data.

4. Write the data to the new file.

5. If there is still data to be read, jump back to step 2.

6. Close both files.

REDIRECTION AND PIPES

Up until now it has been assumed that all input is from the standard input device (the keyboard) while output is to the standard output device (the screen). Output to the printer is also assumed to be to the parallel port.

Any of these defaults can be changed by a process known as *redirection*. Data intended to travel along one route is redirected to another. An extension to this is the process of *piping*, under which the output from one operation becomes the input for another.

DOS includes four basic redirection operators.

- The '>' operator redirects output to a non-standard device or file.

- The '>>' operatore appends the output to an existing file.

- The '<' operator collects input from a non-standard device or file.

- The '|' pipe redirects the output from one operation to become the input of another.

These operations can be combined. For example:

```
DIR SORT >> ALLDIR.TXT
```

Files

This command takes the output from a DIR command (which would normally be directed to the screen), inputs it to SORT (which normally takes its input from a file) and then adds the output to the file ALLDIR.TXT (instead of displaying the sorted data).

Various file functions are illustrated in Figure 17.10 below.

```
;A selection of file-handling routines.
                                 ; Although each one of them ends with a
                                 ;   RET they can be made standalone
                                 ;   by replacing this with INT 20h
                                 ; Filenames could be stored in a calling
                                 ;   routine. Alternatively, DX could be
                                 ;   loaded with address of filename.
                                 ; If routines are to be used in a
                                 ;   program together then the data areas
                                 ;   can be shared, resulting in
                                 ;   considerable savings in space
; -----------------------------------------------------------------
CREATE:                          ; Creates a file

                                 ; Gives error message if file already
                                 ;   exists

                                 ; Entry values: FNAMEC holds ASCIIZ
                                 ;   string with filename to be created
                                 ; Exit values:  None

            jmp createst

fnamec      db '\filename.ext',00h
message     db 'File already exists$'
handlec     dw ?

createst:
            push ax
            push bx
            push cx
            push dx
            xor cx,cx
            lea dx,fnamec        ; Point to filename
            mov ah,5bh
```

Files

```
            int 21h               ; Create file
            jnc ok                ; Jump if no error
            lea dx,message        ; Otherwise, display message
            mov ah,09h
            int 21h
            jmp endcreate
ok:
            mov [handlec],ax      ; If created, save handle
            mov bx,handlec
            mov ah,3eh
            int 21h
endcreate:
            pop dx
            pop cx
            pop bx
            pop ax
            ret

; -----------------------------------------------------------------

REOPEN:                           ; Reopens an existing file

                                  ; Gives error message if file
                                  ;   does not exist

                                  ; Entry values: FNAMER holds ASCIIZ
                                  ;   string with filename to be read
                                  ; Exit values:  None

            jmp reopenst

fnamer      db 'filename',00h     ; Put filename here
message     db 'Cannot open file$'
handler     dw ?                  ; First file
handle2     db '$'                ; Second file
filedata    db 'Filler'

reopenst:
            push ax
            push bx
            push cx
            push dx
            xor cx,cx
            lea dx,fnamer         ; Point to file
            mov al,02h
```

417

Files

```
        mov ah,3dh
                int 21h                 ; Open file
                jnc ok2                 ; Jump if alright
                lea dx,message          ; Otherwise display error message
                mov ah,09h
                int 21h
                jmp endopen

ok2:
                mov [handle],ax
                mov bx,[handle]
                lea dx,filedata         ; Point to data
                mov cx,06h
                mov ah,40h
                int 21h                 ; Write to file
                mov ah,3eh              ; Close file
                int 21h

endopen:
                pop dx
                pop cx
                pop bx
                pop ax
                ret

; ---------------------------------------------------------------

READ:                                   ; Open and read from a file

                                        ; Gives error message if file
                                        ;   does not exist

                                        ; Entry values: FNAMEO holds ASCIIZ
                                        ;   string with filename to be read
                                        ; Exit values:  None

                jmp readst

fnameo          db '\filename.ext',00h  ; Put filename here
messageo        db 'Cannot open file$'  ; Error message
handleo         dw ?
handle2o        db '$'
readdata        db 06h dup (?)
readend         db '$'

readst:
                push ax
```

Files

```
                push bx
                push cx
                push dx
                xor cx,cx
                lea dx,fname0       ; Point to filename
                mov al,00h
                mov ah,3dh
                int 21h             ; Open file
                jnc ok3
                lea dx,messageo     ; Error message for failure
                mov ah,09h
                int 21h
                jmp endread
ok3:
                mov [handleo],ax
                mov bx,[handleo]
                lea dx,readdata     ; Point to buffer
                mov cx,06h          ; Read 6 bytes
                mov ah,3fh
                int 21h             ; Read data from file
                mov ah,3eh
                int 21h             ; Close file
                mov ah,09h
                int 21h
endread:
                pop dx
                pop cx
                pop bx
                pop ax
                ret

; ----------------------------------------------------------------

RECREATE:                           ; Recreate a file and write data to it

                                    ; This file creates a new file even if
                                    ;   a file of that name already exists

                                    ; Entry values: FNAMEZ holds ASCIIZ
                                    ;   string with filename to be read
                                    ; Exit values:  None

                jmp recst

fnamez          db 'filename',00h
```

419

Files

```
messagez       db 'Cannot open file$'
handlez        dw ?
handle2z       db '$'
filedata       db 'File data'
recst:
               push ax
               push bx
               push cx
               push dx
               xor cx,cx
               lea dx,fnamez         ; Point to filename
               mov ah,3ch
               int 21h               ; Create file
               jnc ok4
               lea dx,messagez       ; Error message
               mov ah,09h
               int 21h
               jmp endcreate
ok4:           mov [handlez],ax
               mov bx,[handlez]
               lea dx,filedata       ; Point to data
               mov cx,09h
               mov ah,40h
               int 21h               ; Write data
               mov ah,3eh
               int 21h               ; Close file
endcreate:
               pop dx
               pop cx
               pop bx
               pop ax
               ret

;-----------------------------------------------------------------

RENAM:                                ; Rename file

                                      ; Entry values: OLDNAME and NEWNAME hold
                                      ;    ASCIIZ strings for old and new names
                                      ; Exit values:  None

               jmp renst
oldname        db 'oldname',00h       ; Put old name here
newname        db 'newname',00h       ; and new name here
```

420

```
renst:
            push ax
            push cx
            push dx
            push di
            xor cx,cx
            lea dx,oldname         ; Point to filenames
            lea di,newname
            mov ah,56h
            int 21h                ; Rename
            pop di
            pop dx
            pop cx
            pop ax
            ret

; ------------------------------------------------------------------


DELET:                             ; Deletes a file

                                   ; Entry values: DELNAME holds ASCIIZ
                                   ;   string with file to be deleted
                                   ; Exit values:  None

            jmp delst

delname     db 'filename.ext',00h  ; Store the filename here

delst:
            push ax
            push dx
            lea dx,delname         ; Point to file
            mov ah,41h
            int 21h                ; Delete it
            pop dx
            pop ax
            ret
```

Figure 17.10 File-handling routines

18. *The Serial and Parallel Ports*

The Amstrad PC is fitted with two standard hardware ports. One of these is for parallel output, the other is for serial communications. The layout and use of these two ports is considered in this chapter.

It is important to make the distinction between these *hardware ports* and the *internal ports* mentioned earlier. The internal ports are locations through which data is transferred within the main system; the hardware ports are general communications channels for transferring information to and from the outside world.

The Amstrad PC is fitted with two ports as standard, but could have more connected via the expansion slots. It is able to take up to two additional parallel ports and one more serial port.

When data is transferred via one of these hardware ports it is actually sent to or received from a register (input port). The addresses of these ports are held in memory in the system variable area, from 0400h to 040Dh.

Note that the various interrupts and functions generally work with the standard parallel printer port and serial port. If other ports are available, these can be selected with the DOS MODE command. Any operations directed to the standard ports will then affect the newly-assigned ports. The descriptions in this chapter assume that the standard ports are to be used but the effects are the same if the ports have been re-assigned.

THE PARALLEL PORT

The *parallel port* is generally used for attaching a parallel printer, but can be used by any other parallel device. Basically this port is used for sending one complete byte at a time to the peripheral device. It is a one-way port, incapable of receiving data, although it can obtain certain status information about the receiving device. The programming of this port is very straightforward, since it is up to the device at

The Serial and Parallel Ports

The parallel printer connector

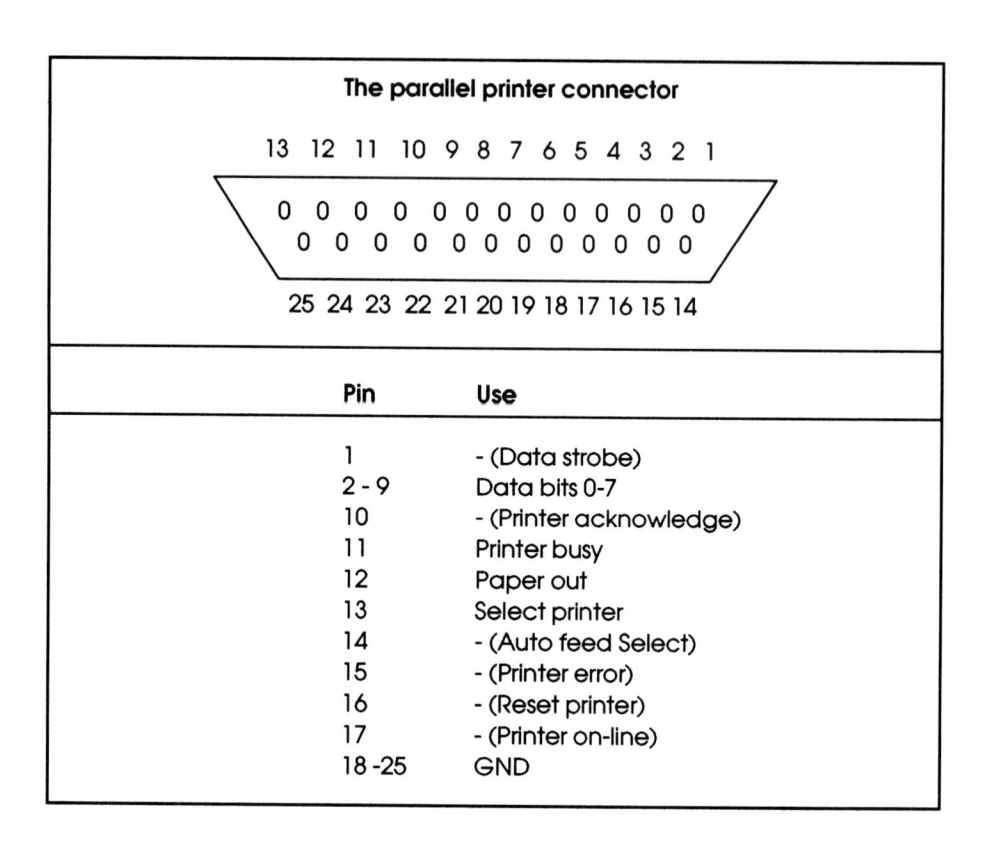

```
13 12 11 10 9 8 7 6 5 4 3 2 1
   0 0 0 0 0 0 0 0 0 0 0 0
    0 0 0 0 0 0 0 0 0 0 0 0
   25 24 23 22 21 20 19 18 17 16 15 14
```

Pin	Use
1	- (Data strobe)
2 - 9	Data bits 0-7
10	- (Printer acknowledge)
11	Printer busy
12	Paper out
13	Select printer
14	- (Auto feed Select)
15	- (Printer error)
16	- (Reset printer)
17	- (Printer on-line)
18 -25	GND

Figure 18.1 The parallel printer connector

the other end to decide how it actually handles the data that it receives.

This printer port is a standard centronics port for sending either 7- or 8-bit data. It is fully IBM-compatible.

Printer connector The parallel port has a 25-pin, female, D-type connector. This connector is identical in every way to its IBM counterpart. The pin layout on this port is shown in Figure 18.1.

PARALLEL PRINTER INTERNAL PORTS Three internal ports are maintained within the PC for storing data to be sent to the hardware port or received from it. Each of these is described below.

Parallel print status port (0379h)	
Bit	Use
7	Not Printer busy
6	Not Printer acknowledge
5	Paper out
4	Printer on-line
3	Not printer-error
2	Not LK1 fitted
1	Not LK2 fitted
0	Not LK3 fitted

Figure 18.2 The parallel printer status port

Parallel data port   The internal port that deals with the actual data that is being sent is 0378h. This port stores a single byte and it is here that information is sent before it is transmitted to the printer. We can test to see what value is about to be sent or has just been sent to the printer. Since this is a read/write port we can also change the value.

Parallel printer control port   The second port is 037Ah. This stores a variety of information, not only about the printer, but about the PC itself as well. The top two bits of this byte mimic the contents of dip switches 7 and 6 respectively. These are read-only bits and cannot be changed.

Bit 5 can be used to determine whether the machine is an Amstrad PC1640 (in which case the bit is clear) or a PC1512 (in which case the bit is set). It can also return the settings of dip switches 9 and 10.

Bit 4 (Enable Interrupt on Acknowledge) is a read/write bit that can be set to determine how the hardware behaves when it receives an acknowledgement signal from the printer. If it is set then the receipt of a 'printer acknowledge' signal forces a hardware interrupt 07h to be issued. It is up to the programmer to devise a suitable interrupt 07h routine, though this is usually done in the device driver. If the bit is cleared then any 'printer acknowledge' signal is ignored.

The Serial and Parallel Ports

Parallel printer status byte	
Bit	**Meaning if set**
7	Printer not busy
6	Printer acknowledge
5	Paper out
4	Printer on-line
3	Printer error
2	Not used
1	Not used
0	Time-out error

Figure 18.3 Parallel printer status codes

Parallel printer status port

The third port stores information about the current status of the print. The port number is 0379h. It is a read-only port so its contents cannot be changed; its values are always input from the printer. The use of the bits is shown in Figure 18.2. In general, the status port is used to tell us about whether the printer is ready to receive data as follows:

- The 'printer busy' bit tells us whether or not the printer is ready to receive a new byte of data.

- The 'printer acknowledge' signal is set when the printer has satisfactorily received the data that was sent.

- The 'paper out' bit is set when the printer's paper-out detector is activated.

- The 'printer selected' bit indicates whether the printer is on-line or off-line.

- The 'printer error' bit is a general purpose error flag.

Note that some of these bits are inverted and therefore their values may not be as initially expected. For example, when the 'not printer busy' bit is clear, this indicates that the printer is busy.

The Serial and Parallel Ports

Not all of this information is sent by all printers. Some of it may be ignored or may have a slightly different meaning. However, there should be no problem as long as a suitable printer driver has been installed.

PROGRAMMING THE PARALLEL PRINTER

Actually sending information to the parallel port is extremely simple. There are only three stages involved. Firstly we must initialise the printer control port, an internal operation. Next we should check the printer status, to ensure that the printer is ready to receive data. Finally, we can send the data. The data can only be sent one byte at a time.

All of this is controlled by interrupt 17h, which has three functions. Each of these uses a set of standard codes, as shown in Figure 18.3. When referring to the standard parallel printer port the printer number should always be set to 0.

Initialising the printer

The initialisation is carried out using function 01h of interrupt 17h.

Interrupt:	17h
Function:	01h
Service:	Initialise parallel port
Entry values:	AH=01h
	DX=port number (0=default)
Exit values:	AH=status code

The initialisation process simply sends two bytes, 08h and 0Ch, to the printer control port, which is numbered 02FAh. If any problems arise then the appropriate error codes are returned.

Checking the printer status

The printer status is set as a direct result of any activity within the printer. For example, when the printer is switched off-line the appropriate bit within the printer is set. This is sent as a signal along the corresponding wire of the 25-way cable. The signal is received at the Amstrad PC's parallel port and the relevant bit in the status port is set. Interrupt 17h is then able to read this register and return the value in AH.

Interrupt:	17h
Function:	02h

The Serial and Parallel Ports

        Service: Check parallel port status
        Entry values: AH=02h
                            DX=port number (0=default)
        Exit values: AH=status code

The meaning of the bits of the status code returned in AH is shown in Figure 18.3.

Sending a byte to the printer

The main function of any parallel port control program is obviously to send data.

        Interrupt: 17h
        Function: 00h
        Service: Send character to parallel port
        Entry values: AH=00h
                        AL=character
                        DX=port number (0=default)
        Exit values: AH=status code

Function 00h sends a single byte, which must have been stored previously in the AL register. Having called the interrupt, the byte will be sent and control will only be returned to the program when either the printer acknowledges that the byte has been received successfully, or when one of the error conditions is set. You are then free to move on to the next instruction. Therefore, the time that actually passes between the interrupt call and the next instruction in the program can be quite a few seconds, even though nothing much is happening. The next instruction should be to check the error code in AH and, as long as it is clear, continue by sending the next byte.

Note that the carriage return character may be interpreted by printers literally as that, taking the print head to the left-hand side but not advancing the paper. In these cases it is necessary to send a line feed character as well.

DOS has just one parallel port function:

        Interrupt: 21h
        Function: 05h
        DOS version: 1
        Service: Send character to parallel port
        Entry values: AH=05h
                        DL=character

Exit values: None

This function is lacking in proper error-checking facilities.

When printing a disk file you will need a buffer in memory where data that can be temporarily stored while waiting to be directed to the printer. This buffer must be large enough to hold a complete sector but performance is usually improved by increasing the buffer size, if memory allows. This is because the process of reading from disk is relatively slow but can be made more efficient by reading several sectors once the drive is up to full speed.

THE PRINT-SCREEN SERVICE

The parallel printer port is also used by the default routine that is called whenever we press the Shift-PrtSc combination. This combination causes an instant hardware interrupt 05h.

Interrupt: 05h
Service: Print screen

The effect of this interrupt is to send a complete copy of the screen display to parallel printer port 0. At any stage we can check the status of the screen dump by inspecting internal port 0500h. This will contain one of the following three values:

00h   Print-screen completed successfully

01h   Print-screen still in progress

FFh   Previous print-screen not completed (time-out error)

The main problem with this service is that it ties up the entire program while it is in effect. It will of course be speeded up if the receiving printer has a buffer.

We can hijack this service for our own purposes. A number of programs exist to change the effect of this key combination; most notable is the GRAPHICS.COM program supplied as part of MS-DOS. This program upgrades the default routines so that they can also deal with the extended ASCII graphics characters; obviously the printer must be able to deal with such codes. It will also send a copy of any graphics screens to a suitable printer, as well as the standard text screens. The time taken for a dump of graphics screen tends to be about six times that of a text screen.

The standard Print-Screen option checks the display mode before sending the dump to the printer. If it is a text mode it sends the characters as ASCII codes; if it is a graphics mode the routine converts the pixel map in memory into a form suitable for interpretation by a graphics printer.

There is one major disadvantage to the Print-Screen operation; if there is no printer attached the system will either hang completely or eventually time-out after some considerable delay. This is an immense irritation to users, particularly since PrtSc shares a key with the asterisk. This asterisk is much more accessible than its counterpart on the '8' key; the fact that the alternative requires a Shift means that it is very easy to try and get Shift-* by mistake and end up with the PrtSc operation. If no printer is attached the machine will hang. If a printer is attached but not on line, the program will eventually time-out. Either way, it provides a frustrating delay.

There are a couple of ways to overcome this problem. One method is to do a check on the printer before the dump routine is called, and ignore the dump call if there is no printer or the printer is off-line. The other approach is to display an 'Are you sure?' message, in the same way as for the reboot. The two methods can of course be combined. An extra option allows the user to interrupt the dump by pressing Ctrl-Break.

Various other alternatives exist for this key combination. For example, the current contents of screen memory may be written away to a disk file or - when it is a screen display that occurs when the disk is in use - may be copied to another part of memory; another key combination can be used to store that part of memory away to disk when it is safe to do so. The advantage here is that other routines can be developed to recall the display from disk or to string together screen displays to set up a rolling demo.

ECHOING OUTPUT TO THE PRINTER

DOS provides a facility whereby all output to the screen can be *echoed* to the printer. This process is effected by pressing either Ctrl-PrtSc or Ctrl-P. From that point on, all data that appears on the screen is also sent to the parallel port. The echo is turned off by pressing Ctrl-PrtSc a second time.

The serial connector

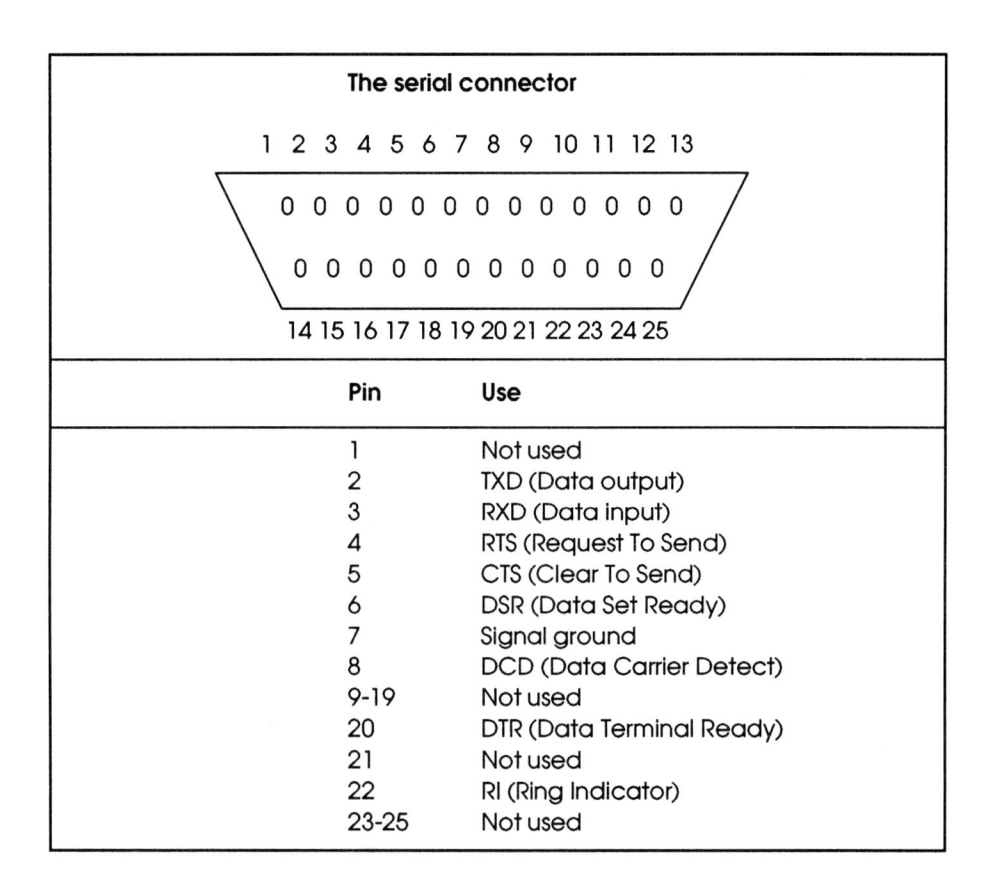

Pin	Use
1	Not used
2	TXD (Data output)
3	RXD (Data input)
4	RTS (Request To Send)
5	CTS (Clear To Send)
6	DSR (Data Set Ready)
7	Signal ground
8	DCD (Data Carrier Detect)
9-19	Not used
20	DTR (Data Terminal Ready)
21	Not used
22	RI (Ring Indicator)
23-25	Not used

Figure 18.4 The serial connector

THE SERIAL PORT

The Amstrad PC's *serial port* is used for any output to a serial device, such as a serial printer, plotter and so on. It is also used for input from devices such as digitisers and, finally, for two-way communications through devices such as modems.

The serial port attached to the Amstrad PC is a standard RS-232C asynchronous port. It should therefore be compatible with most serial devices.

The data transfer code

Serial data transfer byte

Bit	Use
7	)
6	) Baud rate
5	)
4	) Parity
3	)
2	Stop bits (0=1 stop bit, 1=2 stop bits)
1	) Data size
0	)

Baud rate codes (bits 7,6,5)

Bit Code	7	6	5	Baud rate
0	0	0	0	110
1	0	0	1	150
2	0	1	0	300
3	0	1	1	600
4	1	0	0	1200
5	1	0	1	2400
6	1	1	0	4800
7	1	1	1	9600

Parity codes (bits 4,3)

Bit Code	4	3	Parity
0	0	0	None
1	0	1	Odd
2	1	0	None
3	1	1	Even

The Serial and Parallel Ports

Data size (bits 1,0)			
Bit Code	1	0	Size
0	0	0	Not used
1	0	1	Not used
2	1	0	7-bit
3	1	1	8-bit

Figure 18.5 The data transfer code

Unlike the parallel port, data is sent as a stream of individual bits. Unfortunately the way in which various devices send and receive data varies considerably. There are differences in the speed of data transfer, the number of bits used for each character, the method of error checking and so on. This is called the *protocol*. Before any communications can be carried out using the serial port it is necessary to set up these parameters within the computer so that they match those of the receiving device.

The serial connector

The serial port has a 25-way, male D-type connector. Only 9 of the pins are actually used. The use of the pins is shown in Figure 18.4.

The actual way in which a serial cable should be connected varies considerably, depending upon the device with which the communication is to be made. This provides an absolute nightmare for anyone making up a cable but unfortunately there is no easy answer.

PROGRAMMING THE SERIAL PORT

As with the parallel port, there are only a limited number of instructions that can be applied to the serial port, making the programmer's task much easier. We can decide what protocol is to be used; we can send or receive one byte at a time; and we can check to see if any errors occur. All of this is done with

Serial port main status codes (AH)	
Code (hex)	Meaning
1	Data ready
2	Overrun
4	Parity error
8	Framing error
10	Break detected
20	Holding buffer empty
40	Shift buffer empty
80	Timeout

Serial port modem status codes (AL)	
Code (hex)	Meaning
1	Delta CTS
2	Delta DSR
4	Trailing-edge RI
8	Delta line signal detect
10	CTS
20	DSR
40	RI
80	Line signal detect

Figure 18.6 Serial port status codes

hardware interrupt 14h. For the standard serial port we must specify the port number as 0 in DX for each of the functions.

Setting the protocol

Before sending or receiving data we must decide on the protocol to be used. The information relating to the protocol can be set up using the first of the interrupt 14h functions.

Interrupt: 14h
Function: 00h
Service: Initialise serial port

The Serial and Parallel Ports

    Entry values: AH=00h
                           AL=protocol code
                            DX=port number
    Exit values: AH=main status code
                            AL=modem status code

The AL register must be packed with the parameters relating to the type of data transfer. This includes the following:

- The baud rate (speed of transfer; 1200 baud is roughly equivalent to 120 bits per second)

- The parity (the type of error checking)

- The stop bits (the bits sent after each character)

- The character size (7 for standard ASCII or 8 for extended ASCII)

The way in which this code is constructed in shown in Figure 18.5. A similar effect is achieved by a variant of the DOS MODE command.

The serial port status

At any time - in particular after data has been sent or received - we can check the status of the serial port.

    Interrupt: 14h
    Function: 03h
    Service: Check serial port status
    Entry values: AH=03h
    Exit values: AH=main status code
                              AL=modem status code

This function returns two bytes:

- AH is returned with a value after all serial port events and shows the general status of the serial port.

- AL is generally known as the *modem status* and can be reported as required.

The meanings of the various codes are shown in Figure 18.6.

Sending a character

One character at a time can be sent through the serial port, in a similar way to function 00h of interrupt 17h.

435

The Serial and Parallel Ports

>   *Interrupt:*   14h
>   *Function:*   01h
>   *Service:*   Send character to serial port
>   *Entry values:* AH=01h
>   AL=character to send
>   DX=port number
>   *Exit values:*   AH=main status code

Before invoking the function the character must have been placed in AL. The serial port must have been initialised with the correct protocol parameters beforehand.

DOS provides a function to achieve the same effect.

>   *Interrupt:*   21h
>   *Function:*   04h
>   *DOS version:*   1
>   *Service:*   Send character to serial port
>   *Entry values:* AH=04h
>   DL=character to send
>   *Exit values:*   None

This function lacks the error reporting of its ROS counterpart.

Receiving a character

One character can be received in a similar way to that of sending.

>   *Interrupt:*   14h
>   *Function:*   02h
>   *Service:*   Get character from serial port
>   *Entry values:* AH=02h
>   DX=port number
>   *Exit values:*   AH=main status code
>   AL=character received

The character is returned in AL, and any error is reported in AH. Since we don't know quite when a character is going to appear we have to keep checking the AH and AL ports until one or other becomes non-zero.

DOS provides a similar function:

>   *Interrupt:*   21h
>   *Function:*   03h
>   *DOS version:*   1
>   *Service:*   Get character from serial port

The Serial and Parallel Ports

Entry values: AH=03h
Exit values: AL=character

THE TIME-OUT ERROR

Perhaps the most difficult error to deal with is the *time-out* error. The actual length of time that we have to wait before issuing this error is determined by the device driver. Inevitably this seems a rather long period. The reason for this is that the driver must allow for lengthy procedures that may be going on within the printer, such as form feeds.

For example, suppose we send a byte of data, followed by the ASCII character 0Ch (which most printers will interpret as a form feed character) and then another byte. We may have to wait quite a while before the final byte is accepted, since it may take a considerable time for the form feed to be completed. This has to be allowed for in the time-out value. Therefore, if there is any fault with the printer it can be anything up to a minute before the driver decides to issue the time-out error.

It is unwise to reduce this time too much, since any function such as a form feed would result in an error and cause the program to issue an error message to the user. However, the wait can be frustrating for the user and therefore some sensible balance must be achieved. Unfortunately there is no easy solution to this, since different printers will require different time-outs to allow for their standard functions. The more sophisticated printer set-up routines allow the user to select the time-out delay.

The length of time for which the program waits before assuming a time-out error can be calculated from the values in locations 0478 to 047A for parallel printers 0 to 2, and 047C to 047D for the serial ports. The values stored in memory represent the number of half-second intervals to wait. The defaults are 20 (10 seconds) for parallel printers and 1 (0.5 seconds) for the serial ports.

It is also worth noting that different printers and drivers behave in different ways with relation to all these errors.

19. *Device Drivers*

A CPU on its own is of little use to us. To have any function in the real world it must be able to receive information from input devices and send information to output devices; it also needs to communicate with storage devices. Such devices include the keyboard, screen, disk drives, printers, plotters, modems and many others.

All these devices work independently of the computer itself, so the communications between the CPU and its peripheral devices must be carefully controlled. The software used for this communication is discussed in this chapter.

OPERATION OF DEVICE DRIVERS

The CPU outputs information in a standard format; however, output devices vary in the way in which they expect to receive information, so the data from the CPU must be converted into a suitable format. Similarly, input from a device must be converted into a form that the CPU can understand. The translation of data in this way and the setting up of the *protocol* required for communications with a particular device is handled by a program called a *device driver*.

There are two types of device driver:

- Standard device drivers

- Installable device drivers

The first set are drivers that form part of the operating system; the second set are additional drivers to be added by the user.

Standard device drivers

These are an integral part of the operating system and are contained in IO.SYS. These drivers are automatically installed in memory when the system is booted. They cannot be changed (except by changing IO.SYS itself) but they can be superseded by installable drivers.

The standard device drivers are heavily dependent on the characteristics of the computer. Therefore different computers have different drivers, and hence IO.SYS will vary from one computer to another. However, the commands accepted by the device drivers are identical in all cases, so a program written for MS-DOS should run satisfactorily under all the different varieties of the operating system. The only time there is likely to be a problem is with programs that bypass DOS and give instructions directly to the hardware. Such programs may not work on different computers.

The standard device drivers include:

- NUL, the null device

- CON, the console

- COM1 or AUX, the first serial port

- COM2, the second serial port

- LPT1 or PRN, the first parallel port

- LPT2, the second parallel port

- The floppy disk(s)

- The hard disk

The *null* device is used when you want to direct output to a non-existent device or ignore input. For example, when copying files you may direct all messages to be sent to the null device rather than the screen, so that the messages are effectively 'turned off'.

The *console* is a single driver that controls two devices, the keyboard and the screen. Any input must come from the keyboard while output can only be directed to the screen.

Installable device drivers

These are additional drivers which are added at the programmer's or user's discretion. They can either be extra drivers for devices not catered for by the standard drivers or they can be replacements for the standard drivers. The drivers are stored in individual files.

Additional drivers include:

- ANSI.SYS, a driver to amend the behaviour of the screen and keyboard

Device Drivers

- RAMDRIVE.SYS, a driver to handle communications with the RAM disk

- MOUSE.SYS, a driver to control the use of the mouse

Replacement drivers must have the same name as the drivers they are to replace.

As with the standard drivers, the installable drivers must be installed when the system is booted. The drivers must be included in CONFIG.SYS in the form:

```
DEVICE = {file specification}
```

CONFIG.SYS must be in the root directory but the drivers can be in any directory, as long as the full specification is include in the DEVICE command.

Device drivers cannot be added at a later time.

(Note that installable device drivers were not allowed for in DOS 1.)

DEVICE TYPES Device drivers are of two very different types.

Character devices *Character devices* send and receive data one character at a time. These are used for the keyboard and screen, and the serial and parallel ports. The null device is also a character device.

Character devices have *device names*. A device name can be up to eight characters long, following the same rules as a filename, and ending with a colon (:). DOS always checks the list of devices when an operation involving files is requested. The device name takes precedence over the filename, so any attempt to use a file with the same name as an installed driver will fail, as will any attempt to create such a file.

DOS uses this procedure for commands such as:

```
COPY CON: PRN:
```

This command is executed in the same way as any other command but the data comes from the console (keyboard) rather than a file and is copied to the printer rather than another file. (In fact, the colons are superficial in such cases;

441

Device Drivers

Device	Type	Device Name
Null device	Character	NUL:
Console (keyboard & screen)	Character	CON:
First serial port	Character	COM1: or AUX:
Second serial port	Character	COM2:
First parallel port	Character	LPT1: or PRN:
Second parallel port	Character	LPT2:
Floppy disk drive	Block	Usually A: and B:
Hard disk drive	Block	Usually C:

Figure 19.1 Standard MS-DOS devices

DOS recognises the device names quite happily without them.)

In this way DOS treats device names as standard filenames. These filenames are hidden from the user but are actually contained in a hidden sub-directory called *DEV*. DOS does not allow the user to create a sub-directory or file with any name that is used by a device; DEV is also reserved.

Each character device driver can only control one device at a time.

Block devices   Block devices send and receive data in blocks, usually of 512 bytes. These are used to control devices that deal with a large amount of data at a time, such as disk drives and other storage devices.

Block devices do not have names, rather they have drive *identifiers* which are allocated to them when they are installed.

A block device can control more than one device at a time; for example, the driver for the floppy disk drives controls both drives A and B. A different driver is needed for a hard disk or in cases where a second drive has been fitted that is of a different size or type. The RAM drive also has its own device driver.

Device Drivers

REDIRECTING INPUT AND OUTPUT

As with files, it is possible to redirect input and output from devices. The MODE command can be used to redirect other default output on a more permanent basis, for example:

```
MODE LPT1:=COM1
```

As a result of this command, any data that would have been sent to the serial port is now directed to the parallel port until a new MODE command is entered or the system is reset.

Similarly the CTTY command tells DOS to expect input from a device other than the keyboard.

The standard devices are listed in Figure 19.1.

INSTALLATION AND EXECUTION

Device drivers are stored consecutively in memory. The first device is always the null device. This is followed by the installable drivers. Finally there are the standard device drivers.

Each driver contains a header followed by the driver program itself. Amongst other things, the header points to the start of the next driver in the chain so the drivers are all linked. When a request is made for a device DOS searches through the devices in order; therefore any installable driver with the same name as a standard device is located first and the standard device is ignored.

Any request to DOS for the use of a device results in the creation of a *request header*. This is an area of memory, temporarily set aside by DOS, used for communications between DOS and the driver. DOS uses this area to give the driver basic information about what function is required; the driver uses the same area to return information about the success or otherwise of the operation.

STRUCTURE OF DEVICE DRIVERS

The device driver consists of three main parts:

- The *device header* contains basic information about the device and the driver.

Device Drivers

- The *strategy routine* stores away information about the registers when the driver is called.

- The *interrupt routine* is the main part of the driver, which carries out the requests.

The structure of the DOS device drivers is shown in Figure 19.2.

The request header	The request header contains a number of items, as shown in Figure 19.3.
Next device pointer	This is the segment and offset address of the location of the next device. This item points to byte 0 of the next device header. The pointer is stored as -1 (FFFF:FFFF) in the file but the appropriate value is inserted by DOS when the driver is installed in memory. The value of the pointer in the last header is left as -1.
Device attributes word	This word contains various information about the device, such as the device type and whether it is able to respond to particular types of command (see Figure 19.4).
Strategy routine pointer	This is the offset of the strategy routine from the top of the header.
Interrupt routine pointer	This item stores the offset of the interrupt routine from the top of the header.
Device name	For character devices, the device name may be up to 8 characters long (excluding the colon); if necessary it is padded with trailing blanks. For a block device this item stores the number of units controlled by the driver. This provides an opportunity for the programmer to overwrite the standard value and close off a drive from the user.
Length of header	The length of the header varies because the data section at the end depends on the device and the command. The minimum length is 13 bytes (0Dh).
Unit code	This value is valid for block devices only. It indicates the unit to be accessed: for example, the drive to be accessed by the floppy disk driver, or which unit on a subdivided hard disk.
Command code	There are only 20 different commands that can be carried out by any device, each of which has a one-byte code.

Structure of MS-DOS device drivers

Start Byte	No. Bytes	Purpose
0	4	Pointer to next device
4	2	Attributes
6	2	Pointer to strategy routine
8	2	Pointer to interrupt routine
10	8	Device name
18	n1	Strategy routine
18+n1	n2	Interrupt routine

n1 = Length of strategy routine
n2 = Length of interrupt routine

Figure 19.2 Structure of MS-DOS device drivers

The request header

Offset	Bytes	Meaning	Set by
0	1	Length of header	MS-DOS
1	1	Unit code	MS-DOS
2	1	Command code	MS-DOS
3	2	Status	Driver
5	8	Reserved	
13	Variable	??	MS-DOS

Figure 19.3 The request header

Status — This word is set by the device driver, to report back to DOS. The high-order byte indicates the success or otherwise of the command; the low-order byte indicates the nature of any error (Figure 19.5).

Data area — The length of this area is set by DOS, depending on the command to be processed, but the data itself is supplied by the driver.

Device Drivers

Bit	Character/ Block/Both	Use	Meaning if set (=1)	Meaning if clear (=0)
15	Both	Type of device	Character	Block
14	Both	IOCTL commands	Supported	Not supported
13	BLOCK	Format of disk	IBM	Non-IBM
12	CHARACTER	Output until busy	Supported	Not supported
11	Both	Device Open/Close and Removable Media commands	Supported	Not supported
10	Not used			
9	Not used			
8	Not used			
7	Not used			
6	Both	Get/Set Logical Device commands	Supported	Not supported
5	Not used			
4	CHARACTER	Int 29H for fast console I/O	Implemented	Not implemented
3	CHARACTER	Device is current clock	Yes	No
2	CHARACTER	Device is current null device	Yes	No
1	CHARACTER	Device is standard output device	Yes	No
0	CHARACTER	Device is standard input device	Yes	No

Figure 19.4 Meaning of device attributes word

THE STRATEGY ROUTINE — This is a very simple routine, its only purpose being to store the address (segment and offset) of the request header.

THE INTERRUPT ROUTINE — When called, it must save the registers, determine the command by inspecting the request header and then call the appropriate procedure. On completion, each proce

When called, it must save the registers, determine the command by inspecting the request header and then call the appropriate procedure. On completion, each procedure must store a value in the status word and any return parameters in

Device Drivers

\	Device status word
	High order byte
Value	Meaning
80	Error encountered. (Low order byte indicates nature of error.)
02	Device is busy. (Response to command 6 only.)
01	Processing completed without error.
00	Device driver still processing request.
	Low order byte
00	Write-protect violation
01	Unknown unit
02	Device not ready
03	Unknown command
04	CRC error
05	Bad drive request structure length
06	Seek error
07	Unknown media
08	Sector not found
09	Printer out of paper
0A	Write fault
0B	Read fault
0C	General fault
0D	Not used
0E	Not used
0F	Invalid disk change (DOS 3 only)

Figure 19.5 Meaning of device status word

the data area. The interrupt routine must restore the registers before returning to DOS.

Note that interrupt routines are quite limited in the things they can do. Of necessity, since their function is to link two particular hardware devices, they must talk directly to the hardware using the hardware interrupts and memory locations, and by writing to the ports. In general, procedures

447

Device Drivers

cannot call MS-DOS functions. Obviously, if you are using a device driver, calling a DOS function activates another device driver and this sort of nesting can cause major problems.

The only command that can call DOS interrupt functions is command 00h, to initialise the device, and even here the functions that can be used are very limited.

USING A
DEVICE DRIVER

The following procedures are carried out when a device operation is requested:

1. The application program issues a DOS function call.

2. DOS locates the driver by checking each device header in turn and checking the name.

3. DOS creates the request header; the registers ES:BX are set to point to the segment and offset of the request header address.

4. DOS initialises the device driver by issuing a call to the driver's strategy routine.

5. The device driver strategy routine saves the segment and offset address of the request header in local variables, then returns control to DOS.

6. DOS calls the device driver interrupt routine.

7. The device driver interrupt routine acts upon the command and rewrites the request header, before returning control to DOS.

8. DOS interprets the response and passes control back to the application program.

9. The application program takes control, interpreting the DOS response codes as appropriate.

THE BIOS
PARAMETER
BLOCK (BPB)

For each unit to be controlled by a block device there must be a *BIOS Parameter Block (BPB)*. This is an area of memory set aside for storing information about the unit. This stores information such as the number of bytes in each sector and a description of the directory (Figure 19.6).

Device Drivers

Every disk or other storage device has a BPB in its boot sector, lying between the initial Jump instruction and the boot routine. It is the task of the device driver to read this BPB into memory when it is initialised and, later, when the media is changed (for example, whenever a floppy disk may have been replaced).

For each type of media that can be used with a particular device there must be a BPB in memory. The locations of these BPB's are stored as pointers in a table. There is a BPB table and a set of corresponding BPB's for each device.

Note that DOS does not check the drives to see when there has been a change; when it wants to perform an operation and discovers that the media has changed, DOS directs that the new BPB should be read into memory. Thus the BPB in memory should not be taken to be identical to that on the current disk, unless some disk operation has been performed. The same applies to the copy of the directory that is held in memory.

For each unit DOS needs to know where the BPB is stored in memory and one of the tasks of the device driver is to provide this information.

INPUT/OUTPUT CONTROL (IOCTL)

Data can be input and output in two different ways:

- Standard input/output, in which the device simply reads or writes a character or block by directly accessing the ports.

- IOCTL functions, which provide a more sophisticated method of data transfer.

If IOCTL functions are used a memory buffer is set up and all communications between the driver and application programs is controlled by storing information in this buffer. If a driver is written to allow this form of input/output bit 14 in the attribute field of the device header should be set.

Assuming that a device can handle IOCTL functions and that a suitable device driver has been installed, DOS provides a single service to carry out all communications between a program and the device.

Offset	Bytes	Meaning
0Bh	2	Number of bytes per sector
0Dh	1	Number of sectors per allocation(??) unit
0Eh	2	Number of reserved sectors
10h	1	Number of FAT's
11h	2	Number of entries in root directory
13h	2	Total number of sectors on the media
15h	1	Type of media
16h	2	Size of FAT in sectors

Figure 19.6 The BIOS Parameter Block

Interrupt: 21h
Function: 44h
DOS version: 2
Service: IOCTL functions
Entry values: AH=44h
(Various others)
Exit values: (Various)

There are a number of different functions that can be performed by this service. The functions are listed in Figure 19.7, which also shows the registers that are used for passing data to and from the interrupt. The meaning of the device information code that is returned by some of the functions is shown in Figure 19.8. The structure of the IOCTL BPB is given in Figure 19.9 and the device parameter block in Figure 19.10.

THE DEVICE COMMANDS

There are only a limited number of commands that any device is expected to cater for.

Some of these commands are relevant only for block devices. In these cases character drivers should report merely that the function has been completed, by setting the status in the request header to 10h. Other commands are relevant only for character devices, in which case block devices should set the status to 10h.

Device Drivers

Some commands can only be invoked if the relevant bit in the attribute byte has been set.

Command 00h (Initialisation)

This command is used only when the device driver is installed for the first time (when the system is booted). After this it serves no purpose and the space it takes up in memory may be re-used by DOS. For this reason this routine is usually at the end of the driver.

The purpose of this command is to perform any initial operations, such as resetting the software codes of a printer. This is the only command that may use DOS functions, and even these are limited to interrupt 21h, functions 01h to 0Ch inclusive and function 30h.

In addition DOS expects the command to do the following:

- Store the segment and offset address of the end of the main portion of the driver (excluding the initialisation routines) in the data area (bytes 14-17).

For block devices the following operations are also required:

- Set up BPB's for each type of media and a corresponding BPB table.

- Store the segment and offset address of the BPB table in the data area (bytes 18-21).

```
Subfunction:    00
Effect:         Get device information
Entry values:   BX=file handle
Exit values:    DX=device information

Subfunction:    01
Effect:         Set device information
Entry values:   BX=file handle
                DL=device information
Exit values:    DH=0
```

Figure 19.7 The IOCTL functions

Subfunction: 02
Effect: Read from character device
Entry values: BX=file handle
X=Number of bytes to read
DS:DX=Number of bytes to read
Exit values: AX=number of bytes read

Subfunction: 03
Effect: Write to character device
Entry values: BX=file handle
CX=number of bytes
Exit values: AX=number of bytes written

Subfunction: 04
Effect: Read from block device
Entry values: BL=drive number
CX=number of bytes to read
DS:DX=number of bytes to read
Exit values: AX=number of bytes read

Subfunction: 05
Effect: Write to block device
Entry values: BL=drive number
CX=number of bytes to write
DS:DX=number bytes to write
Exit values: AX=number of bytes written

Subfunction: 06
Effect: Get input status
Entry values: BX=file handle
(FFh (not end of file/device ready)
Exit values AL=(00h (end of file/device not ready)

Subfunction: 07
Effect: Get output status
Entry values: BX=file handle
(FFh (not end of file/ device ready)
Exit values: AL=(00h (end of file/device not ready)

Figure 19.7 The IOCTL functions (continued)

Subfunction:	08
Effect:	Check for removable media (DOS 3 only)
Entry values:	BL=drive number
	(01h (fixed)
	(0Fh (invalid)
Exit values:	AL=(00h (removeable)
Subfunction:	09
Effect:	Check for networked device (DOS 3 only)
Entry values:	BL=drive number
Exit values:	DX=device information (bit 12=1 if networked)
Subfunction:	0A
Effect:	Check for networked device (DOS 3 only)
Entry values:	BX=file handle
Exit values:	DX=device information (bit 15=1 if networked)
Subfunction:	0B
Effect:	Delay for locked files (DOS 3 only)
Entry values:	CX=delay count
	DX=retry count
Exit values:	AX=error code (if CF=1)
Subfunction:	0D
Effect:	Device commands
Entry values:	CL=(40h Set parameters
	(41h Write track
	(42h Format track
	(60h Get parameters
	(61h Read track
	(62h Verify track
	CH=08h
	DS:DX=address of parameter block
Exit values:	AX=error code (if CF=1)

Figure 19.7 The IOCTL functions (continued)

Device Drivers

> *Subfunction:* 0E
> *Effect:* Get number of devices
> *Entry values:* BL=drive number
> *Exit values:* AL=(0 (1 drive))
> (last drive (if CF=0)
> AX=error code (if CF=1)
>
>
> *Subfunction:* 0F
> *Effect:* Set drive letter
> *Entry values:* BL=drive number
> *Exit values:* AX=error code (if CF=1)
> AL=(0 (1 drive)
> (last drive (if CF=0)
>
> NB: (1) Drive numbers are coded as: 0=default drive, 1=drive A, 2=drive B, etc.
>
> (2) Entry values for AH (=44h) and AL (=subfunction number) are not shown.

Figure 19.7 The IOCTL functions (continued)

- Store the number of units to be controlled in the device header, overwriting any default value that may be stored there.

Command 01h (Media check)

Block devices only.

This command is used to ask whether or not the media has been changed since it was last accessed.

Every time DOS needs to read from or write to disk it first makes a request for a media check. This is because the disk FAT and directory are stored in memory and DOS needs to know whether or not to re-read this information.

The driver must respond with one of the following values:

- -1 if the media has changed

Device Drivers

Bit	Meaning if set
15	Remote handle (subfunction 0Ah)
14	Device can process control strings
13	Reserved
12	Remote device (subfunction 09h)
11	Reserved
10	Reserved
9	Reserved
8	Reserved
7	Device (0 for disk file)
6	Not end of file
5	Data not processed
4	Special device
3	Clock
2	Null device
1	Screen output
0	Keyboard input

Figure 19.8 IOCTL device information

Offset (hex)	Bytes (hex)	Use
00	2	Bytes per sector
02	1	Sectors per cluster
03	2	Number of reserved sectors
05	1	Number of FAT's
06	2	Number root entries
08	2	Total number of sectors
0A	1	Media type
0B	2	Sectors per FAT
0D	2	Sectors per track
0F	2	Number of heads
11	4	Number of hidden sectors
15	5	Reserved

Figure 19.9 IOCTL BPB

Device Drivers

IOCTL device parameter block

Offset (hex)	Bytes	Use	Values	
00	1	Various	Bit 0= (0	Return BPB as in BUILD BPB
			(1	Return default BPB
			Bit 1= (0	Read all fields
			(1	Read track layout field
			Bit 2= (0	Sector size varies
			(1	Sector sizes identical
			(N.B. Bits 0 and 1 must not both be set)	
01	1	Device type	0: 320K or 360K floppy	
			1: 1.2 Mb floppy	
			2: 720K floppy	
			3: 8-inch, single-density floppy	
			4: 8-inch, double-density floppy	
			5: Hard disk	
			6: Tape device	
			7: Other device	
02	2	Attributes	Bit 0= (0	Removeable
			(1	Non-removeable
			Bit 1= (0	Disk change line not supported
			(1	Disk change line supported
04	2	Number of cylinders		
06	1	Media type	0: Quad density	
			1: Double density	
07	1A	BPB		
21	1	Track layout		

Figure 19.10 IOCTL device parameter block

Device Drivers

- 0 if the driver does not know if the media has been changed

- 1 if the media has not been changed

To a certain extent this is a fairly pointless command. For hard disks the media cannot have changed and the response is always the value 1. For floppy disks the driver cannot tell whether or not the disk has been changed so must return a value 0.

Command 02h Block devices only.
(Build BPB)

This command builds the device's BPB in memory and is requested whenever the media check returns a value of -1 or 0 (that is, the media may have changed).

The driver must read the BPB from the disk's boot area and return the address of the BPB to DOS. When running under DOS 3 it also copies the disk's volume label to memory.

Command 03h Invoked only if attribute bit 14 is set.
(IOCTL Input)

This command is used to set up an IOCTL string, ready for input.

Command 04h Invoked only if attribute bit 14 is set.
(Input)

When this command is received the driver must perform the input that is specified by the IOCTL control string.

Command 05h Character devices only.
(Non-destructive
Read) This command should read a character from the device buffer without changing the contents of the buffer. (That is, the character that has been read will still be at the front of the buffer queue.)

Command 06h Character devices only.
(Input status)

This command is issued when DOS needs to know whether or not the buffer for an input device is empty. The driver should set bit 9 of the status in the request header if the buffer is empty; if there is a character to be read (or if there is no buffer) the driver should clear bit 9.

Command 07h
(Flush Input Buffer)

Character devices only.

The purpose of this command is to clear the buffer of an input device. All characters in the buffer are read and discarded.

Command 08h
(Output)

Invoked only if attribute bit 14 is set.

When this command is received the driver must perform the output that is specified by the IOCTL control string.

Command 09h
(Output with Verify)

Invoked only if attribute bit 14 is set.

When this command is received the driver must perform the output that is specified by the IOCTL control string. It must also verify that the data has been output correctly by reading the data back from the output buffer and comparing it against the data that was output. Any errors should be handled by re-writing the data or returning a suitable error code to DOS.

Command 0Ah
(Output status)

Character devices only.

This command is issued when DOS needs to know whether or not the buffer for an output device is empty. The driver should set bit 9 of the status in the request header if the buffer is full or the device is busy; if the buffer is not full or the device is idle the driver should clear bit 9.

Command 0Bh
(Flush Output Buffer)

Character devices only.

The purpose of this command is to clear the buffer of an output device. All characters in the buffer are discarded.

Command 0Ch
(IOCTL Output)

Invoked only if attribute bit 14 is set.

This command is used to set up an IOCTL string, ready for output.

Command 0Dh
(Device Open)

DOS 3 only.

Invoked only if attribute bit 11 is set.

Whenever a device is opened DOS issues this command. The driver may use this command and the Device Close command in whatever way it wishes, for example to limit the number of

Device Drivers

activities going on at any one time or to initialise a device each time it is opened.

Command 0Eh DOS 3 only.
(Device Close)

Invoked only if attribute bit 11 is set.

Whenever a device is closed DOS issues this command. The driver may use this command in combination with the Device Open command.

Command 0Fh Block devices only. DOS 3 only.
(Removable
Media) Invoked only if attribute bit 11 is set.

The command is used to inform DOS whether or not the media is removable. For removable media bit 9 of the request header status is cleared, for non-removable media it is cleared. DOS issues the command as part of interrupt 21h function 44,08h.

Command 10h Character devices only. DOS 3 only.
(Output Until
Busy) Invoked only if attribute bit 13 is set.

The command outputs data to a device until a busy signal is received. It is generally used for print spoolers.

Command 13h Block devices only. DOS 3.2 onwards.
(IOCTL function)
Invoked only if attribute bit 0 is set.

This command gives a standard IOCTL service. The command is called as part of interrupt 21H function 44,0DH. DOS passes to the device driver the code for the required function and the driver must verify that these are valid.

Command 17h Block devices only. DOS 3.2 onwards.
(Get Logical
Device) Invoked only if attribute bit 6 is set.

The command indicates the number of logical drives assigned to the device. The number returned in the unit code of the request header is one less than the number of logical drives.

Device Drivers

Command 18h Block devices only. DOS 3.2 onwards.
(Set Logical
Device) Invoked only if attribute bit 6 is set.

The command is used by DOS to assign a logical drive letter to a device. The number placed in the unit code of the request header by DOS indicates the logical drive letter (0 for A, 1 for B, and so on). If the value is invalid the driver must reset it to 0.

The way in which the device commands use the request header data area is shown in Figure 19.11.

INSTALLABLE DEVICE DRIVERS

Any new device that is added to the system may require its own device driver, if it requires any special handling that is not catered for by the standard device drivers. Since device drivers are merely pieces of software - and there are a great many of them - it is obviously not possible to attempt to describe all those that exist in any detail. However, there are three installable device drivers that are supplied with the Amstrad PC and are therefore worthy of mention.

ANSI.SYS The ANSI.SYS driver is commonly used on many computers. It is not intended to provide a driver for a new device; rather, its role is to provide enhanced functions for the keyboard and screen.

DOS has very limited facilities for screen output. It does not provide functions to move the cursor or change the display mode, for example. ANSI.SYS is intended to fill these gaps.

The driver works by intercepting all output directed to the screen by DOS and checking it for special command sequences. These commands are executed; any other output is allowed to continue on its way unhindered. (ANSI does not detect commands sent to the screen by the ROS services.)

All ANSI.SYS commands begin with the escape character (1Bh) and an open square bracket '[' (5Bh). The parameters that follow define the command. It is important to note that upper and lower case letters are treated differently.

Device Drivers

Some of the commands require ASCII values. These must appear in the command as a string of decimal numbers. For example, to refer to the ASCII value for 'A' the command would need to include the characters 65 (which needs to be coded as 36h 35h). This curious method of passing values actually makes the entry of commands easier.

All commands are sent to the ANSI driver by writing them to the screen as text. This can be done by putting them in an ASCII file and issuing a TYPE command at the DOS prompt, or by including them in a PROMPT parameter list. Alternatively, they can be included in a program by sending them as a string of text with interrupt 21h, function 0Ah.

While it is feasible to use the ANSI commands, this does mean that they ANSI driver must be installed before the program will run satisfactorily. It is often simpler to issue the corresponding ROS interrupts.

The ANSI commands fall into two categories. One set affects the display, clearing the screen, moving the cursor and so on. The other set (which can be very useful for users) are used to intercept key presses, replacing the standard codes with new characters or strings. They are particularly useful for setting up the function keys to perform a complicated set of instructions.

The full ANSI command set, and the corresponding ROS interrupts, are shown in Figure 19.12.

MOUSE.SYS MOUSE.SYS was covered fully in Chapter 11. The object of this drive is to provide a set of services for programs using the Amstrad mouse. If any other mouse is connected to the Amstrad PC then it will need its own device driver.

RAMDRIVE.SYS RAMDRIVE.SYS sets aside a part of memory to act like a disk drive. The advantages of such a *RAM disk* are that file operations are much faster and another drive is available to the user. This is a useful place to transfer batch files for example, so that they can continue even after disks have been swapped.

The device driver takes care of all details of setting up the RAM disk. The size of the RAM disk is read from the NVR. Any change in the NVR will therefore take effect when the system is next booted (when the driver is loaded).

Device Drivers

Command Name	Offset	Bytes	Set by	Meaning
00h Initialisation	12h	4	DOS	Segment:offset of device filename
	16h	1	DOS	First drive unit: 0 for A, 1 for B, etc (DOS 3 only)
	0Dh	1	D/D	Number of units controlled by device driver
	0Eh	4	D/D	Segment:offset of end of main portion of driver
	12h	4	D/D	Segment:offset of BPB table
01h Media check	0Dh	1	DOS	Media type
	0Eh	1	D/D	Media status: -1 Changed 0 Don't know 1 Not changed
	0Fh	4	D/D	Segment:offset of disk volume label
02h Build BPB	0Dh	1	DOS	Media type
	0Eh	4	DOS	Segment:offset of buffer containing first sector of disk FAT (IBM format disks only)
	12h	4	D/D	Segment:offset of BPB
03h IOCTL input	0Dh	1	DOS	Media type
	0Eh	4	DOS	Segment:offset of transfer buffer
	12h	2	DOS	Amount of data to be transfered in bytes (character devices) or sectors (block devices)
	14h	2	DOS	Start sector (block devices only)
	12h	2	D/D	Amount of data actually transfered in bytes (character devices) or sectors (block devices)
04h Input	0Dh	1	DOS	Media type
	0Eh	4	DOS	Segment:offset of transfer buffer
	12h	2	DOS	Amount of data to be transfered in bytes (character devices) or sectors (block devices)

Figure 19.11 Use of request header data area by device commands

Device Drivers

Command Name	Offset	Bytes	Set by	Meaning
	14h	2	DOS	Start sector (block devices only)
	12h	2	D/D	Amount of data actually transfered in bytes (character devices) or sectors (block devices)
	14h	4	D/D	Segment:offset of disk volume label (DOS 3 only)
05h Nondestructive read	0Dh	1	D/D	Character that was read
06h Input status	-			
07h Input flush	-			
08h Output	0Dh	1	DOS	Media type
	0Eh	4	DOS	Segment:offset of transfer buffer
	12h	2	DOS	Amount of data to be transfered in bytes (character devices) or sectors (block devices)
	14h	2	DOS	Start sector (block devices only)
	12h	2	D/D	Amount of data actually transfered in bytes (character devices) or sectors (block devices)
	14h	4	D/D	Segment:offset of disk volume label (DOS 3 only)
09h Output with verify	0Dh	1	DOS	Media type
	0Eh	4	DOS	Segment:offset of transfer buffer
	12h	2	DOS	Amount of data to be transfered in bytes (character devices) or sectors (block devices)
	14h	2	DOS	Start sector (block devices only)
	12h	2	D/D	Amount of data actually transfered in bytes (character devices) or sectors (block devices)

Figure 19.11 Use of request header data area by device commands (continued)

Device Drivers

Command Name		Offset	Bytes	Set by	Meaning
0Ah	Output status	-			
0Bh	Output flush	-			
0Ch	IOCTL output	0Dh	1	DOS	Media type
		0Eh	4	DOS	Segment:offset of transfer buffer
		12h	2	DOS	Amount of data to be transfered in bytes (character devices) or sectors (block devices)
		14h	2	DOS	Start sector (block devices only)
		12h	2	D/D	Amount of data actually transferred in bytes (character devices) or sectors (block devices)
0Dh	Device open	-			
0Eh	Device close	-			
0Fh	Removable media	-			
10h	Output until busy	0Dh	1	DOS	Media type
		0Eh	4	DOS	Segment:offset of output buffer
		12h	2	DOS	Amount of data to be transfered (in bytes)
		12h	2	D/D	Amount of data actually transfered (in bytes)
11h	Not used				
12h	Not used				
13h	Generic I/O control	0Dh	1	DOS	Major function code
		0Eh	1	DOS	Minor function code
		0Fh	2	DOS	SI register value
		11h	2	DOS	DI register value
		13h	4	DOS	Segment:offset of IOCTL request

Figure 19.11 Use of request header data area by device commands (continued)

Device Drivers

Command Name	OffsetBytes Set by	Meaning
14h Not used		
15h Not used		
16h Not used		
17h Get logical device	-	
18h Set logical device	-	

Note: all segment:offset addresses are stored in reverse order, with the offset stored in the first pair of bytes and the segment in the second pair, in each case the low byte being stored first.

Figure 19.11 Use of request header data area by device commands (continued)

Code	Effect
`Esc[HEsc[J`	Clears screen
`Esc[K`	Clears to end of line
`Esc[2J`	Clears to bottom of screen
`Esc[y;xH`	Moves cursor to (x,y) (col,row)
`Esc[nA`	Moves cursor up n rows
`Esc[nB`	Moves cursor down n rows
`Esc[nC`	Moves cursor right n columns
`Esc[nD`	Moves cursor left n columns
`Esc[s`	Save cursor position
`Esc[u`	Restore cursor position
`Esc[n;nR`	Get cursor position
`Esc[6n`	Get device status
`Esc[a;bp`	Redefine ASCII character a by ASCII 6
`Esc[0;f;"s";13p`	Redefine function key f by string s where F1 = 59, F2 = 60, ..., F10 = 68

Figure 19.12 The ANSI.SYS command set

Device Drivers

These installable device drivers, along with the many others that exist for the vast array of devices that can be attached to any PC, make the Amstrad PC range of computers suitable for countless tasks, and an asset to almost any type of business or the home. With good programming the Amstrad PC can be greatly enhanced; with the range of possibilities provided by the Amstrad and its operating system, programming these computers can be both enjoyable and rewarding.

Index

765A, *see* FDC
8086 instruction set, 86
8086 maths co-processor, 33
8086 Processor, 27
8086 programming, 71
8253, *see* PIT
8255, *see* PPI
8259, *see* Interrupt Controller
8259A-2, *see* PIC
8287-4, *see* DMA

A

AAA, 94
AAD, 94
AAM, 94
AAS, 94
Ability, 25
Accounts Master, 25
Accumulator, *see* AX
Adapter modes, 275
ADC, 92
ADD, 92
Add with carry, 92
Address interrupts, 149
Address mark, 342
Addressing modes, 80
Alarm, 217
Allocating memory, 157
Alt codes, 241
ALU, 29
Ambiguous filenames, 388
Amstrad PC, 25
Amstrad PC range, 22
Amstrad PCW, 22
AND, 95
ANSI.SYS, 460
APPEND, 163
Arithmetic and Logic Unit,
see ALU
Arithmetic operations, 91
ASCII, 66
 adjustments, 94
 characters, 68
 files, 385
ASCIIZ strings, 355
Assemblers, 20, 145
 A86, 145
Attribute byte, 361
AUTOEXEC.BAT, 181
AX, 77

B

Background programs, 162
 accessing, 163
Bad sectors, 336
Base register, *see* BX
Based addressing, 82
Based index addressing, 82
Basic Input/Output System,
 see BIOS
BCD, 94
BCD calculations, 94
Binary:
 addition, 91
 division, 93
 multiplication, 93
 subtraction, 91
Binary coded decimal, *see* BCD
Binary digits, *see* Bits
BIOS, 184
Bits, 55
 clear, 55
 set, 55
BIOS Parameter Block, *see* BPB
Block devices, 442
Boot, 160

Index

code, 183
cold, 169
procedures, 169
program, 169
record, 179, 356
record disk information, 184
types of, 169
warm, 174
Bootstrap, 169
BP, 77
BPB, 448
Branching, 98
Buffer:
  clearing, 247
Building characters, 70
Bus interface unit, 27
BX, 77
Bytes, 55
  moving, 103
  signed, 56

C

CALL, 112
Call interrupt, 113
Call interrupt on overflow, 113
Carry bit, 65
Carry flag, 81
CBW, 108
Central Processing Unit, see CPU
Character devices, 441
Character font, 49
CLC, 96
CLD, 97
Clear carry flag, 96
CLear direction flag, 97
Clear interrupt flag, 97
Clearing the buffer, 257
CLI, 97, 121
Clock, 201
  count, 202

information, 213
Closing files, 401, 410
CMC, 97
CMP, 99
CMPSB, 110
CMPSW, 110
Code segment, see CS
COM files, 145
Command line parameters, 151
COMMAND.COM, 185
  boot routines, 191
Communicating with ports, 112
Compare instructions, 99
Compare string bytes, 110
Compare string word, 110
Comparisons, 98
Compatibility, 23, 125, 199
Complement, 63
Complement carry flag, 97
Components, 23
COMSPEC, 185
CONFIG.SYS, 188
Console, 440
Control codes, 67, 69, 251
Control system, 29
Convert byte to word, 108
Convert word to double word, 108
Count register, see CX
Country, 189
Country-dependent information, 188
CP/M, 25
CPU, 27
CREATE, 416
Critical errors, 158
Critical error codes, 159
Critical-error handler address, 154
CS, 76
Ctrl-Alt-Del, 174, 238
Ctrl-Break, 237
  address, 154
Ctrl-Num Lock, 236

Index

Current drive, 367
Cursor, 310
  information, 313
CWD, 108
CX, 77

D

DAS, 95
Data bus, 29
Data register, *see* DX
Data Segment, *see* DS
Data terminology, 55
Data Transfer Areas, *see* DTA
Date, 206
Date stamp, 364
  changing, 413
DAA, 95
DEBUG, 122, 149
DEBUG commands, 148
DEC, 92
Decimal adjustments, 95
Decimal-to-hex conversions, 60, 64
Decrementing, 92
DELETE, 421
Deleting files, 412
Destination Index, *see* DI
Detailed error codes, 160
Device commands, 450
Device driver, 184, 439
Device header, 443
DI, 78
Digitisers, 24
Dip switches, 36, 48
Direct addressing, 81
Direct control of the speaker, 327
Direct Memory Access, *see* DMA
Direction flag, 79, 108
Directory:
  current 368
  path, 383
Disk:
  architecture, 334
  buffers, 350
  directory, 356
  drives, 24
  parameter table, 331
  resetting, 352
  structure information, 355
  status, 351
  swapping, 411
Display characters, 302
Display mode, 285
Display pages, 294
Display pixel, 318
Displaying a string, 305
DIV, 93
Divide by zero, 122
Divide instruction, 93
DMA, 34
  check, 170
DOS:
  boot record, 183
  version number, 196
DOS sector numbers, 345
DOS Plus, 25
DOS 3.3, 25
Drive:
  current, 367
  specifier, 381
DRIVEPARM, 333
DS, 76
DTA, 386
Duplicate keys, 27
Duplication of file handles, 403
DX, 77

E

ECD, 24

469

Index

Echoing output, 430
End-of-file markers, 385
English font, 49
Enhanced colour display, see ECD
Environment, 187
  variables, 189
Error messages, 387
  language, 171
ERRORLEVEL function, 156
ES, 76
ESC, 114
Escape instruction, 114
Exchange instruction, 104
Exclusive or, 96
EXE files, 145
Executable files, 145
Execution unit, 29
EXE2BIN, 145
Expansion bus ports, 33
Expansion ROM's, 43
Expansion slots, 24
Extended ASCII, 67
Extended ASCII characters, 67
Extended ASCII symbols, 69
Extension, 360
External devices, 24, 32
Extra Segment, see ES

F

FAR call, 154
FAT, 356, 371
  information, 375
FCB's, 403
FDC, 32, 39, 329
FDISK, 339
File allocation table, see FAT
File:
  buffers, 398
  closing, 401, 410
  creating, 393, 404
  delete, 377, 412
  directory, 357
  finding, 392, 405
  handles, 391
  interrupts, 382
  locking, 402
  opening, 393, 404
  pointer, 384
  random, 408
  renaming, 411
  sequential, 384, 406
  size, 410
  specifications, 381
  types, 384
  unlocking, 402
  use codes, 397
File control blocks, see FCB's
Filename, 358
Filters, 414
Flags, 78
  changing, 96
Flags register, 29, 78
  restoring, 97
  saving, 97
Floppy disks, 332
Floppy disk controller, see FDC
Floppy disk organisation, 337
FORMAT, 340
Foreground programs, 162
Formatting, 336
  disk track, 341
Fragmentation, 372
Free memory, 158

G

GEM:
  Paint, 25
  user interface, 25

Index

General registers, 29
General purpose registers, 77
Gigabyte, 59
Graphics displays, 316
Graphics cursor, 311
Graphics modes, 290

H

Halt instruction, 114
Hard disks, 332
Hardware interrupts, 121
HDFORMAT, 339
HD146818, *see* RTC
Hex, *see* Hexadecimal
Hexadecimal, 57
Hexadecimal representations, 58
Hexadecimal notation, 22, 57
Hex-to-decimal conversions, 62
HLT, 114

I

IBM PS/2, 23
IDIV, 94
IGA, 45, 275
Immediate addressing, 80
IMUL, 93
IN, 112
INC, 92
Incrementing, 92
Index registers, 77
Indexed addressing, 82
Indirect addressing, 81
Initialisation of system, 169, 172
Input instruction, 112
Input/output ports, 24

Input/output control, *see* IOCTL
Installable device drivers, 440, 460
Instruction pointer *see* IP
Instruction queue, 29
INT, 113, 120
Integer division, 94
Integer multiplication, 93
Interleaving, 343
Internal Graphics Adapter, *see* IGA
Interrupt:
  00h, 122
  01h, 122
  02h, 122
  03h, 122
  04h, 122
  06h, 266
  09h, 223
  11h, 50
  12h, 51
  18h, 175
  19h, 175
Interrupt:
  flag, 79
  get vectors, 125
  handlers, 117
  lines, 120
  replacing, 124
  replacing vectors, 126
  return, 113
  routine, 446
  vectors, 118
Interrupt controller, 120
Interrupts, 117
INTO, 113
INTR (Interrupt request), 121
IOCTL, 449
IO.SYS, 118, 180, 184
IP, 29, 78
IRET, 113

471

Index

J

JA (JNBE), 99
JAE (JNB), 100
JB (JNAE), 100
JBE (JNA), 100
JC, 101
JCXZ, 101
JG (JNLE), 100
JGE (JNL), 100
JL (JNGE), 101
JLE (JNG), 101
JMP, 102
JNC, 101
JNO, 101
JNP (JPO), 102
JNS, 102
JNZ (JNE), 100
JO, 101
Joystick, 269
JP (JPE), 102
JS, 102
JZ (JE), 100
Jump instructions, 98

K

Key indicator lights, 238
KEYB, 189
  programs, 234
Keyboard, 24, 221
  buffer, 224, 242
  input, 244
  scan codes, 36
  status bytes, 225
  translation table, 230
Key-repeat action, 239
Kilobytes, 57

L

Labels, 91
LAHF, 98
LDS, 104
LEA, 104
Least Significant Bit, *see* LSB
LES, 105
Library files, 145
Light pen, 268
  emulation, 267
Linking, 145
Links, 43
Load AH with flags register, 98
Load effective address, 104
Load pointer, 104
Load string byte, 108
Load string word, 109
Loading addresses, 104
LOCK, 114
Locking files, 402
LODSB, 108
LODSW, 109
Logical operations, 95
LOOP, 102
Loop instructions, 98
Looping, 98
LOOPNZ (LOOPNE), 103
Loops, 102
LOOPZ (LOOPE), 103
Low-high convention, 59

M

Machine type, 49
Maskable interrupts, 121
MASM, 145

Index

Megabytes, 57
Memory, 24, 42
Memory organisation, 70
Memory maps, 44
Mickey, 263
Mnemonics, 85
Modems, 24
Modify allocated memory, 158
Modifying keys, 225
Monetary symbols, 191
Monitors, 24, 273
Most Significant Bit, *see* MSB
Mouse, 24, 253
   buttons, 265
   cursor, 259
   hiding cursor, 262
   initialisation, 171
   speed, 264
MOV, 103
Move instruction, 103
Move string byte, 109
Move string word, 109
Moving data, 103
MOVSB, 109
MOVSW, 109
MSB, 56
MS-DOS, 20, 25
   boot routines, 179
   files, 183
   interrupts, 118
MSDOS.SYS, 180, 185
MUL, 93
Multiplex numbers, 163
Multiplexing, 161
Multiply instruction, 93
Multi-tasking, 161

N

NEG, 92

Negative instruction, 92
Negative numbers, 63
NMI, 36, 39, 121, 122
No operation instruction, 114
Non-maskable interrupt, *see* NMI
Non-volatile RAM, *see* NVR
NOP, 114
NOT, 96
Null device, 440
NVR, 34, 211
   interrupts, 211
   system data, 218

O

Object files, 145
Offsets, 70
Operands, 29, 85
   duplicate, 91
Operating systems, 25
   loading, 169, 178
OR, 95
OUT, 112
Output instruction, 112
Overflows, 65, 122
Overflow flag, 79

P

Page register ports, 34
Pages, 59
Palettes, 298
Paragraphs, 59
Parallel ports, 423
   checking, 170
Parallel printer, 32
   programming, 427

473

Index

Parity checking, 43
Parse the command line, 152
Parsing, 406
Paths, 369
Pausing, 114
PC-DOS, 197
Plotters, 24
PIC, 39
  test, 171
Pipes, 415
PIT, 35, 201
  check, 170
Pixels, 271
Pointer registers, 77
POP, 105
Pop flags instruction, 98
POPF, 98
Ports:
  037Ah, 49
  66h, 175
  A, 36
  B, 36
  C, 36
  checking, 170
  internal, 29
Power supply, 41
POWER-UP procedures, 170
PPI, 36
  check, 170
  ports, displaying contents, 40
PRINT, 161
Print-Screen, 429
Print spooler, 161
Printer connector, 424
Printers, 24
Program:
  ending, 151
  executing, 155
  load, 155
  locating parameters, 154
  terminate, 151
Program flow, 112
Program Segment Prefix, *see* PSP

Programmable Interrupt Controller,
  see PIC
Programmable Interval Timer,
  see PIT
Programming the 8253 timer, 322
Protocol, 434
PSP, 149
  creating, 151
  duplicating, 151
  finding the address, 150
Pseudo-ops, 147
PUSH, 105, 147
Push flags instruction, 98
PUSHF, 98

R

RAM, 42
  'extra' size, 51
  size, 36
  test, 171
RAMDRIVE.SYS, 461
Random Access Files, 385
Random Access Memory, *see* RAM
Random files, 408
RCL, 106
RCR, 106
READ, 418
Read Only Memory, *see* ROM
Reading a character, 309
Reading files
Reading sectors, 346
Real Time Clock, *see* RTC
  HD146818, 34
RECREATE, 419
Redirecting input and output, 443
Redirection, 415
Register addressing, 81
Registers, 72
Registers (ports), 33

Index

Release code, 223
REOPEN, 417
RENAME, 420
Renaming files, 411
REP, 111
Repeat instructions, 111
REPNZ (REPNE), 111
REPZ (REPE), 111
Request header, 444
Reset flags, 178
Resetting the disk, 352
Resident Operating System, see ROS
Resolution, 273
RET, 113
Return instruction, 113
ROL, 106
ROM, 43
    boot routines, 178
Root directory, 357
ROR, 107
ROS, 45
ROS interrupts, 117
ROTATE instruction, 106
RTC, 34
RTC.COM, 210
Running a subprogram, 155

S

SAHR, 98
SAR, 107
SBB, 92
Scan code, 223
Scan string byte, 110
Scan string word, 110
SCASB, 110
SCASW, 110
Screen interrupts, 281
Screen refresh rate, 279

Scrolling, 315
Segments, 70
Segment registers, 29, 76
Selecting monitor, 48
Selecting video mode, 48
Self-testing, 169, 170
Sequential files, 384, 406
Serial connector, 433
Serial port, 431
    programming, 433
Set carry flag, 97
Set direction flag, 97
Set interrupt flag, 97
Shareware, 147
SHIFT instruction, 106
Shift-PrtSc, 238
SHL (SAL), 107
SHR, 107
SI, 77
Sign flag, 80
Software, 25
    bundled, 25
    interrupts, 123
Sound, 321
Sound frequencies, 323
Source files, 145
Source Index, see SI
SP, 75, 77
Speaker, 36
SS, 76
Stack, 72, 105, 123
Stack errors, 123
Stack pointer, see SP
Stack Segment, see SS
Standard device drivers, 439
Status-1, 36
Status-2, 36
STC, 97
STD, 97
STI, 97, 121
Stopping a program, 114
Store AH in flags register, 98
Store string byte, 109

475

Index

Store string word, 109
STOSB, 109
STOSW, 109
Strategy routine, 446
String inputs, 249
String operations, 108
Structure of device drivers, 443
Sub-directories, 357, 365
Subprogram:
  control block, 156
  return codes, 157
Subtract instruction, 92
Subtract with borrow, 92
Supercalc 5, 25
Swapping disks, 411
Syntax of instructions, 85
System board, 27
System bus, 29
System configuration, 48
System RAM variables, 45

T

TEST, 99
Terminate address, 157
Terminate and Stay Resident,
  see TSR's
Text cursor, 310
Text modes, 285
Time, 201, 208
Time stamp, 363
  changing, 413
TIME-OUT error, 437
Timer, 204
Timeslice, 161
Top of stack, 75
Tracing through program, 122
Translate instruction, 104
Trap flag, 80
TSR interrupt, 165

TSR replacement interrupts, 165
TSR shell, 176
TSR's, 164
Two's complement, 65
Type conversions, 108

U

Unix, 25
Unlocking files, 402
US Gold, 25
User RAM, 43, 50

V

Verifying sectors, 348
Vertical retrace, 280
Video connectors, 271
Video ports, 319
Video RAM, 43, 278
Video state, 285
Volatile memory, 43
Volume labels, 365

W

WAIT, 114
Warm boot, 174
Windows, 314
Words, 56
  moving, 103
  signed, 56
  unsigned, 56

Index

WordStar 1512, 25
Write to a file, 400
Writing sectors, 347

X

XCHG, 104
Xenix, 25
XLAT, 104
XOR, 96

Z

Zero flag, 80

Disk Offer

In order to save you from the frustrations of having to key in listings and create your own general utilities the author has prepared a disk containing all the source code from this book plus many other routines, both as ASCII text and as stand alone programs.

The programs include: a text editor, a disk sector editor, a memory viewer/editor, and extended versions of the programs contained in the book.

Also included is A86 and D86, the symbolic debugger. Both of these are Shareware, and although no charge is made, all users should register for these. Registration gets the user a printed manual and software updates.

The price of the author's disk is £19.95 inc VAT and P&P.

To obtain your disks, send a cheque with order to:

SC & E Morris Computer Services,
Butford,
Bodenham,
HEREFORD
HR1 3LG